FEES MUST FALL

FEES MUST FALL

Student Revolt, Decolonisation and Governance in South Africa

SUSAN BOOYSEN

WITS UNIVERSITY PRESS

Published in South Africa by:

Wits University Press
1 Jan Smuts Avenue
Johannesburg 2001

www.witspress.co.za

First published in South Africa in 2016
Chapters © Individual contributors 2016
Images © Individual copyright holders

ISBN 978-1-86814-985-8 (Print)
ISBN 978-1-86814-986-5 (Web PDF)
ISBN 978-1-86814-987-2 (EPUB – North and South America and China)
ISBN 978-1-86814-988-9 (EPUB – Rest of World)

All rights reserved. No part of this publication may be reproduced, stored in a retrieval system, or transmitted in any form or by any means, electronic, mechanical, photocopying, recording or otherwise, without the written permission of the Publisher, except in accordance with the provisions of the Copyright Act, Act 98 of 1978.

Project managed by Hazel Cuthbertson
Edited by Monica Seeber
Proofread by Alison Lockhart
Indexed by Mirié van Rooyen
Cover designed by Hothouse South Africa
Typeset by Integra

All royalties from the sales of this book will be paid into the Wits School of Governance's beneficiary fund for deserving students.

CONTENTS

ACKNOWLEDGEMENTS		vii
PREFACE	David Everatt	viii
INTRODUCTION	Susan Booysen	1

PART ONE: POWER REDEFINED – 'WHAT HAPPENED TO GOVERNANCE?' 21
CHAPTER 1: Two weeks in October: Changing governance in South Africa 22
Susan Booysen

PART TWO: PRIMARY VOICES – 'THE ROOTS OF THE REVOLUTION' 53
CHAPTER 2: The roots of the revolution 54
Gillian Godsell and Rekgotsofetse Chikane

CHAPTER 3: The game's the same: 'MustFall' moves to Euro-America 74
Sizwe Mpofu-Walsh

CHAPTER 4: #OutsourcingMustFall through the eyes of workers 87
Omhle Ntshingila, in conversation with Richard Ndebele and Virginia Monageng

CHAPTER 5: Documenting the revolution 101
Gillian Godsell, Refiloe Lepere, Swankie Mafoko and Ayabonga Nase

PART THREE: THE REVOLT – 'RISING AGAINST THE LIBERATORS', SOUTH AFRICA IN AFRICA 125
CHAPTER 6: Standing on the shoulders of giants? Successive generations of youth sacrifice in South Africa 126
David Everatt

CHAPTER 7: Learning from student protests in sub-Saharan Africa 148
Lynn Hewlett, Nomagugu Mukadah, Koffi Kouakou and Horácio Zandamela

CHAPTER 8: Unfinished revolutions: The North African uprisings and notes on South Africa 169
William Gumede

PART FOUR: POWER AND CLASS REDEFINED – 'SIT DOWN AND LISTEN TO US' 191
CHAPTER 9: To win free education, fossilised neoliberalism must fall 192
Patrick Bond

CHAPTER 10: Bringing class back in: Against outsourcing during #FeesMustFall at Wits   214
Vishwas Satgar

CHAPTER 11: Between a rock and a hard place: University management and the #FeesMustFall campaign   235
Patrick FitzGerald and Oliver Seale

CHAPTER 12: Financing of universities: Promoting equity or reinforcing inequality   256
Pundy Pillay

PART FIVE: JUSTICE, IDENTITY, FORCE AND RIGHTS – 'WE CAME FOR THE REFUND'   269

CHAPTER 13: Excavating the vernacular: 'Ugly feminists', generational blues and matriarchal leadership   270
Darlene Miller

CHAPTER 14: The South African student/worker protests in the light of just war theory   292
Thaddeus Metz

CONCLUSION: *Aluta Continua!*   309
Susan Booysen

APPENDICES

APPENDIX 1: Annotated timeline of the #FeesMustFall revolt 2015-2016   316
APPENDIX 2: Student protest glossary of terms   328
APPENDIX 3: Key features of student protest across historical periods in sub-Saharan Africa   330
APPENDIX 4: Memorandum of understanding between the University of the Witwatersrand management, outsourced workers, and students   335
CONTRIBUTORS   338
INDEX   344

ACKNOWLEDGEMENTS

The authors' and editor's special thanks go to the individual internal readers, Wits School of Governance (WSG) colleagues and those further afield at Wits and the University of Johannesburg, for making time to do a first-round of internal, collegial assessments: Kelly Gillespie, Gillian Godsell, Lynn Hewlett, Darlene Miller, Merle Werbeloff, David Everatt, William Gumede, David Moore and Horácio Zandamela, besides editor Susan Booysen. We all juggled our lenses as we careered between scholarly secondary voices and activist primary voices, found different balances between the two, and generated a body of interpretations and knowledge that we hope will stand the test of time. In many instances we agreed to disagree on the character of the revolt and the justification of the modus operandi. We hope that the result, this book, will stand as a benchmark that captures the richness of interpretations of what unfolded in October 2015 and beyond, and continue to ring out as the inevitable next rounds unfold.

We thank the anonymous Wits University Press reviewers who engaged with the manuscript and went beyond the call of duty to offer insights, critiques and valuable direction for the further development of the manuscript. We trust that the elaborations, elucidations and further anchoring added to the final version has helped capture your respected advice.

Most of all, we, as scholars, thank the student authors as activist-intellectuals for their brave steps to help capture in writing the spirit of the changing times. This volume is merely a 'first chapter' – the 'final chapter' to the unfolding student revolt still needs to be written. We at WSG look forward to playing a role in the coming of age of a new generation of scholars, one that might bring the dreams of South Africa's 1994 and the aspirations of many different generations of left and new left students and scholars closer to fruition.

PREFACE

David Everatt
Head of School, Wits School of Governance

Faced with major and rapid social change, especially when led by students, academic responses vary from diving in holus-bolus to 'wait and see', with many points and ways of behaving in-between, which may include participant observation, non-participant observation, activist-scholarship, 'embedded' scholarship, disinterested observer, hostile critic, and so on. All are open to challenge, and all hold dangers: a loss of historical or of contemporary perspective; a failure to grasp detail or significance, or to distinguish them in the hurly-burly of the everyday; a failure to capture the lived fabric and significance of a social movement; and of course the *ad hominem* judgements, aimed at those not in the charmed circle, or those too deeply in the charmed circle, or those too critical, too uncritical, with the wrong politics, the wrong class, the wrong skin colour, and so on.

These academic scuffles are not merely vicious, as Henry Kissinger (among many others) had it, because the stakes are so low in the academy – quite the opposite. Controlling the narrative is key in any struggle, most particularly in the era of tweets and texts, and in particular for youth-led struggles, normally demonised by elders and erstwhile betters. As the #FeesMustFall movement took shape, controlling the narrative was critical given the movement's decision to try to avoid high-profile individual leaders who would normally set and manage the narrative – the ways in which the goals of the struggle are explained to the public, to the core constituency and to its opponents. This book is not an attempt to take control of the narrative. Embarking on a book about the student movement of 2015, we faced many of the dangers above, and only the reader can judge whether the authors negotiated the many pitfalls facing them. The book makes no apologies for making judgements on many aspects of the various #Fallist movements. As Susan Booysen makes clear in the Introduction, this book is a *scholarly* assessment of a key moment in post-apartheid South Africa. It is not an attempt to snatch away the narrative, to substitute a more moderate alternative, modulated by elders. It began in the heady days when government backed down in the face of an organised, insistent and compelling student-led struggle whose narrative – of legitimate need driven by inequality in the face of a government deeply mired in corruption allegations – was one that we felt deserved academic analysis, and academic space for students to articulate their own understanding of what they had just achieved, as much as for academic practitioners to reflect on what had occurred.

Given the speed of change in contemporary South Africa, we have no idea what may be happening by the time this book is printed and available to readers. The Wits School of Governance offers it as a small contribution to understanding why change is so urgently needed, and how it may be brought about.

INTRODUCTION

Susan Booysen

What did the student revolt of late 2015 to mid-2016 mean for governance in South Africa? How did it affect higher education and national government?

This book dissects the influence of the days of revolt that shook the government. Its voices are those of primary activists and scholars. The book's reflections represent a mere snapshot in time, and we reflect on only a segment of the overall revolt and its impact. The analysis for this volume ends in mid-2016, as disillusionment with the implementation of early gains sets in; as a second cycle of revolt unfolds; and as government and university managements work to persuade a diverse and still-angry student generation that more profound change is on the way.

The students' renewed objections and challenges to the prevailing sociopolitical order – embodying tales of alienation, of anger and of rejection of much of the *status quo ante* – reverberate as this book goes to print. Our relatively early analysis covers the first months of the #FeesMustFall (#FMF) movement. The events of October 2015, along with the 2016 aftermath, deserve in-depth, contextualised consideration. Multiple controversies colour the ongoing developments – not all students, for example, agree on the extent of rejection of the preceding and prevailing orders, nor do all pursue the outstanding goals with equal fervour. We analyse a moving target. Our need for a deeper understanding prevails over the temptation to stall, in order to see what will happen next. 'The next' (and we are certain that there will be further developments) will be just as important to analyse. We hope to continue listening and interpreting.

In convening the voices to write this book, we at the Wits School of Governance (WSG), together with a handful of colleagues at other University of the Witwatersrand (Wits) sites and at the University of Johannesburg (UJ), concluded that we should not wait for the longer-term impacts to show themselves – while the early and illuminating trends congeal. The book itself is an implicit conversation between scholars and activists. We identify, dissect, contextualise and project the trends while offering the reader the opportunity to listen to the primary voices from the student movement, and weigh up the analyses against the primary narratives.

UPRISING, REVOLT OR REVOLUTION?

The 'classification' of this student uprising has a considerable bearing on the theme of governance, both in its relevance to government as such and in the changing relationships between citizen and government that were manifested as outcomes of 'October 2015'. The public intellectual and philosopher Achille Mbembe (2016) notes that 'we have to find for ourselves the vocabulary to name the ongoing student turmoil in South Africa ... In this necessary task of naming and elucidation, what is required is the kind of sympathetic critique that amounts neither to endless praise singing, nor to unconditional alignment with political causes whose full consequences are yet to be known'.

This collection of primary and scholarly voices positions the student action of October–November 2015 generally as an 'uprising' or a 'revolt'. While organisation, mobilisation and the balance of narratives of the #FMF revolt varied from one week to the next, there is consensus that the events found their major antecedent in the #RhodesMustFall (#RMF) movement. At some stages – especially in the two weeks from mid- to late October 2015 – #FMF also resembled a *national* uprising (with its epicentre at Wits). The characteristics of a 'movement' were evident then. The *united* collective action (at times also including outsourced university workers) helped forge change in fees, access, institutional culture and workers' conditions.

The students themselves often use the term 'movement' in relation to their multi-campus, cross-province and international action under the banner #FeesMustFall – and several derivatives and variations of Fallism over time, including #RhodesMustFall in early 2015, #RhodesSoWhite, #OpenStellenbosch, #TransformWits, #KingGeorgeMustFall, #TheStatueMustFall, #FeesMustFall,

#NationalShutdown, #FeesWillFall, #ANCMustFall, #FeesHaveFallen and #PatriarchyMustFall. The ideologies of feminism, the intersectionality of continuous societal injustice, black-African consciousness and identity, and dismissal of liberalism and neoliberalism were the core of the combination of more immediate targets for non-negotiables in the mix of targets for Fallism.

#RMF, originating at the University of Cape Town (UCT), marked a moment of rapid advancement of the movement. #RMF was a 'root' but, more accurately, a forceful occurrence in a sequence of events that epitomises major and fundamental discontent among the youth generally, and student youth in particular. #RMF used vivid actions of faeces-throwing (borrowed from recent South African service delivery protests), mutilation of a statue and the public burning of paintings that evoked memories of colonialism to drive home its abhorrence of the educational and political systems. It then metamorphosed into a movement for decolonisation (the Fallists' radical iteration of transformation, focusing for now primarily on nationalism, racism and associated exclusion) and grew in its hold on the student community and society. It attained profound black consciousness, African-nationalist and pro-black-African tenors. #RMF and #FMF in turn built on the roots of the serial protests against financial exclusions, over many years, at the historically black, far-flung and 'non-Ivy League' universities. Poverty, marginalisation, exclusion and thus possible disqualification from future life opportunities brought in a link to mobilisation on radical causes.

The cross-cutting thrusts of feminism and class solidarity battled for predominance and, at times, attained it in this kaleidoscope of elements of new political culture and reinvigorated demands for change beyond the placating post-1994 'consensus'. It was 'revolutionary' in changing political culture and asserting the links between education and radical politics. The gains were sustained unevenly beyond the October 2015 peak, and the political order prevailed largely, but there was no going back entirely to the *status quo ante*.

Student activists and analysts characterise the events as a 'revolution' only tentatively. Perhaps they could be deemed a *delimited social revolution* or a revolution of values in having brought about certain foundational reconsiderations (Chapter 1 in this volume), including deep probing of the value and validity of the transitional negotiations of the early 1990s. It is partially a generational revolution in that it indicates the born-free (or coming-of-age-free) young South Africans are no longer taking the liberation myth as seriously as do the elders and liberation stalwarts. It also indicates that the neoliberal ideologies (be 'good customers and pay for services' or even 'play by the rules of multiparty democracy and the constitution') are despised.

The notion of Fallism highlights the demand for far-reaching change. The student activist Athabile Nonxuba (2016) defines Fallism as 'an oath of allegiance that everything to do with oppression and conquest of black people by white power must fall and be destroyed'. In this book, Sizwe Mpofu-Walsh (Chapter 3) elaborates that Fallism 'is a nascent, complicated and emerging viewpoint, combining aspects of decolonial thought, black consciousness, radical feminism, and pan-Africanism'. In line with the notion of the 'leaderless revolution' (Ross 2011), Simon Rakei (2016), a UCT student in #RMF, explains:

> ... as a movement we don't have any official members ... it is a leaderless movement. We don't have any formal structures ... the plenary [decides on strategy]. We have a gathering of all the people involved and decide on the way forward ... The plenary chooses representatives [to negotiate with the university]. They change all the time, anyone who decides they want to be in a meeting with management puts their name up.

These flat structures are of value, but also contributed in the 2016 period to the scope for many people, with diverse projects and agendas, to claim the right to speak on behalf of the movement.

THE VOICES, NARRATIVES, UNFOLDING ARGUMENTS AND CHAPTERS

As this volume shows, scholar 'versus' activist is not binary. Instead, the author-contributors cover a continuum. At the poles are the fully-engaged activists and the theory-driven scholars. At various intermediary points are the student activist-intellectuals, the student activist-scholars, scholar-activists, activist-intellectuals, sympathetic or engaged scholars, technocrat-scholars and critical scholars. As the chapters of this book reveal, supported by accompanying brief biographies, there is no disengaged 'neutral' academia in this project. This book represents a tentative step towards recognising that knowledge is generated in multiple forms, and we willingly take the steps to expose our knowledge to scrutiny and critique by emerging scholars who are graduating at the 'University of Resistance and Revolt'. The book fuses the activist-scholars' (the students') lived realities and interpretations of their experiences with more conventional – but never aloof – research and analysis by the academics/scholars. We hope that this delivers both reinvigorated forms of knowledge and compelling reading.

The book evolved through a process of interactions between (and within) activism and scholarship. WSG's campus in Parktown, Johannesburg, was the first site of the 2015 Wits student blockades of campuses. The protest of Tuesday 13 October 2015 concerned student accommodation. The Wits main campus blockades, the official start of #FeesMustFall, began the following morning. As the action unfolded over the next few days, we realised the importance of how national-level government and political governance were being affected and how pillars of *conventional political society* (as political life had worked before the onset of the revolt) were being challenged. We recognised that the onus was on us to explore and unpack what was happening around us in relation to governance (of the state and of universities as – at least in part – extensions of the state), an obvious core aspect of our work at the Wits School of Governance. Several of the chapters have a predominant but not exclusive Wits focus. We give full recognition, however, to the much wider roots of the current phase of struggle for transformation of universities and society.

We confronted the act of writing up reflectively and dissecting the governance aspect of this student struggle, mindful of the dangers of objectifying it. We are, however, *scholars*. We are responsible for deepening, adapting and applying our research and knowledge, and mapping unfolding changes in the world of governance around us. Students recognised a need to engage with such a process of analysis and writing that would help generate new scholarship. The chapters in the primary voices section (Part 2) testify to students interfacing the spaces of activism and scholarship. Some of the student authors became first-time authors of scholarly materials. Even more, the *student voices shaped this book*, and we hope that this signifies the beginning of a process.

Students assume central status in the book. We forefront students' primary voices, and let them relate the narratives of what the students did to power. This collection of voices within a broad, flat structure and diverse movement speaks the issues and reflects the contradictions of the time. These voices articulate the main stream of the revolt. On the two flanks – and not represented among the authors, except by their quoted words – are the students who settled with and reverted into the fold behind the regime, and the protagonists who hope that the spark of arson and destruction will trigger more than just a sociocultural but also a political revolution. In their writings, this book's student and activist authors reveal, with no holds barred, how coloniality, race, patriarchy, structural and physical violence alienate, colour and continue to taint life in South African society and its universities.

The students write, or co-write with workers, their lived experiences in the section that contains the core narratives on 'The roots of the revolution' (Part 2). Students Sizwe Mpofu-Walsh (Chapter 3), Omhle Ntshingila (Chapter 4, in conversation with workers Richard Ndebele and Virginia Monageng), activist-academic Gillian Godsell with student Rekgotsofetse Chikane (Chapter 2), and in another chapter with students Refiloe Lepere, Swankie Mafoko and Ayabonga Nase (Chapter 5), bring the texture of the struggles and the gaping holes in the 1994 'rainbow' into the heart of political praxis and the student revolt.

They explore how the student struggle originated, spread, was received, in some ways stumbled, but is ongoing, sometimes latent but ever-ready to re-erupt as it did on 19 September 2016 following Minister of Higher Education and Training Blade Nzimande's announcement about fees for 2017. As in the rest of the book there is no censorship of voices and their always-varying, on occasion contradictory takes on unfolding realities. The students exercise control over content. The students' research was their lived experiences and their positioning in the battles. These are *their* narratives. In the words of Chikane and Breakey (2015): 'These movements were born from the womb of the moral decay of our universities and their student bodies. Our thoughts, ideas and beliefs ... were forged in the very university spaces that you are in.' This primary voices section is a vivid illustration of the continuous uncertainties of the *exact* effects of October 2015 ongoing.

The primary voices illustrate arguments in the section 'Power redefined – what happened to governance?' (Chapter 1). This chapter stands in the context of 'governance' (also see the last section in this introduction) and presents my research into how the students moved to change governance. The verdict is that governance changed variably, from definitively and irretrievably to haltingly and reversibly. The chapter is interpretative and sets up a framework for linking the perspectives and approaches in the rest of the book to the theme of governance. The analysis unpacks how the revolt extracted concessions from government on zero per cent increases in fees and free education, but then lost impact as the gains entered the conventional government passages of budgeting, programming and piecemeal implementation. The gains and substantive unity on fees were just one dimension of the deeper issue of insufficient access because of poverty and alienation, which, in turn, were attributed to coloniality, race, whiteness, gendered bias and Eurocentric epistemology. It was a modest but reasoned step to move from nonracialism and cross-class unity to the identity politics of black consciousness, African nationalism, intersectionality, assertive feminism and post-patriarchy.

The section 'Rising against the liberators – South Africa in Africa' (Part 3) deepens the dissection of the revolt and its impact on governance. It positions first the 2015–2016 student struggles in historical perspective in South Africa (David Everatt, Chapter 6), taking stock of how the emerging generations of the children of liberation are positioning themselves politically. The chapter argues that in the midst of the ferment the nonracial and multi-class unity of the early phase was 'replaced with an essentialist African discourse that repeated selective Frantz Fanon and Steve Biko quotes, alongside selected elements of American critical race theory, such as the notion that "blacks can't be racist" – but not others, such as the recognition of intersectionality of struggles across multiple planes, not race alone'.

Lynn Hewlett, Horácio Zandamela, Koffi Kouakou and Nomagugu Mukadah (Chapter 7) analyse sub-Saharan Africa's student struggles over time, taking stock of how students influenced politics, policy and governance in Anglophone, Francophone and Lusophone Africa. The chapter demonstrates how the student struggles helped to propel change on significant political, governance and socioeconomic issues and shaped political consciousness – but failed to bring in political orders that differed fundamentally from the objects of the students' initial revolt. Reminiscent of the case of South Africa 2015, the authors observe: 'Universities became the sites where broader sociopolitical grievances were projected and transferred into more precise localised calls for transformation of educational institutions.' The chapter also raises questions about whether the student revolt of 2015 might be 'mere ritual' as the bulk of the protesters prepare to assume their positions as future political elites in middle-class society.

William Gumede extends the analysis into Arabophone Africa (Chapter 8), and interprets the Arab Spring's lessons for uprisings, including those unfolding in South Africa. He highlights that in the Arabophone world young people have taken 'their anger for their current suffering at current governments, not current foreign enemies and past colonial powers'. This contrasts with South African students in the 2015–2016 revolt predominantly taking on colonialism and race, instead of the government of the day. With the South African context of gradually-accumulating frustration and anger, however, the chapter suggests that such turns on government are a distinct future possibility.

The section 'Power and class redefined' (Part 4) starts with Patrick Bond's broad perspective on the fees struggle, interrogating its neoliberal framing (Chapter 9).

Bond reveals many of the thrusts of government's budgetary choices, especially budgetary reallocations to advance a middle-class project. The chapter uses comparative global contexts to help clarify the intricacies of government compromises to the students, concessions which would, in effect, advance rather than undermine the government's neoliberal and middle-class project. Bond cautions that 'the danger remains that once the heat of battle subsides the students will retreat to a relatively class-privileged position instead of pursuing this historic challenge of economic justice'. In this respect the chapter extends the Chapter 1 argument that there is an ideological and political coherence between much of the #FeesMustFall movement and African National Congress (ANC) government.

While #FeesMustFall registered the demands for no fee increases, decommodified education, decolonisation and an end to outsourcing on the national agenda, various narratives have come to the fore reducing #FMF exclusively to the agency of students – portraying #FMF as post-class, identity assertions related to black consciousness and intergenerational shifts. Vishwas Satgar (Chapter 10) argues that such narratives fail to locate the anti-capitalism of #FMF and deny the existence of solidarities and alliances at work within #FMF. He explores this issue by locating #FMF within post-apartheid transformative resistance and through highlighting the role of working-class agency within #FMF, an aspirant middle-class movement. He thus brings class back in for an understanding of the structural dynamics, lived experience and moments of conjunctural resistance of outsourced workers at Wits over a period of fifteen years. His analysis highlights the intersections of class, race and gender among outsourced workers and shows how working-class agency translated into solidarities with students and progressive academics before and during #FMF.

Patrick FitzGerald, a former struggle activist and deputy-vice-chancellor, and Oliver Seale, a university manager, offer the insider views of management (Chapter 11). Among their scholarly insights is that by 2015 crucial political authority wielded by the broader ANC party structures outside of the campus environment had significantly waned – students had less deference to the ANC when it came to acceptance of ANC student fee directives handed to university managements. Writing of the insourcing-outsourcing debate in this chapter, the authors emerge as critical of insourcing. In due course, however, university managements would have little option (under force of the 2015–2016 worker-student alliance) but to re-insource certain categories of workers.

Pundy Pillay (Chapter 12), from an economist's vantage point, discusses, in concrete policy-alternative terms, the band of options existing for relatively free higher education. He demonstrates the squeeze on university funding from the state – hence the dependence on fees and the decision of universities such as Wits and UCT to propose initially a fee increase that would have been approximately double the prevailing rate of inflation. Pillay directs thinking towards the destabilisation threat of 2016–2017: unless the state significantly increases its funding again, this time for 2017, university managements will suffer shortfalls and will try to introduce fee increases – in a climate where #FMF rejects out of hand any increases at all, if not immediate free university education for the poor.

The chapters in this section drive home the fact of the pincer grip in which the universities find themselves: unless their managements get additional massive transfers from the state (while they are fending off assaults on institutional-intellectual autonomy from the same state), they will enter destructive confrontations with both students and academic staff. The students will rightly demand free quality education, and the managements will pass the buck to government and academic staff. The latter will be instructed to 'work harder' and generate third-stream revenue to ensure universities make up income, for example through the addition of distance learning (with its large added student numbers and different work demands) to their existing workloads (see Habib 2016b; Jansen 2016).

The section 'Justice, identity, force and rights' (Part 5) explores the student struggles in the general context of the realisation and the abrogation of human rights. Darlene Miller (Chapter 13) asserts the significance of the gendered aspects of the student protests. She explores the feminism side of the student struggles, providing no-holds-barred insights into the powerful minds of the new generation of African student-activist feminists which stands in the context of key moments in the feminist positioning of the student struggles. The analysis links into details of Godsell and Chikane's Chapter 2, and clarifies the progression from revolt against colonialist imprints and racism to feminist assertion.

Thaddeus Metz's analysis (Chapter 14) delves into the philosophical side of force and violence – from all angles: students, university managements and government – and contemplates the fine balances in adjudging what is fair and what is not. He emerges critical of the modus operandi of segments in #FMF, arguing that expressions of resentment through 'incidents in which buses filled with students were petrol bombed … and in which petrol bombs were thrown at and left inside university buildings' were wrong. His verdict contrasts with the points of view in the primary-voice chapters, where the emphasis is on physical violence (largely in the form of burning material campus symbols and infrastructure) in response to the brutalisation wrought by structural violence.

FROM CONVENTIONAL TO PARTICULAR IN THE REVOLT'S POSITIONING

South Africa 2015 is neither South Africa 1976, nor Algeria of the 1950s-1960s, nor the northern hemisphere Western world of the 1960s New Left revolt. Moreover, it is even more obviously vastly different from the 1850s–1960s, the period when the Old Left captured revolutionary theory and promoted revolutionary praxis from Russia and the Soviet Union to Latin America and Africa. While there is no direct mimesis of theories of radical change or revolution, it is illuminating to trace some of the historical antecedents of South Africa 2015. Much of the culture and financial conditions differ, yet South Africa is going through a similar stage of development, with emerging cities and proletarians over decades coming in from a rural peasant way of life. This student uprising is thus part of a general democratisation trend that the national democratic revolution should have anticipated.

South Africa's 2015 student revolt talked revolution, but is at least in part a movement that simply pushed for the realisation of the country's 1994 liberation and constitutional settlement ideals, at a time when the ruling elite had become complacent in its post-1994 compromises and the middle-class character of society. In its talk about decolonisation and economic liberation the mainstream of the revolt was left of the core of the contemporary ANC, yet in line approximately with many of the positions of *the left-speaking, right-walking* ANC. Black consciousness has also been accommodated unevenly and ambiguously in the ANC. In this context, the section on rising against the liberators explores the ideological foundations and contemporary positioning of #FMF. The comparative African analyses of Chapters 7 and 8 show how different forms of student resistance across Africa reflect aspects of the broad left-student revolt and 'revolutions' the world over. The next comparison contrasts #FMF with the New Left of the 1960s, the Black Consciousness Movement and the 1976 Soweto revolt, and notions of Black Power. This ideological positioning sheds light on the historical emergence of #FMF, showing remarkable ideological similarities with movements in other parts of the world. Yet, the #FMF movement also derived simultaneous particularities from its South Africa-specific party political interfaces.

From the Old Left and New Left to Occupy

The Old Left (1850s–1960s) cohered around one or at most two national or international organisations (such as a social democrat party or a communist party) which were radically anti-capitalist and whose longevity exceeded a century. These parties were structured and organised around a set of principles, and usually had a politically homogeneous membership – with leadership usually dominated by older white men. The youth, mostly students, in the New Left overruled many of the ideas and internal practices of the Old Left, mainly those of the Communist Party and its dogmatist and sectarian Leninism. By contrast, the New Left (1960s onwards) campaigns and movements were decentralised and ephemeral. While the British Labour Party was at one stage called a broad church of the left, that was nothing compared to the 1960s New Left which accommodated socialists, other radicals such as critical theorists, feminists, mystics, anarchists, environmentalists, social rebels and 'political hippies'. Within their ranks, the feminists alone formed a rainbow of liberals, radicals, womanists and lesbians. In its ideological composition the new movement's heterogeneity echoes some of the diversity of the 1960s.

The preferred New Left organisational style was minimalist and non-hierarchical; daily mass meetings decided policy directly. Sit-ins and teach-ins were popular (see Cohn-Bendit 1998). Where organisations sprang up they were almost never national, and almost always faded out rapidly. While small factions used armed rebellion (Black Panthers, The Weathermen, Symbionese Liberation Army) the great majority were peaceful. Ideologically, the Symbionese Liberation Army wished to symbolise the unity of all left-wing struggles: feminist, anti-racist, anti-capitalist. The great majority of the New Left found their organisational home in the Students for a Democratic Society, which rose in the mid-1960s and had had its final convention by 1969. As Dick Flacks (2010) relates about what revolt based on *lived experience* meant to the New Left:

> Our generation saw the established Left as defined by ideology rather than lived experience – and this was just about as true for the whole gamut of those who identified as socialist. Deriving one's political strategies and analyses from ideological foundations resulted in what Mills

called 'futilitarian' politics and in a vocabulary unintelligible to the masses. The main point of claiming the need for a 'New Left' was to envision a way of acting and speaking politically that connected with experience, that was experimental, that had effects on the world that could be seen as good for people's lives.

The new-New Left of the 2010s Occupy movement has clear analogies to the (older) New Left in terms of both content (ideological heterogeneity) and style – loose, ad hoc organisation, if any. Occupy's primary goal, to make the economic and political relations in all societies more flatly distributed, links back in time to the New Left and forward into #FMF and #RMF.

Pan-Afrikanism, black consciousness and feminism

In line with these international-left trends, the entwined #RMF-#FMF (like their new black consciousness left 'antecedent' of half a century earlier), memberships range from small numbers of arsonist militants to a radical but peaceful mainstream, and many thousands of moderates (including silent moderates). Almost all participants are under forty. They do campaigns rather than constitute organisations, and often fragment within months. While in real-time touch by social and digital media across the country, #FMF comprises campus-wide movements that integrate a host of campus-specific organisations, rather than being national in specifics.

Ideological leanings range from black consciousness, pan-Afrikanism (with a 'k' to help signify militancy) and essentialist African nationalism, to feminists, workerists, reformists and Marxist leftists. Occupations and blockages (or sit-ins) are common; the #RMF-#FMF students' style was anti-hierarchical and revolved around regular mass plenaries. The two hashtag movements have their feminists ('The revolution will be led by queer black women', was a Wits slogan) not purporting to represent a majority of women, but openly speaking up and speaking out for small gender minorities. From Wits to UCT, the feminists had to constantly assert their role, being periodically marginalised (see Naidoo 2016), and even manhandled in one snap that went viral. The anti-rape campaigns at Rhodes University and UCT were part of this feminist re-assertion.

Much of the 2015–2016 student revolt is explained through its black consciousness roots and the historical affinity to the student revolt of 1976 (see Hirson 1979). Several national organisations of the 1970s in South Africa, such as the South African Student Organisation (Saso) and Black Community

Programmes (BCP), which gave birth to the Azanian People's Organisation (Azapo), were building radical alternatives to the status quo. The Black Consciousness Movement (BCM) assumed a central role and developed several political and community organisations that aimed at widening the struggle and mobilising black community supporters. These programmes included the BCPs, founded in the early 1970s (see South African History Online). The BCPs engaged in welfare work and programmes of self-help run by blacks for blacks. Steve Biko, one of the icons of the 2015 struggle, was a BCM founder and was centrally involved in running the BCPs. Biko's description of the rationale behind the BCPs reflects much of the rationale for the 2015 revolt, namely the view of 'the Black man' as:

> ... a defeated being who finds it very difficult to lift himself up by his bootstrings. He is alienated. He is made to live all the time concerned with matters of existence, concerned with tomorrow. Now, we felt that we must attempt to defeat and break this kind of attitude and instil once more a sense of dignity within the Black man. So what we did was to design various types of programs, present these to the Black community with an obvious illustration that these are done by the Black people for the sole purpose of uplifting the Black community. We believed that we teach people by example (Biko cited in Bizos 1998: 43).

(The 1960s BCM was pre-feminist, with much talk of the 'Black MAN' reclaiming his dignity. Women's role in the discourse of the time was that of support.)

Black power, whiteness and violence

The #FMF movement carries ideological roots from black consciousness generally, the Black Power Movement from the United States, and also South Africa-specific black consciousness. Whiteness, writes Nyamnjoh (2016: 7) 'far from being a birthmark, can be acquired and lost with circumstances ...'. In the narratives of the black power era – *and* in the heat of the 2015 #FMF struggles – there was little space, however, for arguments that black can be white while the primary battles to reverse oppression were unfolding.

Resonating with South Africa 2015, the Black Power Movement of 1968–1980 was a political movement to defeat the institutionally-framed oppression of black Americans. One of the scholars of the movement, Joseph W Scott (1977), argues that neither economic determinism nor psychology explains whites' systematic institutional defeat of blacks in all areas of competition in American society, and details the tactics that blacks have used to reverse the oppression. The movement carried both violent and peaceful activism – in the 1970s, the movement became more violent and included socialist movements, all working towards black empowerment. The Black Panther Party, bedrock to the movement, was grounded in socialism and advocated the use of violence to achieve its goals of black justice (Marxists Internet Archive 2002) – amid intense debate on the justification for violence. In the US, Black Power-Black Panther action peaked prior to, and contributed to, more roles for black Americans at the centre of American politics.

On the back of substantial similarities in perceived lived experience, the 2015 revolt's references to the 'black child', 'black pain', and 'whiteness' were inspired by US African-American philosophies and theories of black power. They also built on South Africa 1976, in the apartheid-racist-oppressive government setting. The 1976 Soweto revolt occurred under a racist police state which had opened fire on 10 000 schoolchildren. Estimates were that around 575 people (around two-thirds of whom were schoolchildren) were killed and more than 2 000 injured. Arrests, deaths in detention and trials followed the revolt (see TRC 1998). By contrast, the 2015 protests occurred in a democracy, with freedom of the media, amid a fully developed social media network among the protesters.

Violence assumed a secondary and largely reactive place in the 2015–2016 struggles. Blockades, occupations, semi-detention of university managers and barrier lines against the police were far more common than arson or fire bombs (with extremist factions inflicting increased fire damage in the 2016 phase). There were close encounters in confrontations with the police, but no casualties. There was brutality in containing the revolt (Duncan and Frassinelli 2015), also by private security forces. Police and private security fired tear gas and stun grenades, and carried out beatings and manhandlings. Stones were thrown at UJ students, but no student was wounded by police or private gunfire using live ammunition. When protesters were detained this was interpreted as excessive and often brutal, yet detentions were for a limited number of days prior to bail payment or court appearances. Charges of treason were brought against a group of students who led the parliamentary precinct protest of October 2015, but were withdrawn. Such kid-glove police and judicial enforcement was in line with what protesters had become accustomed to in the widespread community protests that characterise South African politics: contain and repulse, but don't forget (there *were* a few exceptions) the bonds of political blood that tie the protesters to the politicians and law enforcers (Booysen 2015).

Party political particularities in the 2015–2016 struggle

Most protesters asserted, across campuses and at most stages of the revolt, their autonomy from both the national political parties and these parties' campus wings. Such non-partisan action contributed to the solidarity (and gains) of October 2015. In many respects, however, the national political parties were omnipresent and played off-stage roles. There were different iterations across campuses, but the ANC and the Economic Freedom Fighters (EFF) were foremost. Despite their black consciousness associations and its centrality in #FMF, Azapo and the Azanian Students' Movement (Azasm) played no known role in either #RMF or #FMF.

The EFF, through its student command structures, was present consistently, although through leaders and actions, rather than *as political party*. The EFF also had a far stronger presence on the northern campuses of Gauteng, North West and Limpopo than on the Western Cape campuses. In one notable instance, the EFF provided buses for a protest from the Cape Peninsula University of Technology (CPUT) to Parliament. Pan Africanist Congress (PAC) activists were involved in the #FMF protests through the Pan-Africanist Student Movement of Azania (Pasma). Pasma, the BLF (Black First Land First) and the ANC youth structures on campuses were also involved in mutual clashes while fighting the #FMF struggle. The Democratic Alliance (DA) and its youth formation were rebuffed. Despite strong presences of black consciousness and Africanist student formations, other associated national political parties were hardly evident (Chapter 1).

A particular aspect of the 2015–2016 revolt was that the students in the driving seats often had a current or earlier form of loyalty to the ANC. This special relationship between many of the students and the ANC helped explain the nature of the revolt, its suspension and moderation in many quarters, and the soft treatment at the hands of law enforcement agencies. As Chapter 1 shows, the tentative settlement towards late 2015 was affected directly by influential students whom the ANC could push to conform to ANC wishes to bring the heady days of October 2015 to a close.

Such party political bonds raise questions about the determination of the bulk of the protesting students to arrive at an entirely new, thoroughly decolonised future in universities and society, or whether they were willing to settle for personal, middle-class spaces in the ANC sun (issues raised in Chapter 10). The 1976 revolt, in comparison, had been one of direct and mobilised revolt that signified the forceful rejection of the status quo in an entirely different context: no moderate or weighted 'negotiation' about the acceleration and reactivation of a reform trajectory was on the agenda. There was a common denominator between 1976 and 2015 in the insistence on quality education and the recognition that education holds the key to (further) liberation. The 1976 revolt was about rejecting the language of the oppressor, and about exclusion through inferior apartheid school education. The theme continued and shifted to post-secondary education in 2015. The activist-intellectuals now focused on lack of access to education and obstacles to completion once admitted. They went deeper into history, into the colonial roots of the education system. They pinpointed structural violence and coloniality and linked these to the incomplete and compromised 1994 transition.

Amid deficient economic growth and massive youth unemployment (estimated as up to 60 per cent) the catching-on of inflationary credentialism (see Collins 1979: 191–204) intensified the chase for university access. The phenomenon was well established in South Africa by 2000 and society saw the requirement for qualifications, including university degrees, for appointment to even modest positions. By 2015–2016, there was immense pressure on youth to get university qualifications to help them into employment. In contrast, back in 1976, even among the privileged white minority, a modest proportion matriculated, and only a small minority went on to university. Among Africans, the proportions were far more daunting, but would change rapidly in the next quarter of a century – by 2000 a supermarket chain, for example, was demanding matriculation for even the lowest job of shelf packers. By 2016, statistics show only marginal difference in the unemployment rates for those who dropped out in Grade 11 and for matriculants (see Yu et al. 2016). In short, by 2016, not merely a middle-class job, but realistic chances of getting *any* job, depended on (but still did not ensure) obtaining a post-secondary qualification. This helps to explain the desperation for aspirant students to not be excluded because they can not afford upfront registration fees, or tuition fees – and, once included, can not cope with the running costs of accommodation, food, transport and books (Many are equally stressed by the poor-quality secondary-level education which has ill-equipped them for post-secondary curricula). These practical necessities help to explain how the support for #FMF extended far beyond direct political and ideological considerations. Yet, mobilisation around black pain, and pushing for recognition of these feelings as a strategy for the change that had not yet materialised (Nyamnjoh 2016) united black – and, on occasion, white – students across class.

GOVERNANCE THROUGH THE LENS OF STUDENT ACTIVISM

Most governance definitions encompass the aspects of authority, decision making and accountability – all of these dimensions of South Africa's political order were challenged in October 2015. Governance, in essence, entails government's ability to rule over citizens, which includes both making rules and enforcing them (Fukuyama 2013).

Governance, practically and conceptually, refers to the way in which authority (the right to make decisions) and voice (the right to participate in decision making) are distributed in a society, a community or an institution (McLennan 2014). Governance thus expresses the process-oriented elements of governing or public decision making that bear political content.

The notions of authority and accountability add the aspect that citizens are *active participants* in governance relationships – they *grant* authority and through their voice they can change the rules, the system itself, and (as a consequence) also the nature and quality of decisions that emanate from that political system. In contrast, many governance definitions prefer to emphasise the top-down and one-sided, 'authoritative' processes of rule making. The World Bank, for example, argues that governance ought to be understood as 'the rule of the rulers, typically within a given set of rules. One might conclude that 'governance is the process … by which authority is conferred on rulers, by which they make the rules, and by which those rules are enforced and modified' (World Bank 2013). Khalid Malik and Swarnim Waglé, for the United Nations Development Programme (2002), use a definition that progresses towards a more *citizen-government interactive* depiction of governance. They stress the principles of legitimacy and voice (with emphasis on constructive participation through legitimate institutions), direction (towards development), performance (serving all stakeholders responsively and effectively), fairness (all humans or citizens have equity in chances to improve their well-being, and legal frameworks for human rights need to be enforced accordingly) and accountability (to the public, along with transparency). This conceptualisation highlights a two-directional view of governance, one that we use in this book when we talk about the students of October 2015 having affected governance in South Africa. When these principles are not being realised, the citizenry – students, workers, service-delivery-deprived communities – have the right, if not the responsibility, to change governance relations. The means will span the spectrum from representations to revolt.

The political scientists Jon Pierre and B. Guy Peters (2000: 61) conceptualise governance as society-centred instead of state-centred, noting that 'governance relates to changing relationships between state and society and a growing reliance on less coercive policy instruments'. Citizens and bottom-up actions therefore have an integral place in the configuration of governance. In contrast with many of the mainstream conceptualisations, our current analysis focuses less on the assumed consensual and convergent action to obtain developmental outcomes, and engages more with notions of antagonistic action. This form of action is captured in the notion of agonism, as developed by the political theorist Chantal Mouffe (2013; 2016): conflict and antagonism have a constitutive role in building democracy. Similarly, government often needs to be pushed – possibly antagonistically – into acting to realise human and developmental rights that range from education to general transformation towards an imagined postcolonial order.

This book thus addresses the changing relations between citizens and government with reference to how power relations and policy – both generally and in relation to educational policy in South Africa – changed in the process of the 2015–2016 student revolt, which captured important dimensions of the exercise of power from below. The students – and a selection of workers and academics – wrought evidence of how policy change can be forced and how powerful figures in universities and government can be brought to heel. For example, after roughly ten days of struggle the ANC government, along with university vice-chancellors, agreed to a zero per cent increase in 2016 university fees. The vice-chancellors of the higher education institutions, in turn, point out that within a few weeks the student action brought reprioritisations of expenditure on higher education that the vice-chancellors had been advocating for over ten years (see Chapter 1).

This book takes the view (with various iterations across authors) that whereas the #FeesMustFall movement first peaked in its activity in late October 2015, an ongoing thirst for activism is evident. The tension, anger and longing for further 'transformation' or decolonisation (whether articulated in terms of class, race or gender, or intersectionally across all dimensions) persist. Students themselves argue that they can resurrect protest at the flick of a twitter handle (anonymous interview with student leader, 2016). Adam Habib, the Wits vice-chancellor and head of Universities South Africa (USAf), recognises that the student movement reflects 'valid concerns about institutional racism and/or the slow pace of transformation at universities post-apartheid' (2016a).

It is also argued that top university structures worked with government to subvert the 2016 phase of the revolt. BFL (2016) relates high levels of suppression, collusion at high university level, and the presence of private security forces on campuses reporting directly to vice-chancellors. As the united fervour of the 2015 phase of the revolt declined it was unclear at the time whether the movement had been thwarted or was merely taking a breather. The bottom line was that the institutional culture had changed, student activism had proven how effective concerted action taken in solidarity can be, and the #FeesMustFall goals were partly achieved and partly suspended. Students were whispering that it was 'inevitable' that another outburst would be in the making. It appeared to be a question of time before the cycle would be repeated, in different iterations and possibly with different outcomes. For now, in this book, we focus on the first of these cycles.

REFERENCES

Bizos, G. (1998) 'Steve Biko'. In *No one to Blame? In pursuit of justice in South Africa*, cited at http://www.sahistory.org.za/topic/black-community-programmes-bcp#sthash.6BNTjmsG.dpuf

Black First Land First (2016) Is Prof Achille Mbembe the Joseph Goebbels of Wits? http://Black1tLand1sr.wordpress.com/2016/01/28/is-prof-achille-m

Booysen, S. (2015) *Dominance and Decline: The ANC in the Time of Zuma*. Johannesburg: Wits University Press.

Chikane, R. & Breakey, J. (2015) Students' decolonisation of varsities has only just begun. *Sunday Times*, 24 May.

Cohn-Bendit, D. (1998) *Wir haben sie so geliebt, die Revolution*. Berlin: Philo.

Collins, R. (1979) *The Credential Society: An Historical Sociology of Education and Stratification*. New York: Academic Press.

Duncan, J. & Frassinelli, P. P. (2015) The right to protest. Pamphlet, Johannesburg.

Flacks, D. (2010) Paul Goodman and the Old New Left. *Dissent*. https://www.dissentmagazine.org/article/paul-goodman-and-the-old-new-left

Fukuyama, F. (2013) What is governance? *Governance*, 26(3), 347–368.

Habib, A. (2016a) Goals and means: Reimagining the South African university and critically analysing the struggle for its realisation. Lecture in the African Voices series. London, University College of London.

Habib, A. (2016b) Address to Senate meeting, 2 June 2016, Johannesburg, University of the Witwatersrand.

Hirson, B. (1979) *Year of Fire, Year of Ash: The Soweto Revolt*. London: Zed Books.
Jansen, J. (2016) Jansen prophesies academic ruination. *Noseweek* Issue #200.
Malik, K. & Waglé, S. (2002) Civic engagement and development: Introducing the issues. In *Capacity for Development. New Solutions to Old Problems*. United Nations Development Programme (UNDP). http://unpan1.un.org/intradoc/groups/public/documents/un/unpan006234.pdf
Marxists Internet Archive (2002) The Black Panther Party – Guerrilla war in the USA. https://www.marxists.org/history/usa/workers/black-panthers/
Mbembe, A. (2016) Theodor Adorno vs Herbert Marcuse on student protests, violence and democracy. *Daily Maverick*, 19 January. http://www.dailymaverick.co.za/article/2016-01-19-theodor-adorno-vs-herbert-marcuse-on-student-protests-violence-and-democracy/#.Vw8tZmNWdcY
McLennan, A. (2014) Concept note on governance. Wits School of Governance. University of the Witwatersrand, Johannesburg.
Mouffe, C. (2013) How to interpret the recent protest movements? An agonistic approach. https://www.youtube.com/watch?v=4sWK2KRhBjo
Mouffe, C. (2016) The politics of passions: The stakes of democracy. The Steve Biko Lectures in Philosophy. University of Johannesburg, 8 March.
Naidoo, L. (2016) Contemporary student politics in South Africa: The rise of the black-led student movements of #RhodesMustFall and #FeesMustFall in 2015. In A. Heffernan & N. Nieftagodien (eds) *Students Must Rise: Youth struggles in South Africa before and beyond Soweto '76*. Johannesburg: Wits University Press.
Nonxuba, A. (2016) In S'thembile Cele, 'The protests will continue, says leader', *City Press*, 21 February.
Nyamnjoh, F. B. (2016) *#RhodesMustFall: Nibbling at Resilient Colonialism in South Africa*. Bamenda (Cameroon): Langaa Research and Publishing Common Initiative Group.
Pierre, J. & Peters, G. B. (2000) *Governance, Politics and the State*. New York: St Martin's Press.
Rakei, S. (2016) In Chris Barron, So many questions. *Sunday Times*, 21 February.
Ross, S. (2011) *The Leaderless Revolution*. London: Simon & Schuster.
Scott, J. W. (1977) *The Black Revolts: Racial Stratification in the USA*. Cambridge, MA: Transaction Publishers.
South African History Online (n. d.) http://www.sahistory.org.za/topic/black-community-programmes-bcp#sthash.6BNTjmsG.dpuf
TRC (Truth and Reconciliation Commission) (1998) Special Report, Glossary Sv 'Soweto Uprising'. http://sabctrc.saha.org.za/glossary/soweto_uprising.htm
World Bank (2013) What is governance? Governance in Middle East and North Africa. http://go.worldbank.org/G2CHLXX0Q0
Yu, D., Kasongo, A. & Moses, M. (2016) South African labour force 1995–2015, Working paper. https://theconversation.com/how-two-crucial-trends-are-affecting-unemployment-in-south-africa-56296?

PART ONE

POWER REDEFINED – 'WHAT HAPPENED TO GOVERNANCE?'

CHAPTER

1

TWO WEEKS IN OCTOBER: CHANGING GOVERNANCE IN SOUTH AFRICA

Susan Booysen

'The people have more power than the people in power.'
— *Protest placard used in student action outside Parliament, October 2015*

'You cannot carry out fundamental change without a certain amount of madness ... it comes from nonconformity, the courage to turn your back on the old formulas, the courage to invent the future.'
— *Thomas Sankara, in interview with journalist Jean-Philippe Rapp, 1985*

INTRODUCTION

The #FeesMustFall student movement that started in late 2015 unleashed social and political power that challenged the established political order, brought university managements to heel, and changed the social fabric of universities and of parts of society. Foundational values were to be reconsidered, and their ideological bases laid bare and cast off; policies were changed and institutions transformed – and the power of direct action to get radical results was affirmed.

October 2015, in the main, changed universities, government's relations with the youth, and government itself.

At the height of the national #FeesMustFall (#FMF) revolt, the protest was taken to the seats of power in Cape Town, Johannesburg and Pretoria. In Parliament, in the African National Congress's Luthuli House and at the seat of government power, the Union Buildings, the political parties and government braced themselves behind closed doors and security fences. In some instances they were shielded by armed security forces, under siege while the revolt unfolded on the streets.

Policy concessions and revisited practices were foremost among the gains – the students extracted significant compromises, substantial compared to what any opposition party, community protest, internal African National Congress (ANC) formation (such as a province or ANC league), or trade union federation had attained on comparable issues in the recent past. The parameter shifts of sociopolitical culture in South Africa were evident, if less tangible than the concessions on educational policy. The students changed the rules of the universities, held government to account and changed both national fiscal planning and higher education praxis. Even more, they served notice that the 1994 settlement was just the opening of the door and not an achievement in own right – that the sociopolitical compact was no longer carved in stone.

The 2015 student uprising, in a powerful intra-university alliance with workers, had far-reaching impacts, therefore, on government and society. The #FeesMustFall movement – bringing in a new iteration of post-#RhodesMustFall Fallism – started as a protest against the announcement on 4 October 2015 by the University of the Witwatersrand (Wits) of its planned 10.5 per cent increase in student fees for 2016. Student anger metamorphosed rapidly into a national campaign. It merged with pre-existing thrusts against the oppressions inherent in coloniality and whiteness, as epitomised in the ongoing presence of the colonialist Cecil John Rhodes (by name or figuratively) on several higher education campuses. It fused with long-standing protests against financial exclusions at the historically black universities – the University of Fort Hare and the Tshwane University of Technology, for example, had been protesting long before the 2015 Fallist movements found their feet. The campaign burgeoned into a powerful mass-solidarity student movement targeted at university managements and national government. The solidarity of action turned out to be short-lived, but the implementation of concessions, the student insistence on *full* implementation and the general impact of the revolt remained.

This chapter investigates in broad strokes the nature and level of change wrought by #FMF. It questions whether the revolt against the prevailing sociopolitical order – especially as it was manifested in higher education – approached 'revolutionary change' in the sense of a social revolution or merely far-reaching change across education and education-worker sectors. It questions whether it is set to be a continuous process of change or whether the movement has become so diversified, infiltrated by political parties, and pulled in irreconcilable ideological directions that its historical significance is fading. The chapter has a particular focus on how the events in the early stages (roughly the eight-month snapshot from October 2015 to June 2016) affected governance. I argue that at this early stage certain impacts are evident, while longer-term influences are still to be concretised. After unpacking the first eight months of the revolt in terms of changes in governance, the chapter develops and then applies an analytical framework. Methodologically, it draws on direct observation of the student action, listening to the unfolding narratives, studying the emerging literature and interpreting the sources.

THE PARTY POLITICAL NON-PARTISAN SETTING OF THE REVOLT

Assessing the student revolt's impact on governance in South Africa is inseparable from party politics, either by 'association with' or due to 'distance from'. The relatively non-partisan nature of the October 2015 phase of #FMF, together with the ANC's closeness to the Progressive Youth Alliance (PYA), helped to get the ANC government to compromise on fee increases and student funding. Much of the revolt originated from the children of the 1994 liberation, many of whom were specifically associated with the ANC's student structures. The ANC and its government had to settle, appease and halt the party political migration of its support base and contain anti-systemic action and the erosion of its hegemony. The ANC strategy, as it unfolded, was to *own* the October phase (and attach its fees and funding concessions to this peak period), and *disown* the continuation of the struggle (see Nkwanyana 2016).

Herein lay some of the keys to explaining the governance-related impact of the revolt, which is also the theme in the rest of the chapter: the protest had a radical thrust and challenged socio-political-economic fundamentals, yet it was not an outright rejection of the legitimacy of the regime (see also Booysen 2013) or its ideological compromises. The ANC and its government therefore had to play to a strategic middle-ground of concede-capture-control, recognising the explosive potential of the revolt and the threat that it could move beyond control – as it did in fact for a week or two (see also De Kadt 2015).

The young generation had been accumulating reservoirs of malcontent. Something had to give way. The young and the impatient, joined by some university workers and academic staff, came to speak truths to power in ways that demanded attention. They trampled on the myth of the miracle of South Africa's 1994 political settlement and overruled the dogma that the former liberation movement turned governing party, the ANC, was fulfilling the 'rainbow promises' of 1994. Coming from backgrounds of post-1994 poverty and/or socioeconomic exclusions, the student youth of 2015 rebelled against a cluster of higher education grievances: unaffordability and hence lack of access (direct and indirect, formal and informal) for the poorest and the unbearable position of the 'missing-middle', too well-off to get public funding yet unable to afford university life. As the authors of Chapter 7 remark regarding student protests elsewhere in sub-Saharan Africa: 'Universities became the sites where broader sociopolitical grievances were projected and transferred into more precise localised calls for transformation of educational institutions.' The grievances in the case of South Africa were 'compressed' (as conceptualised in Chapter 7) and nationalist and neoliberal struggles were contemporaneous. Once the 1994 rainbow faded, the struggles were compressed further, combining with the pressures of intersectionalism, and generalised, beyond structural adjustment economic desperation. The lens of ongoing and intersectional oppressions and alienation due to colonial and apartheid legacies focused the part of the revolt that went beyond the tangible fees/funding issue. Beyond the traditional race and class filters, the students also saw the denial of spaces for intergender and feminist voices, affecting the LGBTIAQ+ (lesbian, gay, bisexual, transgender, intersex, asexual and queer) community.

In a powerful twist on protest against the dual targets of the ruling class's complacency and the tolerated residues of apartheid and colonialism, the protesting youth projected themselves regularly as the neglected 'children of the ANC'. Narratives centred often on the 'condition of the black child', 'black pain', the 'suffering of the children of the workers', and the students' concern about workers as their emblematic 'mothers and fathers'. In Chapter 6 in this volume, David Everatt sees this as 'victimhood'. It is, even more powerfully, anger directed into mobilisation to fight against the delivery and transformational (by now, decolonisation) deficits in the 1994 expectations. This is also to be balanced against the possibility that for many students the revolt was about ensuring their own middle-class ascendance.

The #FMF narratives were complex and strategically calculated. The 2015 narratives were concentric to ANC standpoints yet also projected assertive black consciousness. They positioned the critical mass of students on the side of the ANC government, in a precarious way at a time of cross-class and race solidarity – and before party political alignments resurfaced from roughly November 2015 onwards (also described by Naidoo 2016b: 186–188). Amid tones of black consciousness the narratives voiced angry reminders to the generation of 'liberators' that the youth requires them to make good on the 1994 liberation promises. If not, the revolt gave notice that the rising class of post-secondary-education youth might realign, away from the former liberation movement, and create political homes for themselves in opposition parties or anti-systemic political organisations.

The political parties and their student wings – especially at the height of the October phase of the protest – were forced to keep their distance. A Democratic Alliance (DA) leader, Helen Zille, had to be escorted away from protesting Stellenbosch students. Their message to Zille was 'Voetsek [also 'Futsek' on some posters], you aren't here for us' (*News24* 2015). It contrasted with the #FMF students' relative closeness to the ANC (although the ANC at Wits had sometimes to meet students clandestinely) and high levels of tolerance for the Economic Freedom Fighters (EFF). The EFF was centrally positioned, and pro-EFF students drove the protests in many locations, including in the #OutsourcingMustFall phase. Black First Land First (BLF, the Andile Mngxitama offshoot from the EFF) and the Workers and Socialist Party (Wasp) were active, working to sustain the radical wing of the revolt and propelling a left surge in the slipstream of the revolt.

The ANC's PYA student structure – comprising generally the ANC Youth League (ANCYL), Young Communist League (YCL), Congress of South African Students (Cosas), South African Students Congress (Sasco) and the Muslim Students' Association (MSA) – was foremost in many of the campus struggles. The EFF's student command structures were leading the revolt (mostly in non-partisan presences) at many sites. Equally, the Pan-Africanist Congress's Pan Africanist Student Movement of Azania (Pasma) mobilised both before and during the revolt at many of the campuses. They were radically pro-poor and black consciousness. The DA's Democratic Alliance Student Organisation (Daso) was virtually absent from the 2015 revolt, despite its focus on the black middle class (disproportionately represented on campuses). #FMF was a black-led struggle for radicalism and it brought together the *black* underclasses in solidarity with the *black* middle class and a sprinkling of radical white middle class. The 2015 revolt was simply not doing liberalism, even if that ideology in all probability did well among the passive numerical majorities on many of the campuses.

FRAMEWORK TO ASSESS IMPACT ON GOVERNANCE

My analysis uses three main categories of impact and governance change: foundational and ideological reconsideration; policy and institutional change; and modes of political action (Table 1.1). The analysis recognises differences across the locality of campus and type of higher education institution – it draws out the most tangible changes and trends concerning phenomena that were often unevenly realised at different sites yet cohered to constitute generalised trends.

In terms of *foundational and ideological impact,* the student action induced important forms of reconsideration of the status quo. It questioned the legitimacy of the convenient social compact that emerged from the transitional negotiations of the early 1990s, culminating in the Constitution of South Africa of 1996. Concerns about the ANC's compromises at the time re-emerged in the contemporary student narratives, by now in aggravated form and from young people who had the lived experience (an essential part of the narrative) of continuous poverty, inequality and disappointing opportunities. Substantial numbers of the black youth had risen above these conditions, but emphasised their solidarity and helped lead the revolt.

The debate on insufficient levels of societal change had in the preceding two decades already been legitimised by the ANC in its public narratives around the ANC in government having failed to deliver more definitive change. The ANC had been positioning itself as a leader of this game of identifying apartheid and colonialism to this day as the leading causes of the deferred revolution. In the time of the second Zuma term, 2014 onwards, it increasingly reinvented the liberation struggle – prolonging liberation and propelling liberation narratives into the present, pleading minimal agency in terms of what was not delivered in the first twenty-two years of democracy. Achille Mbembe (2016b) similarly argued (on the ANC positioning itself as both government and protester) regarding the #FMF mobilisation at the Union Buildings and mayhem caused by ANC-aligned youth in breaking down fences and burning portable toilets in the course of street battles: '… if you go to Pretoria you are going against the government. You are going against the ruling party, but then the ANC turns around and says, we are with you …' The students had the benefit of a platform prepared by the ANC, although they used it with more radical intent; their positions on decolonisation, racism and gender transformation amplified their grievances about the foundations of South African society. The student movement also forged reinvigorated ideological critiques, infused with threads of black consciousness, African nationalism and criticisms of the preceding political-economic orders.

The second part of foundational impact relates to the ANC government's mode of operations in a zone of consensual, piecemeal, gradualist policy and delivery. Up to the time of the student revolt (and in some respects thereafter) the ANC government was accustomed to arguing that strategies, policies and plans were in place, that delivery was proceeding (and it always had statistics, even if ambiguously framed, to back up the trend) and that just a touch of patience was needed before delivery would reach even more people. These ANC narratives have been evident in, for example, its election campaigns and, as government, in the president's State of the Nation addresses. The students differed. They forced the ANC government into immediate and far-reaching policy reconsideration in higher education, and gave notice that change in other sectors required urgent attention.

Policy and institutional impact constituted a second category of evidence of change to governance. The students extracted specific public policy changes on the delivery of higher education, and forced policy amplification and implementation that required far-reaching national budgetary reprioritisation. Government had to make good the expectations of the children of the 1994 transition to access free, quality higher education that is relevant to black lives. In the process of insisting on their demands being met (see Table 1.2 on demand progression in the revolt) students successfully challenged the offices of both the president and the minister of higher education and training. Their immediate targets, however, were at the university level. In an Althusserian view (Althusser 2014) of the universities as extensions of the state apparatuses, students subverted the authority of university councils, senates and – at the later, beyond-solidarity phase of the revolt – also the authority of student representative councils (SRCs). The students, as the first line of attack, thus held the universities to account (see also February 2015) for continuously colonial, apartheidist and neoliberal institutional and educational cultures that brought exclusion and alienation at university level.

A third category of governance changes relates to ***protest, direct action and direct accountability***. Using direct action as the means of engagement with the state (and extracting results), the student action added a new axis to public protest in South Africa. Unlike community (or 'service delivery') protest, the student action occurred in the political centre and, with the facilitation of social media, evolved rapidly into a national campaign. Government could not marginalise or ignore the student constituency. Because of the importance of their class and intellectual positions, articulation of grievances and access to both social and conventional media guaranteed that they would publicise demands, embarrass government and threaten to let the revolt spread among angry and jobless young people (see also Naidoo 2015b). There have been no direct ANC or government references to such fear; yet, circumstantially, the state's speed of compromise and counter-action suggests it was real.

The protest elevated direct action over voting. Students could see immediate responses and did not have to wait for conventional and multi-phase policy-making processes to unfold. On accountability, #FMF student action forced national and university leaderships into various forms of humbling demeanour, direct accountability and, at university level, 'capture' by the students. The national leaders included the president, Jacob Zuma; the minister of higher education and training, Blade Nzimande; the ANC secretary-general Gwede Mantashe and a range of university vice-chancellors. The students redefined political accountability in national politics and management answerability in the universities.

Table 1.1: The impact of the 2015–2016 South African student revolt on governance – framework for analysis

FOUNDATIONAL AND IDEOLOGICAL IMPACT	
SYMPTOMS	DEMANDS AND ALTERNATIVES
Deficits of social justice, 1994 settlement falls short, reformism allows coloniality, racism, whiteness, intergenderist intolerance to remain rooted. Intersectionality of ongoing exclusion. Lived experience shows contradictions.	Restitution through an identity-nationalism and black consciousness, to obliterate structural inequalities and injustices associated with colonialism, apartheid and racism. Capitalism questioned, but socialist demands weakly articulated.

SUBVERSION OF COMFORT ZONE OF ANC GOVERNANCE			
Gradualist 'we have a plan', 'we are working on it' placebo is delegitimised. Students demand and get immediate action from the ANC.			
IDEOLOGICAL SUBVERSION			
In: Pan-Africanist 'African nationalism' with African/black-*African*, counter-colonialist, 'forgotten children' foci, biggest reinvigoration of black consciousness since 1976, feminism and LGBTIAQ+ affirmation, consciousness of intersectionality of black oppression. **Out:** Neoliberalism, Rainbowism, whiteness, patriarchy, sexism and anti-LGBTIAQ+-ism.			
POLICY AND INSTITUTIONAL IMPACT			
POLICY – BUDGETARY	POLICY – SECTORAL	OUT-INSOURCING OF WORKERS	INSTITUTIONS
National budget reprioritisation – detracting from other budget items. Reversal of declines in expenditures.	Zero per cent fee increase. Select debt cancellation. Flexibility on registration fees, improved NSFAS funding, and books, accommodation, curriculum reform.	Phased termination of outsourcing of workers in cleaning, maintenance, gardening.	National – president, minister. University management – councils, senates, security systems. University students – SRCs, plenaries.
PARTICIPATION/MOBILISATION CHANGE			
New experiences of people's power: Power of direct action. Actions articulate with broader manifestations of 'parallel' (to official) forms of government.			
Voting less central	Occupy physical spaces	Protest culture	Tentative new alliances of workers and students
COUNTER MOBILISATION			
STATE AGENCIES	POLITICAL PARTY/IES		PRIVATE SECTOR
Fears of contagion to other sectors. Strategy of compromise and contain.	ANC rules in aligned formations in PYA; EFF, Pasma, BLF further programmes through own formations.		Privatisation and commercialisation of higher education.

Table 1.2: Issue progression in the #FeesMustFall revolt

RANKING	DEMANDS, CLAIMS	SEQUENCES
FOUNDATIONAL Challenging coloniality, racism, intergender biases	Angry victims of slow, incomplete liberation; 'address failure of older generation to complete the liberation'. Revisiting 1994 and going further back to pre-1994 colonial roots; 'the post-1994 consensus bred complacency'. Understand oppression in intersectional terms. Decolonise education and post-secondary institutions and the curriculum, and establish new frameworks to drive structural change and institutional renewal. Fight whiteness and racism; amplify and live black consciousness. Let women rise and assume leadership roles. Recognise and create space for inter-genderism. Effect justice for outsourced workers.	Throughout, originating in #RMF, demands and ideals solidify over time.
EDUCATION POLICY Fees and access demands	Zero per cent fee increase. Free education (for the poor), free quality education, take care of the missing-middle. Address corruption in NSFAS. No exclusions through historical debt. No exclusions through inability to pay registration fees. Cater for accommodation, study materials, food.	Starter demands in #FMF, diversifying, details get added.
EDUCATIONAL INSTITUTIONS Question and reject	University councils forced to change decisions. Senate meetings invaded and challenged. Question authority structures like SRCs; reject SRCs – 'they represent a minority on campus'; reinstate the legitimate SRC (NWU). Reject sell-out student organisations.	Becomes an immediate issue when demands were denied at first.

RANKING	DEMANDS, CLAIMS	SEQUENCES
CULTURAL CLEANSING Decolonise or change into the present	Remove hurtful and insulting symbols of the old order, ranging from statues to paintings and building names. Make the African child feel comfortable in higher education. Scrap Afrikaans dominance at nowadays 'multiracial' and black-dominant institutions; 'Tuks FM must play black music'. Revise curricular content work for more inclusive and Africa-centred pedagogical tools. Reactionary white-Afrikaans cultural organisations claim space for language rights. Get demographic representativeness in faculty – appoint and empower black faculty.	As the struggle progresses the students focus on detailed points of friction.
OUTSOURCING Conditions of workers and children	Make all essential service workers permanent employees. Grant these workers and their offspring full and fee-exempted study rights at the institutions of employment. Equalise wages paid across private company employers.	Ongoing struggle over time, the 2015–2016 phase is prolonged to get these concessions.
POLICE AND CAMPUS SECURITY BRUTALITY Excessive force	Condemnation of the mass arrest of more than a hundred UJ students, of vicious suppression of protest, in displays of violent masculine authority; at UWC and NWU security forces moved in in large numbers when students torched or vandalised buildings. Riot units and police snipers were on standby to manage protesting crowds, followed by stun grenades and tear gas; or maintain lower-key presences.	In, especially, the 2016 phase when managements work with some factions to get universities working again.

FOUNDATIONAL RECONSIDERATION OF GOVERNANCE

The student revolt had an unquestionable impact in challenging fundamentals of South Africa's post-1994 socio-political-economic order. The effects were not as immediate as the challenges to policy and educational institutions, yet unleashed demands for incisive corrective action for the shortcomings of 1994. It is possible that these political, social, cultural and moral impacts could continue unfolding for the foreseeable future.

Forcing a review of the sufficiency of the 1994 settlement

The student revolt delivered signs that the social compact of the early to mid-1990s was becoming unstuck. The compact had included that the constitutional compromises of 1993 and 1996 are respected, rule of law prevails, due political and judicial process is followed and that people relinquish force and violence as means to change government and its policies. The #FMF challenged the substantive transformational compromises. Some factions also argued for the use of force and violence (see also Chapter 3 in this volume), believing that cathartic change is necessary to arrive at a new order (a popular student reading of Frantz Fanon, hero among black consciousness followers). There was simultaneously strain on the Truth and Reconciliation Commission's settlements – also branded as sell-out actions.

The older generation had settled into the post-1994 'consensus', accepting discrepancies and inequality (or in effect tolerating slow, incremental advancement), possibly reassuring the people that the ANC government's policies and plans will deliver, that this 'trusted ANC government' is doing all it can (see Booysen 2015: 126–162). The new generation of protesting students was strident in its demand that the missing elements of liberation be delivered. The University of Cape Town (UCT) vice-chancellor, Max Price (2015) acknowledged that for young people from township areas it is clear that the system does not work. These young people have *lived* service delivery problems and protests, the corruption and lack of national leadership. They have acquired a bold sense of anger and impatience. Jonny Steinberg (2015) writes, in the time between #RhodesMustFall and #FeesMustFall, '... for twenty years, there was a consensus in South Africa that the settlement we reached in 1994 was the right one. That is now open to question in ways it has not been before, on the streets and in the lives of ordinary people, especially the young and the aspirant'.

In line with the general Fallist centring of a complex campaign around a simple issue such as fees, the students also put on the agenda ownership and property, and the whiteness and coloniality of much of the character of South African universities (also taken as reflective of institutions of the state). In this positioning they were advancing a battle that the ANC itself was fighting, although from the ANC side in more politically opportunistic ways. Mbembe (2016b) identifies a cultural change, and notes that this new generation brings a new politics into the open, sharpening the antagonisms and getting them resolved.

> And that ... cultural shift ... is more important than anything else, and it signals a new form of politics, at least on campuses. The challenge will be to what extent these new protagonists are capable of linking up with other social and professional categories, workers, the disenfranchised youth. Will they be able to build broad coalitions and put new claims to the state and to society?

The students themselves frequently used revolutionary language, citing selectively from Frantz Fanon, Thomas Sankara, Steve Biko and others and doing political education on the basis of their writing. Leigh-Ann Naidoo (2015a) elaborates in the context of #RMF: 'The RMF movement takes seriously [black consciousness] and Biko and are reading Fanon and Freire, Cabral, Nkrumah, Sankara...' There were degrees of revolutionary promulgation along with mimetical transfers between systems and historical conditions (see Mkhatshwa 2015b). Some used revolutionary and African-nationalist decolonisation language, indicating the fundamental radical-change intent; others use revolution in ways that are compatible with their open display of ANC affiliation while they ask for implementation of the ANC's prevailing policies. Much of the subsequent *non-revolutionary* furtherance of the revolt (settlement on the fees issue and further-access action directed through university institutional channels) could be linked to uprising participants, leaders who projected themselves as 'children of the ANC', still deferring to the parent body.

The managements of the higher education institutions seemed to have been unaware of the extent of alienation and discrimination experienced by large numbers of black students and staff. Universities tended to see themselves as largely transformed courtesy of black student numbers, without due cognisance of the texture of the experience. Wits, for example, '... has become 75 per cent black. In twenty-one years! And this at a university that's historically white' (Tawana Kupe, quoted in Bloom 2015).

On decolonisation, students blended the narratives of alienation, ongoing racial structuring of society and rousing statements on injustice. UCT students adopted the broad decolonisation definition of 'the removal of all unjust systems', including 'patriarchy, racism and capitalism in society' and projected the need for 'the restructuring of society to reflect African systems' (Nxumalo 2015; Appendix 2). These discussions nevertheless were characterised by 'statements [that] ignore the extensive diversity of the economic, circumstantial and educational status of students …' (Letsaolo 2015: 2). Blade Nzimande tried to interpret the 2015 recasting of the universities as a point to get 'dialogues, talks and conversations' going, saying: 'The important thing about student protests is that they are forcing us to re-imagine the university space' (see Monama 2016; also see Mbembe 2016c).

Pushing the ANC out of its comfort zone

At least two aspects of the #FMF revolt pushed the ANC out of its governance comfort zone. First, the new generation had lost trust that the ANC government is unambiguously on track to fulfil the liberation promises. As Lerato Lephatsa (2015) points out, the ANC had 'scripted a narrative that presents it as a progressive liberation movement in governance, thus responsible [for] numerous "gains" achieved in the past twenty-one years'. Second, and interrelated, the student generation signalled its loss of patience, along with demands for immediate action. Such patience is one of the premises that had been binding the ANC's national governance project – contagion, in which the students' disbelief spreads to other sectors, could implode the ANC governance project.

Indications were that the ANC had been unaware of the build-up of the students' hashtag revolution, expecting just another *campaign* to register objections against fee increases (see Mantashe 2015 for the appeal to students not to let the campaign evolve into anarchic violence). The ANC's (2012) theorisation of the 'second phase of the transition to democracy' was not synchronised to the students' 2015 iteration of far-reaching change. The ANC was pushed out of its comfort zone of governance by the students using exactly the same parent-child narrative that constitutes another pillar of the ANC's governance project. In usual circumstances, the ANC is regarded as the caring parent who may not get everything right, yet 'will bring home the food at night' (Booysen 2013). In recent years, the ANC itself has been relying on anti-colonial and nationalistic rhetoric to build explanations for continuous socioeconomic shortfalls in contemporary government delivery and 'transformation', thereby legitimating narratives of the deficits of the 1994 settlement. This helped create fertile soil for the student movement.

Safe-zone protest, with the ANC retaining control

Much of the student movement remained close to the ANC, confirming that the ANC had only felt truly threatened for a brief period from late October to early November 2015. For example, in an interview with the *Sunday Independent* in February 2016, the incoming SRC Wits president at the time, Nompendulo Mkhatshwa, argued about her iconic ANC head-wrap: '… the *doek* has been our thing as women in the ANC … [we] gain strength from it' (2015a; 2016). The most prominent of the Wits leaders, Mcebo Dlamini, treated ANC secretary-general Mantashe with deference when the movement descended on Luthuli House (see Lephatsa 2015).

The ANC-aligned PYA caused divisions in the Wits movement when it was revealed that revolt leaders had been meeting in and with the PYA, beyond the assembly format that generally held sway (see Wits SRC 2015a). ANC national structures had intervened and a meeting was held on Sunday 25 October 2015 at which, it was reported, participants included President Zuma's daughter, Thuthu Zuma, and the current and outgoing SRC leaders at Wits (South African History Online 2016). The ANC structures told the students to 'take charge', 'pull out on a high morale' and 'postpone the matter' (see Gillespie 2015). Student body members of WitsFeesMustFall alleged that the SRC had been bribed, and in response #ANCcapture began trending on Twitter. The SRC (2015b) denied these claims, and averred that no decisions had been made in the meeting. The PYA then turned on #FMF and called on the State Security Agency to probe the #FMF movement, calling it a 'counter-revolutionary movement' intending to 'overthrow a democratically elected government of the people' (Cele 2016). The minister of state security, David Mahlobo (2016), suggested in his 2016–2017 budget vote that he had been following through, stating: 'Some of these protesters are undermining the authority of the state by engaging in acts that seek to provoke the law enforcement agencies hence some people have acted with impunity by killing members of the security agencies.'

The ANC and its associate organisations of the SACP, ANCYL and Sasco also suggested that a 'third force' was behind the movement. The destructive and violent students at the Union Buildings, for example – whom Fallists in the crowd continuously wanted to bring under control – in turn pointed fingers to a 'third force'. Over time the third force was alleged to have been the EFF student command, or unnamed political parties (according to Nzimande, in early February 2016 (Lewis 2016)); or the National Union of Metalworkers of South Africa (Numsa) for allegedly paying for student bus transport to the Union Buildings (said Cosas Gauteng chairperson Lwando Majiza (Ngoepe 2015), or for example, Nzimande in early February 2016). Nico Cloete (2016) more cogently points out the role of political parties, including the ANC, which play out their control and recruitment functions on campuses. His argument articulates with the dissensus that followed the ten days of solidarity in October, a condition that was substantially due to the ANC and its aligned PYA trying to regain lost student territory.

When, in early January 2016, the #FMF movement threatened to disrupt the 2016 South African local government elections if access to free higher education remained unrealised,[1] the ANCYL leadership threatened that #FMF 'will meet the might and wrath of the PYA. No one will ever be allowed to disrupt elections in this country' (Maine 2016). ANCYL president Collen Maine argued that #FMF was supposed to have been a campaign and not a movement (Mkentane 2016). Sasco, in third-force mode, added that it was 'aware of CIA-trained dark forces, who wanted to use the #FeesMustFall campaign as fertile ground for regime change in the country' (Mkentane 2016). The ANC senior leadership and cabinet members had, on various occasions – and especially in the aftermath of the #RhodesMustFall actions – admonished students to follow the law and prioritise legal and administrative processes, and not to 'rip pages' out of their history books.

When its 'children' revolted and forced accountability and policy change on higher education, the ANC struggled for a while to find its feet again – but in order to be seen as remaining in charge, and in good standing with the rising youth generation, it conceded, reprioritised national budgets and fiscal allocations, and appointed a commission of inquiry to help deliver solutions to challenges thrown out through the uprising. The costs included the estimated R460 million of university infrastructural damage up to May 2016 (National Assembly 2016).

Beyond ANC control, but in conjunction with ANC government, university managements in 2016 were in more open and consultative relationships with student structures than previously. In volatile conditions, where students were troubled continuously by financial constraints, managements gathered their own intelligence to help them prevent new outbreaks. Their sources included university media staff reading daily the Facebook accounts of student leaders; vice-chancellors sharing information mutually on campus-specific Fallist trends; and, on occasion, also receiving information from observant outsourced security companies working on campus.[2]

POLICY CHANGE

The most direct #FMF impact on governance was in the realm of policy change. The national budget was reprioritised by reallocating from previously prioritised areas, including basic and vocational education and training (Sachs 2016). University funding increased and student access to higher education improved – all within record time. The revolt triggered a turnaround – funding for higher education had not previously been sufficiently prioritised (see Chapters 11 and 12 in this volume) and national allocations had been on a proportionate decline. However, with the new 'regime' of no fee increases and rapid progress to free education for the poor, the improvements would still be insufficient. In this respect, university managements were victims of the same complacency that was affecting national government (see Lund 2015). Vice-chancellors asked themselves how it was possible that under their watch and despite their ongoing attention to the exact matter of the 2015–2016 protest, the revolt actually happened (see Badat 2016a). They had imagined that they had sufficient trust, that students had infinite patience, and that more substantive change could follow in due course.

Much of the policy success was about getting the government and universities to *implement* prevailing policy commitments to free higher education for the poor, and see government and universities realise institutional (including racial) transformation that had been *envisaged* when the post-apartheid order took root. Some students had a more radical version, though, 'demanding decolonisation and social justice as opposed to incremental change through transformation' (see Naidoo 2015b: 13). Students were occupying the moral high ground, building their campaign on the notion of the unfulfilled promises of the ANC regime, or the expectations young people had had of free education at all levels. Many students emphasised how modest their expectations were. At the Union Buildings protest of October 2015, some stressed 'we are not here to do anything except ask for government to implement policy' (Rappetti 2015). The rage was evident, with some protesters calling President Zuma a traitor, or claiming, as did one poster: 'It is like 1976; it is like Marikana – we are dying all over again'. Others were even angrier, about university coloniality (in curriculum and institutional culture) and an unjust society in general.

The government's reaction at the time was to make compromise offers while promising task teams to investigate pressing matters. Government thus retreated strategically, compromised with the students on a zero per cent fee increase for 2016, further committed to leveraging free higher education for the poor, and made substantial additional contributions to facilitate access. Government forced the National Treasury and universities to find much of the money. At university level the commensurate-with-government steps to get financial access and inclusion leapt forward whereas the long-term sustainability of the rescue measures remained in the balance (Sachs 2016). The thrust to get and advance more black academic staff gained (modest) momentum; and the insourcing of university workers progressed, even if at substantial cost to universities (Jansen 2016) – by mid-2016 Wits estimated that insourcing would add R100 million to its annual budget, and this was the ceiling set by the Wits Council (11 June 2016). The broader issue of decolonising curricula and institutional culture was a paradigmatic shift for universities, although the exact requirements remained to be clarified (Badat 2016b).

The policy base, implementation and extension

Insufficient transformation of higher education prevailed despite the development and adoption of policy in many instances. Policy itself, however, was meaningless without *implementation* – and students insisted (Student debate 2016) on policy being refined, extended and implemented (even constitutional amendments to be instituted) to bring them free higher education. Multiple ANC policy documents demonstrate the existence of a policy base – but it had had insufficient impact on university and student life. This base included the ANC's 2007 conference deliberations and its 2009 election manifesto, 'Working Together we can do more'. It stated that 'the ANC has always stood for' the 'right to access health, education …' and then simply mentioned that the national financial aid scheme 'is helping to improve participation of the poor in higher education' and that '(m)uch needs to be done to improve the quality of health care and education'. Under the heading 'education is at the centre of our efforts', the manifesto restated the Freedom Charter's call. The slogan was repeated in the ANC's 2015 National General Council (ANC 2015a) political report. With emphasis on school education primarily, it stated that there will be '... work towards a free and compulsory education for all children'.

The 2014 ANC election manifesto 'Together we move South Africa forward' referred to higher education and student access elusively, in typical 'ANC-speak': 'Working together with universities and FET [Further Education and Training] colleges we will intensify efforts to support the needs of poor students, including (and through) adequate student funding ...'. The manifesto boasted that student enrolment at higher education level had increased from 495 000 in 1994 to 953 000 in 2012. The proportion of African students grew from 49 per cent in 1995 to approximately 66 per cent in 2010. At that time more than 1.4 million students had benefited from the National Student Financial Aid Scheme (NSFAS).

In their action, the students engaged only minimally with these specific details, but took forward the generic constitutional formulations on educational rights. The 1955 Freedom Charter call, 'the doors of learning and of culture shall be opened!' and the ANC's continuous elevation of the charter as its guiding document supported student demands. The ANC's 1993 Reconstruction and Development Programme (RDP) had urged the incoming government to attend to access and finance for higher education. Thereafter, the 1996 Constitution stopped short of guaranteeing free access to higher education. The 1997 Education White Paper (Council on Higher Education 1997), 'A Programme for the Transformation of Higher Education', was hoped to assert guarantees, but it was soon confirmed to be crying out for review. The 2008 report by the Ministerial Committee on Transformation and Social Cohesion and the Elimination of Discrimination in Public Higher Education Institutions (Soudien et al. 2008) found pervasive discrimination at South African universities. It highlighted that although African students were admitted, the system conspired against them. The 2013 Department of Higher Education and Training White Paper for Post-School Education and Training, entitled 'Building an Expanded, Effective and Integrated Post-School System' (Department of Higher Education and Training 2013), promised to build 'appropriate diversity'. The issue of poor – including lower-middle-class – students who were systematically denied access, or who became financially excluded, as well as the missing-middle of students 'too rich' to qualify for NSFAS support, was the collective elephant in the room.

The concessions that students gained at this time and while broader changes were unfolding were: zero per cent fee increases for 2016; the reorganisation of NSFAS, and better funding for it to assist a much wider range of poor students; special payment terms for students who cannot afford upfront registration fees (and, later, additional flexibility on further payment deals); finding interim funds for tuition of poor students and the children of previously outsourced workers; no exclusion for historical debt (and some debt written off); universities escalating help to source accommodation for needy students; and children of formerly outsourced workers now being incorporated into the system of employee benefits, transport, book allowances and affordable canteen food. SRCs – those of Wits, the University of Pretoria and UJ, for example – launched fundraising campaigns to cover costs for the missing-middle students. These aspects of free education were on the agenda amid the realities of a no-growth economy, high unemployment rates and retrenchments.

Unrealised policy initiatives towards free or accessible higher education

Despite official declarations of the importance of the higher education sector, there are multiple signals that government has been guilty of sectoral neglect (see, for example, Butler-Adam 2015: 1). A 2012 report found that free higher education for the poor is possible and affordable (Department of Higher Education and Training 2012),[3] but it got stuck in the politics of public policy making. The National Treasury regarded it as non-implementable. The National Development Plan (NDP), the current government policy blueprint, also offered some support for broader access in referring to the areas in which South Africa 'already has endowments and comparative advantage such as ... higher education', and in recommending that government should:

> ... provide all students who qualify for the National Student Financial Aid Scheme (NSFAS) with access to full funding through loans and bursaries to cover the costs of tuition, books, accommodation and other living expenses. Students who do not qualify should have access to bank loans, backed by state sureties. Both the NSFAS and bank loans should be recovered through arrangements with the South African Revenue Service.

By the time of the revolt, progress towards these goals was negligible. When, in April 2016, NSFAS presented its 'new plan', student leaders condemned it as 'fundamentally flawed' (Hassan 2016).

Initiatives for free access for the poor failed to get the necessary political support, but the students had the bargaining chip of the power to call #FMF Round Two. The ANC's National General Council (NGC) meeting was dismissive, saying 'higher education has implemented its plans and programmes despite the shortage of skills and resources' (2015: 19). Subsequently, as the protest unfolded, senior ANC and government figures Mantashe and Nzimande issued clarifications: 'We must be able to fund free education because it is not a cost but an investment into the future. Students are the future of the country' (Mantashe 2015) and 'free higher education is not a government policy ... but it is government policy to subsidise the poor until they get their first undergraduate qualification' (Nzimande 2015).

Following President Zuma's meeting with vice-chancellors, chairpersons of university councils, presidents of SRCs and other student representatives in late October 2015, he announced the Commission of Inquiry into Higher Education Funding. It was scheduled to report in late 2016 (later extended into 2017) and was briefed to take into account the Constitution, current education laws, findings of previous task teams, policies, reports and guidelines.

Unpacking the policy concessions

The students gained notable concessions, compared to what would have been feasible for any opposition party, community protest, internal ANC formation (such as a province or ANC league), or trade union federations to attain. The student movement's short-term policy gains and power over unfolding governance generally could be explained by many of the activists playing 'children of the ANC's own revolution'. In addition, for much of the protest the students did not campaign under party political banners, and they did not call for entirely new policies but, rather, for the ANC to make good on stated policy directions. There were multiple reasons why the ANC felt obliged to heed the student demands, including the students' status as a powerful constituency in elections.

Policy concessions are not entirely unusual; the ANC does change policy under pressure, even if not as dramatically and rapidly as in the case of #FMF. For example, in 2015 Cosatu (Congress of South African Trade Unions) resisted policy changes on pension pay-outs and the ANC reversed its initial position. In one roughly comparable *major* policy concession, the Treatment Action Campaign (TAC) forced government to make hitherto unaffordable – and thus inaccessible – antiretroviral treatment available in the public sector (it took roughly five years, however, from the start of the TAC campaign to government's conceding).

TENTATIVE INSTITUTIONAL CHANGE EMERGING

The students' assault on universities challenged and subdued top government and governing party figures – ranging from the president of South Africa, and the minister of higher education and training, to the secretary general of the ANC, and including university structures and figureheads. Even when universities argued that they were autonomous from the state (especially in the intellectual domain and despite their economic dependence on the state), students drew a seamless connection between state and universities. Simon Rakei (2016) of the UCT #RMF leadership collective stated: 'Universities are an extension of the state and part of the state's apparatus', and 'also part of government and should be putting pressure on government. So by putting pressure on universities, it's an extension of putting pressure on the state.'

#FMF pushed for aloof and sheltered politicians and university principals (and, indirectly, academic staff) to account to them. The following accounts are isolated cases but demonstrate nevertheless the power that protesting and unified students could yield over government and university institutions. Students were encouraged by their conquest of the Wits vice-chancellor, Adam Habib. At the protest at Parliament, the seat of legislative power and where the medium-term budgetary framework was being delivered on 21 October 2015, students demanded to be addressed by the minister of higher education and training. Shielded by security and accompanied by cabinet ministers in security portfolios, Nzimande relented – but loudhailer failures and being shouted down by students cut short his intervention. (Government responses and, in the late-2015 and 2016 phase, university responses, were frequently shielded by high-level, also private, security – see Mbembe 2016a.) A day later, on 22 October, students converged on another major centre of power, the ANC's Chief Albert Luthuli House headquarters. They forced secretary general Mantashe to listen (but he was allowed to refuse their instruction to *sit* and listen) to their memorandum. On 23 October, students converged on the Union Buildings, the national seat of executive government. Inside the Union Buildings, students from multiple (but not all) universities and vice-chancellors negotiated with Zuma. Students rejected the deal for a limited 2016 fee increase that their vice-chancellors had struck with Nzimande on 20 October. The vice-chancellors' authority had also been undermined by the executive of government (Badat 2016a), besides the fact that the ANC as party had, by all indications, struck the Union Buildings' deal for a zero per cent increase with ANC government and the Presidency the day before (see ANC 2015b).

Beyond the inner chambers of power at the Union Buildings, student protestors demanded, in posters and interviews, that the president 'come here and account to us', adding 'we are here for free education now, now, zero per cent'. In a live-streamed television interview a protester, applying the 'black child narrative', explained the students' frustration with lack of accountability and relayed their suspicion of the unfolding negotiations: 'As a black child you do anything just to get their attention ... The minister understands the struggle of the black child ... But who knows what they are talking about inside. They could be manipulating us.' Many others echoed the reservations. Initially, it had been the plan that the president would descend to the Union Buildings lawns (albeit still behind physical security barriers and with high-level security forces present) to address the students. Riotous behaviour on the lawns and adjacent streets, however, changed the plans. The minister of police said that that they were trying to get the student leadership (those who were inside the Union Buildings) to come down and 'assure their constituencies' (Bauer 2015).

Another layer of institutional tensions demonstrated the state-institutional tumult triggered by the revolt. On the one hand, it was stated that the National Treasury had been accusing Nzimande (general secretary of the South African Communist Party (SACP)), besides minister of higher education) of stirring up national protest in order to extract more funding from the Treasury. On the other hand, Wits vice-chancellor Habib was alleged to have blamed the 'Premier League',[4] known to be politically opposed to the SACP and Nzimande, for stirring up Wits students (BLF 2016).

At the height of the revolt students chose when they wanted to humiliate, invade or treat with kid gloves. The decisions of university councils, as in the case of the Wits negotiations, were rejected, and revised in line with student demands. At one point, the Wits Senate was invaded and faculty members were subjected to racist attacks. In some cases, students insisted on change at the top: at the Free State University students demanded the resignation of vice-chancellor

Jonathan Jansen (he resigned in May 2016); at UCT the vice-chancellor's office was torched. At other campuses, such as the North West University, the University of the Western Cape and UJ, major campus buildings were destroyed through arson. The legitimacy of SRCs was questioned, especially when SRCs settled and scaled down their protests after gaining the zero per cent for 2016 (see, for example, Lephatsa 2015; Chapter 11 in this volume). They stood accused of representing only the minority of students who had actually participated in their elections. 'Students no longer accept that [an SRC member] elected by a minority of students, can stand up and speak on behalf of the student body' (Naidoo 2016a).

In the overall scheme of things, the institutional change that took effect in the course of the 2015–2016 revolt offered small and tentative illustrations of its influence. Students forged curricular reconsideration and new institutional cultures – longer-term processes that commenced in earnest. Across universities, gains included the insourcing of workers, change in language policies, transformation of senates, and über-prioritising of the recruitment of black-African faculty.

All of the effects, whether they would be lasting or ephemeral, demonstrated how fragile university institutions could be, and how state power hierarchies are short-circuited in times of crisis. As Godsell and Chikane argue (Chapter 2 in this volume), a re-imagining of the university structure was not possible without re-imagining the ideological identity of the university. The revolt showed how at least some of the universities' hierarchical power structures were adjusted and it became widely accepted that coloniality (see Chapter 5 and Appendix 2 of this volume) in university cultures is alienating and exclusionary, *and* needs action. This was the beginning of tentative ideological reframing of crucial structures within the universities.

GOVERNANCE CHANGE THROUGH AFFIRMING DIRECT ACTION

The revolt demonstrated how students, united through mass action and facilitated by social media, could, within a week, escalate issues of free higher education and insourcing of workers from university management level to national presidential level – and get results. The action showed the effectiveness of mass direct action as a means of engaging government. In later phases of the revolt, however, unity frayed, and party political roots and acrimony (re)surfaced. The phase of major policy gains had passed, at least in the current cycle.

The value of protest action affirmed

The student protest of 2015–2016 was a major extension to the repertoires of protest politics in South Africa. Unlike the student protests, community (or 'service delivery') protest has hardly ever demanded a fundamental reconsideration of directions by government and the ruling party and hardly ever resulted in national-level or immediate policy concessions. In contrast, the #FMF action challenged the political system, and within days the movement threatened to subvert university authorities and forced national government into significant policy concessions. The student action hence raised the question: why vote if the impact of direct action can be quick and definitive? In pursuing direct action, the students changed the government–civil society interface of governance.

Ben Turok (quoted in Lund 2015) remarked that the ANC government was 'now faced with two rather powerful forces (labour and youth) which have shown that they can successfully fight for their own'. This had changed the balance of forces, and the ANC needed to 'recalculate'. There have on occasion been suggestions that community protest constitutes a rebellion (Alexander 2010), but community members have been willing to settle with their municipalities when their local or provincial demarcation issues were attended to. The student protests (see Appendix 1) reflected a more fundamental resentment over the shortfalls of the 1994 settlement.

Anarchists and arsonists at times threatened to capture the #FeesMustFall revolt – some suspected of being anomic agents of political parties that used township youth with nothing to lose as proxy agents; others were Fanonist cathartic agents (happy to set fire to buildings and throw Molotov cocktails), or simply out-of-control students and other youth who had graduated at the 'university of township protest'. The spokesperson for the Ministry of Higher Education and Training averred that this 'fringe does not enjoy students-wide legitimacy, they co-opt outside non-students ... to impose their will to students and universities' (Nkwanyana 2016). There are indications, however, that such a fringe may also be much closer to the ANC itself: at the Union Buildings protest, for example, journalists observed that it was Sasco students, students from the Tshwane University of Technology at Soshanguve, and the ANCYL who were burning toilets and breaking through security barriers (Tlhabi 2015; Rappetti 2015).

Student direct action has benefited from their being more centrally positioned than their community-member counterparts. They built a protest platform that ANC government could not ignore. Students are an intellectually-confident community, who know their legal and constitutional rights and are likely to know that concerted mobilisation on a platform of moral high ground is bound to have an effect. They know how to link their societal and university grievances to colonial, capitalist and racial histories. The student revolt – even if it mellowed and became politically diffused – brought a deepening and radicalisation of South Africa's protest project.

The student movement also brought new attitudes towards authority. The brutality of university institutions and processes were emphasised. In the words of Vuyani Pambo (2015), the EFF student command leader at Wits, '(t)he vice-chancellor insists that Wits EFF has been violent when, in fact, it is Wits University that has been ... brutal to the black students, workers, lecturers and its security staff.' In turn, some argued there was an ingrained effort to bring down the ANC government (Satgar 2016 dissects the argument). FitzGerald and Seale (Chapter 11 in this volume) assert 'there is no doubt that national government and institutional governance structures came under severe attack and were subjected to significant strain'. Pambo argued that Wits was targeting the radical students because they wanted to transform and decolonise the university; the Wits vice-chancellor argued that the university cannot tolerate (student) violence, in any form. At the University of North West (Mahikeng campus), brutality played out more party politically: when the university management decided to remove a legitimately elected SRC (due to its EFF links), the angry ousted students turned to arson.

CONCLUSION

The earlier phases of the revolt were remarkably non-party political – young people of several party backgrounds converged to focus on fees and exclusion, and students challenged the ANC government on policy and transformation-decolonisation. Many of the universities were dared to reinvent themselves on the fronts of racism, coloniality, quality education in terms of being post-colonial and Africanist, and failure on equality and justice. At that stage, students told opposition party leaders bluntly that their 'revolution was not for sale'. This did not prevent parties, ranging from the ANC to the EFF, DA and BLF, from trying to capture the action.

For the student formations the issue was to safeguard the 2015 gains in 2016 and beyond. Yet, few appear to have been immune from capture.

The ANC was never far from the action. The student movement was seen consistently as divided between alignment with and loyalty to the 'ANC parent' and the dissident, more radical student formations associated generally with the EFF or Pasma. The ANC as governing party, which needed to contain revolt and reassert control, did re-capture much of the student movement, as seen at Wits.

The texture of governance has, therefore, changed as a result of the student revolt. To be sure, the process was 'one step back, two steps forward', and it remains to be seen what will happen after the Commission of Inquiry into Higher Education Funding makes its recommendations – and to what extent they are implemented, or used as the basis for another round of revolt. In the meantime, the students suspended their revolt after taking the gains, however moderate and piecemeal.

The effect on the ANC as the ruling party remained ambiguous. Political and social culture changed. Several of the faces of governance changed, but not the government. Seeds, however, were sown – the student generation had had a taste of power. Whether that taste will change the way in which power has been implemented, or whether this generation will be co-opted into its embrace, can only be seen as the interregnum unfolds.

NOTES

1. Towards mid-2016, when universities started finalising their 2017 budgets, a senior university functionary reported (personal communication) that vice-chancellors had agreed not to disclose fee increase plans for 2017 prior to the local elections of 3 August 2016.
2. Information from a highly-placed UCT source, on intelligence gathering and sharing between university managements, Cape Town, 12 July 2016.
3. The report surmised that a fee-free university system is achievable with government cooperation. The NSFAS rollout mechanism, the report argued, would be appropriate to facilitate the transition. The report denotes university education as undergraduate degrees, certificates and diplomas; the student beneficiaries would receive cover for tuition, registration, books, accommodation, meals and travel costs; the qualification, over and above academic eligibility for university study, was to be based on a student's household's earnings.
4. An internal ANC lobby group or faction comprising mainly the ANC political leadership of the provinces of the North West, Free State and Mpumalanga. The League is known for its political support of President Zuma.

REFERENCES

ANC (2012) Resolutions by the National Elective Conference.
ANC (2014) Together we move South Africa forward. Election manifesto.
ANC (2015a) Resolutions by the National General Council.
ANC (2015b) Media statements (set of three) issued on 22 October. 09:19: Policing of student protests; 14:26: Statement of the ANC on student protests against fee increments; 20:47: ANC statement following meeting with the Progressive Youth Alliance. By e-mail.
Alexander, P. (2010) Rebellion of the poor: South Africa's service delivery protests – a preliminary analysis. *Review of African Political Economy*, 37(123), 25–40.
Althusser, L. (2014) *On the Reproduction of Capitalism: Ideology and Ideological State Apparatuses* (transl. and ed. G. M. Goshgarian). London: Verso.
Badat, S. (2016a) Contribution to debate on deciphering the meanings and explaining, 10 March, WISER, University of the Witwatersrand.
Badat, S. (2016b) Deciphering the meanings, and explaining the South African higher education student protests of 2015-16. Inyathelo Leadership Retreat, 4 April, Cape Town.
Bauer, N. (2015) Twitter, 23 October.
Black First Land First (2016) Is Prof Achille Mbembe the Joseph Goebbels of Wits? 28 January. https://black1stland1st.wordpress.com/2016/01/28/is-prof-archille-mbembe-the-joseph-goebbels-of-wits
Bloom, K. (2015) The negotiator: A view from the top floor of #FeesMustFall. *Daily Maverick*, 12 November. http://dailymaverick.co.za/article/2015-11-12-the-negotiator-a-view-from-the-top-floor-of-feesmustfall/#.V9VHjZN95sM
Booysen, S. (2013) *Twenty Years of South African Democracy: Citizen Views of Human Rights, Governance and the Political System.* Washington D.C. & Johannesburg: Freedom House.
Booysen, S. (2015) *Dominance and Decline: The ANC in the Time of Zuma.* Johannesburg: Wits University Press.
Butler-Adam, J. (2015) Is the decline and fall of South African universities looming? *South African Journal of Science*, 111(11/12), 1–2.
Cele, S. (2016) #FeesMustFall is treason. *City Press*, 31 January.
Cloete, N. (2016) A 'third force' in higher education student activism. *University World News*, 4 March. http://www.universityworldnews.com/article.php?story=2016030410040021
Council on Higher Education (1997) Education White Paper 3: A programme for the transformation of higher education, July. http://www.che.ac.za/media_and_publications/legislation/education-white-paper-3-programme-transformation-higher-education
De Kadt, D. (2015) This data confirms South Africa's ruling party initially ignored mass protests. *Washington Post*, 23 October. https://www.washingtonpost.com/news/monkey-cage/wp/2015/10/23/this-data-confirms-south-africas-ruling-party-initially-ignored-mass-protests/
Department of Higher Education and Training (2012) *Report of the Working Groups on Fee-free University Education for the Poor in South Africa*, Pretoria. http://www.dhet.gov.za/SiteAssets/Fees%20Must%20Fall/287700266-Final-Draft-Report-of-the-Working-Group-on-Fee-Free.pdf.

Department of Higher Education and Training (2013) White Paper for post-school education and training: 'Building an expanded, effective and integrated post-school system', published in *Government Gazette*, 15 January 2014. http://www.gov.za/sites/www.gov.za/files/37229_gon11.pdf

February, J. (2015) Why is the state not a target of student protests? *Daily Maverick*, 20 October. http://www.dailymaverick.co.za/article/2015-10-20-op-ed-why-is-the-state-not-a-target-of-student-protests/

Gillespie, K. (2015) Zero per cent, the ANC and the new student movement. *The Daily Vox*, 4 November. https://www.thedailyvox.co.za/zero-percent-the-anc-and-the-new-student-movement/

Hassan, F. (2016) Contribution to debate 'A new model for funding higher education', 12 April, University of the Witwatersrand, Johannesburg.

Jansen, J. (2016) Contribution to debate 'How do universities adapt or die?' Inyathelo Leadership Retreat, 4–5 April, Cape Town.

Lephatsa, L. (2015) The ANC's capture of #FeesMustFall. *Daily Maverick*, 30 November. http://www.dailymaverick.co.za/opinionista/2015-11-30-the-ancs-capture-of-feesmustfall/#.Vx0dSXoQsTs

Letsaolo, M. (2015) Transforming our universities. *Rosa Luxemburg Stiftung News*, 1–2.

Lewis, C. (2016) Nzimande blames political opportunists for hijacking protests. SABC News, 1 February. http://www.sabc.co.za/news/a/760098004b86babc9773f777bc6a42c4/Nzimandeundefinedblamesundefinedpoliticalundefinedopportunistsundefinedforundefinedhijackingundefinedprotests-20160102

Lund, T. (2015) A game changer. *Financial Mail*, 29 October–4 November.

Mahlobo, D. (2016) Statement on State Security Agency department budget vote 2016–17, 26 April, Parliament of the Republic of South Africa, Cape Town.

Maine, C. (2016) Media briefing, 14 January, Luthuli House, Johannesburg. http://www.gov.za/speeches/minister-david-mahlobo-statement-state-security-agency-dept-budget-vote-201617-26-apr-2016

Mantashe, G. (2015) Media statement issued at 14:26, 22 October: Statement of the ANC on student protests against fee increments. By e-mail.

Mbembe, A. (2016a) Theodor Adorno vs Herbert Marcuse on student protests, violence and democracy. *Daily Maverick*, 19 January. http://www.dailymaverick.co.za/article/2016-01-19-theodor-adorno-vs-herbert-marcuse-on-student-protests-violence-and-democracy/#.Vw8tZmNWdcY

Mbembe, A. (2016b) Achille Mbembe on the new politics of the South African student. University seminar, 21 January. Interview with Hans Pienaar. *Litnet*. Retrieved from http://www.litnet.co.za/interview-with-achille-mbembe/

Mbembe, A. (2016c) Decolonising knowledge and the question of the archive. Public lectures at the University of the Witwatersrand, the University of Cape Town, and Stellenbosch University. Retrieved from *Africa is a Country*. E-book.

Mkentane, L. (2016) Vow to tackle 'dark forces' during poll. *Cape Times*, 15 January.

Mkhatshwa, N. (2015a) *Destiny*, December.

Mkhatshwa, N. (2015b) In M. Makhubele, Face of the fees revolution unmasked. *The Sunday Independent*, 6 February.

Mkhatshwa, N. (2016) Interview. *The Sunday Independent*, 21 February.

Monama, T. (2016) Talk to one another – Nzimande. *The Star*, 4 March.

Naidoo, L. (2015a) Open letter to Barney Pityana on the #RhodesMustFall movement. *Daily Maverick*, 14 April. http://www.dailymaverick.co.za/opinionista/2015-04-14-open-letter-to-barney-pityana-on-the-rhodes-must-fall-movement/#.VuVqmuYQsTs

Naidoo, L. (2015b) We shall not be moved or led astray: The emergence of the 2015 student movement. *New Agenda*, 60, 12–14.

Naidoo, L. (2016a) Forum at 8. South African Broadcasting Corporation. *SAfm* radio, 18 January.

Naidoo, L. (2016b) Contemporary student politics in South Africa: The rise of the black-led student movements of #RhodesMustFall and #FeesMustFall in 2015. In A. Heffernan & N. Nieftagodien (eds) *Students Must Rise: Youth Struggles in South Africa Before and Beyond Soweto '76*. Johannesburg: Wits University Press.

National Assembly (2016) Questions for written reply. Internal question paper 17 of 2016, 8 June, Parliament of the Republic of South Africa, Cape Town.

News24 (2015) Zille whisked away by police after students tell her to 'voetsek', 23 October. http://www.news24.com/SouthAfrica/News/Zille-whisked-away-by-police-after-students-tell-her-to-voetsek-20151023.

Ngoepe, K. (2015) Planned march to Union Buildings fuelled by 3rd force – Sasco, 22 October. http://m.sowetanlive.co.za/?articleId=15734325&sectionId=32

Nkwanyana, K. (2016) We can struggle and study. *PoliticsWeb*, 16 March. http://www.politicsweb.co.za/opinion/we-can-struggle-and-study?utm_source=Politicsweb+Daily+Headlines&utm_campaign=1c3ecd27ed-DHN_17_March_2016&utm_medium=email&utm_term=0_a86f25db99-1c3ecd27ed-140175425

Nxumalo, B. (2015) #ShutItDown. IOL, 23 October. http://www.iol.co.za/news/south-africa/western-cape/shutitdown-1934399

Nzimande, B. (2015) Roundtable discussion with students, 3 December, Johannesburg.

Pambo, V. (2013) Suspended Wits 7 violent or vexed? *Mail & Guardian*, 18 August–3 September.

Price, M. (2015) On student protests. *New York Times*, 8 September.

Rakei, S. (2016) In C. Barron, 'So many questions'. *Sunday Times*, 21 February.

Rappetti, I. (2015) Live-streamed broadcast by *eNCA*. 23 October, Union Buildings, Pretoria.

Sachs, M. (2016) Contribution to debate 'A new model for funding higher education'. 12 April, University of the Witwatersrand, Johannesburg.

Satgar, V. (2016) What #ZumaMustFall and #FeesMustFall have in common. *Mail & Guardian*, 18 January. http://mg.co.za/article/2016-01-18-what-zumamustfall-and-feesmustfall-have-in-common

Soudien, C., Michaels, W., Mthembi-Mahanyele, S., Nkomo, M., Nyanda, G., Nyoka, N. & Villa-Vicencio, C. (2008) Report of the Ministerial Committee on Transformation and Social Cohesion and the Elimination of Discrimination in Public Higher Education Institutions. Department of Education, Pretoria.

South African History Online (2016) University of Witwatersrand student protests 2015 timeline. http://www.sahistory.org.za/article/university-witwatersrand-student-protests-2015-timeline

Steinberg, J. (2015) Young South Africans harbour new thoughts. *Business Day Live*, 26 June. http://www.bdlive.co.za/opinion/columnists/2015/06/26/young-south-africans-harbour-new-thoughts

Student debate (2016) Contribution to debate on 'A new model for funding higher education', 12 April. University of the Witwatersrand, Johannesburg.

Tlhabi, R. (2015) Redi Tlhabi at Radio 702. Twitter, 23 October. Fees Must Fall protest in Pretoria 'hijacked'. *The Citizen*. http://citizen.co.za/833478/fees-must-fall-protest-in-pretoria-hijacked

University of the Witwatersrand Council (2016) Statement on Council meeting of 10 June by registrar Carol Crosley.

Wits SRC (2015a) Wits SRC addresses the vice-chancellor's 9-point proposal to students and rumours surrounding Sunday's PYA meeting, 29 October. http://www.iol.co.za/news/wits-src-on-habibs-plan-and-the-r40k-1937718

Wits SRC (2015b) Statement on the #FeesMustFall movement. http://www.wits.ac.za/studentservices/studentrepresentativecouncil/27541/wits_src_statement.html

PART TWO

PRIMARY VOICES – 'THE ROOTS OF THE REVOLUTION'

CHAPTER

2

THE ROOTS OF THE REVOLUTION

Gillian Godsell and Rekgotsofetse Chikane

INTRODUCTION

This chapter discusses the roots of the 2015 and ongoing protests in South Africa across three areas. The first area is that of the views, beliefs and experiences of current students. The voice here is chiefly that of Rekgotsofetse Chikane, who was centrally involved in the Fallist movement.[1] Chikane's primary voice brings a particular insight into the philosophies that shaped and grew out of the protests at the University of Cape Town (UCT) and elsewhere. The other two areas are the social and political roots of the protests, and those roots as found in South African university management practices.

STUDENT ROOTS

In public discussions, the Fallist movement and the academic project are often presented as incompatible. This chapter argues that decolonisation is the necessary road towards inclusive academic excellence. Pro-democracy and anti-fee protests worldwide have located themselves within the discourse about the role and purpose of a university for students and society. Across the globe, students are re-imagining the functioning of a university. They are rejecting the dominant ideologies of managerialism, neoliberalism and commodification within universities (Gonzalez 2012).

The South African protests of 2015 were driven by the same process of radical re-imagining. Set within the rapidly changing context of race, class, gender and various intersectional relations on campus, the protests were one facet of a new discussion regarding the role of South African universities in the development of their students. Malia Bouattia (2015: 26), describing the need for radical action to decolonise higher education in the United Kingdom, writes that as '… minor reforms are not working, we require alternatives to structures which mainly benefit straight white middle-class men'. The students in South Africa similarly require, not minor reforms of their institutions, but revolutionary change.

Noor Nieftagodien, chair of the History Workshop and active member of the October 6 movement at the University of the Witwatersrand, explains that this protest is not just about incorporating more black students into the status quo. It is about deep change within the university (Noor Nieftagodien, personal communication, 10 November 2015). South African students are seeking a university where workers, academics and students all feel welcome: a postcolonial university where they 'recognise themselves' and feel at home. As Nqobile Malaza, lecturer at Wits, put it in a Facebook post of 19 October 2015: 'The dream for a transformed society that breathes fairness, equality, equity and social justice is one whose time has undeniably come' (Nqobile Malaza, personal communication, 10 June 2016).

What differentiates the protests of 2015 from other access-related protests that have taken place across campuses over the past decade has been the (sometimes temporary and fluid) ideological solidarity among the various political and non-political student organisations and actors. The dedicated solidarity with workers may be one of the issues that sets South Africa 2015 apart from other student revolutions – stretching from China to Mexico (Castells 2015) – in the twenty-first century.

The root of the student protests of 2015 can be found within the nexus between the efforts of students, workers and academics to change the transformation discourse on university campuses across the country. This discourse has, in the past, often been reduced to what Nicola Rollock (2015), referring to academia in the United Kingdom, calls 'racial gesture politics … which appear to offer serious engagement with the issue of race inequality but in reality do very little'. The mass mobilisation of these varied stakeholders under a single issue was made possible by convergence of their beliefs regarding their roles in achieving transformation within their sectors. Crain Soudien (2010) reminds us that an understanding of the structural and ideological characteristics of the university is necessary if we are to unlock the transformation puzzle.

'Structural' refers to the ordered sociological relations among actors within the university; 'ideological' pertains to the 'beliefs and assumptions which define and articulate understandings of what the nature of the problem and its solutions are' (Soudien 2010: 883). The structural and the ideological have to be understood together. Where previous protests focused only on structural issues within the university, the debate among students and academics has progressed to a point at which the ideology of the university becomes the new area of protest.

Where Soudien sees ideology as a set of beliefs and assumptions, students have begun to understand it in a way similar to Peter Ekeh's interpretation of ideologies in African politics in the 1970s. Ekeh (1975: 94) argues that ideology can be considered as a set of theories based on interests and used both deliberately and unconsciously by intellectuals to distort or pervert the truth in order to advance points or ideas that favour or benefit their own interest groups. The ideological protest of students should be seen as an attempt to speak on behalf of their own sets of beliefs where their interests are not recognised by or within the university.

At UCT, the emergence of #RhodesMustFall and the philosophy of Fallism is a result of discussions and events challenging the transformation discourse on campus over the previous two decades. At Wits, managerialism and outsourcing have been opposed actively since 2000 (Kenny and Clarke 2000; Bezuidenhout and Fakier 2006).

The words of Mahmood Mamdani in 1997 encapsulate the rationale behind the student uprisings: '[T]he university is one of the most racialised institutions in South African society – as racialised as big business. The only difference is that while big business is sensitive to this fact, universities are not. The university is proud of its exclusivity, considering it an inevitable consequence of the pursuit of excellence' (Mamdani 1997: 2). In the pursuit of excellence, universities in South Africa, in particular historically white universities, failed in the role of intellectual arbiter of socioeconomic transformative change in a newly democratic country.

Mamdani's own controversial departure from UCT in 1996 entrenched the belief among students at UCT and other universities that a re-imagining of the university structure was not possible without the re-imagining of the ideological identity of the university beyond the search for excellence. As Isaac Kamola (2012: 149) explains, 'Mamdani's 1998 public demand that a post-apartheid university defines excellence in terms of how well it encourages students to critically engage South Africa's apartheid history directly conflicted with UCT's stated aspirations of presenting itself as a "world-class" university; one that trains skilled workers in a "global knowledge economy" … "excellence" should be conceptualised within the immediate politics of the postcolonial university, and shaped by its constituency, rather than simply imported from external sources'.

In 2011, UCT's student representative council (SRC) hosted a series of discussions called 'To whom does UCT belong?' The purpose was to question and examine the institutional culture of the university, particularly the belief that UCT, as an institution, was inherently anti-black. In 2012, a seminar organised by Mpumi Tshabalala, 'Is UCT Racist?' took the discussions further. During the course of the seminar, a student asked: 'If UCT is not racist, why is Cecil John Rhodes's statue still there?' This statement challenged the university for failing to acknowledge the culture it had created, and in this moment the terms of the conversation about race relations on campus and their broader impact on society began to change. The terms of previous conversations had never been balanced. This imbalance – caused primarily by the role that 'whiteness' has played in tempering discussions – has placed a lid on volatile conversation, which is seemingly only for the few.

The university unrest of 2015 can be traced to the continued use of tempered discussions as proxy conversations for transformation. These conversations maintained the status quo. For students, the proxy conversations took the form of race discussions or workshops, university admissions policy debates and the nature of SRC and management interactions. For academic staff, the discussions took the proxy of employment equity targets, academic tenure and the ever present argument about quantity versus quality. For workers on campus, the discussions were about negotiating outsourcing agreements.

A key moment of the 2015 protests was the ability of #RhodesMustFall to bring the various stakeholders – all engaged in their own proxy wars with university transformation – into discussions that no longer focused on the role the university should play in transformation but, rather, the role the stakeholders had to play in transforming the university.

On 9 March 2015, Chumani Maxwele held a protest at the site of the Cecil John Rhodes statue. This began a week of events eventually leading to the occupation of Bremner Building, the administrative head office of UCT and the formation of #RhodesMustFall, defined on its Facebook page as a '... student, staff and worker movement mobilising against institutional white supremacist capitalist patriarchy for the complete decolonisation of UCT'. But as Christina Pather (2015: 1) notes, the student-led protest was not about Rhodes or his fall but, rather, a 'symbolic physical representation of all that is wrong with our universities and the country'.

In a memo to the University of Nairobi's English Department demanding its abolition, Ngugi wa Thiong'o (1995: 438) wrote:

> ... if the basic assumption that the English tradition and the emergence of the modern West is the central root of our consciousness and cultural heritage ... Here then, is our main question: If there is a need for a 'study of the historic continuity of a single culture', why can't this be African? Why can't African literature be at the centre so that we can view other cultures in relationship to it?

In a similar way, the efforts of the #RhodesMustFall movement were refocused on placing, at the centre, the experience and consciousness of young black adults within a white institution. This meant that other cultures and values (in particular, whiteness) were viewed and experienced in relation to black experience. This act of re-centering began to change both the nature and the manner of the interactions between students and management.

DECOLONISATION, NOT TRANSFORMATION

Driven by Frantz Fanon's belief that '... decolonisation, which sets out to change the order of the world, is, obviously, a program of complete disorder' (Fanon 1963: 36), #RhodesMustFall changed the nature of transformation discourse to a broader discussion of access and the success of black students in an institution seen as a colonial/apartheid artefact disrupting their progress. If this institution was seen as a remnant of the colonial situation, then 'decolonisation ... is therefore the need of a complete calling in question of the colonial situation' (Fanon, 1963: 36). Through the acts of #RhodesMustFall – that eventually led to the fall of the Rhodes statue on 9 April 2015 – the philosophy of Fallism began.

Fallism should be understood as the reinvigorated process in which the decolonisation project has been renewed in the higher education system and in society at large. #RhodesMustFall revived the decolonial project started by James Ngugi, Henry Owuor-Anyumba and Taban Lo Liyong at the University of Nairobi in 1968 and by Mahmood Mamdani during the 1990s (Garuba 2015; Kamola 2012). Though Fallism as a philosophical construction among students is not yet aligned across campuses, there have been attempts to aggregate its understanding with Fallism utilising black consciousness in conjunction with intersectionality as a way of understanding the logic of the movements (Smith 2015: 43). What can be assumed for the time being is that the basic foundations of Fallism reside within the ambit of the decolonisation project of the African university as described by Sabelo Ndlovo-Gatsheni (2013): the radical transformation of the curriculum and institutional frameworks of the university including the values that distinguish and underpin it. It is this radical change in values that has created the space for students to critically link issues of race, intersectionality, radical black feminism, black consciousness, pan-Africanism, gender and sexuality with discussions about access and success within a university. It is in the context of these conversations and discussions that the structural issues of the institution have been questioned.

Fallism locates black consciousness and radical black feminism as integral aspects of the decolonial project. Through the use of intersectionality, Fallism engages and deconstructs what Anibal Quijano describes as the colonial matrix of power which speaks to the control and coloniality of four interrelated domains: the economy, gender and sexuality, knowledge and subjectivity, and authority (Quijano, cited in Mignolo 2007: 156). The work of #RhodesMustFall at UCT, and the emergence of Fallism, have created the space for students on university campuses across the country to begin questioning the manner in which they engage with each other and with management and society.

Through organisations such as Open Stellenbosch, the Black Student Movement at the university currently known as Rhodes University,[2] the Black Student Stokvel at the Nelson Mandela Metropolitan University, Transform Wits and also the October 6 Movement at Wits, the influence of Fallism was extended. Coalitions these organisations created on campuses proved pivotal during the #FeesMustFall protests. Questions of access and success within the university system became entwined with the decolonisation project, examining the deeper issues affecting student throughput rates. The roots of the revolution are constantly fertilised by the growing resentment at the current embodiment of transformation in a post-1994 society. Resentment grew against the use of transformation as a functional response to a deeply ideological problem.

Fallism brought a discussion that had existed exclusively at historically black institutions (HBIs) of higher learning into the context of historically white institutions (HWIs). #FeesMustFall's origins can be traced to the growing discontent among students in HBIs and their relations with the National Student Financial Aid Scheme (NSFAS) (among other financial issues) (South African Press Association 2014; Mama and Feni 2012; Mokoena 2014). Discussions and actions on HWI campuses took on a form and content not previously seen there.

ROOTS WITHIN SOUTH AFRICAN SOCIETY

What brought about this change? Massification brings previously excluded problems onto campus. As Madalena Fonseca (2012: 385) writes about higher education in Portugal after 1974, 'growth in size and diversity ... [brought] into higher education many of the conflicts and contradictions that once flourished in society beyond the university and in the world outside'. In South Africa, two levels of problems, permanent throughout the history of HBIs, began to be reflected on HWI campuses. One level was the problems of poverty: students lacking food, transport, housing and books, on campuses where many staff still expected students to have middle-class resources. The other level is the problem of students who are now ostensibly welcomed on HWI campuses, but discover that they still have no agency or identity. Their delight at getting through the gate changed to despair and anger as they realised that their outsider status and inability to change things, or even to act, remained unaltered.

Ferial Haffajee (2015) recognises this pattern in another context, and describes it as the need for black people, even at senior corporate level, to 'check their blackness at the door' in order to succeed. The political commentator Steven Friedman (personal communication, 7 March 2016) describes the frustration and rage of senior black employees who feel that although they have opportunities denied to their parents and grandparents, race prejudice has not changed since 1994. According to Friedman, these employees feel that they have been invited into the club, only to discover that this club has an A and a B membership, and they are not A members.

The problems of both poverty and exclusion are personified on South African campuses by first-generation students – students who battled to pay fees, who felt alienated on campus and who identified closely with workers. First-generation students come from families in which no one has been to university. Servaas van der Berg (2013) suggests that the best way of estimating first-generation students is simply to count the number of NSFAS bursaries. That is probably an underestimate. Anecdotally, it seems that first-generation students make up a majority of students across South African campuses, although not on every campus.

Increasing numbers of first-generation students in a developing country are not a given. Tadit Kundu (2015) argues that differences in educational levels can persist for generations, and suggests that the correlation of educational attainment between fathers and sons has, in India, been steady between fathers and sons born between 1949 and 1985.

It is a marker of some post-apartheid success that significant numbers of black students are achieving well enough in high school to enter university, and that they are present in large numbers on all South African campuses. Unexpectedly, the changes resulting from educating these new students are not just a hope for the future but are already apparent in the current protests.

STUDENTS, RELATIVES, WORKERS, ACADEMICS: ALL PRECARIOUS

Although fees and outsourcing may seem unconnected, they are linked by an apartheid past and a precarious present. Employment and education are perceived as the highways out of poverty. Fees that prevent students from entering university, debt that bars them from graduating, and precarious employment are roadblocks on these highways.

Joseba Gonzalez (2012: 172–175) warns that it is not only low-level workers who are precarious, but students themselves, and even employees with degrees. He suggests that the function of the modern, economically-oriented university is to train and provide precarious workers for the knowledge economy. He refers to the students as 'the precarious in training ... for flexible production', and labels the university 'a factory of precariousness'. That two precarious groups, students and outsourced workers (see also Chapter 4 in this volume) encountered these impediments to an individual and a group flight from poverty at the same place and time does not yet account for their degree of solidarity. To explain this, we need to look at who the students are. A characteristic of the student/worker interaction in 2015 was that the workers were addressed as 'our mothers and our fathers'. Student Mpho Sithole tweeted: 'These workers are our mothers, they suffered through apartheid and continue to suffer through "democracy"' (Sithole 2015). This is partially a form of respect, but also reflects the life circumstances of many first-generation students for whom a mother, sister, grandmother or aunt may well be in domestic service – a particular form of precariousness. There is a deep personal understanding of, and revulsion for, the abuses endured by this category of worker. Student Simamkele Dlakavu tweeted: 'The joy in our mothers and fathers faces! Thixo wam! what a moment! Wits gets insourcing! #EndOutsourcing' (Dlakavu 2015)

Personal student identification with the experiences of the poorest is not unique to South Africa. The Indian student leader Kanhaiya Kumar, just released from jail, told an audience that as he comes from Bihar state, 'the farmer who works in the fields is my father. It is my brother who joins the army … the policeman, like me, comes from an ordinary family; like me, wanted to pursue studies, yet is working as a policeman' (Kumar 2016).

This sympathy is not an inevitable part of a working-class experience on campus. The explicit connection is in stark contrast to Rose's (2001: 462) account of the contempt of middle-class students in England in the 1960s for a 'culturally conservative working class … porters, cleaning ladies and the kitchen staff … were quite often treated shamefully and with derision'. On South African campuses, specifically the Wits/UJ alliance, the sympathy extended to students taking considerable personal risks – from arrest to expulsion – to support workers' demands. Workers reciprocated, not only demonstrating with students (see Chapter 5 in this volume), but also by contributing money for food for occupying students, and money for bail when UJ students were arrested (Noor Nieftagodien, personal communication, 16 January 2016). This pattern of solidarity is not limited to campuses. Haffajee (2015) describes how solidarity with extended family in dire circumstances affects the way in which middle-class black South Africans describe their own well-being. While uncles still live in shacks, cousins in townhouses do not see themselves as having achieved financial stability.

Debt is an acute form of precariousness. Indebtedness is a growing problem, globally (Kowzan 2010) and locally (James 2014). Student debt is a significant sub-section of this problem. High university fees and unbearable levels of debt are an international concern (Marshall 2012; Hill 2015; Smelzer and Hearn 2015). Debt makes the lives of students particularly precarious. Indebted students have no leeway; their post-graduation choices are constrained by the need to repay. These debt-vulnerable students incur even greater risks through any form of campus activism, which could be an obstacle to graduating or limit post-graduation job opportunities, which may impair their repayment capacity. First-generation students have a particular vulnerability. Family resources have been invested in them; their education is expected to uplift not just themselves but a whole family. Their parents may have vivid apartheid-era memories of the violent consequences of opposing authority.

Indebtedness does not only affect working-class families where first-generation students aspire to higher education as a way out of poverty, but also middle-class and second- or third-generation students (Williams 2006). However, unaffordable fees as an entry barrier, and unbearable debt as an unintended consequence of even an uncompleted degree, are not the whole story. Hueslman et al. (2015) point out that, internationally, although higher education has been viewed as an antidote to inequality, rising fees may mean that student debt actually contributes to inequality. We must focus on the varied forms of this inequality, not only debt-induced, to understand what happened in 2015.

ROOTS IN UNIVERSITY MANAGEMENT

Edward Webster, of the Society, Work and Development Institute at Wits, explained that the protests against outsourcing may be seen as a continuation of the political concern expressed by students at the treatment of workers under apartheid (personal communication, 19 November 2015). The Wages Commission was a branch of the National Union of South African Students, started on English-speaking South African campuses in the early 1970s (Moss 2014), concerned with workers in general, and focusing on sectoral wage hearings. The 2015 revolution was not about workers in general, or workers as a category, but expressed itself in an intensely personal concern with workers on South African university campuses. This can be related to the idea of a personal revolution, discussed in Chapter 5 in this volume.

Outsourcing at South African universities cannot be understood without insight into the deep changes in the public service around the world. For about the last thirty years (Laegreid 2016), from New Zealand to the United States (Moynihan 2006), the public service has increasingly taken on the characteristics of the private sector. This change has many different labels, from managerialism to the New Public Management. Colin Bundy, Wits vice-chancellor from 1997 to 2001, explained that the call in the private sector that organisations should concern themselves with core functions only, and delegate 'non-core' to specialists, appeared relevant to the public sector as well (personal communication, 14 December 2015). The New Public Management, although not a unified or even easily categorised movement (Roberts 2016), favoured delegation and lower-level autonomy to achieve accountability.

Accountability is an important theme of the New Public Management. Noor Nieftagodien (personal communication, 10 November 2015) comments that the question 'who is the university accountable to?' is seldom asked. The answer that comes from the October 6 Movement is that the university should be accountable to students, workers, staff and perhaps parents – and not only to donors, Council, Executive Committee, Senate and Convocation.

Delegation, accountability and proper management of non-core (non-academic) functions were particularly attractive at Wits in 1997. Judge Edwin Cameron, chairperson of the Wits University Council 1998–2008 described Wits as being in an 'institutional crisis', with donors, A-rated researchers, senior black academics and students deserting it for other universities (Edwin Cameron, personal communication, 7 January 2016). The gardens and buildings were neglected, and even the toilets were not properly cleaned. 'We spend more than we earn,' a letter in the *Mail & Guardian* argued as a reason for outsourcing in order to cut costs (Kenny and Clarke 2000).

Managerialism had taken the academic world by storm, globally (Williams 2006) and locally (Bertelsen 1998). Four major South African universities, starting with UCT in 1998 (Kenny and Clarke 2000) had already introduced outsourcing (Colin Bundy, personal communication, 14 December 2015) and other aspects of New Public Management such as centralisation of departments into fewer faculties under more highly paid executive deans, so it is not surprising that it should have been introduced at Wits, as a small part of sweeping organisational reform (Barchiesi 2000).

In South Africa outsourcing offered two advantages to both public and private sector. With the arrival of democracy in 1994, calls for increased egalitarianism provoked the scrutiny of pay differentials within organisations, and a quick way of reducing these differentials was simply to slice off the bottom sector of the wage scale, excluding it from comparison with other salaried workers because they were now employed by someone else. The management of these workers was then delegated to an outside organisation, which also seemed to solve the problem of managing militant unionised workers (hiving bottom-level workers off in this fashion made union organising more difficult, around the world (Drahokoupil 2015)).

The New Public Management as a whole offered something of a panacea for a messy, uncooperative, expensive public sector. Vice-chancellors and university councils with impeccable political credentials adopted outsourcing (Colin Bundy, personal communication, 14 December 2015). At Wits, outsourcing was part of a deep restructuring in which the university was to focus on its core business. In a time of low management morale (Colin Bundy, personal communication, 2015) and high worker militancy, what New Public Management offered was reform, control and, if not exactly order, then at least someone else to manage the disorder.

However, Anne McLennan of the Wits School of Governance (personal communication, 15 December 2015) has pointed out that a problem with delegation of control had already been noted by Henry Mintzberg in 1996, in pleading for 'a shift in emphasis to the normative model, where control is rooted in values and beliefs' (1996: 81). Mintzberg foresaw problems where the New Public Management was presented as a formula, the right way of doing things, without examining whether this formula embodied or developed institutional values. Eve Bertelsen (1998) took this argument further, claiming that the New Public Management was in fact an ideology rather than merely a value. She warned that by the turn of the century, managerialist values would be presented as common sense, thus not open to scrutiny of implementation or, most importantly, of values.

The introduction of New Public Management at university level is, explains Bertelsen (1998: 133), simply 'a localised instance of this larger cultural shift'. Bertelsen also describes the particular difficulties of South African universities, which must contend with a culture of global competition and profitability, 'even as they begin to repair the social and cultural rifts of apartheid through programmes of redress'.

Wits Council minutes (2013) in response to the Letsema Report of 2013 show that outsourcing was initially welcomed at Wits in the hope of efficiency, cost savings and focus on core business. The language of the Wits Review Committee Report of 1999, effectiveness and efficiency, best practice and service providers, is all New Public Management language or the language of managerialism, what Bertelsen (1998: 131) calls 'the language and logic of business'. There are two discourses around the introduction of New Public Management at Wits. One describes it as the means of taking a declining university and putting it on the right road: cutting costs, re-allocating responsibility, taking the management of service workers out of the hands of people incapable of doing it properly. Patrick FitzGerald, Wits deputy vice-chancellor (finance and operations) 2007–2012 (personal communication, 11 January 2016), has concluded that an important part of this discourse was the need, post-apartheid, to move away from the expensive paternalism that paid black service workers a higher wage than the going rate in the industry. This discourse also emphasised the availability of career paths within outsourced industries, and the value of retrenchment packages to all workers, whether or not they were re-employed. Better-paid academics, well-kept grounds, well-managed workers, clean toilets, improving finances – all are described as outcomes of the overall business-like re-organisation of Wits (FitzGerald 2003).

There is another conversation, which focuses on consequences for outsourced workers. The dangers to outsourced workers, and their subsequent grievances, have been documented since 2000 (Adler et al. 2000; Bezuidenhout and Fakier 2006). The university management had hoped for someone else to manage the disruption. What they got was not only management but also policing, detailed in the Tokiso report (Orleyn et al. 2013). This exemplifies Bertelsen's observation (1998: 145) that when managerialism devolves control, what is most likely to be passed on is 'the unpleasant duty of surveillance'. Outsourced cleaners were prohibited from using staff or student toilets, allowed to enter the university by one gate only (no matter where on campus they worked), and barred from eating lunch in any space other than the small room allocated to them (Orleyn et al. 2013; Letsema 2013). These three provisions were overturned after a meeting with then vice-chancellor, Loyiso Nongxa, in 2013 (Deliwe Mzobe, personal communication, 3 December 2015). In addition to these restrictions on their working lives, outsourced workers 'earned a third less in wages and had no benefits' (Kenny and Clarke 2000: 28). To meet their living expenses, they immediately had to borrow money (Deliwe Mzobe, personal communication, 3 December 2015). Conveniently, Supercare, the labour broker employing them, was also a registered credit provider – which, they explained, was in order to protect employees from loan sharks (Orleyn et al. 2013; see also Chapter 4 in this volume).

How did these neo-apartheid conditions come to exist at Wits? Inherent in New Public Management is contestation around authority. This frequently shows up in a pseudo-autonomy, where responsibility is delegated without either fiscal or decision-making authority (Moynihan 2006; Shan Naidoo, personal communication, 14 April 2016). In outsourcing, the authority appears to be absolutely clear: the outsourcing company hires, fires, pays and disciplines – but as soon as any decision is contested, each party, the outsourcing company and the company where the work is done, lays the blame on the other. Both the

Tokiso and Letsema reports provide evidence of Supercare's insisting that the onerous conditions were set by Wits, and vice versa.

The university decisions are purely operational, so never held up to the scrutiny of council, senate, faculty or school meetings. From the perspective of senior university management, the outsourcing decision provides a cloak of invisibility for the outsourced workers. They are not employees, and the story ends there. In reality, workers interact all the time with staff and students. They are seen, and their stories are heard.

The university finally found the practices attributed to Supercare, the initial outsourcing company for cleaning staff, intolerable and terminated their contract in 2013. This would have automatically terminated the employment of all the outsourced cleaners on campus but the workers made themselves and their plight visible, by leaving little notes for all the people with whom they interacted on a daily basis. 'Did you know that we are leaving at the end of the year? Will the new person dust your books and put them back exactly, the way you taught me to?' (Deliwe Mzobe, personal communication, 3 December 2015). In the end, the university made the re-employment of existing workers a condition of the contract with the new outsourcing firm. It is perhaps not surprising that the form of power or agency exercised by the workers was relational. The threat implied in the notes was a disruption of a functional relationship.

The workers' cloak of invisibility could be disturbed by individual relationships. This invisibility also does not really exist for the world beyond the university. In 2013, the university commissioned two reports into outsourcing practices, the Tokiso and Letsema reports. One of the comments in the Tokiso report reads: 'It is the submission of the investigators that it does not hold in good stead that a leading university in Africa is paying the minimum wage ... indeed, it would better promote the local relevance of the university if the university sought to ensure that remuneration is not at a minimum but promoted fairness and efficiency' (Orleyn et al. 2013: 17). The Tokiso Dispute Settlement company was engaged to report on outsourcing. They were intimately acquainted with the outsourcing agreements and practices. Yet they could not help themselves – they saw the workers as Wits employees, capable of inflicting reputational damage on the institution that so fervently believed that it did not employ them.

Although outsourcing is an international practice it acquires particular meaning post-apartheid. The comparisons with black lives governed by pass laws are inescapable. According to Deliwe Mzobe (cleaner, member of the Workers' Solidarity Committee, October 6 and #WitsFeesMustFall movements, deputy chairperson of Wits Insourcing Task Team and MoU signatory), some of the workers have been there for twenty years (Deliwe Mzobe, personal communication, 3 December 2015). These workers nevertheless do not have 'citizenship' of the university. They are subject to an authority external to, and ostensibly independent of, the university. Yet their aspirations are all focused on the university that disowns them.

An outsourced worker explained that she had originally sought employment in a university because it is an educational institution. 'Maybe there I can also get an education.' Aspirations for the future depend on the university's undertaking to waive the fees of the children of permanent staff who qualify for a university education. This aspiration is powerful. 'We followed our mothers as cleaners. But now we are insourced, our children will be educated and not cleaners' (Deliwe Mzobe, personal communication, 3 December 2015).

CONCLUSION

The protests are part of an ongoing battle to decide who has the power to shape the twenty-first-century South African university, and what the nature of that university should be.

Public and university opinion on student pass-rates, or throughput, has portrayed students as being in deficit. First-generation students, in particular, have been seen as inadequate students bringing problems (poor basic education, inadequate language skills, lack of books in the home, absence of computer skills) with them onto an adequate campus. The Fallist movement focuses attention on the problems, previously concealed, which are imbedded in systems and structures on campus. The #AccessMustFall campaign focused on students who are actually passing, but who drop out because of unpaid debts for the previous year or lack of funds for the next year. According to details provided in the Wits management/SRC agreement of 19 January 2016, more than 6 000 students were at risk of being excluded for financial (rather than academic) reasons in 2016 alone. Add to this 'the fundamental issue of the alienation of black students' (Habib 2016) and a narrative begins to take shape which is campus-as-a-problem, even society-as-a-problem, rather than simply student-as-a-problem (Steven Friedman, personal communication, 7 March 2016).

What are the campus problems beyond finance? Writing about inequality in higher education in the UK, Penny Burke identifies problems of structural inequalities, and misrecognition which 'operates at symbolic, cultural and emotional levels, and produces subtle and insidious forms of inequality in higher education' (Burke 2015: 21).

Once they get to university, South African students face previously unimagined barriers. University is to some extent a foreign country for all new students – academic language, concepts, work demands and teaching are very different from high school, and often from the students' expectations. But for many black South African students, the country of academia is not only foreign but hostile. They find little that is familiar in the structures and content they are presented with. This is not unique to South Africa. A UK report on race, inequality and diversity in the academy describes 'how different, even alien, elite universities appear to … students' (Reay 2015: 19). As they perch precariously in this strange and unwelcoming environment it is easy for students to make common cause with precarious workers. The managerialist university has reduced the human stature of both groups and they join forces to fight back. A university is not a factory or a bank or a tax office. People on a university campus, whether they are service workers or postgraduate students, enter the campus with hopes – hopes for what education can do for them, for their families, and for future generations. Hopes for change in their material lives. The current protests are about identifying the barriers to these hopes

NOTES

1 It is important to note that the Falls, or Fallist, collectives, across campuses and nationally, rejected idea of 'leaders', hence collectives and plenaries (see Appendix 2) are some of the organisational principles.
2 The students would like the name of the university to be changed. There is as yet, in 2016, no agreement on this. The students therefore refer to 'the university currently known as Rhodes'.

REFERENCES

Adler, G., Bezuidenhout, A., Buhlungu, S., Kenny, B., Omar, R., Ruiters, G. & Van der Walt, L. (2000) The Wits University support services review: A critique. Wits Sociology of Work Unit.

Barchiesi, F. (2000) Lean and very mean: Restructuring Wits University. *Southern Africa Report*, 15(4), 24–30.

Bertelsen, E. (1998) The real transformation: The marketisation of higher education. *Social Dynamics*, 24(2), 130–158.

Bezuidenhout, A. & Fakier, K. (2006) Maria's burden: Contract cleaning and the crisis of social reproduction in post-apartheid South Africa. *Antipode*, 38(3), 462–485.

Bouattia, M. (2015) Beyond the gap: Dismantling institutional racism, decolonising education. In C. Alexander & J. Arday (eds). *Aiming Higher: Race, Inequality and Diversity in the Academy*. London: Runnymede Trust.

Burke, P. (2015) Widening participation in higher education: Racialised inequalities and misrecognitions. In C. Alexander & J. Arjay (eds). *Aiming Higher: Race, Inequality and Diversity in the Academy*, London: Runnymede Trust, pp. 21–23

Castells, M. (2015) *Networks of Outrage and Hope: Social Movements in the Internet Age.* (2nd ed.). Cambridge: Polity Press.

Corporate Strategy and Industrial Development Programme (2015) Workshop on minimum wages, Wits School of Economics, 2 December.

Dlakavu, S. (2015) Twitter, 1 November. https://twitter.com/simamkeleD/status/660799533572599809

Drahokoupil, J. (2015) *The Outsourcing Challenge: Organising Workers Across Fragmented Production Networks*. Brussels: Etui.

Ekeh, P. P. (1975) Colonialism and the two publics in Africa: A theoretical statement. *Comparative Studies in Society and History*, 17(1), 91–112.

Fanon, F. (1963) *The Wretched of the Earth* (transl. C. Farrington). New York: Grove Press.

FitzGerald, P. (2003) Successes and failures of restructuring, decentralisation and the implementation of a cost centre approach at the University of the Witwatersrand. A case study prepared for improving tertiary education in sub-Saharan Africa: Things that work! Regional training conference held in Accra, Ghana. 22–25 September.

Fonseca, M. (2012) The student estate. In G. Neave & A. Amaral (eds) In *Higher Education in Portugal 1974–2009: A nation, a generation*. Lisbon: Centrao De Investigatio de Politicas do Easino Superior (CIPES).

Garuba, H. (2015) What is an African curriculum? *Mail & Guardian*, 17 April.

Gonzalez, J. (2012) The new wave of student mobilizations in Europe explained as a Fordist-postFordist transition. In B. Tejerina and I. Perugorria (eds) *From Social to Political: New forms of Mobilization and Democratization*. Conference Proceedings, Universidad del Pais Vasco, Bilbao, 9–10 February, pp. 172–201.

Habib, A. (2016) Meeting for staff of the Faculty of Commerce, Law and Management, University of the Witwatersrand, February.

Haffajee, F. (2015) *What if There Were No Whites in South Africa?* Johannesburg: Pan Macmillan.

Hill, C. (2015) Free tuition is not the answer. *New York Times*. http://www.nytimes.com/2015/11/30/opinion/free-tuition-is-not-the-answer.html?emc=edit_th_20151130&nl=todaysheadlines&nlid=35955942&_r=0

Huelsman, M., Draut, T., Meschede, T., Dietrich, L., Shapiro, T. & Sullivan, L. (2015) Less debt, more equity: Lowering student debt while closing the black-white wealth gap. *Demos*. http://www.demos.org/publication/less-debt-more-equity-lowering-student-debt-while-closing-black-white-wealth-gap

James, D. (2014) *Money from Nothing: Indebtedness and Aspiration in South Africa*. Johannesburg: Wits University Press.

Kamola, I. (2012) Pursuing excellence in a 'world class African university': The Mamdani affair and the politics of global higher education. *Journal of Higher Education in Africa*, 9(1-2), 147–168.

Kenny, B. & Clarke, M. (2000) University workers exclude them out. *Southern Africa Report* 15(4), 27–30.

Kowzan, P. (2010) New face of poverty: Debt as a sociological category. University of Iceland. http://hdl.handle.net/1946/6725

Kumar, K. (2016) English translation: Full text of Kunhaiya Kumar's electrifying speech at JNU. *The Wire*, 4 March. http://thewire.in/2016/03/04/english-translation-kanhaiya-kumars-electrifying-speech-at-jnu-23820/

Kundu, T. (2015) How rising returns to education can lead to greater inequality. *Livemint*, 10 December. http://www.livemint.com/Opinion/KeMPddO80uVPZquEkDvgvM/How-rising-returns-to-education-can-lead-to-greater-inequali.html

Laegreid, P. (2016) Review of Hood, C. & Dixon, R. (2015) A government that worked better and cost less? *Governance*, 29(1), 139–140.

Letsema (2013) Letsema report into outsourcing, compiled at the request of the Wits Council. Wits Central Records.

Mama, S. & Feni, M. (2012) Student protests turn violent. *IOL*, 17 January. http://mini.iol.co.za/news/south-africa/western-cape/student-protests-turn-violent-1214650

Mamdani, M. (1997) Makgoba: Victim of the 'racialised power' entrenched at Wits. *Social Dynamics*, 23(2), 1–5.

Marshall, A. G. (2012) From the Chilean winter to the maple spring: Solidarity and the student movements in Chile and Quebec. *The Market Oracle*, 20 May. http://www.marketoracle.co.uk/Article34749.html

Mignolo, W. D. (2007) Introduction: Coloniality of power and de-colonial thinking. *Cultural Studies*, 21(2–3), 155–167.

Mintzberg, H. (1996) Managing government, governing management. *Harvard Business Review*, 74(3), 75–83.

Mokoena, L. (2014) Vaal University closed after student protests. *TimesLIVE*, 9 September. http://www.timeslive.co.za/local/2014/09/09/vaal-university-closed-after-student-protests

Moss, G. (2014) *The New Radicals: A Generational Memoir of the 1970s*. Johannesburg: Jacana.

Moynihan, P. (2006) Managing for results in state government: Evaluating a decade of reform. *Public Administration Review*, 66(1), 77–89.

Mzobe, D. (2015) Address to a workshop on minimum wages organised by the Corporate Strategy and Industrial Development (CSID) research unit of the Wits School of Economics, University of the Witwatersrand, 2 December.

Ndlovu-Gatsheni, S. J. (2013) Decolonising the university in Africa. *The Thinker*, 5, 46–51.

Neave, G. & Amaral, A. (eds) (2012) *Higher education in Portugal 1974-2009: A nation, a generation*. Lisbon: Centrao De Investigatio de Politicas do Easino Superior (CIPES).

Ngugi wa Thiong'o (1995) On the abolition of the English department. In B. Ashcroft, G. Griffiths, G. & Tiffin, H. (eds). *The Post-Colonial Studies Reader*. London: Routledge.

Orleyn, T., Ngcukaitobi, T. & Venter, T. (2013) Tokiso report into allegations of discrimination, victimisation and harassment by employees of contractors to the University of the Witwatersrand. Wits Central Records.

Pather, C. (2015) #RhodesMustFall: No room for ignorance or arrogance. *South African Journal of Science*, 111(5–6), 1–2.

Reay, D. (2015) Time to change: Bringing Oxbridge into the 21st century. In C. Alexander & Arday, J. (eds) *Aiming Higher: Race, Inequality and Diversity in the Academy*. London: Runnymede Trust.

RhodesMustFall (2015) *Facebook*. https://www.facebook.com/RhodesMustFall/info/?tab=page_info

Roberts, N. (2016) Review of Hood, C. & Dixon, R. (2015). A government that worked better and cost less? *Governance*, 29(1), 140–143.

Rollock, N. (2015) Why is it so hard to talk about race in UK universities? *The Conversation*, 9 February. http://theconversation.com/why-is-it-so-hard-to-talk-about-race-in-uk-universities-37299

Rose, J. (2001) *The Intellectual Working Life of the British Working Classes*. London: Yale University Press.

Sithole, M. (2015) Twitter, 7 November. https://twitter.com/phillenda/status/662910961603493888

Smelzer, S. & Hearn, A. (2015) Student rights in an age of austerity? 'Security', freedom of expression and the neoliberal university. *Social Movement Studies*, 14(3), 352–358.

Smith, M. (2015) Black consciousness and feminism – the IFAA Sunday forum: Youth issues. *New Agenda: South African Journal of Social and Economic Policy*, 59, 42–43.

Soudien, C. (2010) Grasping the nettle? South African higher education and its transformative imperatives. *South African Journal of Higher Education*, 24(5), 881–896.

South African Press Association (2014) Countrywide protests over NSFAS funding. *IOL*, 24 January. http://www.iol.co.za/news/south-africa/coutrywide-protests-over-nsfas-funding-1637716

Tejerina, B. & Perugorria, I. (eds) (2012) From social to political: New forms of mobilisation and democratisation. Conference proceedings. Universidad del Pais Vasco, Bilbao, 9-10 February.

Van der Berg, S. (2013) Beyond expectations: Progression of poor students through university. *Focus: Journal of the Helen Suzman Foundation*, 68, 6–12.

Williams, J. (2006) The pedagogy of debt. *College Literature*, 33(4), 155–169.

Wits Review Committee report (1999) Wits Central Records.

Wits University Council minutes (2013) Document C2013/180. Wits Central Records.

Wits Workers' Solidarity Committee (2015) University Workers' Charter, 27 October. http://witsworkerssolidaritycommittee.blogspot.co.za/2015/10/university-workers-charter_27.html

INTERVIEWS (PRESENTED IN TEXT AS 'PERSONAL COMMUNICATION')

Professor Colin Bundy, vice-chancellor, University of the Witwatersrand, 1997–2001.

Judge Edwin Cameron, judge of the Constitutional Court of South Africa, chairman of the Council of the University of the Witwatersrand, 1998-2008.

Professor Patrick FitzGerald, founder-director of the Wits School of Governance 1990–1994, deputy vice-chancellor (Finance and Operations), University of the Witwatersrand, 2007–2012.

Professor Steven Friedman, director of the Centre for the Study of Democracy, Rhodes University and the University of Johannesburg.

Ms Nqobile Malaza, lecturer, University of the Witwatersrand.
Professor Anne McLennan, new public management specialist, Wits School of Governance.
Ms Deliwe Mzobe, cleaner, member of the Workers' Solidarity Committee, October 6 & WitsFeesMustFall movements, deputy chairman of Wits Insourcing Task Team, MOU signatory, University of the Witwatersrand.
Professor Shan Naidoo, chief specialist and head of department in Public Health Medicine, Wits School of Medicine (Prof Naidoo's PhD on the effects of PHM in state hospitals is under examination).
Professor Noor Nieftagodien, chair of the History Workshop and active member of the October 6 movement, University of the Witwatersrand.
Professor Edward Webster, Society, Work and Development Institute (SWOP), University of the Witwatersrand.

CHAPTER

3

THE GAME'S THE SAME: 'MUSTFALL' MOVES TO EURO-AMERICA

Sizwe Mpofu-Walsh

INTRODUCTION

It is the 23rd of October 2015. About 350 people are gathered outside the South African High Commission in London. Familiar struggle songs ring out. This could be a protest at any South African university, but for the British accents, slight chill in the air and faces of smiling police officers in brilliant neon jackets. A collection of students and South Africans abroad under the banner of #FeesMustFall demand to see the high commissioner. A stand-off ensues: the high commissioner is in a meeting and cannot come out, according to a member of his staff. 'We're not leaving until he does,' cry hundreds of voices. The high commissioner eventually emerges, smiling at the crowd as if at a rally. The crowd erupts, out of relief, not reverence, then crouches in silence. A debate follows over whether the high commissioner should sit on the paved floor, or whether he should use a regal chair produced moments earlier by a subservient staffer. Jeers abound as the chair dances its way over the top of the front of the crowd. The protesters want him to sit on the floor *à la* Habib. He does. A memorandum is signed, the international media capturing the high commissioner's every facial twitch. Not since the anti-apartheid struggle has the South African High Commission seen an event like this.

As the London protest spreads on social media, #FeesMustFall in South Africa is preparing to march on the Union Buildings. Rhodes has already fallen at the University of Cape Town (UCT), and Oxford is battling to decide whether to remove its own Rhodes monument. Students at the most prestigious universities in the US also call for the removal of symbols linked to slavery. An old conversation is awaking in new ways.

One of the most neglected aspects of the 'Must Fall' movement is its spread to Euro-America. Oxford has seen sustained protest under the #RhodesMustFall banner since May 2015, centring on a statue of Cecil Rhodes located on its High Street. Under pressure from a campaign called 'Royall Must Fall', the Harvard Law School has abolished its official crest, an ode to the slave-owning Royall family. Significant debates have raged in both Britain and the US over the apparently unapologetic public attitude of universities towards the legacy of slavery and colonialism, spurred on – and in many cases directly inspired – by events in South Africa.

This chapter focuses on the Must Fall movement's advance to the epicentre of colonial nostalgia: elite Euro-American universities. It traces the genesis of the Must Fall moment from its inception at UCT to its culmination outside the Union Buildings. It also reflects on the theoretical importance of the movement's spread from the South to the North, before examining ambiguities that linger over #FeesMustFall's future.

I make these arguments through a series of personal reflections, having been deeply involved in the #RhodesMustFall movement in Oxford. Though I have not been directly involved in the South African student movement, I have followed it closely and maintain close ties with some individuals connected to it. In the spirit of the humility that has characterised these movements, I do not claim to speak on anyone else's behalf, but simply to offer my own views on their significance.

RHODES TO FEES

It is impossible to understand #FeesMustFall without examining #RhodesMustFall. In early March 2015, a group of students marked what they called 'Black Friday' by wearing black clothing and protesting against 'institutional racism' at the University of Cape Town (UCT), actions met mostly with derision and scepticism. On 9 March, students gathered around a statue of Rhodes on the Upper

Campus, holding placards, blowing whistles and sharing messages on social media. What looked like a fleeting moment of dissent was quickly transformed when Chumani Maxwele – then a fourth-year student at UCT – hurled faeces at the statue. A flurry of debate and student activism – unlike what had been seen in several decades at the formerly white universities – followed.

Maxwele's act was treated with disdain by the popular press. It was characterised as irrational, inappropriate and even immoral (Cardo 2015; Kane-Berman 2016). Supporters countered that the act was symbolic: the sight of colonial glorification was a permanent assault on the senses of many black students (Maxwele 2015). Maxwele wanted those who were inured to the Rhodes statue to have their senses assaulted, so that they could appreciate what it was like for him to see the statue on a daily basis. Smell became a token for sight. The protest also echoed previous demonstrations in Cape Town over the city's use of the bucket toilet system in townships – revolted by this demeaning attempt at solving the city's sanitation crisis, the Ses'khona People's Rights Movement had established faeces as a symbol for economic inequality in the politics of Cape Town (Conradie 2014; Nyawasha 2016).

In this context, Maxwele's act had at least five meanings. First, the statue itself became a totem of the persistence of white supremacy and black exclusion at UCT. Second, the faeces became symbolic of black pain, revulsion and disgust. Third, the statue also became a token for the failures of the higher education system to dismantle the remnants of apartheid and colonialism. Fourth, it represented Cape Town's own inequality: a way of bringing struggles happening at the periphery of the city into its centre. Finally, UCT became a symbol of South African society, where black people were forced to assimilate to succeed. In one act, Maxwele had stirred up a social hornet's nest.

#RhodesMustFall had begun as an idea but was not yet a concrete movement. A number of hash tags competed on social media, including #TheStatueMustFall and #RhodesMustGo. In the ensuing furore, a mass meeting was called for students to discuss their experiences of institutional racism. Radical activists, like Maxwele, then began a conversation with reformist elements in formal leadership structures. Feminist and trans-rights movements also played an active role in building what would become a new consensus among students who identified as black. Throughout March, speeches were disrupted, ceremonies halted and libraries disturbed as the #RhodesMustFall movement was officially born.

To their credit, the UCT administration took the issues raised by #RhodesMustFall seriously. In October 2014, the vice-chancellor, Max Price, had cast doubt over the prominence of the statue before Maxwele's protest (Maxwele 2015). And when the debate erupted, although Price's administration did not act immediately, they did begin a formalised campus debate that offered an opportunity for broader discussion and a potential vote. Yet, students pointed out that this approach assumed a fair debate could happen, and black students had already argued that the institution was rigged against them: 'putting this to a simple referendum misses the crux of the issue' (Chikane and Price 2015). The decision to remove the statue eventually reached the UCT Council on 8 April 2015. What followed was a moment of symbolism equal to Maxwele's first protest: the physical removal of the Rhodes statue, watched by crowds flowing onto UCT's main sports fields. A spray-painted Rhodes swung and swayed overhead as onlookers furiously photographed. Rhodes had fallen.

THE BURDEN OF FEES

Unlike #RhodesMustFall, #FeesMustFall confronted an issue that directly implicated both the university administrations and the state. The critique of university administrations stemmed from their decision to shift the burden of higher education funding onto students. Between 2006 and 2012, the state's contribution to the total funding of higher education remained roughly stagnant, at about 40 per cent – yet between 2010 and 2012 tuition fees increased by 27 per cent whereas student enrolment only increased by 7 per cent (PriceWaterhouseCoopers 2012). Vice-chancellors suggested that this shift was because of a falling per-capita state subsidy, but this is inaccurate: the per-capita subsidy fell relative to fees precisely because fees were rising so quickly. Indeed, while the subsidy did fall in some years, in other years it actually increased. In effect, between 2006 and 2012 the state subsidy remained stable, while the contribution of fees to total university revenue increased (PriceWaterhouseCoopers 2012). In years where the subsidy had increased (such as between 2010 and 2012) no concomitant fees relief took place. Since fees continued to rise at levels above inflation, the per-capita subsidy continued to fall in relative terms. A falling subsidy may have explained a portion of fees increases in some years, but it could not explain why fees had risen quite so dramatically at such a constant rate for so long.

Similarly, universities were unduly fiscally conservative. For instance, in the five years leading up to 2010, UCT had consistently overestimated the amount of revenue it would receive, to say nothing of a considerable budget surplus (UCT SRC 2010). This was for several reasons. First, the university relied on the myth that more students meant more costs, which was not necessarily true – since many university costs are fixed, more enrolments can often in reality simply mean more revenue (as the fact that fees outpaced student enrolments has already suggested). Second, the university's 'internal inflation' models were biased: finance departments concocted a basket of goods that always defied inflationary gravity and justified lavish fees increases. When internal inflation figures were found to have been overly conservative, students did not get a break in the following year. Finance departments often relied on economic rhetoric as a smokescreen behind which they could justify fiscal conservatism (UCT SRC 2010). For example, in 2015 the University of the Witwatersrand (Wits) argued that the falling exchange rate forced fee increases in 2015 because of dollar-pegged library expenditures. This argument is spurious (in the several years that the exchange rate strengthened or remained constant against the dollar fees still rose) – and also neglects to mention that the university had doubled its private donations in the previous year. Indeed, as reported by the 2014 annual report of the Wits Council, in 2014 Wits made a profit of about R40 million from interest on net foreign exchange. Even if Wits lost all of its 2014 profits in 2015, this would have had a negligible impact on a budget in the order of billions.

Therefore, students took the fight to universities first, to foreground their complicity in the rising cost of education. Universities responded as they always had, by suggesting that the National Student Financial Aid Scheme (NSFAS) covered fees increases in any case. Until FeesMustFall, this argument continued to convince university elites. But students responded that this problem simply kicked the can down the road through indebtedness, which rose by a staggering 31 per cent between 2010 and 2012 (PriceWaterhouseCoopers 2012). Students who did not graduate were doomed to a life of growing debt and unemployment – the system's safety valve was itself faulty. The critique of governance more generally was clear: those in power, both state and university, were too prepared to transfer costs onto the most vulnerable in society.

When the state made its first concession, on 20 October 2015 – a cap on fees increases of 6 per cent – this was met with opposition from students. The problem was not simply that fees were outpacing inflation; it was that there were increases at all. But the picture was growing increasingly complex as the movement grew larger. A minority in the student movement was content with the cap. Others wanted no increase at all. Yet others demanded a firm commitment to free higher education. Still others wanted it implemented immediately. The debate soon shifted to the question of free education and its feasibility, and involved a more direct confrontation with the state.

'Free education' can mean different things. It could mean free tuition. Or, it could mean free tuition, accommodation, meals, books, study materials and a stipend for living expenses. It could also mean something somewhere between these options. The financial differences between the choices are significant. FeesMustFall has not always been clear about the appropriate alternative. This is to be expected: it is not the students' job to envisage a new model, but that of publicly elected representatives and paid university administrators. In many ways, students have played their part in mobilising against the current model sufficiently to render it politically unfeasible.

The student criticism is also valid: at the very least, state-funded free tuition at universities is not only possible but actually rather inexpensive. Consider that the South African state already grants universities a subsidy of about R50 billion in 2012 prices (PriceWaterhouseCoopers 2102). What would therefore be needed is an amount in addition to the subsidy that would cover the revenue that universities receive in fees. How much is that? In 2012, the amount was about R15 billion (PriceWaterhouseCoopers 2012). In the same year, South Africa's budget was about R1 trillion What would therefore be needed is the political will to find a proportion of 1.5 per cent of the current budget – which could be done by re-allocating funds from other parts of the budget, raising 1.5 per cent in additional tax or issuing a government bond. But this would be to fund free tuition for *all*. If we eliminated postgraduate fees from the equation, and also subtracted students in the top quintile of family incomes from the programme, it would drop to about R10 billion. A pilot project in the first year could focus on a full 10 per cent of needy students and would only cost government R1 billion. New models are possible, but they require the political bravery to try them.

INTERNATIONAL ECHOES

#RhodesMustFall's spread across South Africa, and its precursory role in #FeesMustFall, have received academic attention. Less focus has gone to the movement's spread to elite institutions in Euro-America. On 19 March 2015, as the debate over the Rhodes statue at UCT raged, a group of Oxford students arranged a small protest outside Oriel College, home of a statue of Cecil Rhodes overlooking the High Street. Behind a large painted banner, their fists raised, they expressed official solidarity with #RhodesMustFall at UCT for the first time. Although the image spread across social media, no formal movement had actually yet begun in Oxford. A few weeks later, the philosopher Nathaniel Adam Tobias C̶o̶l̶e̶m̶a̶n̶ called a lunch for Oxford-based race activists at a restaurant opposite the Oxford Union. (C̶o̶l̶e̶m̶a̶n̶ intentionally spells his last name with a line through it, to signify its links with slavery.) The aim of the lunch was to share experiences and deepen the struggle against racial injustice at Oxford. The gathering began with C̶o̶l̶e̶m̶a̶n̶ quoting from Richard Symonds (1986):

> No one has more memorials in Oxford than Cecil Rhodes ... There are two busts and a portrait in Rhodes House, a portrait in Oriel College, a plaque in the Examination Schools, and another on his lodgings in King Edward Street. In the High Street, on top of the building which Oriel erected with his money, his statue is poised above those of Edward VII and George V, Rhodes in his rumpled suit and the King-Emperors in their Coronation robes. He would have appreciated all this, for he was obsessed by a desire for posthumous fame, and liked to be told that his bust resembled that of a Roman Emperor.

As the discussion unfolded, it became clear that a new movement was necessary at Oxford. The university markets its 'diversity' in glossy brochures, but the facts tell a different story: in 2015, the university accepted just twenty-four black British undergraduates into the undergraduate system. A 2013 access to information request revealed that twenty-one of Oxford's colleges did not accept a *single* black student in 2012 (Young-Powell and Page 2013). All this is apart from the extreme idolisation of colonial symbols throughout the university, and the deeply Eurocentric curriculum. Thus, when the statue eventually fell at UCT, about fifteen students decided to formally establish RhodesMustFall in Oxford (RMFO). Secret meetings were held inside the Rhodes Building of Oriel College – a consciously ironic place from which to plan. For a month, RMFO met to plot its first public protest. The eventual idea was to protest at a debate on whether Britain owed reparations to her former colonies, to be held at the Oxford Union. Arriving at the Union Bar on 29 May 2015, RMFO organisers noticed a pre-debate cocktail flyer called 'the colonial comeback'. The accompanying image was of black hands in shackles. Convinced this was a joke, they asked Union authorities whether this was, in fact, an official advert endorsed by the Union. It was.

The flyer was immediately shared on Twitter under the hashtag #RhodesMustFall and was re-tweeted enthusiastically. Soon, several national newspapers were interested in covering RMFO. The protest that evening, which consisted of holding up banners while the proposition (arguing that Britain did not owe colonial reparations) spoke, garnered further attention. The following weeks saw a flurry of media activity, as RMFO pressurised the Union to offer an apology. This came on the first of June, along with a public statement from the Union (unprecedented in its history) in which it admitted to being 'institutionally racist'. Just three days after it had officially launched, RMFO had sparked a charged debate over Oxford's implication in colonial glorification.

Simultaneously, large student protests over racism in the United States attracted global attention. Protests, at institutions like Yale, Georgetown, Amherst and Harvard drew directly from the ongoing South African struggle. The Royall Must Fall movement at Harvard Law School drew its name from a notoriously brutal Massachusetts slave-owning family whose seal formed part of the school's crest. The movement scored a significant victory when, on 15 March 2016 – after months of campaigning – it convinced the Harvard Law School to retire the crest.

Initially, the Oxford protest seemed to have borne fruit. Oriel College released a statement on 17 December saying it would review the statue and remove a plaque celebrating Rhodes. However, as a new vice-chancellor took office, Oriel was forced to backtrack, allegedly because donors had threatened to pull out. This created the impression that a dictatorship of donors controlled university policy, no matter how vociferously students protested.

RMFO then widened its campaign, while retaining its demand for the Rhodes statue to fall. Other demands related to colonial iconography at Rhodes House, All Souls College and Oriel were sent in a series of letters to various officials – all of whom refused not only to entertain the demands but even to engage with RMFO. In e-mails to RMFO, the vice-chancellor, Louise Richardson, called a demand for a panel of academics of colour to review the Oxford curriculum 'invidious', while the warden of All Souls, John Vickers, described the name of the Codrington Library as a 'fact of history like slavery'. The chancellor of Oxford, Lord Patten, compared RMFO to the Islamic State, and suggested that students who criticised colonial iconography should 'study elsewhere'.

(Gayle and Khomami 2016). Oxford has resisted change to a greater extent than UCT or Harvard, but there remains no doubt that RMFO has brought the debate over colonial glorification onto its doorstep.

THEORY

To understand the Must Fall movement's spread to Euro-America through the lenses of Gramsci, Foucault or Marx is already to misunderstand it. Certainly, 'traditional' theory can illuminate certain aspects of the movement, but it cannot capture its anti-hegemonic and unmistakably Southern bent. 'Fallism' is a nascent, complicated and emerging viewpoint, combining aspects of decolonial thought, black consciousness, radical feminism and pan-Africanism. Some have criticised it for incoherence. But no protest movement as wide as 'Must Fall' can claim coherence. The Must Fall umbrella is not, nor does it aspire to be, a body of literary thought, or a full social theory. Rather, it is a programme of political action. Those who unfavourably compare it with student movements in South Africa in the 1970s and 1980s have forgotten just how ideologically disparate those movements were.

There is no doubt, however, that Fallism poses questions for theory, and its spread to other parts of the world should provoke us to search for explanatory lenses. One prism through which to consider this development is 'theory from the South', a viewpoint advanced by authors such as Hountondji (2002), Connell (2007) and Jean and John Comaroff (2012). They argue that a great inversion of the Eurocentric narrative actually explains phenomena in the global North. Far from events and theories originating in Euro-America and applying in the 'rest of the world', the reverse is actually true: Euro-America is evolving towards the global South in crucial respects:

> What if we posit that, in the present moment, it is the so-called 'global South' that affords privileged insight into the workings of the world at large? That it is from here that our empirical grasp of its lineaments, and our theory-work in accounting for them, ought to be coming, at least in major part? That in working the contradictions inherent in the suspect North-South dualism we might be able to move beyond it, to the larger dialectic processes of which it is a product (Comaroff and Comaroff 2012: 114).

Such an inversion of the Eurocentric narrative also involves a direct critique of the global system of knowledge production. Patterns of economic exploitation map onto patterns of theory production and data collection, according to Connell (2007): 'the global division of labour in the production and circulation of knowledge' locates the North as the centre of theory. This leads Southern theorists to orient their writing towards external frames of reference. Hountondji (2009) describes this as a process of academic extraversion which must be reversed:

> The study of Africa, as developed so far by a long intellectual tradition, is part of an overall project of knowledge accumulation initiated and controlled by the West ... It calls upon '*épistémologies du Sud*.'... It calls upon African scholars in African Studies and in all other disciplines to understand that they have been doing so far a kind of research that was massively extraverted, i.e. externally oriented, intended first and foremost to meet the theoretical and practical needs of Northern societies.

RMFO was the consequence of a plan consciously to implant a way of looking at the world into the North, from the South: to subvert the directionality of colonial logic as a theoretical strategy, but also as an ironic political gesture. Yet, if these theorists implore us to imagine *theory* from the South, the spread of RMFO calls us to embrace *practice* from the South; if there is anything original about the spread of the Fallist movements to the North, it is that they represent an important contemporary example of the importation of political strategy and practice from the South to the North.

In this light, the strategy of metaphorical campaigning is perhaps one of the central contributions of the Must Fall movement to the practice of activism and mobilisation. For years, students across South Africa had been protesting against a host of perceived injustices. But no one had understood how to unify these different actions under one banner in a way that could attract sufficient public attention. The thrust of the #RhodesMustFall campaign was a symbolic act. This would later be both emulated and rejected by the #FeesMustFall movement: emulated in the sense that #FeesMustFall latched on to #RMF's strategy of centring a complex campaign around one issue (in this case that of fees) but rejected in the sense that the issue chosen was more directly material. As #RhodesMustFall used the statue of Rhodes to reflect on colonial legacies, #FeesMustFall used fees to show that economic policy was failing the black and poor. Movements around the world adopted this strategy to significant effect across Europe and the United States.

The deep focus on practice is itself a subversion of our traditional understanding of theory. Instead of a set of abstract tenets that emerge from the academy and apply to empirical cases, the MustFall movement reverses the process: practice gives birth to a disparate array of concepts, frames and theories, which compete to explain further practice. Students used whatever theories worked to achieve tangible goals; theory formed around their actions, chaotically and organically. For instance, the Must Fall movement abandoned the rhetoric of 'transformation' in favour of 'decolonisation'. These distinctions were largely rhetorical and tonal, but important nonetheless. Transformation as conceived by the Must Fall movement is largely rejected as a failed project, content with superficial and gradual change. Decolonisation in the context of the South African academy refers not only to a deeper commitment to eradicating the legacies of colonialism and apartheid, but also to eradicating them speedily. Fallism implies immediacy – it means abandoning the politics of gradualism and the primacy of the 'commission of inquiry', and embracing fast and wide-ranging immediate changes to landscapes, demographics, financial models and curricula. RMFO imported the language of 'decolonisation' but also inverted it by focusing on the metropole instead of the periphery.

AMBIGUITIES

Several residual tensions exist under the Fees Must Fall umbrella. First, differences exist over the appropriate attitude towards state power. On one hand, part of the movement insists on launching a radical critique of the state. As seen in protests outside Parliament and the Union Buildings, this strand of the movement is prepared to challenge the political elite directly. By contrast, another strand still owes ultimate allegiance to the ANC, and is therefore less critical of state complicity. This fault line deepened after President Zuma's announcement of the fees freeze, and the introduction of the outsourcing phase of the movement.

A second and related tension relates to #FeesMustFall's connection to formal politics. Some within #FeesMustFall argue that it should remain an independent political force. Other currents are comfortable with overt political party support. Political parties, too, see the movement as a vehicle to advance diverse agendas. As the movement grew to confront the state, it became clear that the ANC's strategy was internal co-option of the Wits movement. Quite how the movement navigates the tenuous balance between confronting deeply political issues while remaining independent of political influence also remains unresolved.

A third ambiguity relates to the place of violence in #FeesMustFall. Some students are committed to the use of violence in extreme circumstances, as seen in protests at North West University's Mahikeng campus. Even at UCT and Wits, protesters have burned buses and damaged infrastructure. Other groups under the Must Fall umbrella are committed to peaceful and non-violent methods. How this tension resolves itself will largely depend on how universities and the state react to peaceful protest. Should universities continue with repressive action, this will spark increasingly violent responses.

The final fault line concerns intersectionality. While certain strands of the movement have prioritised race, or fees, others argue that oppression must be confronted in a multidimensional way. The Must Fall movement has been subjected to a powerful and sustained gender critique. Patriarchy has affected significant strands of the movement, and prompted crucial discussions about rape culture and the subjugation of persons gendered as women inside and outside student movements. New initiatives, such as #PatriarchyMustFall have actively challenged #Rhodes Must Fall. Feminist movements at Rhodes like 'RU Reference List', and at Wits like 'Mbokodo Lead', became a key political force at the beginning of 2016, protesting to foreground the marginalisation of women on university campuses. For Fees Must Fall, tackling financial exclusion while balancing its multidimensional effects on students remains an ongoing challenge.

REFERENCES

Cardo, M. (2015) The sinister underbelly to the 'RhodesMustFall!' campaign. *PoliticsWeb*, 1 April. http://www.politicsweb.co.za/news-and-analysis/the-sinister-underbelly-to-the-rhodes-must-fall-ca

Chikane, K. & Price, M. (2015) Dr Max Price and Kgotsi Chikane discuss the Rhodes statue and transformation at UCT. (Contraband, Interviewer). [Audio clip]. 15 April. https://www.mixcloud.com/UCTRadio/dr-max-price-and-kgotsi-chikane-discuss-the-rhodes-statue-and-transformation-at-uct/listeners/

Comaroff, J. & Comaroff, J. L. (2012) Theory from the south: Or, how Euro-America is evolving toward Africa. *Anthropological Forum*, 22(2), 113–131.

Connell, R. (2007) *Southern Theory: The Global Dynamics of Knowledge in Social Science*. Cambridge: Polity Press.

Conradie, E. (2014) From land reform to poo protesting: Some theological reflections on the ecological repercussions of economic inequality. *Scriptura: International Journal of Bible, Religion and Theology in Southern Africa*, 113, 1–16.

Council of the University of the Witwatersrand (2014) Annual Report.
Gayle, D. & Khomami, N. (2016) Cecil Rhodes statue row: Chris Patten tells students to embrace freedom of thought. *The Guardian*, 13 January. http://www.theguardian.com/education/2016/jan/13/cecil-rhodes-statue-row-chris-patten-tells-students-to-embrace-freedom-of-thought
Hountondji, P. J. (2002) *The Struggle for Meaning: Reflections on Philosophy, Culture, and Democracy in Africa*. Athens, OH: Ohio University Press.
Hountondji, P. J. (2009) Knowledge of Africa, knowledge by Africans: Two perspectives on African studies. *RCCS Annual Review*, 1. A selection from the Portuguese journal *Revista Crítica de Ciências Sociais*.
Kane-Berman, J. (2016) Reaping the whirlwind of RMF. *PoliticsWeb*, 8 April. http://www.politicsweb.co.za/opinion/reaping-the-whirlwind-of-rmf
Maxwele, C. (2015) UCT Rhodes statue sewerage protester explores his reasons for acting as he did. (Contraband, Interviewer). [Audio clip]. 11 March. https://www.mixcloud.com/Contraband_CT/uct-rhodes-statue-sewerage-protester-explores-his-reasons-for-acting-as-he-did/
Nyawasha, T. S. (2016) The nation and its politics: Discussing political modernity in the 'other' South Africa. *Journal of Southern African Studies*, 42(2), 229–242.
PriceWaterhouseCoopers (2012) Funding of public higher education institutions in South Africa. http://www.pwc.co.za/en/higher-education/Funding-public-higher-education-institutions-SA.html
Symonds, R. (1986) *Oxford and Empire: The Last Lost Cause?* Basingstoke: Macmillan.
UCT SRC (2010) Submission to the Council of the University of Cape Town on the student fees decision (Rep.). Student Representative Council, University of Cape Town.
Young-Powell, A. & Page, L. (2013) The absence of black students diminishes the greatness of Oxbridge. *The Guardian*, 4 December. http://www.theguardian.com/education/abby-and-libby-blog/2013/dec/04/black-students-absence-diminishes-oxbridge

CHAPTER
4

#OUTSOURCINGMUSTFALL THROUGH THE EYES OF WORKERS

Omhle Ntshingila,[1] in conversation with Richard Ndebele and Virginia Monageng

INTRODUCTION AND BACKGROUND

Since the introduction of outsourcing in 2000 under the former vice-chancellor, Colin Bundy, insourcing/outsourcing has been a huge debate at the University of the Witwatersrand (Wits). On 11 June 2016, after a prolonged worker and student struggle, the Wits Council (2016) released a statement announcing: '… insourcing will commence on 1 January 2017 or as contracts end' for 1 530 cleaning, catering, security, transport, waste, grounds and landscaping workers. The practice was highly divisive, and was contested both ideologically and in terms of the far-reaching and detrimental effect it had on the lives of workers (see Nkosi 2012).

Bundy had outsourced cleaning, catering and electrical and grounds maintenance to companies such as Supercare (established in 1959 and specialising in cleaning), MJL (an electrical maintenance service company, established in 1994) and Royal Mnandi (established in 1990, and working in the field of food services or catering) (see Table 4.1). The practice of outsourcing seeks to be a cost-effective solution for the institution requiring the services. At the time of the 2015 workers' sit-in, for example, Wits management argued that insourcing would require 'an extra 15 per cent increase in student fees otherwise Wits quality will decline ... This would destroy Wits. Where would future students go?' (Heiberg 2015). It was estimated then that the insourcing of all Wits outsourced workers would cost R150 million per year. Such calculations, however, fail to take to heart that outsourcing has major pitfalls and disadvantages for those who are hired by the outsourcing companies. There is no consideration of whether the outsourcing practices, encompassing service and remuneration are compatible with the values that the university professes to embrace. In the words of Workers' Solidarity Committee (WSC) member Tokelo Nhlapo: 'The university needs to confront the ugly truth that outsourced workers are treated like second-class citizens [on its campuses]. This goes against the values of the university' (quoted in Nkosi 2012).

Because of its fundamentally negative impacts on workers, outsourcing is classified as an agent of capitalism – it contributes to the oppression of workers (see Robinson 2004). Outsourcing at Wits has indeed been a particularly painful system. For example, starting in 2000, 613 workers have been retrenched, and only 259 re-employed by outsourcing companies. In the process, the wages of the re-employed workers were cut drastically: those of cleaners fell from R2 227 a month to about R1 200. These retrenched and now unemployed workers lost their pensions and other non-wage benefits (Workers Solidarity Committee 2011). Even in the cases where the outsourced workers retained their jobs, working conditions were far from favourable. The 'absorbed ones', employed by the new outsourcing companies, faced the challenge of earning low wages without any benefits that they had received previously, benefits such as maternity leave, medical benefits and fully paid scholarships for their dependents to come and study at the university.

Outsourcing has taken away the responsibility from Wits – and from many other institutions of higher learning across South Africa – to actually deal with worker struggles and representation such as trade unions. Equally, outsourcing makes it difficult for workers to have their voices heard in universities, unless 'joint ventures' arise with students and progressive academics within the institutions. Such mobilisation at Wits in late 2015 helped to bring a series of victories to the outsourced workers – ranging from the gradual re-introduction of insourcing by the university to immediate free study benefits for their children.

Table 4.1: Details of the outsource companies

NAME OF COMPANY	SECTOR	SELECT INFORMATION
Royal Mnandi	Catering	Provides catering for main dining hall for main campus at Wits. In 2010, Mvelaserve (Bidvest), the direct holding company for Royal Mnandi, unbundled from the Mvelaphanda Group and listed on the JSE.
MJL	Electrical maintenance	MJL provided Wits with services, but was liquidated in South Africa. MJL stopped paying its Wits workers in early 2015. By May 2015, Wits formally terminated its contract with MJL and used payments owed to MJL to reimburse workers.
Supercare	Cleaning	Supercare provided Wits with services from 2000–2013. Supercare's contract with Wits came to an end in 2013.
Ukweza	Cleaning	When Supercare's contract ended, Ukweza took over the contract. Ukweza has provided Wits with services from 1 June 2013 to date.

What outsourcing has done is to exclude the workers from the Wits community and to decrease their political presence on campus on the basis that they are not fully part of the university. They have been treated as contracted workers and not permanent Wits staff.

Many in the worker, student and academic ranks have found the conviction to fight for workers and their rights. In some instances this happened alongside the student representative councils (SRCs). Here, the Workers' Solidarity Committee (2015) has been playing a notable role. This committee fights for workers' rights on campus, and comprises Wits workers, progressive academics and progressive students. The committee has been actively involved in workers' rights struggles since outsourcing commenced.

Universities across the country experienced the seriousness of the workers' struggle through the nationwide demonstration October 6 (#OCT6). The demonstration took place from the morning until the late afternoon of 6 October 2015 (see South African History Online 2016). A memorandum was handed over to vice-chancellors, pleading with university managements to reverse the fifteen years of exclusion and financial pain that outsourced workers had suffered; this would be done by ending outsourcing and adopting a new workers' charter (see Nkosi 2015). The demonstration brought much excitement to the workers at Wits: the support of students was overwhelming and this resulted in workers, in turn, involving themselves fully in the #WitsFeesMustFall protest that began on 14 October 2015.

All chapters in this book touch on aspects of the worker struggles and the insourcing victories – even if, for now, slow, and modest in implementation – that Wits's #OutsourcingMustFall movement achieved. Central to these victories is the agreement of Sunday 1 November 2015 in which Wits management – on behalf of the institution's Council – agreed to gradual insourcing. It would unfold step-by-step and as existing contracts expired. As the announcement was made, shortly before five o'clock that afternoon, songs of jubilation reverberated through the already informally renamed former Senate House, Solomon Mahlangu House.

The day's victory led the way for workers and students at other South African universities, and in the months to come the Wits example would be used as the benchmark in other unfolding negotiations.

The Wits workers' struggles did not, however, end on that Sunday afternoon in November 2015. The tortuous process of reversing outsourcing would take considerable time. The June 2016 Wits Council announcement was a milestone, but not the end of the road; it is a testimony to the exceptional multi-class worker-student alliance that had campaigned to have outsourcing ended. There are many lessons to be learned from the process, and in particular from the havoc it caused and the hardship it had brought to workers. The rest of this chapter charts the stories of two Wits workers in the time of outsourcing and in the uncertain interregnum that is currently playing out.

THE STORIES OF WORKERS RICHARD NDEBELE AND VIRGINIA MONAGENG

The story of Richard Ndebele, as told to Omhle Ntshingila, 29 April 2016

Richard Ndebele was born in the great Ukhahlamba region of KwaZulu-Natal, in a mountain town called Msinga. Richard grew up there, and matriculated in 1994. After matriculating, Richard did not have the option of continuing his studies because of financial constraints and opted to be an artisan. He became a professional electrician in 1995 and worked in KwaZulu-Natal until 2001, when he moved to Johannesburg in the hope of better pay. Unfortunately, he landed up in the electrical company MJL that exploited black labour in order to make a profit. He was then deployed to work at Wits from 2011, doing electrical maintenance. Richard found that there was a tendency at Wits to regard the profession of artisans as work done by those in a lower class of society, to underestimate them and to frown upon them as individuals.

Interviewing Richard was not easy, as his life story not only reflected his own personal scars but those of other workers as well. His voice is that of workers who have never been recognised, who have been forgotten or who are never heard in society. Richard decided to write his own story on paper, not only to get his own voice heard, but to stand in the place of many workers who needed a collective voice to join their fight for their rights and dignity in corporate South Africa.

Writing about the workers' struggle is like sharing a piece of Richard's pain, a pain that did not start with him but has existed for many years throughout many generations in many families. Much has happened in Richard's life, a life like that of many other workers in companies from which the universities procure services. Richard felt a deep concern for those he had worked closely with in his six years at MJL, his former colleagues with whom he had formed deep relationships. Richard is a hard-working man, an honest man who happened to fall victim to exploitation as his salary (which excludes benefits such as health care) does not reflect the amount of work he does for the company and university. A father and a husband, Richard understands his role in society as being the one who must provide for family and make sure that ends meet. Throughout our conversation, Richard stressed the pain of not knowing what is ahead for him and his family, especially his children, as he felt that companies such as MJL decide the fate of your children depending on the type of salary you receive. Richard is in distress not only because of his immediate family, but also his extended family back in KwaZulu-Natal, for whom he provides basic needs such as groceries and other household goods.

It is important for Richard that the community must know, in his words, that 'even though we are living in a democratic country, exploitation of workers is still very high in South Africa. Workers are not exploited by ridiculously low wages for their long hours they work, but are exploited by their employer's privilege in many ways'. Richard was referring to the equality gap between the outsourced workers and those who own the means of production, and the fact that there is little if any bargaining power for outsourced workers. Like many other outsourced workers, Richard has gone for months without pay. Even with the salaries they get, workers like Richard cannot change their lifestyles much – they only get enough to survive. 'It's frustrating to work under people who don't consider you as a fellow human being, but just see labour and profits,' Richard said. Most of Richard's colleagues around the university will not even speak out about the exploitation they experience daily, for fear of losing their jobs and then being unable to put food on the table. Those who do speak out run the risk of being categorised as troublemakers within the companies that employ them. 'If you are vocal you can be victimised and can even get fired,' says Richard. He continues:

> This is important, you reading *this* is important, me writing *this* is important. If we don't speak up about our pain and frustration no one will, no one will ever know the wrong that is being done to workers of the university, no one will ever stop the corruption. This is not just my story. It's the beginning of a legacy.

Richard's story now enters the eventful days of May 2015 at Wits, starting with negotiations and a strike, and ending with an occupation and a settlement of sorts. Richard tells the story of the origin of the MJL workers strike in full detail, and was happy to share his experience. The Wits-MJL outsourced workers had requested that their employer, George Croswell, and the Wits management meet to negotiate insourcing for the MJL-Wits outsourced workers. The National Union of Metalworkers of South Africa (Numsa) attempted to help the Wits-MJL outsourced workers, but left negotiations early. The negotiations continued without Numsa, Richard on his own representing all the Wits-MJL outsourced workers. The workers realised that their demands were not being taken seriously, however, when the university blocked their access cards as soon as Numsa left. The blocking was not linked specifically to Numsa's departure, but to the fact that the company was no longer rendering services to Wits. The workers now had no access to the university. It was confirmed: they had lost their jobs. Wits management refused to relent and insource them.

This was therefore the beginning of the MJL outsourced workers' occupation of the eleventh floor of Senate House (for additional details, see also Nkosi 2015; Steenkamp 2015).

Richard resumes:

We thought Numsa, Wits and George [Croswell] had agreed on something that we knew nothing about, as George had disappeared. Then we received an e-mail from university management stating that our services with Wits had been terminated with immediate effect, and Wits wanted us to return our access cards immediately. We responded to the e-mail stating that we were not going anywhere until negotiations had been concluded. Soon after that e-mail was sent, our access cards stopped working and we could no longer gain access onto the university campus, with no explanation as to why from our employers or the university. We wanted a response to our e-mails, and an understanding of why we were being chased out while negotiations were still unfolding. Those actions taken by the university led us, the MJL workers, to then decide to occupy eleventh floor [of the former Senate House, where the university's top management holds fort].

A few student leaders, those of the [ANC-aligned] Wits Progressive Youth Alliance (PYA) and the Wits Economic Freedom Fighters (EFF), including the SRC president at that time, Ms Shaeera Kalla, joined the occupation. Other student leaders would sit day-by-day by the lifts at the eleventh floor in solidarity with our occupation. The MJL workers' issues were not new to student leaders. They were familiar with our situation on campus, since we have been working with them to find solutions to our company's [and our related] problems. Everyone knew that MJL was being liquidated, but the university was not doing enough to save our jobs, our lives and those of our families. Before the strike, from 8 May 2015, we had been meeting with management about our demands and concerns, without ever getting effective responses from management. We, then, as MJL outsourced workers together with WSC, took it upon ourselves to get a petition with over 2 000 signatures of both workers and students on campus and handed it over to the vice-chancellor, Professor Adam Habib, on 13 May. It demanded that the university ... must absorb us back into the system and MJL workers should be hired directly by the university. We were calling for insourcing. This was the university's response: 'While the university completely sympathises with the plight of workers, we are unfortunately not in a position to employ MJL workers. If we were to employ workers, we would be setting a precedent that would compromise us financially.'

Richard continues:

The university was then too arrogant to accept the petition or even entertain our demands. Even after we ended the occupation, we were still negotiating with the vice-chancellor and Professor Tawana Kupe, but nothing came out of it. The university evidently protected the companies they get services from more than they cared about the workers. The university is late in responding to our demands, and this for us shows that they undermine outsourced workers. During negotiations, the student leaders and other key players in our struggle were thrown out of the meeting. I was then forced to take the lead and represent the workers. All I wanted was to expose [what we see as] the corruption that happens between the university, vendors and the workers inside the university. We kept on fighting; I fought till the last minute. And I must say, leading a strike is not an easy thing, I was scared of saying the wrong things and putting everyone's job at risk. Being the leader of the strike, I was not only putting my own life at risk but the future of my family as well, because I risked losing employment. But I kept on fighting because I was fighting for the very same future of my family that I was also scared of jeopardising. I soon was regarded as a troublemaker by management, and my employer wanted me out of his company. But that did not bother me, as I knew who I was. I am an honest man who wants justice for those who are exploited, and was no longer going to keep quiet and watch employers and the university undermine workers and their [struggles]. The truth I had come to realise during our two-day sit-in of the vc's office is that the university doesn't care about the poor and outsourced workers, but cares more about cutting costs. The outsourced workers of the MJL were costing Wits too much to keep any longer, and us being retrenched would have a far worse impact on the lives of our families than [on the lives of] those who owned our labour. The university itself could not operate without those workers, so these workers deserve to be treated better, with dignity.

Negotiations ended and MJL was no longer at Wits. Most of my colleagues have not found employment till today. I was lucky as I am currently working for a labour broker that MJL has been using for many years. But I know it won't last because it's not permanent. I am not under a contract; I have no benefits and no job security. I still have to find a job outside the university because here with the labour broker, there is no life for me and [therefore] no future for my children. We had asked the company to stop using the labour broker a long time ago, because that in itself is form of exploitation. We don't like it and don't accept it. I believe that worker solidarity, working together with students and progressive academics, is the only way we can have a bigger impact on the university … to change things. We need to be brave and say enough is enough. The university must get rid of all the outsourcing companies. The only solution is the university insourcing, because workers have been exploited enough, black people have been used enough. It's time to speak up, if not for ourselves then for our children.

The story of Virginia Monageng, as told to Omhle Ntshingila, 29 April 2016

Virginia Monageng was born in Alexandra, Johannesburg, in 1962. She grew up in this township area, but attended school in Meadowlands, Soweto. She only finished her schooling up to Standard 9 (Grade 11 today) as her father passed away and she stopped going to school to take care of her mother, who became sick after the death of her father. Virginia was the only child, so the responsibility of taking care of her mother fell to her. She could not further her studies or even get a better-paying job. Virginia became a cleaner in 1988. This was the only job that accommodated a person with her level of education. Under apartheid, and amid ongoing poverty, Virginia could not dream beyond just providing for her family. It was unfair, her life was very unfair. Simply being black and oppressed was a burden enough, but her father's death added more weight to that burden. Still, life moved on for Virginia. Her first job was at Imperial Motors at Cresta Mall. The pay was terrible, says Virginia, considering the amount of work she was doing. She applied for a job at the University of the Witwatersrand. At that time, Wits was using a vendor called Supercare and Virginia was hired in 2000. From 2000 until 2013, Virginia worked for Supercare.

Virginia experienced Supercare as a hostile company: it never wanted to listen to the workers' concerns and demands. She observes:

> It always pretended to be a super-power in the university, and its voice was of course louder than ours. Whenever a worker spoke up, [she or he] would get fired and I really feared for my job. I soon became silent myself.

But the year 2007 changed my perspective; it made me brave enough to stand up for my rights and those of others. The vendor had not paid us for three months, so we decided to also not come to work for three months. It was difficult as I was the sole breadwinner at that time, with four children at home to feed. But I had faith in our protest action.

The university still didn't take all our demands into consideration, before or after the demonstration ended. We therefore did the same demonstration in 2010, but only for a month because of pressure to provide for our families. We then heard that the university had given the cleaning tender to another company, Ukweza, and many people started losing their jobs. I was one of the lucky ones who got absorbed into the company Ukweza and kept my employment – and my low pay. I thought things were going to change, but nothing changed except the vendor. It was very sad, to know that the company did not absorb everyone into their system, it was really unfair.

Virginia talks about her ambitions for her children and grandchildren, and about the sadness and frustration of being unable to do more.

This motivated me even more to be active in Workers Solidarity on campus, and contribute in any way I could to improve the lives of workers on campus. But that's just the face value of the struggles I face every day. My biggest struggle is providing for myself and my family. When a small salary is involved there is not much one can do with it. I tried providing for my two older sons, but unfortunately, because their father was absent and not able to take care of them, everything fell on me. They had to drop out of technikon, because of financial constraints, and they unfortunately were not able to obtain external funding. The marks they matriculated with also did not qualify them for entry to the university. I am not sure whether to blame my sons or the flawed education system in our country. This has caused them to fall into the same job types that I have, just in order to take care of themselves. I now have a grandchild who is in Grade 8. He is looking forward to coming to university, and the only way I can make that dream come true is if I don't retire before he is at least in his second year of studies. It will be cheaper for our family, as the university has agreed to allow workers' dependents to come to Wits for free [education]. But the truth is I am old, tired and very weak. I don't know how long I can survive the working hours and the actual labour itself.

But I am praying that God carries me through until I see my grandchild coming to university and graduating. Even though I have been cleaning toilets inside Senate House for the past sixteen years of my life, I still enjoy working at a university because I get to interact with the younger generation. I get a chance to pour out my wisdom and encouragement to the students. They are friendly, even if some of them do treat us, the cleaners, like we don't exist, or like we are not human beings. That's the part of my job I don't like.

WORKERS' STRUGGLES THROUGH THE STUDENT LENS

These two Wits worker stories are also the everyday lifestories of many black workers among us. It may be the teacher from Grade 8 who taught you economics, or the cleaner you pass by in Senate House each day but do not really notice. What we as young South Africans are only now starting to take note of is that colonisation brought pain and inequality around the world. Its impact has left multiple generations scarred with poverty, unemployment, racial division, exclusion and many other social ills that our continent is facing today.

South Africa is considered a land of hope. Yet, as is tangible in these worker stories, it is a land suffering from its own covered-up wounds inflicted by colonisation and the apartheid system. It is now bleeding through the cracks. We see evidence of it in the higher education system and the models used to keep universities functioning. We see neoliberalism at work, but neoliberalism cannot work in a country where inequality is still a huge issue and where white privilege is still a very big part of our everyday lives. The system works to exclude the previously disadvantaged, through measures that range from upfront fees for registration at universities and no guarantees of free education for the poor, to an economy that is still in the hands of the unelected few, land redistribution that proceeds at a snail's pace, and the many workers who are still outsourced. Low wages keep our people enslaved to white capital and those who own the means of production. Low wages mean that quality of life stagnates or declines. It means that the children of the workers are entrapped, as the stories of Richard and Virginia illustrate. This results in undignified living, with no hope.

In many of the institutions of higher education, workers have for a long time been kept as slave-like employees rather than individuals with rights. The undignified worker initiations at the University of the Free State (UFS) offer further evidence. There was an outcry at the UFS, but far less action followed. The private sector is still showing little interest in meeting the demands of workers while they await insourcing.

In June 2016, Wits announced that its Council had formalised the reversal of outsourcing, with effect from January 2017, and that there would be a top-up of wages in the period leading up to 2017. Advocate Dali Mpofu, the chairperson of the Wits Insourcing Task Team, had led the process. The new minimum was set at R7 500 for 2017. This was a victory for workers and the students who had supported them, especially as the monthly minimum wage of R2 731 across all the private-sector bargaining councils, and R2 362 across all the sectoral determinations, were regarded as the minimum wage in South Africa in early 2016 (BusinessTech 2016). Cosatu had also called for a national minimum worker wage of from R4 500 to R6 000, while the Economic Freedom Fighters (EFF) wanted a national minimum wage of R4 500 in 2016.

The Wits insourcing minimum wage announcement potentially signalled that the university now wishes to end its ways of treating and remunerating the workers in the Wits family. As students, we stand firm that Wits cannot be proud of being a top class university in Africa (see *Wits Vision* 2022) when workers are treated as third-class citizens in our institution. We shall watch over the rapid and fair implementation of the June agreement.

Wits thus joined several other South Africa institutions of higher education that had already formalised agreements on insourcing (see also UCT 2015). In February 2016 at the Tshwane University of Technology (TUT), a hundred outsourced workers accepted the insourcing offer given by TUT management, with a starting minimum wage of R5 000 (Bateman 2016). On 20 January 2016, the University of Pretoria also signed an insourcing agreement, which applied to all service workers within the university (UP 2016). The University of Johannesburg (UJ) signed in November 2015 to end outsourcing, and has to date signed specifically to insource all gardening services (UJ 2016).

Nonetheless, the outsourced Wits workers have taken an initiative to help tackle their own problems: they raised R100 000, are in control of the funds, and are looking forward to using this money to improve their lives on campus and those of their children by investing it in their and their children's education.

Since #Oct6 and #FeesMustFall, Wits has looked at worker demands such as allowing their children free university education until their final year of study, and has responded to them. Beyond this, it is important to accept that it will be a resolute 'never again'. The university must be mindful not to perpetuate exploitation and other forms of alienation in its own backyard. We trust that the June 2016 agreement will prove that the university recognises it was not enough simply to hire companies with outsourced workers and then to plead innocence about the labour practices that those companies follow. For too long have the voices of the unheard been bulldozed by white monopoly capital – and, now, by empowerment capital affected by white capital, which creates more animosity and will eventually spill over to future generations, causing more than racial tension alone. The system on which we have built our democracy has to be revisited, to be channelled by and influenced by the people.

It has now been two decades of democracy, yet many Wits workers have been burdened by extreme exploitation and alienation through for-profit logic. They are tired of this, and so are their sons and daughters in the universities. We take lessons from the courage of leaders like Richard Ndebele and Virginia Monageng who stood up against the injustices. The workers' stories show that political freedom is not enough to improve lives. Frantz Fanon (1963) stated: 'Each generation must, out of relative obscurity, discover its mission, fulfil it, or betray it' (see also, in relation to the current student struggles, Maserumule 2015). The words of Fanon, coupled with Richard's and Virginia's stories and the victory of June 2016, highlight that it is now the task of *our* generation to advance the struggle for economic emancipation. My well-being is meaningless without the well-being of workers in all universities in South Africa. The suffering of Richard and Virginia will be a constant reminder of our duty to our nation.

NOTE

1   In the process of writing this chapter, Omhle Ntshingila was mentored by Susan Booysen.

REFERENCES

Bateman, B. (2016) Outsourced workers finally accept TUT's insourcing agreement. *Eyewitness News*, 11 February. http://ewn.co.za/2016/02/11/Protesting-outsourced-works-accept-TUTs-insourcing-agreement

BusinessTech (2016) The real minimum wage in South Africa. http://businesstech.co.za/news/wealth/111781/the-real-minimum-wage-in-south-africa/

Fanon, F. (1963) *The Wretched of the Earth*. (transl. C. Farrington). New York: Grove Press.

Heiberg, T. (2015) Wits reaches an agreement with MJL electrical workers. *Vuvuzela*, 29 May. http://witsvuvuzela.com/2015/05/29/wits-reaches-an-agreement-with-mjl-electrical-workers/

Maserumule, M. H. (2015) Why Steve Biko's Black Consciousness is gaining ground in SA. *Rand Daily Mail*, 4 September. http://www.rdm.co.za/politics/2015/09/04/why-steve-biko-s-black-consciousness-is-gaining-ground-in-sa

Nkosi, B. (2012) Wits takes hard look at controversial outsourcing. *Mail & Guardian*, 9 November. http://mg.co.za/article/2012-11-09-wits-takes-hard-look-at-controversial-outsourcing

Nkosi, B. (2015) Wits vice-chancellor says state can help end exploitation. *Mail & Guardian*, 26 May. http://mg.co.za/article/2015-05-26-wits-vice-chancellor-says-state-can-help-end-exploitation

Robinson, W. I. (2004) Global class formation and the rise of a transnational capitalist class. In *A Theory of Global Capitalism: Production, Class, and State in a Transnational World*. Baltimore: Johns Hopkins University Press.

South African History Online (2016) University of Witwatersrand student protests 2015 timeline. http://www.sahistory.org.za/article/university-witwatersrand-student-protests-2015-timeline

Steenkamp, J. (2015) Workers stage a sit-in at Wits. *SABC News*, 29 May. http://www.sabc.co.za/news/a/57bfe400488c962dafb4af5b3432783c/Witsundefinedworkersundefinedstageundefinedsit-inundefinedandundefineddemandundefinedemployment-20152905

University of Cape Town (UCT) (2015) Newsroom/daily publications. http://www.uct.ac.za/dailynews/

University of Johannesburg (UJ) (2016) Joint UJ and Labour Memorandum of Agreement on the insourcing of outsourced services and the transfer of workers to UJ. *UJ Newsroom/daily publications*. http://www.uj.ac.za/newandevents/Pages/Joint-UJ-and-Labour-Memorandum-of-Agreement-on-the-insourcing-of-Outsourced-Services-and-the-transfer-of-Workers-to-UJ.aspx

University of Pretoria (UP) (2016) Diversity, not division, in lecture halls. *Mail & Guardian*, 29 April. http://mg.co.za/article/2016-04-29-diversity-not-division-in-lecture-halls

University of the Witwatersrand Council (2016) Statement on Council meeting by registrar Carol Crosley. Released by spokesperson Shirona Patel.

Wits Vision 2022 (n. d.) University of the Witwatersrand. https://www.wits.ac.za/media/wits-university/footer/about-wits/governance/documents/Wits%20Vision%202022%20Strategic%20Framework.pdf

Workers' Solidarity Committee (2011) Draft report on the conditions of outsourced workers at Wits University. http://witsworkerssolidaritycommittee.blogspot.co.za/2012/04/draft-report-on-conditions-of.html

Workers' Solidarity Committee (2015) University Workers' Charter. Presented to the management of Wits and UJ, 6 October 2015. http://witsworkerssolidaritycommittee.blogspot.co.za/

CHAPTER

5

DOCUMENTING THE REVOLUTION

Gillian Godsell, Refiloe Lepere, Swankie Mafoko and Ayabonga Nase

INTRODUCTION

'A way of looking at the world that creates a space in which dialogue and contestation are truly possible, in which new ways are constantly explored and created, accepted and rejected, and in which change is unpredictable, but the idea of change is constant.' This is how the former chief justice, Pius Langa (2006), described transformative constitutionalism. Such ideas of dialogue, change and contestation apply equally to transformation battles on university campuses, and this chapter will describe some of the different forms which the dialogue took, chiefly on the campus of the University of the Witwatersrand (Wits).

The three student authors of this chapter, Refiloe Lepere, Swankie Mafoko and Ayabonga Nase, were all involved in different ways in the 2015 protests at Wits: producing plays on the Wits Great Hall steps, marching, occupying and providing legal assistance to University of Johannesburg (UJ) workers and students. The chapter therefore offers a medley of voices, combining academic discussion of protest in South Africa and elsewhere with insider elucidation, viewpoints and theoretical references.

The emphasis is on documents, from the fleeting (such as a student play performed only once) to the permanent, such as the Memorandum of

Understanding (MoU) signed between Wits management, workers and students (2015). Protests cannot be understood by relying on written documents alone. This is because so much communication takes place beyond the printed word, and because some crucial issues cannot be communicated in formal documents.

Students demanded decolonisation of all aspects of the university (see also Chapters 2 to 4 in this volume). Their protest sought change in tuition costs, university governance, curriculum and the character and content of teaching. The student challenge to the way universities in South Africa currently operate was not limited to university interactions with students, but included the well-being of the workers on campus, particularly outsourced workers.

As well as demanding social transformation, the students challenged the manner in which words and symbols become documents of protest, using new media, performances and other artefacts in making meaning of historical events such as the protest. 'The mobilisation of words can actually change how people act collectively,' argues Sidney Tarrow, who studies social movements. In his book on the language of contention (2013: 3), Tarrow explains that words 'reflect the contexts of social and political change'. However, language does not only reflect; it also structures. Symbols, including (but not limited to) words, structured and reflected the student protests grouped under the label #FeesMustFall. In analysing the documents of the protest, this chapter focuses on their meaning in counter-storytelling, and what the themes in the documents elucidate in terms of framing content in contemporary South Africa.

DOCUMENTS OF THE PROTEST

Social science methodology textbooks now include a wide range of artefacts, from sculpture to songs, as suitable for academic document analysis (Wagner, Kawulich and Garner 2012). The information technology specialist Ralph Sprague (1995: 30) defines a document as 'a set of information pertaining to topic, structured for human comprehension, represented by a variety of symbols, stored and handled as a unit'. This definition suggests that documenting is a process of choice and illumination.

In a review of books discussing protest, Katherine Everhart (2012: 110) urges scholars to think analytically about 'varied forms of protest such as sit-ins, street protests, occupations, and artistic performances'. Researchers need to study a wide range of communications carefully, as not only do they reveal the social movement, they shape it. Markus Prior (2009) reminds us that as well as acting as 'receptacles of content' documents are also 'agents in networks of action'. Importantly, though documents are intended to be read as objective, they are in fact the product of a social context, and many documents are biased.

Printed documents

During the 2015 protests at Wits, printed documents dominated communications from university management, and management dominated the field of printed documents ranging from press statements, through e-mails and circulars, to court documents. The initial documents, including the legal documents discussed below, were hostile to the protest, but the final document of 2015 was the joint MoU, a document both resulting from and demonstrating cooperation and compromise between management, workers and students.

At first, the communication was linear, based on the university's disseminating information and instructions. This soon changed and communication became more nuanced. A turning point in the university discourse was the Statement (2015) to vice-chancellors and ministers originating at Wits and signed initially by 400 academics:

> We stand with students in their fight for the democratisation of our universities ... our students are leading the national debate on education, and we insist that they deserve our respect and attention ... [student] commitment and self-control has gone unseen by many university managers, government leaders and the media who have misrepresented students as uninformed, irresponsible or irrational.

This statement transformed students from isolated troublemakers to important members of the academic community. The problem shifted from halting the activities of protesters, to incorporating their concerns into the interests of the university.

Following barricading, toyi-toying and confrontation at entrances and exits of Wits, on Thursday 15 October 2015 the university management circulated a notice, via e-mail and posters stuck up on campus. In terms of the Trespass Act 6 of 1959, students were requested to immediately discontinue; failure to do so would lead to the university taking 'necessary action' which would include Wits's employing the services of the South African Police Service. Pierre de Vos, (who teaches Constitutional Law at the University of Cape Town (UCT)) argues that 'as long as such protests remain[ed] peaceful and as long as they pose[d] no immediate threat to persons or property, it [was] morally unconscionable to use force to break them up – no matter how inconvenient the protest may be for others' (De Vos 2015). The Regulation of Gatherings Act 205 of 1993 requires organisers to give notice of a gathering to a responsible officer. It does 'not allow the police as a matter of course to use force to break up peaceful gatherings where there are no reasonable grounds to believe that the protest or demonstration threaten persons or property' (De Vos 2015). In order to allow the police on campus, the universities had to use interdicts and, in the case of Wits, the Trespass Act, a piece of legislation dating from 1959 and originally introduced to curb 'loitering' by black people. The university's usage of the apartheid law on students speaks to the institution's initial intent to strong-arm and threaten students and staff to desist from protesting, as well as denying them full citizenship of the university.

Following the notice on the trespassing law, on Thursday 29 November 2015 Wits instituted an urgent court application at the South Gauteng High Court by way of an interim interdict. Wits requested that the court rule that students refrain from acts of violence and vandalism, including 'disrupting lectures and tutorials; preventing any person from entering or leaving the university; causing damage to the property of the university, its staff and students; and harassing, intimidating, threatening or assaulting any of the University's staff and members of the public in any manner'. The Legal Resources Centre (LRC) acted for Wits students and opposed the interdict. Speaking to News24, the university spokesperson, Shirona Patel, said the purpose of obtaining the interdict was to 'allow police to come in and intervene because police told us [the university] they cannot act against perpetrators without an interdict' (Tandwa 2015). The interim interdict was granted. During the following week in court the university instructed their attorneys to discharge the temporary court order, following discussions between the university management and the students. The interim order was subsequently dismissed, and police were not allowed on Wits campus during 2015.

Subsequent to student protest action, on 23 October 2015 the University of Johannesburg (UJ) sought and was granted a temporary interdict – carefully worded in the same language and containing the same content as the Wits interdict. On 4 November 2015, Servest (Pty) Ltd, a cleaning company contracted with UJ, obtained an interdict from the Labour Court against its employees, cleaners at UJ. The interdict essentially prohibited all protest action by workers and classified this action as an unprotected strike. These two interdicts followed on the initial University of Cape Town (UCT) interdict of 19 October 2015.

On Friday 6 November 2015, workers and students from UJ, together with students and staff from Wits, were arrested for participating in a protest outside their campus. They were detained at Brixton Police Station and charged with 'public violence' and 'contravening interdicts'. The Centre for Applied Legal Studies (CALS), based at Wits, represented the group of 141 workers and UJ and Wits students. Lawyers deployed by the Muslim Lawyers Association, the Socio-Economic Rights Institute of South Africa (SERI), Section27 and Right2Know were also present. From the time they went in for the identification process, after the initial arrest until the following day, no lawyers were allowed to consult with those detained. Those arrested were warned to appear at the Johannesburg Magistrate's Court on Monday 9 November 2015 at eight in the morning. CALS represented the #Brixton141 at the Magistrate's Court where the charges were eventually withdrawn by the state early that afternoon.

The court documents, together with the notices, legitimise the university in justifying the inclusion of law-enforcement officials as actors in the protest. The inclusion of these documents in this chapter is to highlight the extent to which the university used official documents to create a stand based on an absolute moral judgement. However, even documents generally accepted as 'objective' may be biased and can be seen as a reflection of the institution's rejection of transformation and change, as well as determination to define protest as 'violent', and thus justify counter-measures on moral grounds.

The university documents were unidirectional, used established channels, and emanated from a single authority. The use of social media allowed students a multi-form of communication. There was no one sender of documents, one all-knowing producer of knowledge, one creator of records. This came to characterise the collective nature of the #Falls movement.

Open letters

Open letters fill an interesting space between formal print and social media. The appearance of the letter is formal, but Internet and other social media spread the document, and make possible formal participation by others. An Open Letter to Wits management and SRC dated 25 October (2015) revealed the rifts and challenges between students. This letter, #Letuswrite2015, highlighted the costs to students of the continued protest, and was signed by 3 000 students. While identifying with the campaigns for lower fees and supporting workers to bring an end to outsourcing, the students raised problems arising from delayed end-of-year examinations, ranging from the expiry of visas for foreign students to possible ineligibility to write Board Examinations for Chartered Accountants in 2016. The open letter was supported on Twitter. Palesa @palesa_parisma tweeted 'Tell them @Noksipedia; We have hustled to get this years fees paid, now please #LetUsWrite. Leave this battle for another day'. Lesego tweeted @SegoMolabe 'WITSIES LETS UNITE. #LetUsWrite.'

Worker documents

Key to the continuation of protest once no fee increase was agreed on, and therefore the reason for #LetUsWrite, was that the students linked their demands to the workers' struggle at the university (see also Chapters 4 and 10 in this volume). The voices of workers themselves were largely absent from written documents. Deliwe Mzobe, worker leader, is heard on YouTube, explaining the consequences of outsourcing (2015). A workers' charter was produced as early as October, by the Worker–Student Solidarity Committee (2015). The charter protests outsourcing and offers a different vision of a public university.

Posters #allworkandnopay depicting the workers' plight, were prepared by @projecthoopoe and by #October6, using statements from workers. Examples are:
- 'I support my whole family back at home in Venda … I will be a bachelor for life, I can't even buy myself clothing'.
- 'I am buried in debt … I work for that garnish order'.
- 'We will always live in shacks'.

Formal agreements

The MoU (see Appendix 4) signed at Wits on 13 November 2015 embodies the student/worker protests in important ways. The signatories tell a large part of the story: Wits management, a representative of the outsourced workers, and a representative of the protesting students. Although unions and SRC have a place on the task team, they were not central to negotiations. The representatives of both students and workers were individuals who played a key role in the protests. Working outside existing structures is not unusual in twenty-first-century protests. Castells (2015: 4) describes an occupying movement across 82 countries and 951 cities, a movement, which 'ignored political parties …

and rejected all formal organisation'. However, without a formal leadership, the ability to compromise and agree, and to make demands, is often absent. This makes the signing of an MoU at Wits quite unusual within the international protest movement. The memorandum covers matters of immediate concern to protesters,

Figure 5.1:   Poster advertising mass meeting, University of the Witwatersrand, November 2015.

such as deferment of examinations; medium-term plans such as constituting an insourcing task team; and the long-term dream of a different society. The signing of the formal agreement sets this protest apart from protests around the globe, from Iceland to Tunisia. The agreement incorporates representatives from formal structures in the insourcing task team, but does not limit participation to them.

Although this MoU is necessary for understanding the campus unrest, it is not sufficient. We need to move beyond the printed word, and beyond the issues of control, fees and outsourcing, to gain insight into what happened on South African campuses in 2015, and what is likely to happen next.

Protesters' documents

Communicating the messages of a protest is always crucial. Traditional methods of communication such as posters and banners were employed alongside graffiti, performance art, songs and – most importantly – social media. Blogs, Twitter, Instagram, YouTube and Facebook emerged as important reporting tools during the protests.

Social media as documenting

During the #FeesMustFall protests (according to Ferial Haffajee (2015: 160) this movement spread across seventeen campuses in ten days) social media platforms became sites for counter-storytelling. Using personal stories, metaphors, videos and photographs, students and workers were able to create their own counter-narratives interpreting their community and discourse. The use of social media revealed very personal stories that would otherwise have been missed by mainstream media. Hashtags consolidate personal stories under a common label. They help social media users to classify the sentiment on a particular topic and a hashtag 'also serves as a symbol of community membership' (Zhang, Wu and Yang 2012). Using social media may bring people closer to political or other topics that might otherwise be too public and distant for them.

In using the hashtag #FeesMustFall, communities were formed and counter-narratives were created. Counter-storytelling, rooted in critical race theory, is defined by Daniel Solorzano and Tara Yosso (2002: 26) as 'a method of telling the stories of those people whose experiences are not often told'. Stories that are often told become the dominant narrative and so it is important to have counter-narratives as well, to expose, analyse and challenge deeply entrenched characterisations of race, gender and privilege. In a sense, counter-stories promote what journalists call 'human stories' (McQuail 2010). These narratives put a human face to the experiences of oppressed and marginalised people. Writing about cyber activism during the Iran protest of 2009, Henry Jenkins (2012: 4) argues that 'the daily flow of messages about mundane matters left people using social network sites feeling stronger and having personal ties to their friends, the flow of political messages through Twitter left them feeling more directly implicated in the protest'. Similarly, Tai Wei Lim (2014: 95) describes how 'social media tools became platforms and public spaces of political expression through creative contents' during the 2014 Yellow Umbrella Revolution in Hong Kong. The hashtags wove ideas and thoughts from individual, isolated screens into a clear communal issue.

As well as creating communities, social media sharing and reporting by the students helped to establish new methods of reporting. The uptake on social media platforms by students started to question notions of documenting and who gets to tell the story. The self-documentation of their activities and protest also pushed against the storytelling boundaries often held so tightly by journalists. During the protest, much of the mainstream news media perpetuated a single narrative that lacked the personal perspective of the heart of the movement. In a tweet on 16 October 2015, *The Daily Vox* (2015a) challenged the 'disdainful' mainstream media portrayal: 'The protest has not been characterised by recklessness or destruction.' Mmamalema Molepo brings this need for a personal narrative to light on 11 November 2015 in a status post on Facebook: 'We must help our mothers and fathers tell their stories too. The media doesn't care about them. We must tell our stories; we must help them tell their stories. We can't afford to have people tell our stories for us when our stories are always being distorted to suit an exclusionary and incriminating narrative.' Nqobile Malaza, a Wits lecturer, writes in a Facebook post in October 2015: 'The dream for a transformed society that breathes fairness, equality, equity and social justice is one whose time has undeniably come' (Nqobile Malaza, personal communication, 10 June 2016).

The platforms provided forums for ordinary students to document their protests, and they spread the news about activities such as gatherings and requests for donations. They also provided photographic and video evidence of police brutality and institutional violence. Through these platforms, students were able to disseminate their own stories, words and images to each other and, most importantly, to those not immediately involved with the protest. From these students' perspective, cycles of oppressive communication between the oppressed and those in power needed to be broken.

WhatsApp Groups

University authorities used legislation and interdicts, including interdicts against hashtags, as instruments of control. Public interest law groups, with a proud history of assisting students who defied the apartheid government, were constrained by both ethical and practical considerations when students defied university authority. This problem was solved by a WhatsApp group channelling help to students at different universities from legal groupings with no conflict of interest at that particular university. WhatsApp groups were also viewed by student leaders as a secure method of communication, among themselves and between universities.

Performance art as documentation

One of the important counter-narratives was a portrayal of the university through the eyes of black students. As the protest momentum and energy faltered, artworks were created – fine art, poetry, theatre and music performances inspired by the protest. Varied forms of protest are common in the twenty-first century. A wide range of creations, from graffiti to performance pieces, giving voice and character to protests, has been described (see Lim 2014; Everhart 2013; and Solomon and Palmieri 2011). These creations often confirm shared themes of protests.

Heavily interwoven into South Africa's past and present are discussions around race and racial binaries. A performance art piece performed at Wits by Swankie Mafoko, Zukolwenkosi Zikalala and Matshepo Khumalo (2015) brought to light the nature of these binaries within higher tertiary education institutions. This piece was developed from conversations about how different departments in the university privileged knowledge systems that alienated students. Readings prescribed for students as course packs (bound collections of journal articles and book chapters) were experienced as presenting an erasure of black experience, historically and even in the present. The response to this was a performance piece centring on washing 'colonial course packs'. The performance was a layered attempt at speaking visually, beyond language, not only to the colonial epistemologies within the universities, but also to the issue of the outsourced cleaners – hence the washing and the mopping up. In addition, Zikalala and Khumalo subverted the historically violent tradition of 'blackface' and painted their faces and bodies white. The message was that of 'whitening' themselves in order to make it through the institution. This symbolically referenced issues of economic capital, and the cultural capital that white people in South Africa still have in institutions of higher learning.

The Brazilian theatre director Augusto Boal (1979: 132) speaks of spectators being freed from the state of passive observation and becoming actors themselves, ceasing to be objects and becoming subjects. 'The spectator is encouraged to intervene in the action' as spectators on the day were allowed to intervene in the action that took place on the steps of the Wits Great Hall. They were invited to continue helping Mafoko to wash course packs that contained colonial content, or content they felt needed to be stripped away from the curriculum. They were also given the option of helping Zikalala and Khumalo to continue painting themselves with white paint or removing it from their bodies completely. Lastly, with the same water used to wash the course packs, spectators were given the option to come and wash Mafoko's hair, symbolising the need for the decolonisation of the mind alongside that of the curriculum. Many, at first, stood observing the action, some too emotional to engage, but slowly, one, then two and others came forward to participate. Commenting on this type of act, Boal states how 'the *Poetics of the Oppressed* is essentially the poetics of liberation: the spectator no longer delegates power to the characters either to think or to act in his place. The spectator frees himself; he thinks and acts for himself!' (Boal 1979: 155). The performance allowed the use of the body to reflect and replicate a silence experienced by some students where their freedom and future is concerned. The intention was to mobilise students and give them a voice again. A tweet read: 'fee-free education isn't just a destination, it's a journey (Mbhele 2016). The fight is to free our education completely, permanently and ultimately free society'.

The piece addressed and questioned the silence that the university requires from young black people daily in order to succeed. In *Black Skin, White Masks* the Afro-Caribbean philosopher and revolutionary Frantz Fanon explores the othering of the black man, the 'negro'. He communicates how the black man cannot exist as an entity of his own but lives in relation to the white man, 'for not only must the black man be black; he must be black in relation to the white man' (Fanon 1986: 82–83). The play at Wits highlighted this othering by looking at the conflict some students experience between the desire to decolonise and transform the institutions they occupy and the pressure to constantly abandon their own black identities in order to adopt a white perception of what blackness means or should be. Students felt they were required to die to their blackness in order to give birth to new identities of blackness embedded within whiteness. As Fanon stated (1986: 170), 'he who is reluctant to recognise me opposes me'.

Figure 5.2: Actor in whiteface in Mafoko, Zikalala and Khumalo's performance piece 'Hypervisibility' (Photograph by Levy Pooe).

Owing to the growing fatigue around the failure to recognise the needs and voice of young black people, art became the medium that would best articulate and re-live the trauma of having to survive this every day. Through art, the hearts of those who had turned their backs against the movement could be recaptured, and the story that the media did not tell could be 'televised'. The powerful medium of art could give the movement a second wind, and mobilise students once again.

Occupying

Occupying spaces, from Mong Kok to Wall Street, has been a characteristic of global protest movements in the early twenty-first century (Chomsky 2012, 2015; DeLuca, Lawson and Sun 2012; Chow 2015). Manuel Castells (2015: 11) explains that, for a networked or cyber movement, occupying a physical space is particularly important. Occupied spaces have symbolic meaning, and create communities operating according to their own rules, what Castells calls 'instant communities of transformative practice'. The protesting Wits community did not only operate as a cyber community – they were physically present on campus. But by changing the name of Senate House to 'Solomon Mahlangu House', the community drew 'us and them' lines. Any person referring to that space instantly defined themselves as an insider or an outsider, depending on the name they used. The name was not chosen randomly. Solomon Mahlangu was hanged by the apartheid government in 1979 at the age of twenty-three after having been found guilty of murder and treason according to the common purpose doctrine. His youth makes him appealing to other young people, who quote his words on the gallows: 'My blood will nourish the tree that will bear the fruits of freedom' (see, for example, South African History Online 2016).

Inside their space, the students studied, and cleaned up after themselves, and conveyed this by means of pictures posted on Facebook, Twitter and Instagram. The cleaning-up as a counter-narrative to media images of looting and violence (*The Daily Vox* 2015b) is reminiscent of the tweets depicting protesters in Tahrir Square carefully fitting into place the paving stones they had thrown during the night, and washing everything down with disinfectant. Lim (2014: 93) reports similar images for the Yellow Umbrella Revolution: images of protesters cleaning the streets, apologising to the public for inconvenience caused, and reading textbooks 'emanate soft power to the local and global audience through concepts of social responsibility, democratic ideals and quiet strength'. These visuals counter the narrative of mob mentality with images of passionate, careful and educated individuals.

Senior students and sympathetic academics at Wits made themselves available to tutor protesters occupying Solomon Mahlangu/Senate House, to help them prepare for exams. This tweet from @tutors_witsfees indicates times and venues for tutoring in anthropology, sociology, philosophy, politics, media studies and psychology: 'Please note that the venue is CB15 and not CB14'. Subsequent complaints by climatologists and pharmacists that they had been forgotten were dealt with by @ragingpoet, who tweeted 'I've sent messages out but it may be the case that someone isn't identified until tomorrow' (Danai 2015).

Songs

Lim (2014) points out that songs and performance have an invigorating and sustaining role to play in protests. The students sang songs familiar in the South

African political landscape, songs of the struggle. @SeadimoTlale: 'numbers increasing at Brixton. Comrades chanting senzeni na. Come stand in solidarity for #Brixton 163 with us'. The songs brought to consciousness the unfinished business of the mass democratic movement – not only were they songs from the ruling party archives, but they were also the same songs the movement sang when oppressed. The *Daily Vox* (2016) listed six songs which both defined and motivated #FeesMustFall protesters: the anthem of the revolution was 'Iyoh Solomon', a praise-song for Solomon Mahlangu; other songs sung regularly were 'Senzeni Na'; 'No woman, no cry'; 'Amakomanisi'; 'Siyaya' and 'Abalalanga'. When the weeping UJ workers were released from Brixton Police Station, the waiting crowd sang 'Mama don't cry' for them (Nieftagodien, personal communication 2015). The songs appealed to collective struggle memory – and also functioned to mobilise the students to action: @thedailyvox: 'iyooh Solomon. The crowd outside the Brixton Police Station is in full voice.'

In writing about protest and soul, Hank Johnston (2009) notes that music mobilises people to action. Songs of the struggle, about hope and life in a society free of oppression also have a power to unite. The translator and expert on Latin-American revolutionary songs, literature and poetry, Robert Pring-Mill (1987), explained that the label 'protest song' for Nicaraguan struggle songs was a misnomer – the songs were meant to inspire hope, not merely to protest. They are not only about resistance but also about a past, a present and a future all in one moment. The songs carry with them the intense trauma of the past, the present reality and the possible future – bleak or hopeful.

THEMES FROM THE DOCUMENTS OF THE PROTEST

The documents reveal what the protests were about and how they functioned. The students used various artefacts to make their voices heard. However, a problem with documents is the amount of information recorded. In writing about the massive volume of data out there in the world, Noam Chomsky (2012: 104–105) argues that for one to properly reflect on the messages and documents shared, '[u]nless you know what you are looking for, and you store it properly and put it into context, it's as if you never saw it. There is no point in having a lot of data available unless you can make some sense out of it. And that takes thought, reflection, inquiry.' The following are themes that were harvested from the documents of the revolution.

Violence

Although violence had no hashtag, the possibility of violence, the prevention of violence, what constitutes violence, the causes and effects of violence and the fear of violence all permeated the protests. This fear is implicit in the assurances by university managements that 'the safety and security of our staff and students remain paramount' (Wits Executive Management 2015). An emphasis on safety implied the possibility of violence, when the vice-chancellor of UJ reassured students and staff that 'the university needs to create a conducive environment for exams to take place' (Rensburg 2015).

A dominant narrative during the #FeesMustFall protests in October and November 2015 highlighted the peacefulness of students, but not of police. The students maintained that '... the large majority remain peaceful' (Iaccino 2015). De Vos wrote an opinion piece in the *Daily Maverick*: '#FeesMustFall: Police violence has no place in peaceful protests', condemning police heavy-handedness (2015). This condemnation was echoed by Habib (2015): 'We were dismayed to see the excessive police violence against protesting students at Parliament and elsewhere in recent days. At Wits, we have kept the police off campus because we do not believe that force should be used to prevent the expression of legitimate demands by protesters.'

Nonviolence became a measure of the validity of the protests, and appealed to many who saw it as constructive and effective. Although 'everything that has happened is a true reflection of the country's grievances ... the violence deters us from our common goal,' suggests student Khumo Liphoko in a Facebook post (Khumo Liphoko, personal communication, 20 October 2015). The value of disruption versus riot is captured by Wits alumna Thato Khaole writing on Facebook: 'Protest, be it hostile or peaceful, is meant to be DISRUPTIVE to the status quo ... protest however should not be DESTRUCTIVE ... to turn this from an issue of access to education to an issue about "us" and "them" is ignorant and counterproductive' (Thato Khaole, personal communication, 17 October 2015).

However, as the protest turned from fee increment to outsourced wages to decolonisation and patriarchy, another narrative emerged: nonviolence as a slow and ineffective mechanism for achieving student goals (Ndlozi 2015). 'Peaceful protesting is a luxury only available to those safely in mainstream culture,' wrote Darlena Cunha, referring to the Ferguson riots in the US (Cunha 2014). This new narrative suggested that nonviolence was answered with unrecognised forms of violence from the universities, which required 'receipts for their poverty' just to apply for financial aid, excluding many because of the lack of money to pay the 2015 fees.

One of the few explicit discussions of violence from the side of the security guards, or 'bouncers' (a permanent fixture on most campuses by the end of 2015) is the account by Jane Duncan and Pier Paolo Frasinelli (2015) of human rights violations at UJ. This document describes engagements ranging from spraying pepper into protesters' faces, to 'pushing a line of protesters onto a pedestrian bridge ... an intensely dangerous manoeuvre ... with a danger of causing a fatal accident'.

'Concerned Academics' (2015), an article signed by forty-six Wits academics, offers a different interpretation of violence on the Wits campus. They describe provocation by members of the public, and state that 'students and student leaders remained calm, organised and mostly peaceful'. They also describe management behaviour as provocative when promised meetings were changed at short notice and this was poorly communicated. Does the violence lie in barricading entrances, or in driving directly at students barricading entrances? Does it lie in national inequalities, both compressed and magnified on campuses where some students drive expensive cars and others have no food (Godsell 2015)? Are only nonviolent protests valid, and moral? These are the burning questions explored beyond the official documents.

#FeesMustFall: Protest of shame

The protest produced an inescapable storyline of personal black experience through performances and song. The black middle class in South Africa only emerged post-1994. There have been many assumptions about the class's access to capital and resources, but those assumptions are blown out of proportion. The black middle class has to clash and compete with both the black poor working class in the townships and a white middle class that is established and enjoys more resources. The protest brought home the reality that the ability to compete in a market-driven economy is close to impossible for the black middle-class students. The students realised that actually they were poor. This message was as startling to those students who considered themselves middle class as it was to outsiders. In *The Genesis of Shame*, Velleman (2001) argues that in the story of Adam and Eve, shame is not inherently present in the human but, rather, introduced through outside knowledge. The students who engaged in the protests were in a similar predicament to Adam and Eve, suddenly needing to cover a nakedness of which they had previously been unaware.

Max du Preez (2015) describes the black middle class as 'the ones we have been waiting for – on [whom] we base our hopes for stability and progress in the long term'. They do not, however, have the material conditions to bring about that long-term progress. They have been called middle class, but they knew that they had no material basis (clothing) to cover their being. The fee structure at the institutions then led them to receive knowledge of their nakedness – no money. Hence the protest became a protest of shame.

The students stood, fully aware of their shame and fully exposing themselves in placards: '10%? There aren't ENOUGH sugar daddies to fund us Habib'
- 'When my parents bank account is like, Dololo.0'.
- 'According to Habib's Constitution Section1.A. Rule 18(a) 50 – 76 'Only rich people must be educated'.
- 'My mother earns R2 000 a month, where must she get R10 000 for my registration?'
- 'Are the rich the only ACADEMICALLY DESERVING?'
- 'Post racism society says 'you are poor go get a degree.' Colonial elitist Universities says; 'You are too poor to take yourself out of poverty' #WeArefucked #ShutItDown'.

Stories were told through the placards. The sharing by the black students of stories about their single mothers, who could be the outsourced workers, speaks powerfully to the idea that while imaginary students were easily welcomed into the institutions of higher learning their actual beings, naked and poor, were not as easily accepted. Hank Johnston (2009) argues that participants in a protest seldom interpret their own actions as part of a broader critique of social life under contemporary capitalism. For many students, however, the assessment of neoliberal policies in South Africa and in the university became an integral part of their protest commentary.

Students highlighted the shameful and embarrassing processes of the National Student Financial Aid Scheme (NSFAS), the national funding body. As a student funded by NSFAS you must prove that you are poor, while other bursaries or funding opportunities require you to prove your strengths and abilities. Such oppressive acts leave students in an emotional quandary. What should they choose to do? Take up the loan or hide their poverty? Either choice will have serious repercussions for them.

The issue of debt as shame is not confined to South Africa. Jeffrey Williams (2006: 156), writing about 'the pedagogy of debt' in the US, notes that in the twenty-first century talking about money is forbidden. Debt is 'shameful, reflecting your failing ... you're a spendthrift or you're not good enough.' And so the effects of debt on individual students, on their families, and on the whole project of higher education, go undiscussed.

#RainbowIsDead

Social media posts required viewers to look carefully at the same space and time as was occupied by black and by white people. The protest revealed that the bubble of an equal society had burst. The past and the present were placed right next to each other and there was an intruding reality that they were the same. Not much had changed.

South African rainbowism – 'the unity, the sameness, and rainbow nation' (Gqola 2004: 6) – has been fashioned with the idea that all are alike and will soon be equal. Under apartheid, structural racism meant clear lines of inequality. Since the advent of democracy, there have been legislated policies to promote social equality. The view of many of the protesting students, however, was that material conditions in South African society entrench inequality. The assumption that democracy brought with it fairness and equal access was questioned by the protesting students.

A photograph during the #FeesMustFall protests showed white students forming a human shield around black students. This photograph took the viewer back in time – to the anguish, shame and violence of the recent past. What body is malignant? Which body is allowed to exist without violence or questioning? Which body is subject to violence and terror?

#Hope

The protest was not only about what was not wanted (high fees and outsourcing). It was also about a better future: a university that worked better for the students, and a country more attuned to the needs of its citizens. Castells (2015: 16) writes: '... the more ideas are generated from within the movement, on the basis of the experience of their participants, the more representative, enthusiastic, and hopeful the movements will be'. This hope is embodied in tweets between two student leaders at Wits: 'Another world IS possible' tweeted @Anele_Nzimande on 30 October 2015. To which @Zukiswa responded 'And she is SURELY on her way'. Without access to social media, the hope embodied in this private-but-public conversation would not be part of the protest narrative.

#Transformation

This covered a wide range of concerns, from decolonising the university to a protest against managerialism, discussed in more detail in Chapter 2 of this volume. The protest against managerialism was embodied in this banner hanging at the public meeting at Wits on 1 November, stating 'We are students, not customers'.

Figure 5.3: Banner hanging in Solomon Mahlangu House (formerly Senate House) at mass meeting, University of the Witwatersrand, 1 November 2015 (Photograph by R. M. Godsell)

Jenni Case (2015) argues for the reinstatement of the public good as the aim of the university. She suggests that employability as an outcome has narrowed the functioning of the university, rendering students less rather than more able to function in a rapidly changing society. The argument against managerialism opens up questions of what and who the university is there for, as well as the manner in which it functions.

Gender relations were part of the transformation debate, to the extent that #PatriarchyMustFall was included in the first UCT interdict against students (UCT 2015), along with #RhodesMustFall and #FeesMustFall and, rather bewilderingly, the UCT Trans Collective.

CONCLUSION

The documents discussed in this chapter cross the spectrum from the intentionally public to the intensely private. The performance by Mafoko, Khumalo and Zikalala was available only to the students who watched it on the day it was performed. This performance served the dual process of helping the performers to articulate for themselves key aspects of the protest, and allowing their audience to reflect and to participate. At the other end of the continuum, press conferences, while also giving management a chance to reflect on and articulate their view, were publicly aimed at passive participants.

Social media hold a particularly interesting space in the public/private continuum. Although the communication is available to the public, an effort must be made to access it. Unless it is reported in the media it does not shape the perceptions of the general public, but only of those who choose to participate – even if the participation is only by means of viewing. It is ephemeral, and a particular communication at a specific time may be overlooked. But it is also permanent, and can be accessed later (even this permanence is misleading, as tweets and posts can be deleted).

Communicating protest issues in 2015 was not about presenting pre-printed posters to the public. Personal, direct social media communication allowed the students to articulate issues for themselves, and to incorporate others' stories into the protest narrative. This meant that the narrative was both confused and nuanced. Important sentiments, such as the shame of a middle class unable to pay fees, and the alienation of students offered a colonial curriculum presented in a patriarchal system, could emerge through such a personal narrative, but the representativeness of these communications could not be gauged. Clarity and consensus emerged with printed documents such as the MoU, although many important issues are excluded from these.

The public presentation of the protest was limited to what should be ended – outsourcing and fees. Analysing a wider range of communications allows some insight into the positive goals of the protest: a re-imagined university offering an enhanced education, and a welcoming campus, for students and workers.

REFERENCES

Boal, A. (1979) *Theatre of the Oppressed*. London: Pluto.
Case, J. (2015) Re-imagining the curriculum in a postcolonial space: Engaging the public good purposes of higher education in South Africa. Keynote address at the Higher Education Learning and Teaching Association of South Africa (HELTASA) annual conference 17–20 November.
Castells, M. (2015) *Networks of Outrage and Hope: Social Movements in the Internet Age*. Cambridge: Polity Press.
Chomsky, N. (2012) *Power Systems*. London: Penguin.
Chomsky, N. (2015) *Occupy*. London: Penguin.
Chow, P. (2015) Police-related statements during the Umbrella Movement in Hong Kong – 'laying hands down' or an attempt at discursive formulation. *Inter-Asia Cultural Studies*, 16(3), 470–487.
Concerned Academics (2015) Students showed true leadership. Article signed by 46 academics, University of the Witwatersrand. http://www.bdlive.co.za/opinion/2015/10/23/students-showed-true-leadership
Cunha, D. (2014) Ferguson: In defense of rioting. *TIME*, 25 November. http://time.com/3605606/ferguson-in-defense-of-rioting/
Danai (2015) Twitter, 27 October. https://twitter.com/ragingpoet/status/659074930949148672
DeLuca, K., Lawson, S. & Sun, Y. (2012) Occupy Wall Street on the public screens of social media: The many framings of the birth of a protest movement. *Communication, Culture and Critique*, 5, 483–509.
De Vos, P. (2015) #FeesMustFall: On the right to mass protest and the use of force by the police. *Constitutionally Speaking*, 26 October.
Duncan, J. & Frasinelli, P. P. (2015) The right to protest? An account of human rights violations during #FeesMustFall, #OccupyUJ and #EndOutsourcing protests at the University of Johannesburg. http://www.r2k.org.za/wp-content/uploads/Account-of-human-rights-violations-at-the-University-of-Johannesburg-final.pdf
Du Preez, M. (2015) Rhodes and the rage of the black middle class. http://www.news24.com/Columnists/MaxduPreez/Rhodes-and-the-rage-of-the-black-middle-class-20150331
Everhart, K. (2012) Youth activism and resistance in contemporary times. *Qualitative Sociology*, 35, 109–111.
Everhart K. (2013) Ocup(arte)!: Cultural engagement in the University of Puerto Rico student movement, 2010. In B. Tejerina and I. Perugorria (eds) *From Social to*

Political: New Forms of Mobilization and Democratization. Conference Proceedings, Universidad del Pais Vasco, Bilbao, 9–10 February, pp. 329–344.

Fanon, F. (1986) *Black Skin, White Masks*. London: Pluto.

Godsell, S. (2015) #WitsFeesMustFall op-ed: On violent protest and solidarity. http://www.dailymaverick.co.za/article/2015-10-19-witsfeesmustfall-op-ed-on-violent-protest-and-solidarity/#.V1mFuJN942I

Gqola, P. (2004) Where have all the rainbows gone? *Rhodes Journalism Review* 24, 6–7.

Habib, A. (2015) Wits University supports students' demands for more funding for higher education. Circular from Prof Adam Habib, vice-chancellor and principal, 22 October.

Haffajee, F. (2015) *What if There Were no Whites in South Africa?* Johannesburg: Pan Macmillan.

Iaccino L. (2015) FeesMustFall protest as it happened: South African students violently clash with police. *International Business Times*. http://www.ibtimes.co.uk/south-africa-fees-must-fall-student-protest-turns-violent-attack-police-journalists-1525361

Jenkins, H. (2012) Twitter revolutions. *Spreadable Media*. http://spreadablemedia.org/essays/jenkins/#.Vo3PP8B97-k

Johnston, H. (2009) Protest cultures: Performance, artefacts, and ideations. In H. Johnston, (ed.) *Culture, Social Movements and Protest*. Farnham: Ashgate, pp. 3–29.

Khaole, T. (2015) Personal communication, 17 October.

Langa, P. (2006) Transformative constitutionalism. Prestige lecture delivered at the University of Stellenbosch, 9 October.

Lesego (2015) Twitter, 28 October.

Lim, T. (2014) The aesthetics of Hong Kong's 'Umbrella Revolution' in the first ten days. *East Asia*, 32, 83–98.

Liphoko, K. (2015) Personal communication, 20 October.

Mafoko, S., Zikalala, Z. & Khumalo, M. (2015) 'Hypervisibility'. Live performance on Central Block steps, University of the Witwatersrand, 30 October.

Mbhele, M. (2016) Twitter, 10 January. https://twitter.com/MbeMbhele/status/686295612279664640

McQuail, D. (2010) *McQuail's Mass Communication Theory*. London: Sage Publications.

Memorandum of Understanding (MoU) (2015) Wits University management, student representatives, and outsourced workers, 12 November. www.feesmustfall.joburg/news/

Molepo, M. (2015) Facebook, 11 November. 'We must help our mothers and fathers tell their stories too'. https://www.facebook.com/mamz.molepo?fref=ts

Mzobe, D. (2015) 'Effects of outsourcing on workers'. YouTube. Youtu.be/nRHe1Otp8tY 4:19pm, 29 October.

Ndlozi, M. (2015) The #FeesMustFall movement, Liberalism and the pursuit of peace. http://www.dailymaverick.co.za/opinionista/2015-11-09-the-feesmustfall-movement-liberalism-and-the-pursuit-of-peace/#.V1otvZN942K

Open Letter to Wits Management and SRC (2015) Final-year Law students. #LetUs Write2015, https://docs.google.com/forms/d/1FmeSE01pCp2OepcDNELwsl05 gFi1Qg2Hva7jk_kgb98/formResponse https://twitter.com/SegoMolabe/status/659180640374509568

Palesa (2015) Twitter, 26 October. https://twitter.com/Palesa_parisma/status/658611837278228480

Pring-Mill, R. (1987) The roles of revolutionary song: A Nicaraguan assessment. *Popular Music* 6(2), 183.

Prior, M. (2009) Improving media effects research through better measurement of news exposure. *Journal of Politics*, 71, 893–908.

Rensburg, I. (2015) Violent attacks on students continue at UJ. *Destiny Connect*. http://www.destinyconnect.com/2015/11/06/violent-attacks-on-students-continue-at-uj/

Solomon, C. & Palmieri, T. (2011) *Springtime: The New Student Rebellions*. London: Verso.

Solorzano, D. G. & Yosso, T. J. (2002) Critical race methodology: Counter-storytelling as an analytical framework for education. *Qualitative Inquiry*, 8(1), 23–44.

South African History Online (2016) Solomon Kalushi Mahlangu. http://www.sahistory.org.za/people/solomon-kalushi-mahlangu

Sprague, R. H. (1995) Electronic document management: Challenges and opportunities for information systems managers. *MIS Quarterly*, 19(1), 29–49.

Statement to vice-chancellors, minister of higher education and training, Blade Nzimande, and the minister of finance, Nhlanhla Nene (2015) http://www.amandla.mobi/student_struggle.

Tandwa, L. (2015) Wits gets urgent interdict to allow police to step in. http://www.news24.com/SouthAfrica/News/Wits-gets-urgent-interdict-to-allow-police-to-step-in-20151030

Tarrow, S. (2013) *The Language of Contention: Revolutions in Words 1688–2012*. New York: Cambridge University Press.

The Daily Vox (2015a) Special editorial: The Wits protest is not just about university fee, 16 October. http://www.thedailyvox.co.za/special-editorial-the-wits-protest-is-not-just-about-university-fees/

The Daily Vox (2015b) Twitter, 6 November. https://twitter.com/thedailyvox/status/662706874794557440

The Daily Vox (2016) Six protest songs to brush up on before #FeesMustFall returns. http://www.thedailyvox.co.za/six-protest-songs-to-brush-up-on-before-feesmustfall-returns/

Tlale, S. (2015) Twitter, 6 November. https://twitter.com/SeadimoTlale/status/662709055278878720

UCT (2015) Interdict. Downloaded 16 March 2016. https://www.uct.ac.za/downloads/uct.ac.za/SKM_554e15101916420.pdf

Velleman, J. D. (2001) The genesis of shame. *Philosophy & Public Affairs*, 30(1), 27–52.

Wagner, C., Kawulich, B. & Garner, M. (eds) (2012) *Doing social research: A global context*. McGraw-Hill Higher Education.

Williams, J. (2006) The pedagogy of debt. *College Literature*, 33(4), 155–169.

Wits Executive Management (2015) Update on Activities at Wits this morning. *VCO News* University of the Witwatersrand, 28 October.

Wits Fees Tutors (2015) Twitter, 27 October. https://twitter.com/tutors_witsfees/status/659064784114069504

Wits Workers' Solidarity Committee (WSC) (2015) University Workers' Charter. http://witsworkerssolidaritycommittee.blogspot.co.za/2015/10/university-workers-charter_27.html

Zhang, Y., Wu, Y. & Yang, Q. (2012) Community discovery in Twitter based on user interests. *Journal of Computational Information Systems*, 8(3), 991–1000.

Zukiswa (2015) Twitter, 30 October. https://twitter.com/theladyzook/status/660133096025677825

PART
THREE

THE REVOLT – 'RISING AGAINST THE LIBERATORS', SOUTH AFRICA IN AFRICA

CHAPTER

6

STANDING ON THE SHOULDERS OF GIANTS? SUCCESSIVE GENERATIONS OF YOUTH SACRIFICE IN SOUTH AFRICA

David Everatt[1]

INTRODUCTION

The struggle to overthrow apartheid was generated and populated by youth. From the transformative power of the African National Congress Youth League in the 1940s to the 1976 Soweto uprising through successive waves of youth- and scholar/student-driven school boycotts, consumer boycotts and into the low intensity war that accompanied the 1990–1994 interregnum, young people placed their futures on hold and their lives on the line, to bring down apartheid. But what have these generational cohorts – many now well into late adulthood – received in return? And what lessons, if any, should the current wave of student protesters learn from this history?

This chapter uses a large sample survey (n = 27 485) of people of all races living in Gauteng, the economic and demographic heartland of South Africa, to identify successive (and current) cohorts of youth, so as to understand their situation after twenty-one years of democracy. It starts with the '1976 generation', and includes those who were involved in the successive uprisings of the 1980s, the youth of the 1990–1994 interregnum, and the so-called 'born frees'. The chapter looks at their demographic situation, and lingers on some psychosocial variables such as racial views, alienation, anomie, xenophobia and so on;

and it seeks to understand whether this generational struggle will achieve more lasting gains than those which preceded it.

YOUTH STRUGGLES

Young people – youth, 'young lions', 'lost generation', 'marginalised youth', 'born frees', students, Gen X or Y, millennials or whatever labels are appended – have consistently led progressive movements for change, whether in the struggle for democracy in South Africa, the different struggles that made up the 'Arab Spring', the Occupy movement, and so on (Rizvi 2012; Everatt 2013; Wyn and Cahill 2015). Successive surveys in South Africa and elsewhere have shown that young people support democratic values and principles in larger proportions and with greater fervour than their adult counterparts in the same surveys (Everatt 2013; Wallace and Kovatcheva 1998; Helve and Holm 2005). But youth are not an undifferentiated mass; 'youth' is a label that covers people in a specific age cohort, and while some characteristics are common (psychosocial and emotional development, experimental and risk-taking behaviours, for example), 'youth' as a cohort are as complex, nuanced and differentiated as any other age group in society.

Because of their precarious socioeconomic and cultural location, however, youth provide a lens that magnifies many challenges in society – they are commonly better educated yet suffer far higher unemployment than older people; are regarded as non-credit worthy, unreliable and risky recipients of investment, and despite truisms such as 'youth are the future' they are more commonly understood in terms of the latent threat they represent (see various contributions to Wyn and Cahill 2015; in South Africa, see *inter alia* Marais 1993; Everatt and Sisulu 1993; Van Zyl Slabbert et al. 1994; Marks 2001; Ward, Van der Merwe and Dawes 2012). They are most likely to suffer from the ills of a society, including higher than average unemployment and susceptibility to a range of diseases.

South Africa's liberation history is punctuated by moments of youth-led resistance, ranging from the 1976 uprising led initially by schoolchildren and students, through to the school boycotts of the 1980s, the youth-enforced consumer boycotts of the 1980s, part of the response to the call to make the state ungovernable, to the primarily youth-populated self-defence and self-protection units that fought on opposing sides during the 1990–1994 low intensity war in the then Natal and Pretoria-Witwatersrand-Vereeniging (PWV) regions.

Throughout the period, while a tiny number of young whites broke with apartheid, the overwhelming majority of young white men were conscripted to make up the apartheid regime's defence force. While the '1976 generation' rose up against the attempt to enforce Afrikaans education, and many more were inspired by black consciousness, many emerged in the 1980s and 1990s as champions of the nonracial vision espoused by the ANC and the internal United Democratic Front (UDF). A conscious political effort was made to avoid a racial essentialism and its seemingly unavoidable corollary, race war.

Young people are often brave, principled and fuelled by a sense of fairness and justice; but young people are also gang members, xenophobes and criminals – and make up the mobs that break the heads of opposition political parties or rival groups. Youth fought for liberation, and youth fought for the apartheid armed forces. In sum: there is no point engaging in a study of youth, or students, with a halo obscuring the cohort being studied. Youth, like adults, can be angel, demon or both, depending on circumstance and perspective.

For these reasons – and more, some good, some markedly less so – young people fascinate 'adult' society. This may be due to their fearlessness and risk-taking behaviour. Their opaque cultural rites, language, dress, music, art and speech are part of a general resistance to doing as they are 'meant to' or making themselves available for 'adult' scrutiny and judgement. Their codes make their world impenetrable, and deliberately so; their bold, often aggressive attacks – either for or against the status quo – are admired and feared. They are also preyed upon by predatory adults, whether for sex, violence, to act as foot soldiers, as abusers of addictive substances leading to entrapment in criminal gangs, sex work, trafficking, voyeurism and other morbid adult afflictions.

Above all, however, one fact holds true across different countries, contexts and time periods – that very few, if any, youth-led struggles *for youth-defined goals* are ever successful. This is true even when youth fight for their own goals nestled within a broader struggle. When young people storm the barricades or take up weapons as part of a broader struggle (such as against apartheid) they are lauded; but when the struggle moves out of the trenches and into the boardrooms young people are reminded that they are meant to be seen but not heard, and are shifted (more or less politely) aside for adults – usually older men – to take over.

The same is true of other sectors, most obviously women; but in the 1990s a global moral consensus had emerged around the notion of gender equality, and remarkable champions of women's rights and/or gender equality led the struggle and ensured that their goals were (at least partially) enshrined in new constitutions, laws, programmes and so on. A politico-legal gender machinery was constructed, and substantial resources were invested in gender equality. For youth, however, no moral consensus has existed or does exist; and youth leaders may shine, briefly, as leaders of youth, but are rapidly absorbed into larger political, social or other formations, and shed their focus on youth – or they simply age, and grow beyond a point where they can legitimately claim to represent the sector.

Youth (as a sector) failed signally to gain traction in the post-apartheid governance or government machinery. This is worth remembering precisely because the 2015 student movement was the first youth-led struggle for (in this case) student-specific (as opposed to youth) demands that succeeded (Chapter 1 in this volume offers details). The apparent failure to claim a genuine victory by the student movement is somewhat perplexing.

Youth struggles at the onset of democracy

In the late 1980s and early 1990s, the two large Christian church groupings, the Southern African Catholic Bishops' Conference (SACBC) and the South African Council of Churches (SACC), shared their concerns about what was happening to young people who were labelled 'the lost generation', having boycotted school, often been exposed to and/or participated in violence, and had limited future prospects. The church bodies formed the Joint Enrichment Project (JEP), and tasked it with understanding the then youth cohort (broadly defined as from eighteen to thirty years of age) and developing solutions to the challenges they faced. After February 1990, this took a policy turn: the challenge was accurately to capture the needs of all youth (all races, urban/rural, male/female, younger and older ends of the cohort, etc.) and develop policy proposals for inclusion in what eventually became the Reconstruction and Development Programme (RDP), the election manifesto of the African National Congress (ANC)-led alliance.

After three years of youth mobilisation, political work across the party spectrum, a media charm campaign geared at developing public support for youth (in a deliberate attempt to shake off the pejorative 'lost generation' tag and replace it with an acceptance of youth agency) and the development and later publication in book form of policies for youth development approved at successive 'marginalised youth' conferences attended by the great and the good, youth got nothing of any substance.

It is a maxim of African political studies that women, children, the disabled and the insane are normally grouped together in the smallest and least resourced ministry (Straker 1992; Everatt and Sisulu 1993; Everatt 1994). Occasionally, sport or arts and culture are added to the mix. This is normally done by governments wanting to look representative but not wishing to be distracted from the real stuff of politics by too much concern with these socially marginal groups. This was exactly what the marginalised youth movement battled against, calling for youth-sensitive 'desk officers' to be located in every government ministry and department and thus ensure the mainstreaming of youth. In the event – not least because of ANC infighting over who would become minister of youth – even this was more than youth actually received. The RDP, which described itself as 'an integrated, coherent socio-economic policy framework [that] … seeks to mobilise all our people and our country's resources toward the final eradication of apartheid and the building of a democratic, non-racial and non-sexist future' (ANC 1994), was 147 pages long when it appeared. It covered an enormous range of topics from education to policing to nutrition. 'Youth Development' appeared within the Human Resource Development section, given a total of six paragraphs, which covered a page and a half. It was offered as a sub-section of 'Arts and Culture', and came immediately after 'Sport and Recreation'. Youth had been put firmly in their place.

That there was a failure by youth and their leaders to read the signals should not have been surprising. The first speech Nelson Mandela made directly to young people boiled down to a simple message: go back to school. A noble and consistent theme of Mandela's, it nonetheless ignored the facts on the ground – where many young people were being armed and trained to fight in the Inkatha/ANC conflict (itself fuelled by apartheid agents and resources) – and it sounded suspiciously like 'the old men are home and will take over now', which is precisely what was happening. Youth have an instrumental value, but their agency is more commonly regarded with caution by those seeking to retain the status quo. Youth agency, history shows, is more feared than admired, and older leaders feel a constant need to guide and shape it. As soon as negotiation became more important than confrontation, the value and popularity of the 'young lions' declined – their demands found diminishing purchase and they were expected to resume their culturally allotted place, visible but silent.

In 1994, there were some 11 million young people aged between sixteen and thirty, the cohort treated as 'the youth' (with a higher-than-usual upper end to the cohort to include many of those who had lost out on educational and similar opportunities as part of the struggle against apartheid). They comprised roughly a quarter of the South African population. Despite this demographic weight, the RDP had little of substance to offer them. They were cited (along with women, farmworkers, the elderly and others) as a possible target of affirmative action programmes. It noted that they required economic and educational opportunities, scarcely a profound insight. The RDP made no mention of a youth ministry; rather, it proposed the formation of a national youth council with the task of 'coordinating youth activities, lobbying for the rights of young people, and representing South Africa internationally'. At government level, the RDP primly stated that 'appropriate government departments must more forcefully represent youth interests'. The call for 'desk officers' to mainstream youth concerns across all ministries was entirely ignored (Everatt 1993; Everatt and Orkin 1993; Truscott and Milner, 1994).

Black youth – particularly black, male, urban youth – played a key role in the popular mobilisation and uprisings of the mid-1980s, which were a turning point in the decades-long struggle against apartheid. With the onset of negotiations in the 1990s, however, the particular political contribution of black youth, as the 'foot soldiers' of the anti-apartheid struggle, was increasingly seen as unnecessary. Political organisations seemed unable or unwilling to develop creative means of enlisting the energy and commitment of youth in the new politics of the interregnum, beyond on the barricades. Youth were politically demobilised, but offered no alternate channels of expression or action. As Chapter 1 in this volume argues, the student uprising of 2015 has already had more success, in that it forced the state to abandon planned fee increases, and forced universities to make a whole series of concessions (over insourcing of workers, curriculum reform, language policy, upfront payments and so on). It won, where others lost out. But our recent history provides a cautionary tale for the medium-term (let alone longer-term) success of the student movement.

When youth were addressed as a sector, it was generally in the context of the potential threat they were seen to represent, rather than the complexities and needs of the generation. For example, when the funeral of assassinated Communist Party leader Chris Hani saw street battles between police and youth, within weeks more than fifteen proposals for organising youth had been produced by a range of organisations, ranging from community service corps to enforced physical exercise to straightforward labour camps for black youth (Everatt 1995: 4). Despite many newspaper column inches, however, nothing concrete was done. A few weeks later, youth returned to the *status quo ante*. The struggles of youth in the pre-democracy period were aligned to those of the progressive movement, yet they failed to win any long-standing victories. The students of 2015, many of them children of former youth activists, took on the ANC-led state, and won important gains – a first – and now face the challenge to sustain momentum, broaden the struggle, and ensure that public sympathy is not lost.

THE 2015 STUDENT MOVEMENT

Again, history provides a warning. Students, like youth, are not universally admired – they attract similar morbid fascination, often combined with a negativity deriving from 'student' being in many eyes synonymous with 'lazy', 'spoiled', 'privileged' and so on. There is also a rump of conservative revisionism, which began to emerge even in the early 1990s, as the gains of the 'marginalised youth' movement ebbed. For example, on the eve of democracy, the Human Sciences Research Council (HSRC) produced a paper arguing that 'the problem' lay with 2 to 5 per cent of well-educated young black South Africans. Their social position was seen to be at odds with their relatively high education, and as a result their frustrated expectations would leave them 'status-incongruent' (De Kock and Schutte 1994).

The argument is similar to those made elsewhere about the upper middle class, highly educated members of the Baader Meinhof Gang (correctly, the Red Army Faction (RAF)), for example – and for obvious reasons. RAF members came from the radical student movement of the late 1960s and early 1970s, were distinctly bourgeois, well educated, and fought against an establishment they saw as the Third Reich in mufti – the inclusion of former Nazi Party members in very senior positions of state was regarded as evidence of the need to topple the pro-capitalist, anti-Soviet and anti-left German establishment. The parallels between the RAF and the fears of apartheid apparatchiks, many guaranteed their jobs by the infamous 'sunset clause' but beset by fears of a black *oorstroming*, would have resonated widely. If a South African 'youth revolution' were to be avoided, the authors advised (De Kock and Schutte 1994: 27–28), affirmative action programmes had to absorb these 'status-incongruents … as speedily as possible' so that they did not organise other youth. The goal was clear: government was being told to act against well-educated black students, to ensure that 'the possibility of a youth revolution is very slim.'

The narrative offered by the HSRC team was fundamentally wrong in its analysis of a highly educated minority of black students leading a youth revolution; but the 'status incongruence' rings true. The difference is that an entire generational cohort felt 'status incongruent': the children of liberation (many the children of struggle activists and leaders), two decades into democracy, found that for a great many black students, as for the non-student youth around them, little had changed. Emancipation was not accompanied by rupture: business as usual appeared to be the order of the day. Home life for many remained mired in poverty and debt, where apartheid spatial planning ensured that home was miles away from university; incessantly rising fees were the norm, often followed by financial exclusion for the poor; and the university itself remained a very white, middle-class, Eurocentric institution, even as the demographics of the student body changed quite dramatically (albeit unevenly across different universities).

As the #FeesMustFall movement ratcheted up its protests, students of all races and classes joined in: the gross inequalities of post-apartheid South Africa may not be lived by all, but were visible to all. The legitimacy and logic of demanding an end to fee increases, which most damaged the poorest, was shared across students of all classes and races, and increasingly by the public beyond universities. Students were 'status incongruent' (as were their parents) with the entire post-liberation, unequal capitalist society, where skin colour delineates life chances. Many white students could appreciate the argument, even if for them the privileged life was largely unchanged. The student movement won broad-based student, academic and public support for opposing a system that consistently worked against those most in need.

By late 2015, when the state conceded a zero per cent fee increase for 2016, the student movement presumably had few illusions about who might be its allies, and its enemies. That students may in their turn be demonised is self-evident. As argued in several chapters in this book, the substantive danger remains party politics, and the ways in which it permeates and plays out its own fights using the student movement and campus-based struggles as a proxy. Organised behind a supra-political demand such as a zero per cent fee increase, students united their own constituency and won considerable public support. However, party politics was never far away, and soon formations aligned with the ANC, or the Economic Freedom Fighters (EFF), and former EFF leaders, all began fighting to be 'the most radical' voice, take the most extreme position, and dominate media coverage. Elected student representative councils (SRCs) were drawn into the one-up game, facing the danger of being seen as 'sell-outs' if they negotiated (let alone settled) with management, on anything. The unifying demand regarding fees, which was self-evidently socially just, was soon lost in the mire of political mud-slinging, the fragmentation of demands and groups, and increasingly violent and racist tactics and slogans.

Allies and alliances are important in any struggle, as is strategy: by early 2016 it was apparent that an Africanist narrative was dominating an increasingly fractured student movement, with 'fuck whites' painted on university walls and T-shirts – shirts worn by white as well as black students. Although the protests began in unity they broke up in racial and class antagonism, in part reflecting the party politics at play within the movement, as well as the inevitable internal contradictions of a student movement in such an unequal society. The failure of #FeesMustFall to confront class within its ranks is an indicator of the fragility of the alliance, as was said in an interview on 26 April 2016 by a #RhodesMustFall leader.

In most student and youth uprisings under apartheid, political leadership had been provided by 'charterist' leaders (from the UDF and ANC-aligned grouping). They emphasised nonracial unity rather than Africanist exclusivity. The 1976 generation rose up in the absence of any substantive leadership, as black consciousness leaders increasingly faced the repressive apparatus of the state, which had already decimated the ANC. When young people left the country to seek support, weapons training and the like, the ANC was the primary exiled movement to absorb these Africanist students in numbers – and steadily turn them towards an acceptance of the Freedom Charter, including the clause that had led to the Pan Africanist Congress (PAC) breaking away from the ANC in the late 1950s, namely that 'South Africa belongs to all who live in it, black and white'.

The contrast with 2015 was dramatic. The ANC, entirely implicated in the post-liberation project and, as government, the target of unified student hostility, was incapable of playing any substantive role. It was the problem and could not be part of the solution. It had effectively dismantled the mass democratic movement, and no 'receiving' structures existed to assist, nurture and provide strategic political education or guidance to student leaders. Foundations (in the names of ANC stalwarts) and nongovernmental organisations (NGOs) in support of racial unity against a common enemy were allowed to applaud from the sidelines but not to provide steer. The churches and other religious bodies were also able to provide support, but no more.

The student movement – or the #FeesMustFall movement – was a 'movement' for about two to three weeks. During that time, students united across class and colour, and won massive public sympathy and support behind a single, clearly articulated goal. The combined pressure of protest and public opinion saw government blink – and concede. At that point of victory, the movement lost unity, stopped pursuing a single clear, publicly supported goal, and class differences within the student body were clear as, for example, buses taking students back to the University of the Witwatersrand (Wits) had bricks thrown at them by other students who felt that Wits students had hijacked their own long struggle against fees at other less prestigious institutions. The movement, having won a zero per cent increase, fragmented into various Fallist factions – some calling for patriarchy to fall, others for white supremacy to fall, others focusing on their particular institution (be it colonial heritage or language and so on), and the brief moment of unity was over.

Having won the zero per cent fee increase concession from government, the movement soon began focusing on multiple demands – for decolonising the academy, for dismantling 'whiteness', for insourcing workers, and more. Senate meetings were invaded by students, universities shut down, study and examination timetables substantially disrupted, and sporadic violence broke out across the campuses. Universities responded in a range of ways, but many led with their own security (rather than dialogue, or as a threatening presence looming behind negotiation) which enflamed passions. In the midst of the ferment, the nonracial and multi-class unity of the early phase vanished, replaced with an essentialist African discourse that repeated selective Frantz Fanon and Steve Biko quotes, alongside selected elements of American critical race theory, such as the notion that 'blacks can't be racist' – but not others, such as the recognition of intersectionality of struggles across multiple planes, not race alone. As some elements within the Fallist movement began demanding that 'white bodies' need to be removed from committing further harm to 'the African child', a discourse of victimhood and racist essentialism began to emerge.

By early 2016, as the academic year began, the movement faced the danger of replacing agency with a self-reinforcing victimhood in which 'the African child' was the hapless victim of whiteness, white monopoly capital, and white 'colonisation'. The 'enemy' had shifted from an exploitative capitalist state, managed by the ANC, that transferred the costs of education onto students, to 'whiteness' in all forms, even where those forms were only visible to the *African* child – not the Indian or coloured child. Some began discussing anti-white genocide as 'a rational choice', as did a student leader at a Wits School of Governance public event on 26 March 2016. The movement, which had enjoyed substantial public sympathy and united students, increasingly offered racist tropes as it fragmented and shed the broad-based support it had formerly enjoyed.

Many banners waved during the 2015 #FeesMustFall protests cited the 1976 uprising, deliberately echoing the most prominent student protest in South African history. Many parents of 2015 protesters had been in the class of '76, or later school boycotts (which came in successive waves starting in the late 1970s and throughout the 1980s), and came out to show their support. The remainder of this chapter asks the question: what happened to the youth protesters of previous decades, and how do they compare to the born frees and millennial youth of today? What, in short, has democracy provided to those successive generations of brave young people who took on apartheid with sticks and stones?

Methodology

Official data are of limited help in this specific endeavour, not least because most Statistics South Africa (StatsSA) data are derived from head of household interviews, and very few pose attitudinal or psychosocial questions. This chapter therefore makes use of the 2013 Quality of Life survey commissioned by the Gauteng City-Region Observatory (GCRO).[2] The full realised sample comprised 27 485 respondents, interviewed across the whole of Gauteng province. The remainder of the chapter is a snapshot of the situation in Gauteng only, not South Africa generally, an important point to bear in mind: Gauteng has the largest population share in South Africa, is also the smallest province spatially, contributes well over a third of gross domestic product, and is home to three major metropolitan municipalities. Gauteng has virtually no rural areas – it is too small, densely populated and networked for that. Unlike other provinces with a major metropolitan municipality – such as Cape Town in the Western Cape – Gauteng has no large rural hinterland, but rather comprises a continuous urban extent, tailing into peri-urban areas at some of its border points with nearby, more heavily rural provinces.

In order to understand the contemporary status of youth from past decades, the sample was recoded into age cohorts that mirrored (roughly) key moments of the anti-apartheid struggle – the '1976' generation, the 1980s generation called on to make the apartheid state 'ungovernable', those who were youth in the 1990–1994 interregnum, when many youth were involved in violent struggle; the 'children of democracy' who were children/teenagers during the transition from apartheid to democracy, and finally the 'born frees', in essence all respondents under the age of twenty at the time of the survey fieldwork (and thus born from 1994 onwards). Those older than the 1976 cohort (those aged between sixteen and twenty-four in 1976) were classified as 'older' – the focus of the chapter is on waves of struggle that were led by, or significantly populated by youth, which really begins in 1976.

Each cohort was recoded into a single variable. A simple technique was used, taking actual age (as given by respondents) and working backwards to define who belonged to youth cohorts in previous years.

Table 6.1: Contemporary status of youth cohorts mirroring key moments of the anti-apartheid struggle.

YOUTH COHORT	AGE
Born frees	14 to 19, born after 1994
Democracy's children	20 to 34, therefore aged 1 to 15 in 1994
Youth of 1994	35 to 42, therefore aged 16 to 23 in 1994
Youth of 1986	43 to 51, therefore aged 16 to 24 in 1986
Youth of 1976	52 to 61, therefore aged 15 to 24 in 1976
Older cohort	62+

For pre-1994 cohorts, the full age span – sixteen (sometimes fifteen) to twenty-four years of age – was recoded into a single variable; the mid-point was taken to be the key year, so for the '1976 generation', fairly obviously, 1976 is the mid-point – the youngest respondent in this cohort was fifty-three years of age in 2013, but would have been sixteen in 1976, where the oldest would have been twenty-four in 1976 and would have been sixty-one in 2013. The mid-point for the 1980s 'ungovernability' cohort is taken to be 1986 (reflecting the intensity of protest and viciousness of state repression, rather than ANC leader Oliver Tambo's call for ungovernability, which occurred in 1984). One large cohort is inserted, 'democracy's children', denoting anyone who grew up during the transition (this deliberately includes those who were children at the time). The youngest respondent in this group was twenty in 2013, having been born in 1993. These are distinct from the 'youth of 1994' – more precisely, anyone from sixteen to twenty-four during the 1990–1994 interregnum. More recent cohorts are of necessity smaller – the 'born frees' included respondents who were nineteen, eighteen and a few seventeen and sixteen year-olds (in 2013), but with a 1994+ cut-off point.

Life circumstances

Some factors do not require explanation or analysis, but remind us that young men outnumber young women, a situation that is reversed over time: men made up 53 per cent of born frees, but 45 per cent of the oldest cohort – a reminder of women's longevity, which sees them in the majority nationally, though not in Gauteng (what is true in Gauteng is not always true for South Africa).

Table 6.2: Youth cohorts drawn from sample.

COHORT	% OF TOTAL SAMPLE	FREQUENCY
The 'born frees': respondents under the age of 20 at the time of the survey	4.1	1 129
'Democracy's children': respondents who were children during the transition from apartheid	39.3	10 807
'1994': respondents who were youth during the transition	17.8	4 882
'1980s': respondents who were youth during state of emergency	15.1	4 156
'1970s': respondents who were youth during the 1976 uprising	12.1	3 314
Older	11.6	3 197

Youth provide a lens that magnifies challenges in society more generally. In many instances, conditions – objectively measurable external conditions, at least –

improve over time, as youth age. If we look at housing, for example, we find that in Gauteng, just 5 per cent of the oldest cohort lives in informal dwellings (95 per cent live in formal dwellings) but this rises to 8 per cent of the 1976 generation, 11 per cent for the youth of 1986 and 17 per cent for the youth of 1994, peaking at 20 per cent for the children of 1994, before dropping to 12 per cent among the smallest cohort, the born frees. In part, the explanation lies in the fact that apartheid locked generations within tiny township houses whereas democracy has allowed young people to set up their own households elsewhere. However, their options are severely limited as delivery of 'RDP houses' (yet more matchbox houses in new townships) cannot keep pace with demand, and rumours abound of corruption in allocations. That leaves younger people, notably those lacking the financial resources required to buy their way out of poverty into suburbia, with few possibilities beyond informal shacks.

On this single, simple item, therefore, the reader can see how young people, including students, may see a world around them that is deeply discriminatory – and racialised – and, perhaps most striking, unchanged from the world their parents inhabited. Speaking about housing in Gauteng, the Organisation for Economic Cooperation and Development (OECD) noted:

> Low-income black Africans disproportionately live in deprived neighbourhoods compared to low-income residents of other population groups in the Gauteng city-region, which infringes upon the ability of black Africans to take advantage of economic opportunities and social networks of less disadvantaged areas. Within a typical high poverty neighbourhood in Gauteng, 98.3 per cent of the population is black African, followed by whites (1.26 per cent), coloured (0.27 per cent), and Asians (0.09 per cent) ... black Africans are overrepresented in high poverty zones by 25 per cent while whites, coloured, and Asians together are underrepresented by -18.1 per cent (OECD 2011: 28).

And lest we consider affordability a relatively easy hurdle for a province with a burgeoning black middle class, the OECD had a salutary warning to offer:

> Compared to other large cities in the OECD, indicators suggest that Gauteng's homeowners pay an extremely high cost for housing relative to their income ... Typically those economies where individuals need over five times their annual salary to buy a home are ranked 'severely

unaffordable', which is followed by 'seriously unaffordable' (4.1 – 5.0), 'moderately unaffordable' (3.1 – 4.0), and 'affordable' (3.0 or less). Using this methodology, the area could be characterised as 'severely unaffordable' with high rates in Gauteng (23.1). The rate for townships in Gauteng (4.9) is characterised as 'seriously unaffordable' (OECD 2011: 28).

So whether young black Gautengers want to buy a house in a suburb ('severely unaffordable'), which students may reasonably presume to be part of their life course, or they want to do so in a township ('seriously unaffordable'), they face the fact of racialised and unequal distribution of existing stock, and severe cost barriers in either case. Given that students are groomed to be future societal leaders, prospects are gloomy indeed.

No wonder we find that 55 per cent of the oldest cohort live in dwellings they own and have fully paid off, true of 37 per cent of the 1976 generation and 28 per cent of the youth of the 1980s, and (reflecting the class contradictions within the student movement) true also of 21 per cent of the youth of 1994, 20 per cent of democracy's children and 28 per cent of born frees. But where almost no older respondents (from the youth of the 1980s and older) are in the private rental market, this is where significant proportions of born frees (12 per cent), democracy's children (18 per cent) and the youth of 1994 (14 per cent) can be found – and often renting informal shacks, not smart apartments. Looking only at these three youngest cohorts, we find that they comprise 84 per cent of all respondents living in shacks and paying rent for the privilege; and they comprise 74 per cent of those living in their own shack, not paying rent.

This triggers a series of negative life circumstances – informal dwellings are likely to be at considerable distances from universities based in city centres, requiring transport costs; are least likely to have piped water into the dwelling – 21 per cent of born frees and 30 per cent of the children of 'democracy's children' access water from stand pipes more than 200 metres from their dwellings, for example – or decent sanitation and the basic needs that populated the 1994 RDP. Meeting those needs, the RDP argued, would 'open up previously suppressed economic and human potential [which is] … essential if we are to achieve peace and security for all' (ANC 1994: 6–7). For the students of 2015, there seemed little evidence of or promise for the realisation of their potential. With Gauteng households spending an average of 20 per cent of income on transport (OECD 2011) it is unsurprising that students have been known to sleep in toilets and lecture theatres in order to avoid finding transport money.

Twenty-two years into democracy, large numbers of young black South Africans see little or no change in their life circumstances, and face enormous barriers to the 'better life for all' promised by the ANC in 1994. Across the different age cohorts, for example, is a consistent complaint that unemployment, crime and lack of basic services are key problems facing their communities. Cost is an issue; but the racialised patterns of spatial configuration in combination with cost – making a suburban home a dream way, way beyond the realistic hopes of most Gauteng residents (and a life of debt for so many who 'make it') – have created a toxic mix that feeds easily into narratives of the damage done to the African child. Whether that damage, in 2015–2016, is being done by an undefined but easily sloganeered 'white supremacy', or an ANC government after two decades in power, is open to question.

In a context of widespread unemployment and an unequal and racialised distribution of goods and services, it is notable that while a small proportion of born frees (5 per cent) have run up personal debt, this rises to 28 per cent among democracy's children, 41 per cent of the youth of 1994, 39 per cent of the 1986 cohort and 31 per cent among the 1976 cohort. Debt may drop slowly over time, but it remains high – 30 per cent of the older cohort are in debt – and for the younger cohorts, is primarily credit card, loan shark or personal loan based (for older cohorts, including the youth of 1976 and 1986, debt is more commonly incurred by paying home loans, car purchases, and so on). Taken with slow economic growth and mass unemployment, this debt trap is of substantial concern – not least because in every cohort (bar the born frees, where debt is lowest) a fifth of respondents who have debt say they cannot pay it back. Debt is real: 14 per cent of respondents in debt had had to skip a meal owing to lack of funds in the year before being interviewed, and a similar proportion had been unable to feed their children (among those with children) in the same period. Very real damage is being done to these children born two decades into democracy.

'Headspace'

If socioeconomic status is a concern, so is mood. On the one hand, Gautengers are active citizens. Measuring participation across all types of meetings people might attend – formal government-created structures (such as Integrated Development

Plan (IDP) meetings), to ward councillor-called meetings, to school governing body, block and street committees and so on – we find that while 46 per cent of the older cohort had taken part in any meeting in the year before being interviewed, this was true of 45 per cent of the born frees, 43 per cent of the children of democracy, 50 per cent of the youth of 1994, 54 per cent of the 1986 cohort and 51 per cent of the 1976 cohort. Moreover, most planned to vote in the then imminent 2014 provincial and national elections, ranging from 97 per cent of the born frees to 95 per cent of the 1976 generation. It is worth remembering that the 2014 election saw the ANC's worst-ever performance at the polls.

That students would protest against government, and that they would win widespread support in so doing, should not have come as any surprise. Dissatisfaction with government – all spheres, national, provincial and especially local – is running at record levels in Gauteng, and has grown steadily over time. In Figure 6.1, the levels of dissatisfaction for all age cohorts show that between four and five in every ten respondents had a negative rating for all spheres of government. This has found an outlet in service delivery protests, of which Gauteng has the highest number in the country; but it is a smouldering frustration, which partly explains the support won by the #FeesMustFall movement, which reflected a widely-shared frustration with government. Asked which sphere of government had done most to improve the quality of life of respondents, a common response was 'none of them' – true of 44 per cent of born frees, rising slightly among older cohort, and returning to 44 per cent among the 1976 cohort.

Young people are commonly seen as apathetic, or apolitical, not least because they often prefer their own methods and forms of engagement and are rarely satisfied with the formalities of voting every five years or sitting in long, dull if worthy meetings (Everatt, Marais and Dube 2010; Wyn and Cahill 2015). Gauteng youth and older cohorts, however, still regard politics as important – we saw above that intention to vote was high, and the notion that 'politics is a waste of time' (a Likert item in the survey)[3] was rejected by 54 per cent of the born frees, 46 per cent of the children of democracy, 47 per cent of the youth of 1994 and the 1986 cohort, rising slightly to 48 per cent among the 1976 cohort.

While politics is seen by the various youth cohorts as an efficacious mechanism to effect change, pessimism runs high. In response to the statement 'the country is heading in the wrong direction', agreement with the sentiment rose from 58 per cent among born frees to 61 per cent among the 1976 cohort. If dissatisfaction with government was a key challenge, a specific item of massive concern was corruption. The Likert item stated that: 'corruption is the main threat facing our democracy', which is not specific to governmental corruption – but the question was asked at a time when allegations of corruption against senior politicians from the president downwards were rife. In response, between 89 per cent and 91 per cent of all cohorts agreed or strongly agreed with the statement.

Racial issues, unsurprisingly, were evident among the different cohorts. The most obvious are levels of agreement with the proposition that 'blacks and whites

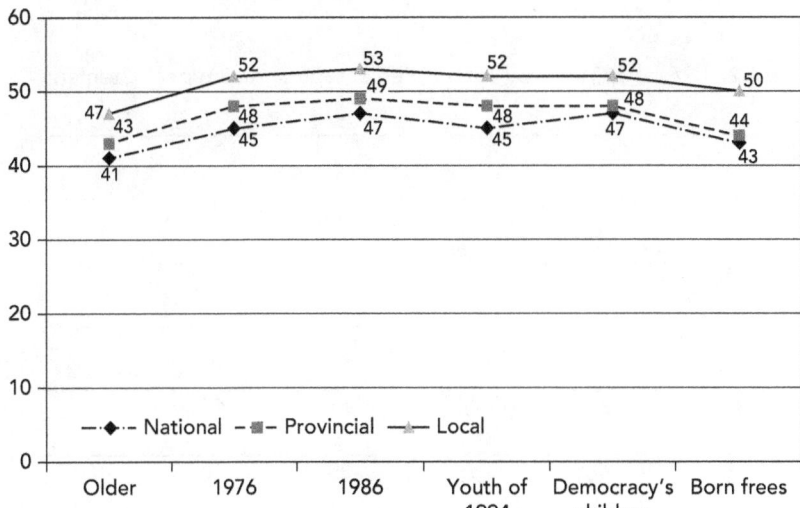

Figure 6.1: Dissatisfaction with the three spheres of government (by cohort).

will never trust each other', ranging from 63 per cent among the born frees to 59 per cent among older respondents. But black/white was only part of the issue, as the Black Consciousness Movement (BCM) leader Steve Biko stated in the 1970s:

> The importance of black solidarity to the various segments of the black community must not be understated. There have been in the past a lot of suggestions that there can be no viable unity amongst blacks because they hold each other in contempt. Coloureds despise Africans because they (the former), by their proximity to the Africans, may lose the chances of assimilation into the white world. Africans despise the Coloureds and Indians for a variety of reasons. Indians not only despise Africans but in many instances also exploit the Africans in job and shop situations (Biko 1971).

As Biko concluded, the racial divide and rule of apartheid had created 'mountainous inter-group suspicions among the blacks'. Posed with a second Likert item that stated that 'coloured people are playing an important role in building the new South Africa', between 41 per cent and 43 per cent of respondents rejected it. Posed with a third, that 'Indians do not deserve to benefit from affirmative action', between 28 per cent and 30 per cent of the sample agreed or strongly agreed with the statement. Racial suspicion continued to abound, and beyond the obvious black/white divide; anti-white sentiment is certainly strong but, more importantly, makes for easy slogans.

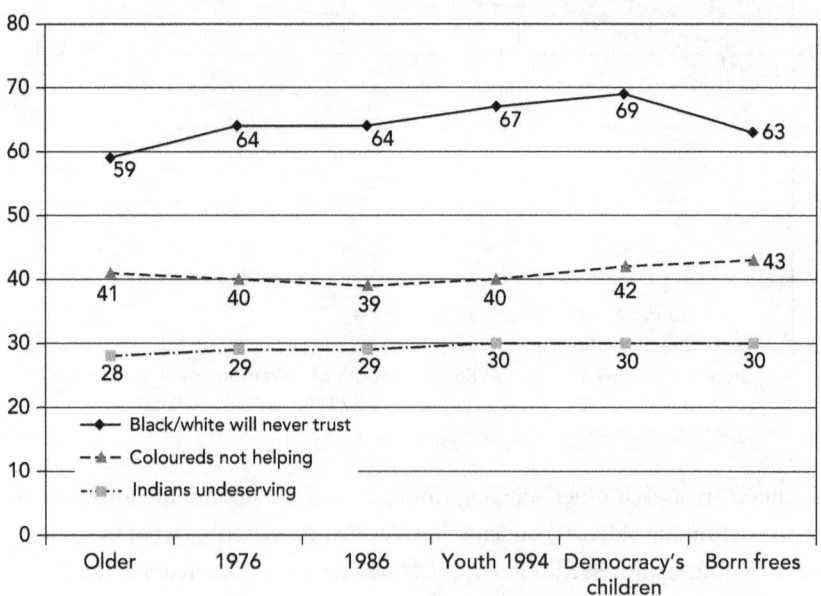

Figure 6.2: Racial attitudes by cohort: Percentage agreeing per statement.

The notion of unity among the formerly oppressed seems to have suffered, while mistrust between blacks and whites is very high. This prefigured the late 2015/early 2016 racialisation of the Fallist splinter groups, and the adoption of a discourse of black – that is, African-only – victimhood.

Material conditions and psychosocial attitudes created a toxic mix. This included anger at government, fuelled by the slow pace of delivery (especially for younger people), the fiscal debt net that surrounds them, and the desire to engage politically – but in *opposition*, not in support of an ANC government increasingly seen as corrupt and leading the country in the wrong direction. This in turn fed into and was informed by a mixed bag of racial hostilities, disconnect from the state, and a sense of powerlessness. Asked about anomie – 'people like me cannot influence developments in my community' – between 33 per cent (born frees) and 31 per cent (other cohorts) agreed or strongly agreed, suggesting that while people participate widely, as we have seen, they do not see a link between that participation and any resultant change. Thankfully, in every instance the proportion who 'agree' comprise the vast bulk; approximately 3 per cent in each cohort strongly agreed with the statement. It is these outliers that are real cause for concern. The ANC as government had failed signally where it had succeeded as liberation movement, in empowering the powerless, and linking their actions to outcomes – including the ultimate victory over apartheid.

Respondents were also asked about alienation, the notion that 'no-one cares about people like me'. Here the outliers were larger, comprising 8–9 per cent of every cohort. The born frees were least likely to agree and/or strongly agree (33 per cent did so), but this rose sharply to comprise 40 per cent of the children of democracy, 41 per cent of the youth of 1994, dropping back slightly to 38 per cent among the 1986 and 1976 cohort respectively.

The survey data indicate why a combination of socioeconomic circumstances and attitudes created conditions in which the student movement could break through to reach the broader public, since #FeesMustFall echoed other struggles against ever-increasing user fees, taxes, tariffs and the like; in a context where perceptions of corruption threatening democracy were ubiquitous. But those same data (and other data not analysed here, including widespread misogynist, homophobic and xenophobic attitudes) also indicate the fault lines that were to split the movement after its moment of victory.

CONCLUSION

The #FeesMustFall movement is remarkable in that it bucked the trend of youth and/or student struggles failing to achieve their sectoral gains even when embedded in a broader struggle. This struggle stood on its own feet – and won. The inequalities students face – how they live, where they live, their levels of debt, combined with a slow (or absent) transformation at universities playing off underlying racist views within society – were all understandable to the broader public. Moreover, unlike localised service delivery protesters, the students were articulate, disciplined in the face of state hostility, and presented a clear, understandable and legitimate message: we simply cannot afford to study and live.

But precisely because it was not embedded in a broader struggle, the movement had no broader, society-wide strategy for change, and 'give us our land' and 'kill whites' became the dominant if hollow slogans of 2016. The ANC as government is directly culpable, having dismantled civil society and ensured that no robust structures existed to act as ally or partner in developing strategy or goals or principles. That students in 2016 can be applauded for understanding that decolonisation means 'burn down the university' (Andile Mngxitama, speaking at the 2016 Strini Moodley memorial) – literally – is indicative of the paucity of ideas that afflicts what was once a movement.

The challenge facing the student groupings – into which they have now fractured – is either to develop a strategic approach to alliances and set goals that can be attained or to embrace the diversity of movements that have emerged and continue to do so, including feminists, queer movements, ecological and 'green' activism, LGBTIAQ+ (lesbian, gay, bisexual, transgender, intersex, asexual and queer) movements and so on. It may well be that #FeesMustFall reversed the long-bemoaned 'death of civil society' and heralded its birth instead among a new generation born free but seeing itself everywhere chained to an unequal, racist and violent society. That in turn may be misplaced optimism, and we may yet descend further into racial essentialism and victimhood. All societies demand youth acquiescence – but it is theirs to change, for the better of all.

NOTES

1 Thanks to Cathi Albertyn for long argumentative discussions while walking the dogs and whatever good points there might be in this chapter.
2 The author was the executive director of GCRO at the time, and he cautions that readers should be aware of potential bias that may result from this fact.
3 A scale for responses, in survey research, on individual preferences or attitudes, towards the given subject.

REFERENCES

African National Congress (ANC) (1994) *The Reconstruction and Development Programme.* Johannesburg: Ravan Press.

Biko, S. (1971) The definition of black consciousness. South African History Online. http://www.sahistory.org.za/archive/definition-black-consciousness-bantu-stephen-biko-december-1971-south-africa

De Kock, C. & Schutte, C. (1994) The African youth in the present-day South Africa: Integration or youth revolution? Human Sciences Research Council. Mimeo.

Everatt, D. (1993) Putting youth on the national agenda. Joint Enrichment Project. Mimeo.

Everatt, D. (ed.) (1994) *Creating a Future: Youth Policy for South Africa*. Johannesburg: Ravan Press.

Everatt, D. (1995) Youth and the reconstruction and development of the 'new South Africa'. Paper prepared for the Henry J. Kaiser Family Foundation. Case (Community Agency for Social Enquiry), Braamfontein. Mimeo. {PRIVATE}

Everatt, D. (2013) Ring of fire or puff of smoke? Youth in Gauteng. In H. Helve (ed.). *Youth and Youth Transitions*. London: Tufnell Press.

Everatt, D. & Orkin, M. (1993) Growing up tough: A national survey of South African youth. Case (Community Agency for Social Enquiry). Mimeo.

Everatt, D., Marais, H. & Dube, N. (2010) Participation – for what purpose? Analysing public participation in governance in Gauteng. *Politikon*, 37(2–3), 223–249.

Everatt, D. & Sisulu, E. (1993) *Black Youth in Crisis: Facing the Future*. Johannesburg: Ravan Press.

Helve, H. & Holm, G. (2005) *Contemporary Youth Research*. Aldershot: Ashgate.

Marais, H. (1993) The new barbarians (the criminalisation of youth). *Work in Progress*, 90, (July/August).

Marks, M. (2001) *Young Warriors: Youth Politics, Identity and Violence in South Africa*. Johannesburg: Wits University Press.

Mngxitama, M. (2016) Speaking at the 2016 Strini Moodley memorial. *News24*, 20 May.

Organisation for Economic Cooperation and Development (OECD) (2011) Territorial review of the Gauteng city-region, South Africa. Paris: OECD.

#RhodesMustFall (2016) Student leader, anonymous. Interview, 26 April.

Rizvi, F. (2012) Mobilities and the transnationalisation of youth cultures. In N. Lesko & S. Talbut (eds). *Keywords in Youth Studies*. New York: Routledge.

Straker, G. (1992) *Faces in the Revolution: The Psychological Effects of Violence on Township Youth in South Africa*. Cape Town: David Philip.

Student leader (2016) Wits School of Governance public event, 16 March.

Truscott, K. & Milner, S. (1994) Youth, education and the world of work. In D. Everatt (ed.). *Creating a Future: Youth Policy for South Africa*. Johannesburg: Ravan Press.

Van Zyl Slabbert, F., Malan, C., Marais, H., Olivier, J. & Riordan, R. (1994) *Youth in the New South Africa: Towards Policy Formulation*. Cape Town: HSRC Press.

Wallace, C. & Kovatcheva, S. (1998) *Youth in Society: The Construction and Deconstruction of Youth in East and West Europe*. London: Macmillan.

Ward, C. L., Van der Merwe, A. & Dawes, A. (2012) *Youth Violence: Sources and Solutions in South Africa*. Cape Town: UCT Press.

Wyn, J. & Cahill, J. (eds) (2015) *Handbook of Children and Youth Studies*. Singapore: Springer.

CHAPTER

7

LEARNING FROM STUDENT PROTESTS IN SUB-SAHARAN AFRICA

Lynn Hewlett, Nomagugu Mukadah,
Koffi Kouakou and Horácio Zandamela

INTRODUCTION

Much is often made of South Africa's exceptionalism and its outlier position on the continent. In contrast, this chapter argues that examination of the recent student protests of South Africa, the continent's 'last born', is enriched by understanding the history of student protests elsewhere in Africa. In the chapter, we review the literature on student protests in sub-Saharan or 'middle Africa' (Mamdani 2008), drawing selectively on insights from Francophone, Lusophone and Anglophone regions. Reviews of student protests in Africa mostly categorise them in terms of political and historical periods: the colonial period; the post-independence period (1960–1985); the structural adjustment, protest for democratic reform and economic decline period (1985–2000); and the post-2000 period of multiparty democracy (Federici, Caffentzis and Alidou 2000; Luescher-Mamashela and Mugume 2014). Mahmood Mamdani (2008) labels the first three periods as colonial, nationalist and neoliberal.

This chapter looks at significant forces that have shaped student movements in Africa as reflected in dominant academic and political literature. We examine student protests and looking at how they were shaped by political developments, particular policies and various governments' provision of and coordination of policy in higher education – governance in Francis Fukuyama's (2013) terms. African countries share a historical experience of colonialism and subsequent periodic responses to it. Although the nature of the colonial experience may account for the differences in performance of higher education systems across the countries (Mamdani 2008), the colonial experience shaped the structure, organisation and governance of higher education systems and the production of the nationalist elite that would rule after independence. In most countries, post-independence, students were part of the new elite and also saw themselves as protecting its gains against external forces – but they also began to act as the social conscience and voice of the broader society. Student protests have responded to and – in some cases – shaped responses to externally driven and internally driven political and economic events in particular historical periods.

In this chapter we discuss the key features of these periods in terms of politics, public policy and patterns of governance, and include a table summarising these features (see Appendix 3). We examine each historical period in terms of these three issues and identify the patterns of student protest. Exploring these experiences helps to inform the debates in this book, particularly as they relate to relationships between and consequences of approaches to funding universities and student fees, relationships between student protests and broader economic policies that have been adopted, the expansion of their postcolonial student intakes without adequate funding, the ideological and economic triggers of student protests, and their short-term and longer-term outcomes.

PRE-INDEPENDENCE PHASE AND COLONIAL ERA – THE 1900s TO 1960s

Although the genesis of higher education systems in Africa lies within the colonial antiquity of the continent, its formation can be traced back to the advanced forms of educational traditions in Egypt, Ethiopia and Timbuktu (Woldegiorgis and Doevenspeck 2013: 35; Rodney 1972). Indigenous education was pragmatic and centred on the institutionalisation of innate identities, fostering imperatives of self-government shaped by African philosophy, religion and civic culture (Ajayi et al. 1996: 5). With the annexation of the continent, education was changed to exhibit the foreign ideology of its coloniser, enforcing new form and content and invalidating the existing established forms of African education. It is from the derivative accounts of dominant academic and political literature that we examine how the historical and political legacies of colonisation have shaped higher education and influenced the agency of student movements on the continent as we know them today.

In looking back at the experiences of colonial hegemony in sub-Saharan Africa, it emerges that the development of education systems was guided by Eurocentric education policies wavering between 'assimilationist 'and 'adjustive' philosophies (Clignet and Foster 1964: 191). It was through the missionary interests of the Protestant, Anglican and Catholic churches that education was first established (Frankema 2012: 337). Not only did it serve for the proselytisation of the African populace but it also facilitated the production of 'schooled' natives or *auxiliaires d'administration* to work within the bureaucracy, aiding the administrative services of these colonies (Urch 1971: 253). This characterised the British colonial system. The French shaped their educational policies for the primary purpose of constructing a colonial order that would inculcate its imperialist identity and beliefs while expanding its culture through the creation of *évolués* – Gallicised elites who would serve as functionaries for its colonies. Grounded in egalitarianism, their assimilation policy was to ensure the harmony of humankind through the efforts of the colonisers to 'civilise' the political institutions and culture of Africa (Serequeberhan 2010). The Portuguese also followed the French assimilation philosophy, selecting a few (the indigenous elites, 'sons of monarchs', referred to as *assimilados*) who became the political intermediaries to assist the colony to expand its influence and control. Access and the type of education offered were restricted so as to ensure that formal schooling would not destabilise and challenge colonial control (Devarajan, Monga and Zongo 2011: 135). Although there was spirited resistance against the enforcement of European ethnocentric education, the opposition was soon condensed as new African elites emerged that embodied modernist images of sophistication and had access to most of the valued positions in society.

Higher forms of education were for a few carefully selected individuals within specific social and ethnic groups, with the majority, in the case of British colonies, given the most basic level of education offered by the missionaries (Colin 1968). Young African elites were sent overseas to European countries such as the United Kingdom and France to acquire knowledge and skills (Read 1955: 173). In most of Africa during the colonial era, higher education was in its elementary state, with few universities and degree-awarding colleges. Egypt, Morocco and Mali were the exceptions as they had higher education institutions that predated the deluge of Europeans onto the continent. Most educational activity in sub-Saharan Africa was linked to missionary efforts (Page 2004: 669) with the British establishing some of the earliest post-secondary institutions in sub-Saharan Africa. These institutions included the South African College (now known as the University of Cape Town), which was founded in 1829 and Lovedale College, which was established by missionaries in 1841. The British colonial legacy of indirect rule was decentralised, and characterised by language of instruction being mainly the local languages, with English taught as a subject (Cogneau and Moradi 2014). The French established sub-university educational systems considered 'glorified secondary schools', merely extensions or metropoles of its institutions in France. The Portuguese did not establish any higher education institutions in their colonies until the early 1960s – the University of Luanda and University of Lourenço Marques, were for the sole purpose of educating the children of the settlers (Woldegiorgis and Doevenspeck 2013: 37). Both the French and the Portuguese exercised more direct rule, indicative of centralised governance, and did not diffuse the local realities of the colonies into their systems of education (Bilodeau 1955: 18; Gifford and Weiskal 1971). Colonial languages were enforced as the sole medium, which enabled them to exert what they deemed their 'civilising mission' across colonies (Brown 2000). It is from this background that we begin to locate and unravel the history of student activism in Africa.

Moncef Chenoufi (1968) dates the first student movements to the early 1900s and locates their origins in North Africa (see also Chapter 8 in this volume). Student movement activities were also noted in African student associations made up of students studying overseas, such as the Union of African Descent, the Gold Coast Students Union, the Nigerian Progress Union and the West African Students Union, which were the first established between 1917 and 1925 (Unesco 1994: 35). In the British colonies, for example in Uganda, students from Makerere College founded the African Welfare Society. Early student movements in African institutions were conservative, with most student dissent confined to sociocultural issues affecting their experiences within the university, including demands for better living conditions, transformation of outdated education systems and other local, political conflicts. None of the concerns that these students raised pertained to the broader ideological or national political issues taking place on the African continent, as they were unable to identify with the realities in their home countries.

Between 1935 and 1960 there was a sense of revolutionary change, which led to a marked increase in African student movements. After the Second World War systematic boycotts and a wide range of anti-colonisation movements emerged, which also provided an impetus for active student engagement in the politics of the day. Movements were located in countries such as Zimbabwe, Mozambique, Angola, Cape Verde, Kenya (the Mau Mau uprising from 1952–1960), Guinea-Bissau and the South African colony of South West Africa (Namibia) (Anderson 2005; Talton 2010). African student movements were spurred into enhancing political education and mobilising students to establish a united front with other citizens against the colonial powers. A handful of African student resistance movements emerged in overseas institutions that started questioning and challenging the colonial repression in the African states. Political consciousness in higher education systems on the continent became more palpable. Saheed Adejumobi (2007: 106) describes how students expressed nostalgia for social and political transformation in 'revolutionary proportions' – they used a variety of strategies to express themselves, including street demonstrations, boycotting classes and organising student congresses where they would discuss the struggle back home. They widely used strategies such as the writing and dissemination of information that would propel citizens in these countries to oppose the power and control of the colonial governments and expand the ideology of pan-Africanism. The African students in the diaspora started forming the intelligentsia that catalysed student insurrections in their home countries (Zeilig 2007) and the West Africa Student Union, a well-known anti-colonialism pressure group (Nwaubani 2001) based in London, became the teaching ground for a number of nationalist leaders such as Kwame Nkrumah who led Ghana to independence in 1957 (Federici, Caffentzis and Alidou 2000: 90).

There is insufficient information for tracing the exact origins of student movements in sub-Saharan Africa. What most literature reveals is that there was definitely far greater fervour and activism exhibited by students in North Africa than by their counterparts in the South (Unesco 1994: 16). Alessia Lombardi (2011: 6) states that the nature, structure and dynamics of student movements might have been greatly influenced by the extent and spread of higher education. In North Africa there were more higher education institutions – potentially what Seymour Lipset and Philip Altbach (1967) describe as 'fertile grounds for student political awareness and participation' – than in other parts of Africa during the colonial era – which possibly explains the nature and dynamics of youth movements in that region and the paucity of evidence of the emergence of student activism in sub-Saharan Africa. They argue that higher education exposes students to new knowledge, new skills and new ideologies, which evoke a sense of 'consciousness'. This assertion also attests to James Coleman's (1954) observation of how nationalist movements in many African countries have been largely orchestrated by intellectuals and the middle class. Michael Burawoy (1976: 78) states that student protests need to be understood 'as the outcome of the interaction of a specific student consciousness and the structural contradictions which inhere in the functions of the higher education institutions'.

NATIONALIST/POST-INDEPENDENCE ERA – 1960s TO 1980s

The dawn of independence led to the proliferation of learning institutions that radically transformed the education landscape on the continent as more young people from all parts of society were given the opportunity to access the education that had been for the few. In most former British colonies (Omari and Mihyo 1991) and in Francophone countries, education systems were not radically transformed; most of what the education models offered was retained and reproduced. In Lusophone countries the liberated governments were determined to rewrite history by changing the Eurocentric perspective in education and decolonising people's minds (Cabecinhas and Feijo 2010: 31).

Although most educational institutions still bore institutional legacies of the former colonial powers, higher education institutions assumed the role of reinstating African identity to the newly liberated states, redressing the ill effects of colonisation and building national economies (Omari and Mihyo 1991; Federici and Caffentizis 2000; Hanlon 1991; Abrahamson and Nilsson 1994). The role of higher education institutions became crucial as there was a need to bridge the knowledge and skills gap in the government administration that had been left after the exodus of the colonial supremacies (Omari and Mihyo 1991; Abrahamson and Nilsson 1994).

In these early years of post-independence there was little growth of student movements. Students displayed elitism (Bathily, Diouf and Mbodj 1995) and were accorded a 'high level of social prestige' (Munene 2003: 120). Three states (Mozambique, Tanzania, Kenya) introduced free higher education using government coffers to subsidise the costs – which translated into no fees, and the provision of free accommodation and food. The liberated governments sought to address populist demands of free education as a 'compensatory legitimation strategy' (Hughes 1994) and to provide more equitable access (Langa et al. 2016). By the late 1970s, state funding for higher education in sub-Saharan Africa began to dwindle, and became increasingly expensive and unaffordable.

This was compounded by a sustained decline in economic growth from the mid-1970s until the 1990s (Langa et al. 2016). The declining economic performance in most countries led to cutbacks and resulted in larger numbers of students in increasingly overcrowded residences and classrooms, crumbling infrastructure, a decline in the learning environment and a brain drain of academic staff. Reviews of the period document the widespread decay of higher education institutions and the poor quality of instruction and research (Langa et al. 2016; Nkinyangi 1991).

In this period, students became political actors (see Zelig 2007). University students abandoned ivory-tower mentalities and began to engage systematically in political action, including violent confrontation (Unesco 1994). They saw themselves as playing a vanguard role and as the social conscience of the new nation states (for example, Ghana, Kenya and Nigeria) – and in Francophone countries (for example, Senegal, Cameroon) they opposed the interference of formal colonial masters in the governance of their countries.

Diverse national and international reports (Nkinyangi 1991; Federici and Cafentzis 2000) reveal that student revolts were widespread in African institutions of learning during the 1970s and 1980s. Between 1970 and 1979 major student protest occurred in some twenty-nine sub-Saharan countries (three-quarters of the countries of sub-Saharan Africa). Towards the end of the 1970s in many countries, the political elite and ruling parties began to clash with more radical students and, in some cases, with academic bodies (for example, at Uganda's Makerere University) as student expectations of high-status employment and a place in the elite began to be eroded by global recession and internal corruption and decay (Zeilig 2009). Between 1980 and 1989, incidents of student upheaval were reported in over twenty-five sub-Saharan countries (Nkinyangi 1991). There were widespread clashes between students and government, and the focus of student politics shifted to expressions of general political discontent coupled with protests about institutional governance and resourcing, and the direct effects on students' material well-being. The sparks for many of the protests were bread and butter issues of impoverished students and inadequate accommodation, crowding, food and hunger (Nkinyangi 1991) – and then also about fees and grants as governments progressively reduced the fees subsidisation of the previous period and introduced co-payments and loans (Langa et al. 2016). Students began to challenge the power configurations where the state was imposing high-level state control of the universities. Governments acted by counter-force, trying to limit and fragment the efforts of student activists (Klopp and Orina 2002).

The widespread economic crisis caused by the adoption of structural adjustment programmes (SAPs) became the pinnacle of political resistance by students as masses demanded democratic reformation in African states. The nascent efforts of students to voice their grievances in view of the SAPs did not go unheard, as it agitated a wave of political movements across the continent. A number of countries also experienced nationwide demonstrations that were directly linked to the adoption of the SAPs by their governments. These protests were part of the greater discontent expressed by citizens against the economic policies that saw several state entities and various industries and businesses collapse. The cutbacks in funding for higher education driven by SAPs and government compliance with them translated into the end of the free fees era in many countries, affecting the less wealthy students. This, as Federici and Caffentzis (2000), Klopp and Orina (2002), Nkinyangi (1991) and Langa et al. (2016) note, had severe implications for educational conditions and access.

Nkinyangi (1991) notes that narrow educational concerns gave way to the expression of more broadly based social and economic questions and the rise of violence in student demonstrations, and he points to the implications for student movements of the solidarity that emerged in some countries between students and other social groups. Student politics in sub-Saharan Africa began to intersect with national politics. Student organisations had strong links to the dominant liberation parties and in some countries a typical response from the state was to try and co-opt emerging student organisations. This happened, for example, in Ghana and Francophone Africa, while in Tanzania student organisations were aligned as youth wings of the dominant political party. The students joined arms with broad political protests that were reacting against what they viewed as artificial, materialistic, conformist and undemocratic societies (Zeilig 2007). This also happened in the former Portuguese colonies – Mozambique is a good example (Hanlon 1991). Universities became the sites where broader socio-political grievances were projected and transferred into more precise localised calls for the transformation of educational institutions. The key issues around which students mobilised, along with other social groups, initially concerned both national and broader African concerns of democratic transition, opposition to apartheid further south, and resistance to capitulating to foreign interests.

Nevertheless Omari and Mihyo's (1991) broad argument should not be missed. They argue that for the last three decades many African countries have been engaged in both gradual and radical educational changes of structure and micro-level institutional innovations, although not always well synchronised by levels and types of education. Unesco (1994) and Nkinyangi (1991) observe that what is generally notable about student protest during the first two decades of independence is how student activism focused less on internal educational matters than on Africa's and their countries' wider global concerns of social philosophies of development, foreign policy, the politics of Cold War and relations with superpowers, and the South African question.

There are several strands to the commentary on student activism during this period. Some see it in terms of a resurgence (or rise) of pan-Africanism against corrupt and authoritarian regimes and external economic and cultural interference (Federici et al. 2000). Others see it in terms of hybridising disparate social forces mobilising around bread and butter issues (Nkinyangi 1991) and a third strand sees it as a recomposition of the African proletariat – vanguardism and new forms of protest (Omari and Mihyo 1991).

THE NEOLIBERAL AND 'DEMOCRATIC' PERIOD – 2000 TO THE PRESENT

The post-independence period in Africa, from the 2000s to the present day, is characterised by two main driving forces towards higher education and their consequences for student protests. The first set of drivers, external to Africa, includes globalisation, with African universities linked to wider global communities, liberalisation, privatisation and regime change. The second set of drivers, internal to the fast-changing dynamics of Africa, includes increasing poverty, inequality, access challenges, social change, the politics of multiparty democracy and the emergence of different culturally, socially and politically driven student movements.

This section of the chapter attempts to capture the dynamics of the key comparative characteristics across the educational cultures of Anglophone, Francophone and Lusophone regions by examining politics, policies and governance. The politics of this era has been marked by greater twenty-first-century openness, democracy, multiparty activity and civic participation in a pluralistic political environment in Africa (Kpundeh 1992). The growing wave of multiparty systems was an endeavour to create open and transparent nations and usher in newer approaches to broader-based inclusive participation in African societies. The idea of democracy started to permeate political practices and governance debates. This greater openness of the political sphere released space for young people and student politics to contribute to the politics, policies and governance of educational systems which, in turn, led to diverse student organisations calling for policies on autonomy and decentralisation of the operations of universities. Discrepancies within the politics and policies to reach educational goals often led to discontent and potential protests (Luescher-Mamashela and Mugume 2014). The African student intelligentsia and diaspora spread worldwide protest in a networked fashion to claim the legitimacy of their political rights, and the student protests have used to their benefit the digital dividends of globalisation and a networked society to rally effectively around their causes (Castells and Gustavo 2005).

The reach of higher education systems increased, with a mix of public and private provision, across nations such as Ghana, Nigeria, Kenya, Uganda, Tanzania, South Africa and Zimbabwe. In Francophone Africa, a similar spread took place, but with a dominant public sector controlled by government. In the later period of the 2000s, a wave of private institutions with mixed languages of instruction (where English became increasingly the leading language of instruction) emerged. There have been calls to rebrand the moribund network of nations that have French as their official language and cultural identities built around French culture (Attali 2014). In Lusophone Africa, this period is characterised by a dominant colonial Portuguese educational system where higher education systems remain public and controlled by the state. This was the case in Angola, Cape Verde, Guinea-Bissau and Mozambique.

Although the assimilationist educational approach of Francophone Africa began opening up to a postcolonial curriculum, it is still strongly tied to the French educational system and, more recently, into the wider Francophone cultural approach (French Senate 2013). A more liberal French-language system increasingly incorporating other dominant languages such as English and other European languages was being adopted in the late 1970s and 2010s. For instance, many African nations are adopting English as an official language. 'Most recently Rwanda, long a French-speaking country, has switched to English as an official language. Burundi and Gabon are switching from French to English, and South Sudan is adopting English' (Plonski, Teferra and Brady 2013). Similarly, Lusophone Africa exhibited the same assimilationist approach as the French. It is becoming more open to the English language and other global languages of instruction. Since Portugal's integration into the European Union (EU), Lusophone countries have benefited from the EU's liberal policies of multiparty politics, liberalisation and privatisation that have affected the educational systems in these countries and opened room for inclusion of English (Veiga, Rosa and Amara 2006).

In Anglophone Africa, mainly in Commonwealth countries, the decentralised educational policies have become increasingly integrated into regional policies. English has become the dominant regional language of instruction and communications although national voices have also emerged to re-focus on local African languages. Most education systems have moved from one official language to a diversified dual system that incorporates both private and public institutions. Consequently, the bid to expand educational access to a wider population has come at higher expense to the state and private investors, especially in Rwanda (Plonski, Teferra and Brady 2013).

With expanding access comes the issue of equity of quality, gender, finances and locations and with the increasing trend towards privatisation and 'pay-as-you-go' education systems fee-paying education gradually becomes *de facto* policy (Gradstein, Justman and Meier 2005). Consequently, higher education is still characterised by elitism and exclusiveness. The universities are either resource-rich or provide poor quality education. Discontent has grown, mainly at poor universities, and student protests have increased and spread to richer universities (Gavin 2007).

In Francophone Africa, national and regional educational systems still remain centralised and modelled on the French. The French language remains largely the only language of instruction at national and regional levels. Generally, the states remain the principal custodians of educational policies, but they cannot afford to expand and fund bloated educational systems. The grudging move towards privatisation in Francophone countries still faces numerous challenges with fee-paying educational systems, given the high poverty level of the people (Momboisse 1977). Growing discontents have led to student protests across many countries: Côte d'Ivoire, Cameroon, Madagascar and Senegal (Momboisse 1977).

In Anglophone Africa, the relationships between governments and states were not clearly delineated. Increasingly liberal policies led to the growing autonomy of educational systems. Centralised governance systems of education were relaxed by the economic dictates of international institutions such as the World Bank and the International Monetary Fund to privatise education and liberalise higher education on fee-based access for sustainability (Babalola, Lungwangwa and Adeyinka 1999; Reimers 1993; World Bank 2010). University governance became characterised by a mix of centralised and liberal policies (Luescher-Mamashela and Mugume 2014).

Student protests in the multiparty democracy era have grown more diffuse in terms of their leadership and governance. The style of protest leadership has changed from one strong person to a model wherein leaders emerge briefly and then disappear, or are very short term. There is also more diversity of gender and ethnicity. There has been evidence of multiple agendas that have changed into more layered demands after the core issue that initially started the protest is overtaken by different agendas. For instance, in Zambia student protest demands have gone from a single to multiple issues – as in South Africa (see Gavin 2007; Omari and Mihyo 1991).

More importantly, and in general, communications, media and information technologies have played a fundamental role in student protests. Old media and new media, especially social media combined with a sustained democratised political environment, have strengthened student protests, improving networked communication and fortifying solidarity between student movements globally (Castells and Gustavo 2005). Communication strategies relying heavily on social media and information technologies have made it difficult for governments to control students' agendas. The African student protest movements benefit from the dispersed yet deeply networked diaspora to form a powerful intelligentsia of contestation and protest.

LEARNING FROM OTHER AFRICAN COUNTRIES

The precipitating factors of the South African protests and their emergence at this particular time in history are not unfamiliar when viewed through a historical lens and the phases of struggle experienced elsewhere in sub-Saharan Africa. A key difference is the 'compression' of the nationalist and neoliberal periods that other countries went through. In South Africa, the post-1994 'independence' period, the adoption of neoliberal economic policies and the multiparty context have been experienced as contemporaneous. We discuss how this experience has influenced the nature of student protest, specifically in relation to funding, access, activism and autonomy.

Policies – funding and access

As with the university students in the nationalist phase of other newly independent countries, the South African protests reflected the concerns of the children of the political, economic (and racial) elite and what post-1994 has brought them (or failed to bring them), socially and economically (see also Chapter 6 in this volume). The initial post-independence period across the continent involved an acceptance of assumptions about nationalist or socialist states setting nationalist and developmentalist agendas for universities and having both the finances and ongoing willingness to fund student fees, accommodation and living expenses in the interests of access and national development. However, this was only possible when accommodating small numbers of students (Wangenge-Ouma 2012). In many newly independent countries in Africa where there were relatively homogeneous (elite) student groupings financed by the state, early protest primarily occurred in response to ideological issues related to the growing authoritarianism of the liberating parties and the continuing influence of the West and former colonialists.

Post-1994 South African students never experienced this 'no fees' heyday of their African counterparts. Neoliberal economic policies and the 'self-imposed structural adjustment programme' (Barrell 2000) introduced in the 1990s in South Africa combined with global recession and the decline of the South African economy to force universities to pass rising costs on in the form of fee increases (particularly when faced with declining subsidies). The spark for the first wide-scale student protests was a complex combination of welfare, survivalist and ideological factors encapsulated in the #FeesMustFall movement. Governments across the continent, in contexts of poor economic performance and pressure from the Bretton Woods institutions, adopted policies to increase student access to higher education rapidly and in large numbers. The resulting imposition of cost-sharing (familiar to South African students who pay fees) resulted in widespread student hardship and resistance. The Bretton Woods institutions are widely blamed for their role in imposing conditionalities in the harsh economic climate of the 1970s and 1980s that were used by governments to end the no-fees era (Federici et al. 2000) but these interventions occurred in political contexts of mismanagement, corruption and poor financial planning in many countries.

The rapid and underresourced expansion of access without appropriate resourcing was a key contributor to the decline of public higher education in many parts of sub-Saharan Africa, leading to the loss of quality academic staff and the movement of fee-paying students to the more stable, less protest-ridden, burgeoning private university sector in many countries, leaving the majority of weak public institutions for the less well off (Wangenge-Ouma 2012; Zeilig 2007). Similarly, in South Africa the precursors to, and harbingers of, the protests of 2015 were the ongoing protests in the historically black universities (HBUs) where the incompatibility of declining state subsidies, rising costs and massively increased enrolment of students was experienced most harshly (in the context of a 30 per cent student increase between 1999 and 2003) (Koen, Cele and Libhaber 2006). Government allocations per full-time student fell at an average annual rate of 1 per cent in real terms between 2000 and 2009 (Wangenge-Ouma 2012; Jansen 2016).

This cocktail of increasing student numbers and declining financial contributions from the state in conditions of a stagnant economy and demands for zero fees (or at least greater subsidisation of fees) are portents of the kinds of pressures on higher education quality and delivery that have undermined the quality of higher education provision elsewhere on the continent. There are already signs of responses from university administrators indicating that some of the paths followed in other African countries may be repeated in various forms – diminishing subsidies, increasing numbers of students, pressures on infrastructure, introduction of parallel programmes (massive open online courses or MOOCs), part-time provision, income-generating courses) and pressure for reductions in academic pay, conditions and numbers.

Politics – multiparty tensions and student activism

Some argue that the demise of one-party rule and the reintroduction of multiparty politics in many parts of sub-Saharan Africa changed the position of students from playing a central role as national opposition (and a vanguard speaking as national social conscience) and limiting the impact of their protest (Munene 2003). Research on the period from 2000 in South Africa and elsewhere on the continent highlights that there are increasingly more complex relationships between student leaders and political parties that influence the levels of autonomy students are able to maintain, their personal opportunities, their influence and their unity or lack thereof (Luescher-Mamashela and Mugume 2014). That research concludes that in some instances students are able to take advantage of their membership of a political party better to represent student interests. Where resources are exchanged and there is trust students might be assisted by this, but it might also increase the parties' expectations of, and control over, student leaders. How South African student protests are resourced (literally and in kind) and the duration and nature of this resourcing are areas for further exploration. Another possibility is that political parties take on some of the responsibilities of representing student interests – for example, putting pressure on university management and administration. There are also dependency relationships where students end up losing their ability to authentically represent students' interests on campus. Recent events on campuses on the continent and in the recent South African protests suggest variations of all of these (Luescher-Mamashela et al. 2011). More recently elsewhere in Africa there has also been more evidence of multiple agendas and greater divisiveness of ethnicity, tribalism, gender and religion – particularly noted in Zimbabwe (Hodgkinson 2013).

Contemporary protests in sub-Saharan Africa have also involved increasing levels of violence from the state (in both multiparty and effectively one-party contexts) (Kohstall 2015) and varying modalities of violence from students. The nature of these violent acts is complex and worthy of further analysis. The case of Zimbabwe may be instructive here as groups of 'hardcore student activism' and 'activist masculinities' fought state repression and dominated student politics, particularly in gender terms (Hodgkinson 2013: 882).

Various forms of domination, intimidation and exclusion may also be becoming more evident (see also Chapter 5 in this volume) and are under-examined. In South Africa it is becoming clear that it is less possible to talk of united student action than diverse and competing groups or 'movements' (Badat 2016) of students coming together (or not) over particular issues. Student protests also have to be read in the context of broader societal protest – both in South Africa and elsewhere on the continent. Students in many countries still see themselves as the social conscience because of their elite status, and protests do not exist separately from broader societal struggles. Another key observation for South Africa from recent student protests, particularly from the Arabophone (North African) protests and the Arab uprisings is how student protests can rapidly shift from pockets of resistance to multi-sectoral mobilisation in politically unstable and authoritarian regimes facing global and local economic pressures and decline (Kohstall 2015).

Governance – autonomy and university governance

Like their counterparts elsewhere, South African students have different and complex relationships with the ruling elite, and different levels of anger and frustration that can be exploited. There are sections of the student elite that have close relationships with the ruling party and turn to it to put pressure on university management and administration. Political parties are increasingly at centre stage. Student leaders are inserted into multiparty politics, and political parties turn to students for prestige, votes, recruitment and a new generation of politicians. This has occurred where universities have limited autonomy and there is centralised party-political recruitment (Luescher-Mamashela and Mugume 2014).

The history of developments in university autonomy is instructive. Academic communities that were shaped under colonialism and postcolonial one-party rule or despotism attached value to academic freedom and autonomy, and academics and administrators paid a high price for their principles by being exiled, jailed or eventually becoming part of the continent's intellectual brain drain (Zeleza 2003). Whereas student activism around educational issues has mostly centred on curriculum change (particularly contesting the content and ideology of colonial curricula in Anglophone countries), there has often been less support for academic struggles around autonomy and academic freedom. Students, some academics and some politicians saw the question of institutional autonomy as being used to defend intellectual elitism, as content that was not relevant to context and privilege, so intellectual debates on the nature of academic freedom did not receive much attention outside the universities.

A response was greater interrogation of the relations between university, society and the political sphere (Mamdani and Diouf 1994) and linking of social responsibility and intellectual freedom with particular national discourses surrounding these issues (Codesria 1996). In South Africa currently, these debates have (re)arisen with some student groupings and members of government explicitly associating the autonomy of institutions with colonisation (Sasco 2015). Elsewhere on the continent, expressions such as these became legitimating discourses justifying state intervention in university autonomy, freedom of speech and even banning and suppression. Current draft higher education legislation (the Higher Education Amendment Bill of November 2015) could allow for greater legislative power over universities. Opposition to academic freedom and institutional autonomy is often both pragmatic and political, and involves diverse internal and external constituencies, so a challenge for its protection is to build constituencies inside and outside the university that will support it if and when it is undermined (Zeleza 2003). Where this did not happen elsewhere in Africa it was easily eroded, receiving little public response or support.

The complexity of the South African student protests of 2015 and early 2016 makes speculative predictions as to their significance, particularly in relation to their potential as a stimulus for far-reaching, sustainable social, political and economic change. Reflecting on the nature of student political protest in Africa in the 1980s and early 1990s, commentators have noted that these struggles were not only pro-democracy (see Federici and Caffentzis 2000; Hardy 2016). In addition, students were also not all children of the elite: the no-fees policies that were threatened by the cost-sharing policies most affected students whose parents were peasants and lower-paid civil servants (for example, in Zimbabwe and Tanzania).

Consequently, students were able to work with civil society and trade unions, open the space for civil society to press for political reform, recreate organisations when they were banned (Daddieh 1996) and work with other groupings to bring about multiparty configurations. The response from African governments was often intimidation and violence, and committed students paid a high price when confronted by state violence, suffering torture, arrest, ruined or interrupted careers, and death (Daddieh 1996). Various governments co-opted (or attempted to co-opt) student movements that had emerged and bolstered the existing compliant national student groupings and the youth wings of one-party and authoritarian states in Ghana and Côte d'Ivoire, for example (Mawuko-Yevugah 2013; Daddieh 1996). However, when multiparty elections took place students (and their teachers) often formed the core of emerging political parties (for example in Côte d'Ivoire and Zimbabwe), which 'truncated' potential student activism (Hwami and Kapoor 2012). Some of the most recent research on student governance in the post-2000 multiparty political context in South Africa and elsewhere in Africa shows varying outcomes for student governance and activism (Luescher-Mamashela and Mugume 2014) with limited possibilities for securing agreement in times of protest.

As with protests elsewhere on the continent (historical and contemporary), the South African student protests have opened up contradictory spaces: the possibility arises of alliances with other sectors of society for resistance to try and bring about different economic and/or political orders, but also the possibilities for co-option by political parties and elites distributing patronage. Across the continent, the long-term success of working with civil society and opposition parties has been limited, and combinations of party patronage, coercion, violence and economic pressures on students have often blunted autonomous and critical student voices.

REFERENCES

Abrahamson, H. & Nilsson, A. (1994) *Moçambique em Transição, um Estudo da História de Desenvolvimento Durante o Período 1974–1992*. Maputo: CEEI–ISRI.

Adejumobi, S. A. (2007) *The History of Ethiopia*. Westport, CT: Greenwood Publishing. https://www.academia.edu/9063290/The_History_of_Ethiopia

Ajayi, J., Lameck, K., Goma, G. & Johnson, A. (1996) *The African Experience with Higher Education.* Accra: The Association of African Universities.

Anderson, D. (2005) *Histories of the Hanged: The Dirty War in Kenya and the End of Empire.* New York: W. W. Norton.

Attali, J. (2014) *La Francophonie et la Francophilie, Moteurs de la Croissance Durable.* Paris: Direction de l'information légale et administrative.

Babalola, J. B., Lungwangwa, G. & Adeyinka, A. A. (1999) Education under structural adjustment in Nigeria and Zambia. *McGill Journal of Education,* 34(1), 79–98.

Badat, S. (2016) Deciphering the meanings, and explaining the South African higher education student protests of 2015–2016. http://wiser.wits.ac.za/system/files/documents/Saleem%20Badat%20-%20Deciphering%20the%20Meanings%2C%20and%20Explaining%20the%20South%20African%20Higher%20Education%20Student%20Protests.pdf

Barrell, H. (2000) Back to the future: Renaissance and South African domestic policy. *African Security Studies,* 9(2), 82–91.

Bathily, A., Diouf, M. & Mbodj, M. (1995) The Senegalese student movement from its inception to 1989. In M. Mamdani & E. Wamba-Dia-Wamba (eds) *African Studies in Social Movements and Democracy,* pp. 368–407.

Bilodeau, C. (1955) Compulsory education in Cambodia. In C. Bilodeau, S. Pathammavong & Q. H. Lee *Compulsory Education in Cambodia, Laos and Vietnam,* pp. 9–67. Paris: Unesco.

Brown, D. S. (2000) Democracy, colonisation and human capital in sub-Saharan Africa. *Studies in Comparative International Development,* 35(1), 20–40.

Burawoy, M. (1976) Consciousness and contradiction: A study of student protest in Zambia. *British Journal of Sociology,* 27(1), 78–98.

Cabecinhas, R. & Feijo, J. (2010) Collective memories of Portuguese colonial action in Africa: Representations of the colonial past among Mozambicans and Portuguese youths. *International Journal of Conflict and Violence,* 4(10), 28–44.

Castells, M. & Gustavo, C. (2005) *The Network Society: From Knowledge to Policy.* Washington, DC: Johns Hopkins Center for Transatlantic Relations.

Chenoufi, M. (1968) Les deux séjours du Chaykh Mohammed Abdouh en Tunisie. *Cahiers de Tunisie,* 16th year, 57–96.

Clignet, R. P. & Foster, P. J. (1964) French and British colonial education in Africa. *Comparative Education Review,* 8(2), 191–198.

Codesria (1996) The state of academic freedom in Africa 1995. Dakar: Codesria. http://www.codesria.org/spip.php?article787

Cogneau, D. & Moradi, A. (2014) British and French educational legacies in Africa. CEPR Policy Portal. http://www.voxeu.org/article/british-and-french-educational-legacies-africa

Coleman, J. S. (1954) Nationalism in tropical Africa. *American Political Science Review,* 42(2), 404–426.

Colin, T. M. (1968) *The Lonely Africa.* New York: Clarion Books/Simon & Schuster.

Daddieh, C. (1996) Universities and political protest in Africa: The case of Côte d'Ivoire. *Issue: A Journal of Opinion,* 24(1), 57–60.

Devarajan, S., Monga, C. & Zongo, T. (2011) Making higher education finance work for Africa. *Journal of African Economies,* 20(3), 133–154.

Federici, S. & Caffentzis, C. G. (2000) Chronology of African university students' struggles: 1985–1998. In S. Federici, C. Caffentzis & O. Alidou (eds) *A Thousand Flowers:*

Social Struggles Against Structural Adjustment in African Universities. Trenton: Africa World Press.

Federici, S., Caffentzis, C. G. & Alidou, O. (2000) *A Thousand Flowers: Social Struggles Against Structural Adjustment in African Universities*. Trenton: Africa World Press.

Frankema, E. H. P. (2012) The origins of formal education in sub-Saharan Africa: Was British rule more benign? *European Review of Economic History*, 16(4), 335–355.

French Senate (2013) L'Afrique est notre avenir. Rapport d'Information. No 104, Session Ordinaire de 2013–2014, Paris, France.

Fukuyama, F. (2013) What is governance? *Governance*, 26(3), 347–368.

Gavin, M. (2007) Africa's restless youth. *Current History*, 106(700), 220–226.

Gifford, P. & Weiskel, T. C. (1971) African education in a colonial context: French and British styles. In P. Gifford & W. R. Louis (eds) *France and Britain in Africa: Imperial Rivalry and Colonial Rule*. New Haven: Yale University Press.

Gradstein, M., Justman, M. & Meier, V. (2005) *The Political Economy of Education: Implications for Growth and Inequality*. Boston: MIT Press.

Hanlon, J. (1991) *Mozambique: Who Calls the Shots?* London: James Currey.

Hardy, S. (2016) A brief history of student protests. *CHRONIC Chimurenga*. http://chimurengachronic.co.za/a-brief-history-of-student-protests-2/

Hodgkinson, D. (2013) The 'hardcore' student activist: The Zimbabwe National Students Union (ZINASU), state violence, and frustrated masculinity, 2000–2008. *Journal of Southern African Studies*, 39(4), 863–883.

Hughes, R. (1994) Legitimation, higher education, and the post-colonial state: A comparative study of India and Kenya. *Comparative Education*, 30(3), 193–204.

Hwami, M. & Kapoor, D. (2012) Neocolonialism, higher education and student union activism in Zimbabwe. *Postcolonial Directions in Education*, 1(1), 31–66.

Jansen, J. (2016) Jansen prophesies academic ruination. *Noseweek*, June, 12–13.

Klopp, M. J. & Orina, R. J. (2002) University crisis, student activism, and the contemporary struggle for democracy in Kenya. *African Studies Review*, 45(1), 43–76.

Koen, C., Cele, M. & Libhaber, A. (2006) Student activism and student exclusions in South Africa. *International Journal of Educational Development*, 26(4), 404–414.

Kohstall, F. (2015) From reform to resistance: Universities and student mobilisation in Egypt and Morocco before and after the Arab uprisings. *British Journal of Middle Eastern Studies*, 42(1), 59–73.

Kpundeh, S. J. (1992) *Democratization in Africa: African views, African voices*. Washington, DC: National Academy Press.

Langa, P., Wangenge-Ouma, G., Jungblut, J. & Cloete, N. (2016) South Africa and the illusion of free higher education. *University Worldwide News*, 402. http://www.universityworldnews.com/article.php?story=20160223145336908

Lipset, S. M. & Altbach, P. G. (1967) Student politics and higher education in the United States. In S. M. Lipset (ed.) *Student Politic*, pp. 199–242. London and New York: Basic Books.

Lombardi, A. I. M. (2011) The influence of higher education on decolonisation protests: A survey of sub-Saharan Africa, 1950–1960. Master's dissertation. University of Utrecht. http://dspace.library.uu.nl/handle/1874/254878

Luescher-Mamashela, T. M., Kiiru, S., Mattes, R., Mwollo-Ntallima, A., Ng'ethe, N. & Romo, M. (2011) *The African University and Democratic Citizenship: Hothouse or Training Ground*. Cape Town: African Minds.

Luescher-Mamashela, T. M. & Mugume, T. (2014) Student representation and multiparty politics in African higher education. *Studies in Higher Education*, 39(3), 500–515.

Mamdani, M. (2008) Higher education, the state and the marketplace. *JHEA/RESA*, 6(1),1–10. www.codesria.org/IMG/pdf/1-mamdani6-1-2008.pdf

Mamdani, M. & Diouf, M. (1994) *Academic Freedom in Africa*. Dakar: Codesria.

Mawuko-Yevugah, L. (2013) From resistance to acquiescence? Neoliberal reform, student activism and political change in Ghana. *Postcolonial Text*, 8(3 & 4), 1–17.

Momboisse, R. M. (1977) *Riots, Revolts and Insurrections*. Springfield: Charles C. Thomas.

Munene, I. (2003) Student activism in African higher education. In P. Altbach & D. Teferra (eds) *African Higher Education: An International Reference Handbook*, pp. 117–127. Bloomington: Indiana University Press.

Nkinyangi, J. A. (1991) Students protest in sub-Saharan Africa. *Higher Education*, 22, 157–173.

Nwaubani, E. (2001) Review: *West Africans in Britain, 1900–1960: Nationalism, Pan-Africanism and Communism* by Hakim Adi. *Canadian Journal of African Studies*, 35(1), 160–162.

Omari, I. M. & Mihyo, P. B. (1991) *The Roots of Student Unrest in African Universities*. The Hague; Nairobi, Kenya: Man Graphics.

Page, W. F. (2004) *Encyclopaedia of African History*. New York: Routledge.

Plonski, P., Teferra, A. & Brady, R. (2013) Why are more African countries adopting English as an official language? African Studies Association Annual Conference, Baltimore. www.booksforafrica.org/assets/documents/2013-ASA-Conference-English-Language-in-Africa-PAPER.pdf

Read, M. (1955) Education in Africa: Its pattern and role in social change. *The Annals of the American Academy of Political Science*, 298, 170–178.

Reimers, F. (1993) Education and structural adjustment in Latin America and sub-Saharan Africa. *International Journal of Education and Development*, 14(2), 119–129.

Rodney, W. (1972) How Europe underdeveloped Africa. London: Bogle-L'ouverture. http://abahlali.org/files/3295358-walter-rodney.pdf

Sasco (2015) Education is not a privilege, it's a right #FeesMustFall. Statement issued 16 October 2015. http://www.sasco.org.za/show.php?include=pr/2015/pr1016.html

Serequeberhan, T. (2010) Africa in a changing world. *Monthly Review*, 61(8), 26–38.

Talton, B. (2010) *African Resistance to Colonial Rule*. Africana Age: African and African Diasporan Transformation in the 20th Century. Schomburg Centre for Research in Black Culture and the New York Public Library. http://exhibitions.nypl.org/africanaage/essay-resistance.html

Unesco (1994) The role of African student movements in the political and social evolution of Africa from 1900–1975. Paris: Unesco. https://www.unesdoc.unesco.org

Urch, E. G. (1971) Education and colonialism in Kenya. *History Education Quarterly*, 11(3), 249–264.

Veiga, A., Rosa, J. R. & Amara, A. (2006) The internationalisation of Portuguese higher education: How are higher education institutions facing this new challenge? *Higher Education Management and Policy*, 18(1), 113–139.

Wangenge-Ouma, G. (2012) Tuition fees and the challenge of making higher education a popular commodity in South Africa. *Higher Education*, 64(6), 831–844.

Woldegiorgis, E. T. & Doevenspeck, M. (2013) The changing role of higher education in Africa: A historical reflection. *Higher Education Studies*, 3(6), 35–45.

World Bank (2010) *Financing Higher Education*. Washington, DC: The World Bank.
Zeilig, L. (2007) *Revolt and Protest: Student Politics and Activism in Sub-Saharan Africa*. London: I. B. Tauris.
Zeleza, P. T. (2003) Academic freedom in the neo-liberal order: Governments, globalization, governance, and gender. *Journal of Higher Education in Africa*, 1(1), 149–194.

CHAPTER

8

UNFINISHED REVOLUTIONS: THE NORTH AFRICAN UPRISINGS AND NOTES ON SOUTH AFRICA

William Gumede

INTRODUCTION

On Saturday 18 December 2010, Mohamed Bouazizi, a youth selling fruit and vegetables at a street stall in the provincial town of Sidi Bouzid, Tunisia, set himself alight, after police confiscated his produce. The twenty-six-year-old Bouazizi had a university degree but had struggled to find work, so set up a stall, without a licence. The police demanded a bribe. When he refused, the police confiscated his scales, and slapped him and insulted his late father (see Whitaker 2010; Lageman 2016). When Bouazizi tried to lay a complaint at the government offices he was refused entry. In frustration he set himself alight. Youths angry at Bouazizi's treatment started rioting, smashing cars, shops and official buildings.

The burning figure of Bouazizi and the protests in sympathy with him were posted on social media, Facebook and mobile phones across the country (Daragahi 2011; Whitaker 2010; National Public Radio 2011). Al Jazeera, the pan-Arab television station, broadcast activists' recordings (Daragahi 2011; Whitaker 2010; National Public Radio 2011). As in the case of South Africa's 2015–2016 student revolt, the protests by a diverse collection of youth (inclusive of students) spread using social media via mobile phones to disseminate the message of revolt and government brutality. Unlike in

South Africa – where the protesters took aim, alternately, at university fees and the continuing apartheid legacy of stark racial inequalities in higher education – the North African protesters took aim at the government, and demanded the fall of the Tunisian president Zine El Abidine Ben Ali. He fled a month after the protest started. The protests in Tunisia then spread across North Africa – and several regimes collapsed under the force of the protest. In South Africa, the government was shaken yet remained in power unambiguously.

The North African youth had a broad set of demands for national political, social and economic change. A combination of the delayed effects of the 2007–2008 global financial and Eurozone crisis, rising inequality and high levels of corruption, combined with oppressive regimes, pushed together young people, with little prospects of jobs, and financially hard-pressed middle classes, to call on regimes run by small elites who controlled almost every sphere of society for democratic, social and economic reforms that would end the disenfranchisement of their rights (Gumede 2011; AfDB 2011; ESCWA 2103; Boutayeb and Helmert 2011). Crucially, in the North African uprisings the youth was a decisive group spearheading the protests against *authoritarian regimes*.

Students were not the vanguard, but as part of the youth they joined with professionals, workers and opposition movements in a cross-sectorial opposition movement. They often went to protests as 'friends', not as a homogeneous protest group. Merging into the general protest and overcoming specific demands helped to make the uprising successful (Kohstall 2015: 62).

In the uprisings against unpopular governments in North Africa, new social media, mobile phones and the Internet that could circumvent the official media, and the rise of new independent media such as Al Jazeera, helped spread the message of revolt (Dergham, as cited by National Public Radio 2011; Gumede 2011; Whitaker 2010; Medien 2016). Where leaders and regimes did not fall because of the youth uprisings, they were sufficiently under pressure to implement political, social and economic reforms (Medien 2016; Perry 2016; Daoud 2015).

It is clear therefore that there are a number of fundamental differences – but also some similarities – between the North African uprisings and the 2015–2016 South African student protests. Both movements used social media to great effect as a mobilising tool. The South African student uprisings brought together middle-class and working-class students and different political formations – and in some cases were multiracial too. These uprisings excluded youth outside higher education. Students did take up the demands of blue-collar university workers, protesting against outsourcing. However, the South

African student #FeesMustFall (#FMF) uprising at its peak was largely single-issue driven – scrapping tuition fees rather than calling for systemic societal, political, social and economic change, as was the case in North Africa. The antecedent #RhodesMustFall and #FMF beyond its October 2015 zenith nevertheless protested against the major systemic issues of inequality and exclusion. The South African student movement did not build broader society-wide opposition coalitions, as was the case with the North African youth, who allied with broader civil society, professional organisations, trade unions and, in some cases, even opposition parties.

THE SPARKS OF THE NORTH AFRICAN UPRISINGS

Although Bouazizi's setting himself alight provided the spark for the North African uprisings, a number of revolts against failing economic conditions had already been brewing. In 2007 and 2008, Egypt and Tunisia were gripped by strikes, for example. Where outbreaks occurred, violent state repression followed in many cases. The South African student protests of 2015–2016 share aspects of this North African phenomenon in that they were situated in the broader, but separate, waves of spontaneous and organised public protests against economic conditions (and service delivery), yet the South African protests did not go as far as bringing a regime to its knees (see Chapter 1 of this volume).

In Egypt, from September 2007 doctors, university lecturers, textile workers and public servants went on strike, threatening the regime's monopolistic power. A general strike in the central delta city of Mahalla, against the president, Hosni Mubarak, took place on 6 April 2008. The strike was against rising food prices, the declining buying power of salaries and rising inequality between the governing elite and ordinary people (Slackman 2008). Organisers mobilised support for the general strike on Facebook and through sending SMS messages headed 'April 6' (Ibrahim 2012).

In 2008 protests over corrupt hiring practices at the state-owned phosphate mines in Gafsa, Tunisia, lasted for six months. The protesters complained about lack of democracy, corruption, unemployment and lack of basic services. They embarked on sit-ins, erecting a tent city. The General Union of Tunisian Workers (UGTT) played a key role disseminating the information about the protests through YouTube videos. The state violently suppressed the protests. Nevertheless, the North African uprisings spread from Tunisia to Egypt in January 2011, with protesters calling for bread, freedom, social justice and human dignity. By February 2011, the Egyptian president Hosni Mubarak was forced to step down.

Algeria was less affected by the 2011 North African youth uprisings. Protests, on a smaller scale, calling for better public services, did take place – and are still a regular phenomenon. Youth uprisings occurred in Algeria in 1988 when the youth rebelled against the Algerian liberation movement turned government, the National Liberation Front (FLN). The complacent FLN, presiding over a one-party state, proved to be autocratic and corrupt in power, and mismanaged the economy.

The 1988 Algerian uprisings forced the FLN to introduce democratic reforms such as allowing opposition parties and free elections, and initiating economic reforms. In December 1990 it passed Law 90-31 which allowed freedom of association, but the associations had to get a permit from government to establish themselves, and permission for public meetings had to be requested from the Ministry of Interior and the local prefect (Cavatorta 2009). In the subsequent 1990 local government elections (the first multiparty elections in the post-liberation era) the FLN, the party of liberation, was defeated by the Islamist Salvation Front (ISF), which won the majority of the local councils. In the parliamentary elections the following year, the ISF completed their clean sweep, winning 188 out of 231 seats, with the FLN puffing in third. In December 1991, the military – dominated by FLN cadres – staged a coup against the ISF, sparking the Algerian civil war.

The FLN, as a party, formally opposed the military dictatorship, but later supported it. After the end of the military dictatorship, the FLN lost the 1997 parliamentary elections, but subsequently returned to victory in 2002, lost the 2004 presidential elections, and won the 2009 presidential elections led by Abdelaziz Bouteflika. In the 2004 presidential elections, which it had lost, the FLN had nominated Ali Benflis, running against Bouteflika, who won. The post-coup Algerian ruling regimes oversaw a 'controlled' democracy, which allowed multiparty politics, but censored critics (Daoud 2015). Bouteflika was re-elected in 2014 for a fourth term as president.

When the 2011 North African uprisings occurred, the FLN was fully back in control in Algeria. The FLN government, like African liberation movements turned governments in sub-Saharan Africa (including South Africa), effectively used the twin threats of the former colonial power, France, returning and the 'imperialist' Western countries (particularly, the United States) of pushing regime change to exploit the resources of North Africa (fears which run deep in African countries that have been colonised over extended periods) to keep the

Algerian population submissive. The Algerian government also suggested that the Western powers were behind the North African uprisings.

The US-led invasion of Libya to depose Muammar Gaddafi was portrayed as 'proof' of Western imperialism. During the 2011 North African uprisings the Algerian government used oil largesse to introduce new reforms, providing social security, free housing and low-interest loans. More recently, the regime has used the threat of terrorism to marshal people behind it. Ethnic divisions between Arabs and Berbers are a regular phenomenon.

In 2011, Moroccan youth formed the '20 February movement' and took to the streets to demand democracy, social justice and jobs, behind the slogan: 'The people want the end of autocracy. The people want the end of corruption' (El Amrani 2014). The Moroccan monarch, King Mohammed VI, at the head of the Arab world's longest-serving dynasty, pursued a conciliatory strategy and used less violence against protesters – without, however, losing overall power. He promised new democratic reforms, including new elections, a new constitution and the introduction of multiparty politics. He reduced the powers of the monarch in favour of an elected prime minister. He also introduced new social reforms, such as improving the powers of women in families and the workplace.

Rebellions broke out in Libya and, with the help of Western-led armies, opposition forces deposed Muammar Gaddafi, after a forty-two-year rule. Antigovernment protests began in February 2011, turning into a civil war between Gaddafi loyalists and the opposition. Western countries, under Nato, led by the US, intervened; the government was overthrown in August 2011, and Gaddafi killed in October 2011. African leaders wanted to negotiate a ceasefire between Gaddafi and his opponents, but were ignored. African leaders argue that the Western countries intervened to protect their oil interests – and if they had not done so a compromise could have been negotiated which could have prevented the country subsequently plunging into chaos (Thabo Mbeki, quoted in Monare 2012).

CONDITIONS THAT CONTRIBUTED TO THE NORTH AFRICAN UPRISINGS

Inequalities are not only confined to income and wealth (Sen 1977). Many of the inequalities in North Africa, as in the rest of Africa, are multiple and intersecting (Kabeer 2014; Paz Arauco et al. 2014). These inequalities are multiple in that they were manifested in economic, political, regional and social spheres – and intersected with one another (Kabeer 2014; Paz Arauco et al. 2014), in ways reminiscent of the 'intersectionality of oppression' that became one of the South African focal points (as argued in Chapter 2 in this volume). In the literature, three forms of political inequality are generally focused on, and these will also form the framework for the rest of this chapter's discussion. The first is lack of political representation and inclusivity, whether on the basis of region, ethnicity, religion, class, race, gender or other discriminatory practices (Bird 2003; Bartels 2005; OSCE 2007). The second is lack of political participation in formal and informal political processes (Lehman Schlozman, Verba and Brady 2012; Dubrow 2014). The third is inequality in power – where political power is concentrated in the hands of small elites (Dubrow 2014; Schutz 2012).

Economic inequalities

In the decade preceding the uprisings, all the North African countries that experienced youth uprisings had implemented Washington Consensus-style economic reforms, with structural adjustment programmes which, like elsewhere in Africa, included privatisation, trade liberalisation and reduction of subsidies to the poor (Springborg 2011; Heydemann 2004; Mourad Sika 2013). The structural adjustment reforms in most North African countries were implemented through top-down decrees (Ansani and Daniele 2012). They increased inequality between the rich elite, linked to the authoritarian regimes, and ordinary citizens. They were simultaneously accompanied by political repression (Ansani and Daniele 2012). These programmes led to the formation of '"networks of privilege" and "crony capitalists" on the one hand, and increasing restrictions on freedom and modes of demobilisation on the other' (Kohstall 2015: 60). In fact, the structural adjustment programmes reinforced the economic power of the elites allied to the ruling regimes.

Figures from the 2013 United Nations (UN) report on the Millennium Development Goals showed that poverty in North Africa had remained high throughout the two decades before the uprisings. Close to 40 per cent of the population in the region were without means to secure basic food (Achcar 2013: 31; ESCWA 2013: 5). In Egypt, poverty levels increased from 16.7 per cent in 2000 to 21.6 per cent in 2008 (ESCWA 2013: 6). Unemployment levels across North Africa were high (IMF 2011: 10) before the uprisings. It was estimated also that before the global and Eurozone financial crisis in 2007–2008 unemployment in North Africa was comparatively higher than any other region (IMF 2011: 39). The youth had the highest levels of unemployment in the region, at 26 per cent (ESCWA 2013: 10). One-third of young people were in work (IMF 2011: 39; UNDP 2015: 41), and a quarter of women were in work (ESCWA 2013: 9).

According to World Bank data, 21 per cent of the youth were unemployed in Algeria, 25 per cent in Egypt, 18 per cent in Morocco, and 30 per cent in Tunisia. More than 19 per cent of women in the region were unemployed. In Egypt, more than 45 per cent of women were unemployed (UNDP 2015: 41). More than 30 per cent of university graduates were unemployed in Tunisia and Egypt (World Bank 2014). More than 40 per cent of women with tertiary education in Egypt were unemployed (World Bank 2014). The youth unemployment level in Libya stood at 17 per cent. Inflation in Libya was 12 per cent in 2009 (Liste, Kolster and Matondo-Fundani 2012).

North African graduates generally struggled to secure jobs. More than 30 per cent of university graduates were unemployed (World Bank 2014). Better-educated youth entered the job market but there were insufficient work opportunities. One journalist wrote: 'They are victims of an educational system that has succeeded in providing them with qualifications that can't be used and expectations that can't be met' (Whitaker 2010).

As elsewhere in Africa, the informal sectors soaked up most of the unemployed (UNDP 2013: 111) – three-quarters of new entrants to the labour market in Egypt joined the informal sectors (Wahba 2010: 34). In the North African countries the social contract in which ordinary people accept autocratic regimes in return for economic welfare and peace fell apart following the economic crises caused by the 2007–2008 global and Eurozone financial crises (Whitaker 2010; Gumede 2011).

Although, in the decade preceding the uprisings, poverty and unemployment jumped, the region at the same time experienced relatively high growth rates. The UN described the increase in poverty levels combined with rises in GDP per capita in Egypt over the period before the 2007/2008 global and Eurozone financial crisis as a 'paradox' (ESCWA 2013: 6). In Tunisia and Morocco real GDP per capita grew between 14.7 per cent and 23 per cent (ESCWA 2013: 6).

Many young people and professionals from North Africa could, in the past, easily migrate across the Mediterranean to Europe to seek better prospects. However, economic difficulties in most of Europe have meant that these countries have blocked entry barriers for the young from Africa – the phenomenon of 'fortress' Europe (Gebrewold 2007; Carr 2012).

One observer wrote: 'That is Mubarak's Egypt, where about half the population lives on $2 a day or less, and walled compounds with green lawns and swimming pools and names like Swan Lake spring up outside cities. It is a place where those with money have built a parallel world of private schools and exclusive clubs, leaving the rundown cities to the poor' (Slackman 2008). Middle classes in the region nevertheless started to feel the pinch of difficult economic circumstances.

Political inequalities

Before the 2011 uprisings all of the North African countries had repressive, patronage-based and paternalistic regimes. For decades, small elites have dominated political, economic and social power in North Africa (Hanieh 2013). A general climate of fear prevailed in the North African autocratic regimes. The Egyptian president Hosni Mubarak and the Tunisian Zine El Abidine Ben Ali were named among the world's most symbolic cases of grand corruption by Transparency International (2015). In Tunisia, Zine El Abidine Ben Ali, at the head of the party of independence, the Democratic Constitutional Rally (RCD), ran the country as a police state. The party had an office in every city and the smallest village. A cult developed around Ben Ali, who came to power in 1987, and who was defended at all costs by the party and members, no matter his transgressions.

Tunisian nationalists founded the Destour (Constitutional) Party in 1920 to fight French colonialism. Younger, more radical members, led by Habib Bourguiba, broke away in 1934 and founded the Neo Destour Party, which became the leading movement in the fight for independence, embarking on armed struggle in the 1940s, and securing freedom in 1956. The party changed its name to the Destourian Socialist Party (PSD) in 1964. From 1963 until 1981 the party was declared the only legal party in Tunisia. Opposition against Bourguiba and the party's autocracy emerged in 1981, when student groups rebelled. The party also faced formal opposition in the form of the Tunisian Communist Party, the Movement for Popular Unity and Hizb ut-Tahrir, the Islamic Tendency Movement.

Ben Ali, then prime minister, took control of the party and government in an internal coup on 7 November 1987, after he declared Bourguiba medically unfit to govern. Ben Ali's leadership was as autocratic as that of Bourguiba. He had promised a clean, democratic and accountable government, introduced a two-term presidential limit and initiated a 'road-map' for gradual political opening – but this did not happen. He changed the Constitution again to allow presidential terms for life. Tunisia was 'run and owned by a club of rich and powerful families' (Sadiki 2010) closely connected to Ben Ali.

Citizens in the region lacked political representation and voice. Political participation in the political processes was absent. Opponents of the regimes were routinely imprisoned, tortured and killed. The media, civil society and opposition were restricted, if not harshly oppressed. The official media were fawning. There was an official media blackout of the early days of the youth uprisings after Bouazizi set himself alight (Whitaker 2010).

Algeria was governed by a one-party state, the FLN, the former liberation movement turned government. From 1991 onwards, the military dominated Algeria with a restricted multiparty system. In Algeria the small elite of military leaders, politicians and businessmen and women are known as '*le pouvoir*': 'Power passes between different "clans" or groupings of influential figures bound by diverse ties, from revolutionary solidarities to school relationships to family and regional divisions' (Lebovich 2015: 2).

Some North African autocratic regimes used religion, tradition and culture to retain power, rather than autocratic regimes with economic patronage, as exemplified in the 'rentier state' phenomenon (Skocpol 1982; Daadaoui 2011; Anderson 1991; Antoun 2006; Ross 1997). These states use 'popular Islam' to perpetuate their 'legitimacy and political authority' (Daadaoui 2011). The political scientist Mohamed Daadaoui (2011) maintains that countries such as Morocco have effectively managed to subtly 'recast history and deploy culture', whether through the use of 'history writing or the reinterpretation of folklore and symbols' to 'exercise and maintain political authority', or through maintaining a 'hegemonic discourse' along the lines of Antonio Gramsci's postulation (Bates 1975).

In this hegemonic discourse the unjust behaviour of the authority and the poor conditions of the populace are embellished to justify the situation, argues Daadaoui (2011): this is done through religious, cultural and traditional justification. These North African states have 'reconstructed, synthesised and even invented symbols that appeal to the populace at large' to perpetuate their legitimacy and control, and their populace's acceptance of their authority (Daadaoui 2011). Marc Howard Ross (1997) has succinctly articulated this phenomenon as the autocratic regime exercises its 'culturally constituted' authority through 'regularised procedures that members of a community consider more or less legitimate, meaning that they have been arrived at by a procedure they consider fair, although the issue may continue to be highly contested' (Ross 1997: 47).

Morocco had been an absolute monarchy. The king was called 'commander of the faithful', and criticising him was a crime. The monarchy, and the network of families and close allies associated with it, ran the country through a patronage system referred to as the 'makhzen' (Daadaoui 2011). The Moroccan monarchy successfully used the 'shared meanings' of culture, traditions, symbols and identity to position itself as the sole conduit for identity, religion and authority. The monarchy had become 'sacrosanct', and positioned itself as the legitimate vassal of both Islam and Moroccan identity, which limited the ability of opposition groups to contest its legitimacy (Daadaoui 2011). The journalist Rachid Elbelghiti observed that the uprisings were civil movements by young people who had grown tired of political, economic and social stagnation: 'Through different creative forms of protest, they demanded freedom, dignity and social justice' (2016).

In Egypt Hosni Mubarak's National Democratic Party was dominant and only smaller parties and the Muslim Brotherhood were allowed to operate – under restrictive conditions. Egypt was for a long time run under emergency powers, legalised by the 1971 Constitution, which allowed the government to declare a state of emergency to (supposedly) ensure 'stability' (Roth 2012). The state used these powers to suppress legitimate opposition, media and civil society. Under Law 84/2002, the government could, for example, close down any civil society organisation, or confiscate or freeze their assets or block their funding if deemed a threat to the state and to 'stability' (Roth 2012).

Many North African regimes have been in power because the army has been loyal to them. In the cases of Egypt and Tunisia, once it became clear to the army that the regimes had lost the support of powerful overseas backers, they changed allegiances, or at least remained neutral. In Algeria and Tunisia, specifically in Algeria, independence and liberation movements in government used the oppression by former colonial powers to hold onto political power. In ways that resemble some of the 'enemy' narratives of South Africa's African National Congress (ANC) (see Gumede 2005), some North African countries consistently created an 'external enemy', whether the old colonial power, or current Western powers, specifically the US and Israel, 'to make the anger towards them [autocratic governments] less, and make the angry young people who have no jobs, no good schools, no housing, divided, not only towards the government, but also towards other external enemies ... In this way, there is a separation in the minds of North Africans between government use of the past and the reality of their present-day suffering' (Githens-Mazer 2009: 1021).

Most of North Africa's autocratic regimes were supported and propped up by industrial and former colonial powers. In January 2011, the French foreign minister, Michele Alliot-Marie, offered to send French forces to support Tunisia's Ben Ali against the uprisings (Willsher 2011). Over the past few years, Tunisia's supposed economic 'miracle' – in spite of political autocracy – was toasted by multilateral organisations and Western powers. Egypt was a strategic focus for the US and the regime there was flush with foreign aid. Even Libya joined the US-led 'war on terror' and became an ally of Western powers – which shored up Gaddafi's powers ahead of the rebellion against his rule.

Regional and social inequalities

In most of the North African countries colonial regional development disparities continue, with the urban coastal areas more wealthy than the rural interior regions (AfDB 2011: 16; Joyce 2013). One analyst suggests that in Tunisia: 'Regional inequality was and continues to be a driving factor behind Tunisia's economic and political crisis. So long as Tunisia's inlands remain ignored relative to its more developed coast, discontent and unrest will plague its political and economic recovery' (Joyce 2013).

In Morocco, poverty has been disproportionally spread between regions. Before the 2011 uprisings regions such as Centre-South, Centre-North and Tensif had seen a 13 per cent increase in absolute poverty (AfDB 2011: 12). In Morocco, 69 per cent of the farming units consist of less than five hectares, and hold 23 per cent of the total land; while under 1 per cent of farmers have units of fifty hectares, and in total hold 15 per cent of the land (AfDB 2011: 12). In Morocco, urban literacy is double that of the rural areas (Boutayeb and Helmert 2011). The average per capita income in urban areas in Egypt is 67 per cent higher than in the rural areas (Verme et al. 2014).

North African countries also have stark gender gaps in economic participation, educational attainment, health and political empowerment (World Bank 2013; Ncube and Anyanwu 2012: 14). According to figures from the African Development Bank, North African countries have 'the most unequal gender unemployment rates among the regions of the world' (Ncube and Anyanwu 2012: 11, 14). Women's participation in the labour market in North Africa is 25 per cent, whereas the global average is 50 per cent (World Bank 2013: 11). In Morocco, for example, urban males are almost five times more likely to be literate than rural women (Boutayeb and Helmert 2011).

IMPACT OF THE 2007–2008 GLOBAL FINANCIAL AND EUROZONE CRISES

The global financial and Eurozone crises had a serious impact on the North African economies – both oil and non-oil producing (Drine 2009; AfDB 2011; Ncube and Anyanwu 2012), amplifying existing inequalities in the region, where more than 56 per cent of GDP is from oil exports, 14 per cent from international tourism and 7 per cent from remittances (Drine 2009). The oil-exporting North African countries have higher levels of GDP per capita, large foreign exchange reserves and comparatively lower unemployment. Algeria, an oil-exporting state with large foreign reserves, was less affected, as it has a low exposure to global financial markets. Nevertheless, in 2008 Algeria ran a surplus on its current account of 28 per cent, which had changed to 10 per cent by 2012 (Saif and Choucair 2009). Algeria's hydrocarbon exports fell. Hydrocarbon makes up 97 per cent of Algeria's exports and 70 per cent of its fiscal revenues. Following the financial crisis, Algeria put together an emergency stimulus, which included a ban on consumer credit and imports and required foreign investors to have a minimum local ownership of 51 per cent. Algeria used its oil wealth to provide social goods, such as cheap loans for public housing, welfare and public subsidies – and so stave off public uprisings.

Prior to the global financial and Eurozone crises Egypt suffered from high levels of poverty, inequality, corruption and unemployment. In 2008, around 18.9 per cent of the Egyptians were stuck in poverty (World Bank 2008). However, roughly the same proportion was just above the poverty line, vulnerable to plunge into poverty from internal or external economic shocks (World Bank 2008). Its inflation rate had been around 10 per cent for three decades (Liste, Kolster and Matondo-Fundani 2012). After the global financial and Eurozone crises, Egypt's stock exchange fell by 56 per cent (ILO 2009). Employment was affected. The International Labour Organisation (ILO) estimates that more women (53 per cent) than men were affected (ILO 2009). The rise in unemployment also heavily affected the youth. In 2008, unemployment for the age group twenty to twenty-five rose to 28 per cent.

More than 70 per cent of Morocco's exports go to Europe. The global financial crisis meant that this slowed (Atieno and Mitullah 2010); and Morocco's reform packages to counter the impact of the financial crisis largely failed because of 'ineffective implementation and narrow scope' (Atieno and Mitullah 2010: 13). By June 2009, foreign investment had dropped 34.5 per cent. Foreign direct investment (FDI) flows from the EU to Morocco declined 37 per cent in 2010. By 2011, 30 per cent of those aged between fifteen and twenty-nine were unemployed. Before the 2011 crisis, Tunisia had managed its macroeconomic fundamentals better than its peers. By December 2011, however, Tunisia saw a decline in all economic sectors. FDI fell by 27 per cent, manufacturing by 12 per cent, tourism by 40 per cent, mining by 50 per cent and remittances by 12.5 per cent, while unemployment jumped from 13 to 20 per cent.

This cumulative set of North African trends demonstrates the economic dire straits that preceded the uprisings. There were rapid declines, caused by both domestic and global conditions. In addition, politics of oppression and constraints on political expression and general political rights were widespread. Such conditions reveal important differences in the settings of the North African (more generalised) uprisings and the South African revolt (specifically students, along with modest numbers of university workers). The South African revolt certainly also emerged in the context of economic hardship and frustration with opportunities that do not arise, but occurred in conditions of mixed relations with those in power – ranging from hostile and intensely challenging to congenial and cooperative. The South African revolt also came to be suspended: for the time being it appeared that the regime remained safely entrenched. In contrast, and as highlighted in the next section, several of the North African regimes succumbed in ambiguous ways to the force of the uprisings.

PEOPLE'S POWER, BUT UNFINISHED DEMOCRACY

The North African uprisings did not turn into genuinely lasting democracies. Upheavals and repression continued, in new manifestations. In most cases, the autocratic regimes ousted by people's power are often soon replaced by similarly autocratic movements and leaders – as can be seen in places like Egypt, where there are now elections, the president is constitutionally limited to only two terms, and has a parliament with diverse political representatives – but women are still vastly underrepresented in public office. After the 2011–2012 parliamentary elections, women made up only 2 per cent of the lower house of Parliament (World Bank 2013). State repression is widespread. Dissenting voices are quashed. Criticising the security services has been criminalised. Detentions without charges are frequent. Many activists are facing travel bans (Perry 2016).

Immediately after the Arab Spring upheavals, the generals who took over from Hosni Mubarak were accused of wanting to hold on to power (rather than immediately returning power to civilians), and using the same violent methods to crush opposition. In the first elections in Egypt after the Arab Spring uprisings, Islamist parties and other conservative parties with patriarchal views on women and youth, and very narrow notions of human rights and democracy, secured electoral victories. Egypt's post-Arab uprising president, Mohammed Morsi, of the Muslim Brotherhood, attempted to force the adoption of a new constitution that would give him sweeping new powers. He was deposed in a military coup in 2013, for misrule.

The gains won by Egyptian independent trade unions were also reversed when the military junta introduced a 'counter-revolutionary' rule. Following the uprisings, Egyptian worker activists formed an independent trade union and worked towards abolishing the state-run union – however, military leaders undermined the new trade unions (Gaber 2011). During the 2014 Egyptian presidential elections the Muslim Brotherhood was banned. Although young women were at the forefront of the uprisings their rights in the post-uprising dispensation were curtailed. Raghida Dergham (2011), a respected newspaper columnist, pointed out that while women had fought with men to bring change, they were being sidelined after the uprising.

Elbelghiti (2016) says the Moroccan youth uprisings 'succeeded in breaking the wall of fear and stripping away the "holiness" of political actors'. However, 'we failed in achieving the ultimate goal: to position Morocco on the path towards democracy'. To appease the uprisings the Moroccan king introduced democratic reforms, including establishing an Equity and Reconciliation Commission with the goal of restoring justice, including financial justice, to those unjustly prosecuted by the regime. The king also reformed the family code to give women more rights in families, such as an equal right to ask for a divorce. In its November 2011 elections, the opposition Islamist Justice and Development Party (its leader, Abdelilah Benkirane, had opposed the uprisings) came to power. Although the king's reforms also included the separation of powers, power remains firmly in the institution of the king. All the existing opposition parties – ranging from Islamist to liberal parties – maintain close ties with the king (Al Jazeera 2011). The King and the Islamist Justice and Development Party insisted that even if a new democratic constitution is introduced, the fundamental laws should be based on Islam. Human rights and civil society organisations and activists are routinely harassed. Ending corruption was one of the key aims of the Moroccan 20 February movement but the post-uprisings government has made few inroads into tackling corruption. Ahmed el-Haij, the head of the Moroccan Association of Human Rights has said: '… the state does not tolerate dissident voices' (Bozonnet 2015). El-Haij fears that the government wants to crush the last remnants of Morocco's 20 February movement, which organised the youth uprisings (Bozonnet 2015).

Following the North African uprisings, Algeria introduced religious freedom. It made Tamazight, the language of Algerian first peoples, the second official language and new codes have been introduced to bring gender parity in public employment. Tunisia has made the most democratic progress following the uprisings; it successfully drafted a new democratic constitution. New reforms in 2011 prescribed that an equal number of men and women participate as candidates in the elections, and women received a quarter of the seats in the Constituent Assembly (World Bank 2013). Tunisia set up a Truth and Dignity Commission to investigate human rights violations under the regime of Ben Ali. The former Tunisian ruling party, the Democratic Constitutional Rally, the party of independence, has been banned, disbanded and its assets liquidated. Tunisian civil society groups, organised under the umbrella of a formal coalition, Quartet, which included the trade union federation, the Human Rights League and the lawyers' association, played a key role in the post-uprisings period, and in 2013 cobbled together a compromise which saw the Islamist government step down, a new Constitution drafted and elections held.

CONCLUSION

In drawing insights for South Africa from this chapter one needs to ask: Why have the North African uprisings not translated into fully-fledged democracies? The nature of pre-uprising activism by civil society and opposition parties appears to substantially influence the extent to which the democratic gains of the uprisings are consolidated. Previous experiences of democratic reform also play a key role.

The North African uprisings have been driven by spontaneous civil groups, youth and the middle classes. They brought different ideologies, classes and sectors together under the umbrella of the civil movement. There were no formal vanguard organisations leading the movements. The North African uprisings were not led by organised opposition parties, popular people's fronts or traditional civil groups such as trade unions. Political youth groups or professional organisations were not at the forefront – although they became key participants. Over time, in North Africa, during autocratic regimes, civil society outside government was dominated by Islamist groups.

During its armed liberation struggle against France, Algeria had a rich web of civil society allied to the liberation struggle. Displaying a gender activist dimension, Tunisia, governed by the party of independence, the Socialist Destourian party, had (in spite of its autocracy) introduced reforms to protect women's rights, had made efforts to reduce the gap between the rich and the poor and had expanded education broadly. Tunisia, related to its left liberation struggle politics, had prior experiences of activism and civil society agitation and had an organised trade union movement, even though the Socialist Destourian party had made it the workers' wing of the party.

As in Tunisia, once the party of liberation came to power Algerian civil society was co-opted into the governing party – if it wanted to exist (Jamal 2007). In many cases, 'civil society' organisations were also established by governments.

That well-developed organised civil society groups – outside the Islamist ones – were missing in these revolutions was perhaps the biggest weakness of the North African uprisings. Of course, the presence of well-developed and structured civil groups does not automatically ensure that revolutions will turn into democracy – although one reason why Tunisia in the post-uprising period made more democratic progress is that its rich civil society network, activism and protest history provided the movement with the tools to construct a more robust post-uprising democratic dispensation – but its absence allowed movements that were organised before the North Africa uprisings (such as Islamist movements and the military) to take power in the vacuum left when the regimes were ousted. The North African protesters were unable to turn their movements into formal structures that could take power – and transform the political, social and cultural systems of their societies. Prior to the 2011 uprisings, Islamist parties were often the existing opposition to governments. Dergham (2011) summarises: 'When the youths went to Tahrir Square (Egypt) and other places they wanted a modernist future ... Suddenly they were encroached upon by the very well-organised and well-experienced Islamist parties'.

Instructively, a generation ago, the 1988 mass youth uprisings in Algeria (which were also spontaneous, unorganised and consisted of different ideologies and classes), turned into an Islamist movement, the Islamic Salvation Front (ISF) in 1989. The ISF went on to become an opposition party, taking up the cudgels for the poor in opposition to the governing elite (Roberts 2002: 3). The Islamist parties and the military that took power in North Africa in the post-2011 uprisings present alternatives to the old autocratic regimes, to liberation nationalist ideologies and to Western style liberalism and the associated donor-community-driven prescriptions.

The alternative they present, however, is merely a different ideology, namely Islamist, but with the same pre-uprisings political, economic and society arrangements, bar few reforms and new faces. They do not bring a new progressive economic, social and democratic transformation agenda – as envisaged by the activists participating in the uprisings. Clearly, North African youth and civil society movements fighting for democracy, social change and equity will have to think about remaking themselves into political parties ready to take power – as did the Islamist social movements.

Although in many North African countries the revolutions appear unfinished, the uprisings did lay the foundations for new domestic and regional consciousness, assertions and expectations for democratic rights, social justice and accountability. The uprisings also signal the end of the ability of governments to deflect their own shortcomings to former colonial powers and external powers – and people falling for it. It will be increasingly difficult for leaders to use religion, traditions and culture to get oppressed citizens to accept poverty, lack of rights and corruption. In Morocco, ordinary people have begun to criticise the monarchy. The institution of the monarchy is no longer 'sacred' – in itself a leap forward for democracy. Governing regimes – with the threat of possible revolt, will feel they have to be accountable, even if it is sham accountability.

It also means that young people will direct their anger for their current suffering at current governments, not foreign enemies and past colonial powers. South Africa's student uprisings have generally focused their anger at symbols of apartheid and colonialism. Of course, the power structures of colonialism and apartheid are largely still intact – and such symbols are stark reminders of lived racial, social and economic inequalities. Nevertheless, it is crucial that the South African student movement also aims its firepower at failures by the current government. If not, the South African government will, as in the pre-North African uprising period, deflect its own shortcomings to former apartheid and external powers – and therefore not accept accountability for its own failures.

REFERENCES

Achcar, G. (2013) *The People Want*. London: Saqi Books.
AfDB (African Development Bank) (2011) Poverty and inequality in Tunisia, Morocco and Mauritania. Economic Brief. Tunis: AfDB.
Al Jazeera (2011) Thousands in Morocco call for poll boycott. 20 November. http://www.aljazeera.com/news/africa/2011/11/20111120184442342660.html
Anderson, L. (1991) Absolutism and the resilience of the monarchy in the Middle East. *Political Science Quarterly*, 106(1), 1–15.
Ansani, A. & Daniele, V. (2012) About a revolution: The economic motivations of the Arab Spring. *International Journal of Development and Conflict*, 2(3), 1–24.
Antoun, R. T. (2006) Fundamentalism, bureaucratisation and the state's co-optation of religion: A Jordanian case study. *International Journal of Middle East Studies*, 38(3), 369–393.
Atieno, R. & Mitullah, W. V. (2010) *The Global Economic Crisis and its Impact on the Economy, Labour Markets, Migration and Development in North and West Africa*. Geneva: International Labour Organisation.
Bartels, L. M. (2005) Economic inequality and political representation. Woodrow Wilson School of Public and International Affairs. http://citeseerx.ist.psu.edu/viewdoc/summary?
Bates, T. R. (1975) Gramsci and the theory of hegemony. *Journal of the History of Ideas*, 36(2), 351–366.
Bird, K. (2003) The political representation of women and ethnic minorities in established democracies: A framework for comparative research. Working paper presented for the Academy of Migration Studies in Denmark (AMID), Aalborg University. https://www.hks.harvard.edu/fs/pnorris/Acrobat/stm103%20articles/Karen%20Bird%20amidpaper.pdf

Boutayeb, A. & Helmert, U. (2011) Social inequalities, regional disparities and health inequity in North African countries. *International Journal for Equity in Health*, 10(23).

Bozonnet, C. (2015) Political stability in Morocco cannot silence the murmurs of discontent. *The Guardian*, 9 March.

Carr, M. (2012) *Fortress Europe: Dispatches from a Gated Continent*. New York: The New Press.

Cavatorta, F. (2009) The civility and un-civility of the relations between secular and religious NGOs in Algeria. Paper prepared for the BRISMES workshop Liberation, Domination, Expression: Micro-political processes. University of St Andrews, 8–9 February.

Daadaoui, M. (2011) *Moroccan Monarchy and the Islamist Challenge: Maintaining Makhzen Power*. New York: Palgrave Macmillan.

Daoud, K. (2015) The Algerian exception. *New York Times*, 29 May.

Daragahi, B. (2011) Tunisia's uprising was three years in the making. *Los Angeles Times*, 27 January.

Dergham, R. (2011) The Arab Spring: A year of revolution. National Public Radio, 17 December. http://www.npr.org/2011/12/17/143897126/the-arab-spring-a-year-of-revolution

Drine, I. (2009) Impact of the global economic crisis on the Arab region. *UNU-Wider*. https://www.wider.unu.edu/publication/impact-global-economic-crisis-arab-region

Dubrow, J. K. (2014) *Political Inequality in the Age of Democracy: Cross-National Perspectives*. London: Routledge.

El Amrani, M. (2014) Morocco's spring: Gone but not forgotten. *Al Jazeera*, 4 April. http://www.aljazeera.com/blogs/middleeast/2014/02/98501.html

Elbelghiti, R. (2016) My Arab Spring: Clinging to hope in Morocco. Interview by El Amraoui. Al Jazeera, 22 February. http://www.aljazeera.com/news/2015/12/arab-spring-clinging-hope-morocco-151209063158008.html

ESCWA (Economic and Social Commission for Western Asia) (2013) *The Arab Millennium Development Goals Report: Facing Challenges and Looking Beyond 2015*. New York: UN Publications.

Gaber, Y. (2011) Egypt's labour movement takes a tumble. *Ahram*, 10 December. http://english.ahram.org.eg/NewsContent/1/0/28840/Egypt/0/Egypts-labour-movement-takes-a-tumble.aspx

Gebrewold, B. (2007) *Africa and Fortress Europe: Threats and Opportunities*. London: Ashgate.

Githens-Mazer, J. (2009) The blowback of repression and the dynamics of North African radicalization. *International Affairs*, 85(5), September, 1015–1029.

Gumede, W. (2005) *Thabo Mbeki and the Battle for the Soul of the ANC*. Cape Town: Struik Random House.

Gumede, W. (2011) Africa rising: Will the popular uprisings in North Africa go south of the Sahara? Briefing paper. London: Foreign Policy Centre.

Hanieh, A. (2013) *Lineages of Revolt: Issues of Contemporary Capitalism in the Middle East*. Chicago: Haymarket Books.

Heydemann, S. (ed.) (2004) *Networks of Privilege in the Middle East: The Politics of Economic Reform Revisited*. Basingstoke: Palgrave.

Ibrahim, E. (2012) Sixth of April 2008: A workers' strike which fired the Egyptian revolution. *Ahram*, 6 April. http://english.ahram.org.eg/NewsContent/1/64/38580/Egypt/Politics-/th-of-April--A-workers-strike-which-fired-the-Egyp.aspx

ILO (International Labour Organisation) (2009) *Global Employment Trends*. Geneva: ILO.

IMF (International Monetary Fund) (2011) *Regional Economic Outlook: Middle East and Central Asia*. World Economic and Financial Surveys. Washington DC: IMF.

Jamal, A. (2007) *Barriers to Democracy*. Princeton: Princeton University Press.

Joyce, R. (2013) The regional inequality behind Tunisia's revolution. *Atlantic Council*, 17 December. http://www.atlanticcouncil.org/blogs/menasource/the-regional-inequality-behind-tunisia-s-revolution

Kabeer, N. (2014) Social justice and the Millennium Development Goals: The challenge of intersecting inequalities. *Equal Rights Review*, 13, 91–116.

Kohstall, F. (2015) From reform to resistance: Universities and student mobilisation in Egypt and Morocco before and after the Arab uprisings. *British Journal of Middle Eastern Studies*, 42(1), 59–73.

Lageman, T. (2016) Mohamed Bouazizi: Was the Arab Spring worth dying for? *Al Jazeera*, 3 January. http://www.aljazeera.com/news/2015/12/mohamed-bouazizi-arab-spring-worth-dying-151228093743375.html

Lebovich, A. (2015) Deciphering Algeria: The stirrings of reform? Policy brief, European Council on Foreign Relations, Brussels.

Lehman Schlozman, K., Verba, S. & Brady, H. E. (2012) *The Unheavenly Chorus: Unequal Political Voice and the Broken Promise of American Democracy*. Princeton: Princeton University Press.

Liste, J., Kolster, J. & Matondo-Fundani, N. (2012) Political transitions and new socioeconomic bargains in North Africa. Economic brief. African Development Bank, Tunis.

Medien, K. (2016) Narrating the 'Arab Spring' – five years on. *Discover Society*, 29, February.

Monare, M. (2012) Mbeki warns South Africa. *Sunday Independent*, 7 October.

Mourad Sika, N. (2013) Dynamics of development and uprisings in the Arab World. *Mediterranean Quarterly*, 24(4), 43–67.

National Public Radio (2011) The Arab Spring: A year of revolution. *All Things Considered*, 17 December. http://www.npr.org/2011/12/17/143897126/the-arab-spring-a-year-of-revolution

Ncube, M. & Anyanwu, J. C. (2012) Inequality and Arab Spring revolutions in North Africa. African Development Bank. *Africa Economic Brief*, 3 (7), July.

OSCE (Organization for Security and Co-operation in Europe) (2007) Effective participation and representation in democratic societies. Warsaw: OSCE. http://www.osce.org/odihr/24995

Paz Arauco, V., Gazdar, H., Hevia-Pacheco, P., Kabeer, N., Lenhardt, A., Quratulain Masood, S., Naqvi, H., Nayak, N., Norton, A., Sadana Sabharwal, N., Scalise, E., Shepherd, A., Thapa, D., Thorat, S., Hien Tran, D., Vergara Camus, L., Woldehanna, T. & Mariotti, C. (2014) *Strengthening Social Justice to Address Intersecting Inequalities in the Post-2015 Agenda*. London: Overseas Development Institute.

Perry, D. (2016) Arab democracies? Not so fast, say some. *The Big Story, AP Analysis*, 9 April. http://bigstory.ap.org/article/14048cba70214fb1be30157252b9b665/ap-analysis-arab-democracies-not-so-fast-say-some

Ravallion, M. (2014) Income inequality in the developing world. *Science*, 344 (6186), 851–55.

Roberts, H. (2002) Moral economy or moral polity? The political anthropology of Algerian riots. Working paper no. 17. Development Research Centre, LSE.

Ross, M. H. (1997) Culture and identity in comparative analysis. In M. L. Lichbach & A. S. Zuckerman (eds) *Comparative Politics: Rationality, Culture and Structure.* Cambridge: Cambridge University Press.

Roth, K. (2012) Time to abandon the autocrats and embrace rights: The international response to the Arab Spring. New York: Human Rights Watch. https://www.hrw.org/world-report/2012/country-chapters/africa-americas-asia-europe/central-asia-middle-east/north-africa

Sadiki, L. (2010) Bin Ali Baba Tunisia's last bey? What will be the fate of the political succession in Tunisia? Will the ingredients for misrule continue to prevail? Al Jazeera, 27 September. http://www.aljazeera.com/indepth/opinion/2010/09/20109238338660692.html

Saif, I. & Choucair, F. (2009) Arab Countries Stumble in the Face of Growing Economic crisis. Washington DC: Carnegie Endowment.

Schutz, E. A. (2012) *Inequality and Power: The Economics of Class.* London: Routledge.

Sen, A. (1977) From income inequality to economic inequality. *Southern Economic Journal*, 64, 384–401.

Skocpol, T. (1982) Rentier state and Shi'a Islam in the Iranian revolution. *Theory and Society*, 11(3), May, 265–283.

Slackman, M. (2008) Day of angry protest stuns Egypt. *New York Times*, 6 April. http://www.nytimes.com/2008/04/06/world/africa/06iht-egypt.4.11708118.html?_r=0

Springborg, R. (2011) The precarious economics of Arab springs. *Survival: Global Politics and Strategy*, 53(6), 85–104.

Stiglitz, J. (2013) *The Price of Inequality.* London: Penguin.

Transparency International (2015) Vote out grand corruption. Unmaskthecorrupt.org. London.

UNDP (United Nations Development Programme) (2013) Humanity divided: Confronting inequality in developing countries. New York: UNDP.

UNDP (United Nations Development Programme) (2015) Perspectives on inequality challenges in the Arab region. Issues brief for the Arab Sustainability report. Cairo: UNDP.

Verme, P., Milanovic, B., Al-Shawarby, S., El Tawila, S., Gadallah, M. & El-Majeed, E. A. A. (2014) *Inside Inequality in the Arab Republic of Egypt: Facts and perceptions across people, time and space.* New York: World Bank.

Wahba, J. (2010) Labour markets performance and migration flows in Egypt. European Commission Directorate-General for Economic and Financial Affairs, Labour Markets Performance and Migration, Egypt, Palestine, Jordan, Lebanon. Occasional Papers No. 60. Brussels: European Commission.

Whitaker, B. (2010) How a man setting fire to himself sparked an uprising in Tunisia. *The Guardian*, 28 December. http://www.theguardian.com/commentisfree/2010/dec/28/tunisia-ben-ali

Willsher, K. (2011) French minister defends offer of security forces to Tunisia. *The Guardian*, January 18, London. https://www.theguardian.com/world/2011/jan/18/french-minister-tunisia-offer

World Bank (2008) *Economic Growth, Inequality and Poverty: Social mobility in Egypt between 2005 and 2008.* Policy Note. Washington DC: World Bank.

World Bank (2013) *Opening Doors: Gender equality and development in the Middle East and North Africa*. MENA Development Report. Washington DC: World Bank.

World Bank (2014) *Corrosive Subsidies. Middle East and North Africa Region Economic Monitor.* Washington DC: World Bank.

PART
FOUR

POWER AND CLASS REDEFINED – 'SIT DOWN AND LISTEN TO US'

CHAPTER
9

TO WIN FREE EDUCATION, FOSSILISED NEOLIBERALISM MUST FALL

Patrick Bond

INTRODUCTION

The most inspiring and surprising social movement to shake the South African state since the Treatment Action Campaign of the early 2000s was #FeesMustFall in October 2015. The primary demand – free tertiary education – is audacious. There are various cost estimates, depending upon demand-related assumptions or simply the prevailing political agenda: a spokesperson for the South African minister of higher education and training, Blade Nzimande (who was at the time opposed to fee-free universities), estimated R100 billion a year, although the 2013 figure from the same office was just R23 billion (that is, R27 billion in 2016 inflation-adjusted rands) (Petersen 2015). But even the centre-right Democratic Alliance estimated in late 2015 that free (albeit means-tested) tertiary education would cost R35 billion per annum (Bozzoli 2015). The students' secondary, immediate demands were that there should be a zero per cent fee increase in 2016 (effectively a 7 per cent+ decrease in fees, given rising inflation) and that all university staff should be paid properly and 'insourced'. The outsourcing in the early 2000s of low-paid cleaning, security, gardening and similar staff at most institutions had been repeatedly contested before 2015, but never successfully.

As argued below, these tens of billions of rands that should be considered for investment in the students' future compare favourably with *hundreds* of billions allocated by state agencies to mega-projects that are largely fossil-intensive (especially based upon coal and oil). The resulting climate change will irrevocably harm the current student generation's future. But will the students come to this realisation, and will it lead to creative political strategies that link issues and constituencies with just as radical a potential as was witnessed in 2015?

Unfortunately, the exceptional mobilisation in October 2015 had degenerated, at the time of writing in April 2016, to a situation characterised by divide-and-conquer student defeats at the hands of the ruling party and its allies in the Progressive Youth Alliance (PYA). The latter had control of most student representative councils, which in 2016 insisted that there be no further disruptive #FeesMustFall protests on the scale of October 2015. Meanwhile, opportunities to broaden the movement in relation to service delivery protests and the new left trade unionism were not being adequately explored. Socialist Youth Movement leader Trevor Shaku (2016) called for a reconstituted Free Education Movement, for, he claimed, the main problem with #FeesMustFall was that:

> the adventurist and populist leadership have, with lack in clear revolutionary tactics and strategies, mismanaged and thus ruined the favourable moments for harnessing the momentum. The results have been despair in what could have been nourishing of confidence for future local campaigns, and certainly national campaigns like free education. Recognising all this, the government tried to turn the concession forced out of it to its advantage by trying to drive a wedge between the mass and the militant minority ... the movement must link itself with other civil society movements fighting in the two other theatres of class struggle – communities and workplaces.

The despair should not be terminal, because in October 2015 just such alliances had been forged on campus and, to the amazement of much of society, the students' and workers' secondary demands were largely won within months. President Jacob Zuma announced a zero per cent fee rise for 2016 after his Union Buildings offices were besieged on 23 October 2015. In part because of the race and class backgrounds shared by most university students and workers, their common cause led to a string of insourcing victories. In only a few universities, (self-proclaimed impoverished) have managers been slow to agree on insourcing or have been duplicitous in its implementation, and in one high-profile incident workers and PYA students at Tshwane University of Technology physically fought each other at the campus gate due to a February 2016 labour strike that briefly prevented student access to buildings.

However, an era of apparent university austerity is one adverse unintended consequence of the students' short-term success, since the R2.3 billion additional 2016 funding for zero per cent fees was not sufficient for all the additional costs – for example, repairing several hundred million rands' worth of damage allegedly done by student protesters (though insurers pick up the bulk of that), or insourcing expenses. The latter were estimated by the University of KwaZulu-Natal (UKZN) management at R80 million per year alone following a dramatic increase in wages for lower-paid workers to a R6 000 per month average.

Renewed battles with Treasury loomed, for in February 2016 the most important constraint emerged to fulfilling the prior October's promises: national fiscal austerity. In turn, that austerity slows – and potentially reverses – two costly processes underway since the mid-1990s: making universities more racially and gender diverse (some are outrageously skewed, for example the University of Cape Town (UCT) with no black African women professors of South African citizenship out of more than 250 senior faculty), and making them more internationally competitive in terms of research output – which biased funding rewards those academics with high publishing levels in the neoliberal incentive-based payment system. The onset of university austerity is not surprising, for conventional wisdom held that, as Wits School of Governance visiting professor Graeme Bloch (2015) claimed in *The Conversation*, 'There are many problems for the government, including the state of the world economy, which ensures that there is not enough money' for free university education. Moreover, although a major commission studied the matter for the higher education minister, its report was buried for three years (Petersen 2015). This, in turn, reflected the (former communist) finance minister Pravin Gordhan's vulnerability, as a newspaper revealed in November 2015:

> Asked … why the findings of the report [about free tertiary education] and government's decision not to implement the policy were not released to the public in 2013, [Nzimande's spokesperson] replied: 'It is a public document, but due to the nature of the report, we decided not to make it public. Obviously we would have been setting the finance minister up against the public if that decision and report was released' (Petersen 2015).

If so, then can the finance minister can be more transparently understood ('set up') by students, when he is working 'against the public' interest, in contrast to the interests of South Africa's massive fossil-intensive industries (which continue to get generous state subsidies notwithstanding their role in planetary destruction) and international financial markets? The latter are ably represented by the Moody's, Standard & Poor's and Fitch Group's ratings agencies which put enormous explicit pressure on Gordhan to lower the budget deficit in 2016 – or by the likes of Goldman Sachs, Absa and Investec which have more implicit backroom persuasion techniques. Along with the Chinese state, whose ownership of Standard Bank suffered a large devaluation (Bruce 2016), the latter three institutions' local chief executives were sufficiently powerful to be given credit for installing a new finance minister (Gordhan) in mid-December 2015, after another powerful network – the Gupta family and their patronage allies – had installed their candidate (Desmond van Rooyen) four days earlier.

In this context of debate over which corporations have succeeded in 'state capture', the students' partially-successful battle for more funding from Treasury deserves full attention. In the next section of this chapter, we review the student forces arrayed against fiscal austerity and university fee increases in 2015, and disputes over whether the South African state is making a sufficient contribution to cover the cost of higher education. These critiques of state spending highlight aspects of state subsidies that harm the next generation insofar as they contribute to climate change, which will damage the current youth's futures, as shown in the third section. Then, drawing on the 2016 budget, in the fourth section we can identify other constituencies currently suffering austerity. Finally, in the concluding section, it is useful to ask (no matter if it is purely hypothetical), whether there is a scenario in which these forces unite to demand a different fiscal regime.

The need for an alternative narrative arises at a time of ferocious liberal attacks on Zuma and his Gupta patronage allies, and likewise by those forces on Gordhan (including threat of the finance minister's arrest). The liberal attacks have been joined by many progressives within a '#ZumaMustFall' movement that emerged immediately following the December 2015 finance minister shuffle, and that appeared likely to regain momentum after 783 corruption charges against Zuma were reinstated in April 2016. But the movement needed to consider the dangers of prioritising a good-governance agenda without reference (aside from the National Union of Metalworkers' warnings) to the likelihood that a *more* neoliberal, anti-poor agenda would result if Deputy President Cyril Ramaphosa replaced Zuma. In the process, Gordhan was insulated from most public criticisms, since he and his deputy Mcebisi Jonas – also a former leftist – are widely recognised as the fiscally responsible 'good guys' against the Gupta-related forces of state capture, nuclear spending and parastatal malgovernance.

As a result of this conjuncture, the most sophisticated and militant of the residual #FeesMustFall network, perhaps in alliance with South Africa's numerous other left-leaning forces, might consider giving much greater attention to reviving the successful strategies and tactics of 2015. Those student innovations included uniting with working-class and poor people (the outsourced university workers); taking physical space (blocking roads near campuses); and choosing targets that are national (not merely campus-based), including the Treasury. It is in these three strategic turns that the pressure on Gordhan can be increased, to make the hypothetical united front of activists *against neoliberalism – and with it, fossil-centric capital accumulation* – potentially feasible.

In short, if the strong momentum gathered in October 2015 was quickly destroyed by a variety of political dilemmas, some of which were internal to the student movement but some also external, at least one of the ways forward is for students and their civil society allies to better interrogate the power of financiers, mining houses and smelters – which are the beneficiaries of the budget at the expense of the students' present and future interests.

ARGUMENTS FOR FISCAL INVESTMENTS IN THE YOUTH

The focus on the fiscus is terribly important (in part because it is so rare), and this was recognised by several thousand students who began national-scale #FeesMustFall advocacy on 21 October 2015 when they stormed the parliamentary precinct in Cape Town. It was the day of the budgetary mid-term review. Prior to Pravin Gordhan, the 2014–2015 finance minister was Nhlanhla Nene, whose response that day – formally articulated in his budget speech – was that student protests were 'unconstructive'. The word was perhaps chosen by the Treasury's neoliberal speechwriters; it scornfully reveals a vast distance between those championing the austerity logic in Treasury on the one hand and, on the other, the logic of society's ascendant leadership at the elite universities, as well as the logic of the 63 per cent of society judged by University of Cape Town (UCT) economists to be living below the poverty line (Budlender et al. 2015).

As Reuters (2015) news agency tellingly reported, Nene 'downplayed the effect of university students storming Parliament as he delivered his medium-term budget on the credit rating of Africa's most advanced economy. "What matters for the ratings agencies is our response as government in addressing these challenges," he said about the students' demands to keep tuition fees unchanged.' The response taken by government security officials against the students that afternoon was described by many journalists as police brutality. Blade Nzimande (besuited) told the students briefly from behind a protective fence that they should accept a 6 per cent increase as a victory. They booed him, and he later joked, 'If these students don't accept this, we will start our own movement, students must fall' (and after intense criticism, he subsequently apologised). Also revealing 'what matters', in February 2015 Nene had relaxed exchange controls, allowing wealthy individuals to take R10 million out of the country each year, up from R4 million, while at the same time cutting grants to poor people by 3 per cent in real terms.

Having made an exceptionally powerful statement, different groups of students then marched in their thousands to the Johannesburg and Durban headquarters of the African National Congress (ANC) on 22 and 23 October, and finally demonstrated – more than ten thousand strong – at Zuma's Pretoria office on 23 October. There, restraining fences were torn down by some of the activists. Tyres and latrines were burned, and police once again responded with stun grenades, rubber bullets and water cannons. Refusing to come out to address the crowd, Zuma instead held a press conference where he conceded to the students' demand for a zero per cent fee increase in 2016 following several universities' attempt to raise prices into double digits. (It was the University of the Witwatersrand's 10.5 per cent increase that on 4 October 2015 spurred the original national awareness of the crisis, although at the University of KwaZulu-Natal two weeks earlier the burning of the administration building was already an indication of extreme opposition to higher 2016 fees.)

In late 2015, Nzimande used adult and vocational education 'surpluses' to fund most of the R2.3 billion required. In February 2016, the main state budget line item for 'university education' was R39 531 603 000 (R39.5 billion), an increase of 21 per cent from R32.8 billion in 2015, and with inflation in 2016 estimated at 7 per cent this amounted to a real rise of 14 per cent (Nene's October 2015 medium-term budget had pegged a nominal increase of just 6.3 per cent annually for the coming three years.) No other major budget line item was boosted so substantially. The largest share of the increase, however, was not for operating grants, but for the National Student Financial Aid Scheme (NSFAS) which, largely in loan form, anticipates repayment. Its budget allocation rose 78 per cent from R6.3 billion to R11.2 million (after inflation, a 71 per cent rise). But the loans must be repaid, a process the NSFAS has reportedly found extremely difficult to enforce given how many people graduate from university without job prospects.

Even with such a large increase, the amounts appear to be well short of a reasonable state contribution to higher education. The 2013 report of the Ministerial Committee for the Review of the Funding of Universities found that state 'funding is not sufficient to meet the needs of the public university system ... Government should increase the funding for higher education, to be more in line with international levels of expenditure' (Department of Higher Education and Training 2013). The same mandate to correct the universities' race and class access bias came from Ramaphosa at the October 2015 higher education summit in Durban:

> Africans account for 79 per cent of the population in the country, yet their gross participation rate in higher education is less than 15 per cent. The low participation rate of the majority of South Africans is untenable – both from a social justice perspective and in terms of meeting the demands of the twenty-first century and the needs of our economy. Higher levels of funding and the expansion of the capacity of the higher education system will be needed in future to ensure that higher levels of participation of African and coloured students are achieved.

A statement released simultaneously by the Democratic Alliance's Belinda Bozzoli (2015) concurred:

> [the Ministerial Committee] found that South Africa's budget for universities as a percentage of GDP was only 0.75 per cent, which is lower than the Africa-wide proportion of 0.78 per cent, the world-wide proportion of 0.84 per cent and the proportion spent by Organisation for Economic Cooperation and Development (OECD) countries of 1.21 per cent. The report also noted that between 2000 and 2010, state funding per full-time equivalent student fell by 1.1 per cent annually in real terms, while fees per each of these students increased by 2.5 per cent annually in the same period ... While President Zuma announced that a Task Team will be

established to find short-term solutions to student funding challenges, this Task Team will be set up to fail if it does not include representation from Treasury. More needs to be done, urgently.

The penultimate sentence is vital because even the centre-right DA – usually very supportive of the government's neoliberal bloc – alleges that the National Treasury has been hiding during this ferocious debate. Behind the fiscal conservatism of Treasury (in Pretoria) are the men they report to in the biggest financial institutions and credit rating agencies (mostly in Sandton). But those men have experienced an exceptionally profitable period, and their ability to disguise profits through misinvoicing and related tax-avoidance techniques is well understood, though it continues apparently unabated. The students were making demands upon the state at a time when the economy was slowing and fiscal revenues – especially from corporate taxation – were declining. But this is certainly one area where the broader class struggle could be pursued in future, with students joining many other constituencies to demand higher and more rigorous taxation, tightened exchange controls, and more courageous economic regulation of transnational and local corporations.

ARGUMENTS FOR NOT INVESTING *AGAINST* THE YOUTH

Until most of the mining and smelting corporations were nearly destroyed by the 2011–2015 commodity price crash, large firms operating in South Africa enjoyed what the International Monetary Fund (IMF) (2013) recorded as among the world's highest profit rates. By many accounts, this was not honestly-acquired wealth, for according to surveys by PriceWaterhouseCoopers (2016) in both 2014 (Hosken 2014) and 2016, Sandton elites remain intent on committing economic corruption at the world's fastest rate. In December 2015, the Washington nongovernmental organisation Global Financial Integrity (2015) recorded an average $21 billion in annual illicit financial flows from South Africa from 2004 to 2013, and in March 2016 the leaked 'Panama papers' began to unravel some revealing relationships between South Africans and tax havens (albeit the tip of the iceberg). Several specific firms had earlier been named by activists and researchers as being guilty of invoice manipulations ('transfer pricing') and other tax-avoidance strategies: MTN and Lonmin (both of which were led – as board chair and main minority investor, respectively –

during the offshoring period by Ramaphosa), the other two major platinum firms (Implats and Amplats) (AIDC 2015) and De Beers (Bracking and Sharife 2014). The corporations do not pay a particularly high primary tax rate – 28 per cent – compared to the 48 per cent they paid during the last decade of apartheid, when exchange controls were the main way the state ensured capital stayed within the country. After 1994, deregulation of exchange controls occurred on more than three dozen occasions, a situation that could easily be reversed in line with international trends. *The Economist* magazine proclaimed a newly 'Gated Globe' because of resurgent capital controls imposed by many countries following the 2008 turbulence, notably including China in mid-2015 and early 2016 as its stock market lost trillions of dollars in notional values.

Treasury also funds many incentive schemes for corporations' benefit, and these are utilised but without many obvious backward or forward linkages into the economy (such as cheap electricity to BHP Billiton/South32 and Anglo American Corporation, auto industry subsidies and the steel industry's increased tariff protection). Were it not for state and parastatal infrastructure spending, the levels of gross fixed capital formation would be at record lows. Yet, at the time students were protesting for more resources, South African corporations had acknowledged reserves of R700 billion in what was essentially idle cash, suggesting that the profit motive for the 'real economy' had become far too low, compared to what corporate treasurers can earn by parking their cash in speculative investments, for example in the Johannesburg Stock Exchange (which hit a record 55 000 index level in October 2015) and real estate (which outstrips nearly all world markets). There was certainly no shortage of savings in South Africa's economy, given how rapidly the stock market's and property's value had grown as a result of speculative financial bubbles, at a time when investment in the real economy withered.

To illustrate further, as a clear signal to students about where Treasury's priorities lay, among the most generously subsidised projects are those in the state's Presidential Infrastructure Coordinating Commission (PICC) programme that promotes, first, exceptionally destructive coal exports via Richards Bay, mainly by multinational corporations; second, the Durban port-petrochemical complex's expansion; and third, iron-ore exports. Yet there is vast world over-capacity in coal, shipping and steel, leaving South Africa's second major steel producer (Evraz Highveld) in bankruptcy and the largest (Arcelor Mittal) sharply cutting back on its main foundries' output. But these white elephant mega-projects continue to get the largest share of state, parastatal and private infrastructure funding.

The PICC, led by the economic development minister, Ebrahim Patel, will coordinate state spending of more than R1 trillion. Although there are excellent small-scale initiatives within the PICC's Strategic Infrastructure Project portfolio, many of the largest are highly dubious and require more aggressive watchdogging by civil society. There is an aura around the word 'infrastructure,' no matter for what purpose, as if the state has an open-ended mandate to 'build it, and they will come'. The precise winners and losers are rarely interrogated. As former e.tv head Marcel Golding revealed in his court battle over control of the station in 2014, Patel's infrastructure mega-projects were promoted generously on eNews just prior to a national election in exchange for Patel's offering set-top box tender favours to Golding (that were never delivered). With this extent of structured fiscal corruption, students can play an extremely useful role in society by drawing attention to the ways that state subsidisation of irrational mega-projects imposes opportunity costs – including foregone education funding – that deserve a rethink and then a budget reprioritisation.

To illustrate, Gordhan's budget speech (2016) noted: 'Transport and logistics infrastructure accounts for nearly R292 billion over the next three years under Minister Peters's oversight. Transnet is acquiring 232 diesel locomotives for its general freight business and 100 locomotives for its coal lines.' But when the highest-priority PICC project – an expanded 464 km railroad link from the Waterberg coal fields in Limpopo to Richards Bay that will carry an anticipated 18 *billion* tonnes of coal over its lifespan – was envisaged, the price of coal was rising. It reached a peak of $170/tonne in 2008 but then dropped to a level in early 2016 of around $50 per tonne. Transnet chief executive Siyabonga Gama estimated in 2011 that the rail line could raise the area's coal exports from 4 to 80 million tonnes a year (Flak 2011). But even the industry's leading insider expert, Xavier Prevost, admits that coal exports had become a money loser by 2015 (Creamer 2015). (Cynics may argue that the subsidisation is critical to state-connected coal corporations such as the Guptas' Oakbay and the former Ramaphosa firm Shanduka, or that the vast bulk of the spending is in KwaZulu-Natal, with the rail line running not far from Zuma's Nkandla homestead.)

The second highest-priority PICC mega-project will also cost hundreds of billions of rands: the South Durban Dig Out Port (on the old Durban airport site). This project aims to increase annual shipping-container traffic from levels of 2.5 million (stagnant from 2010 to 2016) to a new capacity of 20 million by 2040, according to the National Development Plan (other experts suggest 12 million is more reasonable). The project will also double oil refining capacity in South Durban (a residential area already saturated with toxins), with the new Transnet oil pipeline from Durban to Johannesburg originally estimated to cost R6 billion having been redirected from white to black neighbourhoods by the then CEO Maria Ramos, ultimately costing R24 billion by the time it is complete in late 2016. Once again, the port expansion is being subsidised generously with taxpayer funds, yet the Baltic Dry Index – the main measurement of shipping demand and pricing – is at an all-time historic low, having peaked at above 12 500 in 2008 and fallen to below 300 by early 2016. Either the South Durban investments will become yet another of Durban's white elephant projects (like the airport, Dube Trade Port, and Point redevelopment) or, if it is miraculously successful in raising the level of traffic by millions of containers in the coming quarter-century, the project's success will have the effect of de-industrialising many South African manufacturing zones adversely affected by the import wave.

In these two specific instances, the vast subsidies that Treasury and Transnet will provide to the corporate sector do not contribute to the present younger generation's prosperity and environmental conditions. On the contrary, they are much more likely to harm their prospects, through climate change and through fewer labour-intensive manufacturing job opportunities. The student movement should easily be able to raise these as fiscal concerns, and they should resonate with the broader society. After all, in the Pew Research polls of South African public opinion, two issues have consistently ranked as the highest in the recordings of the society's concerns about the world: climate change and international economic volatility (Carle 2015). South Africans are justifiably concerned about carbon-intensive economies – of which theirs is among the world's worst – and about local vulnerability to the kinds of global economic swings that reduce commodity prices and the value of firms operating in South Africa by such extreme amounts. Shareholders in Lonmin witnessed the price falling more than 99 per cent from peak in the 2008–2011 period to trough in 2015, Anglo American more than 90 per cent and Glencore more than 85 per cent.

These desperate, carbon-intensive big businesses – especially the group Ben Fine and Zav Rustomjee (1996) termed the minerals-energy complex (not just the Gupta family but the much bigger set of mining houses operating in South Africa) – remain extremely powerful when it comes to subsidy allocations. For example, the world's largest mining house, BHP Billiton ('South32', formerly South Africa's Gencor prior to 1990s mergers), still gets electricity at one-tenth of the price of ordinary consumers, and at peak consumes 5 per cent of the grid's output. When the Energy Intensive Users Group of mining houses and smelters (responsible for 44 per cent of consumption) needed an increase in electricity supply, Eskom turned to privatised electricity producers for renewable energy instead of using its own resources. In spite of their reported opposition to a nuclear deal apparently struck by Zuma in Moscow in 2014, both Nene (2015) and Gordhan (2016) made a R200 million down-payment on what are likely to be Moscow-sourced Rosatom reactors that could easily cost in excess of $100 billion, as well as the first funding tranche for another pro-corporate investment, the Brics (Brazil, Russia, India, China and South Africa) New Development Bank (NDB), whose target capitalisation (spread among five countries) is $100 billion. One Brics bank director, Tito Mboweni, is on record saying that the nuclear deal 'falls squarely within the mandate of the NDB' (Bloomberg News 2015).

In short, the students could readily have demanded – and still can – that the state and parastatal budgets be restructured to reflect:
- the students' educational needs as a younger generation preparing for employment, so that the state's human capital investment will be valued in a skills-scarce national economy
- the collapse of the prices of many exported raw materials, which should, in turn, be reflected in a redesigned National Development Plan, PICC and Transnet infrastructure investments (the largest items mentioned in Gordhan's February 2016 Budget Speech; Bond 2016)
- the danger that if such investments continue to be made, the minerals-energy complex will grow stronger and the country's contribution to climate change will also rise beyond the 34 per cent cut in emissions (below 'growth without constraints') during the 2020s that was repeatedly promised by Pretoria negotiators at the United Nations climate summits, which in turn will endanger the country's future as other countries also fail to honour their commitments (Bond 2012).

UNITING WITH OTHER CONSTITUENCIES PEERING OVER THE FISCAL CLIFF

Students opposed to the low level of university funding and the simultaneous use of taxpayer funds on projects such as carbon-intensive infrastructure can at least make common cause with numerous social forces also firmly opposed to the austerity trend. These include those community activists and patients of the public health system who have been witnessing the degeneration of fiscal support in their sectors of municipal finance, housing, water and healthcare.

Again, consider the context, this time bottom-up. The #FeesMustFall movement's first short-term victory comes at a time that the ANC is confronting unprecedented economic pressure and social unrest. The GDP growth rate fell from just 1.5 per cent in 2015 to an estimated 0.4 per cent in 2016, at a time of a 1.3 per cent population growth rate and no hope of an upturn in the foreseeable future. South Africa is the most income-unequal of any major country, and 'tokenistic' grant payments (for example, R350 per month for most beneficiaries, who are children), 'free basic services' and an unfunded national health insurance make little or no difference, and sometimes (as in water provision) have had the *opposite* effect because of Pretoria's social policy neoliberalism (Bond 2014). The rise in social grant payments offered by Nene and Gordhan was consistently below an inflation rate that by 2016 was anticipated in double digits for poor people, with much higher food, electricity and transport costs than affect wealthier South Africans. Anger has risen across the subaltern spectrum, and the World Economic Forum's *Global Competitiveness Report 2015–2016* judged the South African working class as the most militant on earth – the same position among 140 countries held since 2012, when thirty-four mineworkers were massacred at Marikana – not long after the South African Police Service had reported that in 2014 nearly 2 300 protests turned 'violent' (in police terminology) (Africa News Agency 2015). The 2015 police record of violent protests was far higher, at 3 542, in part due to the student upsurge.

The August 2016 municipal elections will reflect how difficult the ANC has found either suppression or satisfaction of the protesters. Can students unite with their generational peers who are not in university, and who so regularly take to the streets against all manner of local grievances in the townships, shack settlements and shop floors where most unrest is recorded? (The potential is certainly reflected in the way that cultural reflections of dissent, including use of fire and excrement, moved in 2015 from townships to campuses.) The possibilities of such unity were observable once, starting on 4 October 2015 at Wits, when the casualised university workers were explicitly identified as allies by progressive students. (Earlier attempts at such alliance-building at sites such as UCT and UKZN were not successful beyond a handful of student supporters of insourcing.)

But there are important reasons for caution. The rough class structure of black 'African' society is usually expressed as a small but rising (and debt-encumbered) lower middle class, the working class and the huge unemployed and low-income majority (again, with a 63 per cent poverty rate). The students generally come from the first generation of university attendees, and it is no insult to posit that they aspire to move from the working class to the middle class or, in the case of students at the technical universities, to acquire stronger artisanal skills. Their ability to view the ceilings they face, and to contest various aspects of the university education they receive, is reminiscent of the great massification of universities in Europe and North America during the 1960s, when many of the radical leaders were from first-generation, working-class backgrounds. That they reject the implicit promise of ANC rule – a guaranteed career and black empowerment benefits – is important in material and ideological terms. Their recognition that a university degree is certainly not a guarantee of employment, and their ideological antipathy to nationalist, populist politicians, together give these students the same kind of potential for national leadership that the 1950s ANC Youth League soon attained, breaking through ossified leaderships who fail to spell out the struggle in terms that the wider society is ready to listen to. That they take up 'decolonisation', raise 'the land question' and demand redistribution to address the entirety of persistently racist, sexist social relations also reflects this maturity.

However, the danger remains that once the heat of battle subsides the students will retreat to a relatively class-privileged position instead of pursuing this historic challenge of economic justice. Geographically, one of the main divide-and-conquer strategies adopted by the apartheid regime and big business for about a decade starting in the mid-1980s onwards, was to spatially segment the housing market and encumber the higher echelons of the black working class with debt (Bond 2000; 2014). The impact, today, is that many townships and shack settlements are no longer home to the higher-paid shop stewards and other experienced labour leaders who, in the 1980s, had been both worker and community activists, conjoining their union leadership with their roles in the South African National Civic Organisation. It was not atypical for the civic and trade union officials to wear two hats, and to turn their geographic segregation to advantage. The spatial compression of class, until the Group Areas Act was overturned in 1991, in turn allowed the progressive activists much more coherence in their anti-apartheid protests. Demands for access to water and sanitation, electricity, housing and transport regularly featured as combined worker-community protest rationales.

The political genius of neoliberalism lies, in part, in its fragmentation of opposition. Since the mid-1990s, the most important barrier to making generalised community demands against the Treasury has been the 'popcorn' character of protests: they are segregated, atomised, ideology-free and very rarely link up even with neighbouring activism. Indeed, many turn explicitly xenophobic when, instead of a municipal target, immigrant shop-owners so often become the subject of community anger. Emanating from thousands of violent protests, especially since the late 1990s when urban neoliberalism took on its main features (Bond 2000), there have been sporadic but nearly entirely unsuccessful attempts at organising up-scale. To, illustrate, recall the metropolitan Gauteng anti-neoliberal coalition known as the Anti-Privatisation Forum (APF). It was founded in 2000 after the University of the Witwatersrand Urban Futures conference, in part by radical students who – like Prishani Naidoo and Ahmed Veriava – were, by 2015, lecturers involved in #FeesMustFall. But notwithstanding exceptional victories in specific sites, including Johannesburg metropolitan-scale service delivery policy, the APF had become moribund by 2012, in part due to organisational failure (McKinley 2012).

The United Front was a 2014 innovation that reflected the prior failure of communities to unify across space and of social movements to unify across sector. It was funded initially (but inadequately) by the National Union of Metalworkers of South Africa (Numsa), which itself became one of society's most vital independent radical forces after denouncing the ANC Alliance in late 2013. By 2016, however, the Front had failed to find its footing notwithstanding (largely paper) membership of 400 radical social change organisations. Part of that problem was the inability of Numsa leaders to generalise their ambition to establish a strong independent left in civil society. To some extent this reflected internal debates about whether a new workers' federation (announced in May 2016) or even a workers' party should take precedence. But Numsa also faced financial problems following a R90 million shortfall on its income due to the expiry of some bargaining agreements. In any case, there were approaches to the student movement in late 2015 but the discussions and offers of assistance did not materially change conditions, probably because, like most of society, even Numsa and the United Front were unprepared for the extraordinary upsurge in student protest.

The other dilemma for students was that they had multiple political tendencies: the PYA with its South African Communist Party (SACP) and ANC Youth League dominance; the Economic Freedom Fighters; pan-Africanist youth; and independent progressives. The Numsa/Front was just one of various competing projects. The splits in the student movement that resulted from competing tendencies have been partially documented, but the overall question remains: do students have the potential to again cross-class boundaries by uniting with low-paid workers, take physical space as semi-liberated sites to build that unity, and generate a national movement that takes on national targets such as Treasury?

If so, that would allow several constituencies to find unity in political demands that could include fiscal policy. In February 2016, after all, Gordhan cut the real budget available in 2016–2017 (and beyond) not only for social grants but also for municipalities – including the R53 billion equitable share and R14 billion municipal infrastructure grant that redistributes from centre to local (4 per cent) – for water (12.4 per cent) notwithstanding bulk and retail supply crises across the country, and for housing (12.5 per cent). He cut the already tokenistic national health insurance scheme to the bone. In this context of austerity, an oppositional programme could rise, taking on Treasury, the Reserve Bank and also the ratings agencies and financiers who apply such pressure, based on three arguments:

- the state has the ability to raise sufficient funding to meet social needs
- the social spending component of the fiscus has been far too low
- interest rates should be decreased, which would allow for more state borrowing (although exchange controls would need to be re-imposed to curtail capital flight) and also reduce South Africans' extreme debt load, including that of recent graduates whose repayment rates are miserable.

First, state borrowing could be substantially raised. In the last comparison available (Barclays Capital 2012), both the total accumulated public debt and annual deficit are below that of most peer economies and far below the wealthy countries' debt levels. In historical terms, the South African public debt today is by no means at an excessive level.

Second, in comparative terms, South African social spending (as a share of GDP) typically ranks in the lowest five countries among the Organisation for Economic Cooperation and Development's rankings of the forty major economies, about half the rate that Brazil and Russia spend, for example, and a seventh as much as France (Bond 2014).

Third, interest rates are far too high and as a result debt repayment charges (for the state and students alike) are far beyond what they should be. Since the mid-1990s, when exchange controls were liberalised, the Reserve Bank has adopted a policy of imposing excessively high interest rates so as to attract foreign funds. The main way that the largest Northern governments (US, EU, Japan, UK) dealt with their own recent fiscal squeeze was printing currency (a practice termed 'quantitative easing'). Bank bailouts required many trillions of dollars of direct and indirect subsidies after 2008. In contrast, the South African Reserve Bank aims to keep inflation in the 3–6 per cent band, using extremely high interest rates, which are entirely inappropriate given the economically depressed state of the economy. At the time of the student protests in October 2015, only Brazil, Russia, Turkey, Indonesia and Pakistan (among those which can be measured by ten-year government bonds) had higher interest rates. The situation worsened, as several Reserve Bank rate increases were imposed in 2015–2016.

However, if students and their allies in civil society advance the arguments made above, they will face both intellectual and policy resistance. First, there is the fatuous Reserve Bank (2015) claim that 'the very low savings ratio of South Africa requires relatively high interest rates'. Yet, as noted above, there are plenty of loose savings available in South Africa, as witnessed by how much money sloshes around in the Johannesburg Stock Exchange and in real estate, which in both cases are at the very top range of the world's most speculative markets (Bond 2014). The amount corporations hold in cash is said to approach R1 trillion, as they lack profitable investment outlets. Alleged savings shortages are not a factor, in reality.

Neoliberals do have one valid rebuttal to these arguments: if interest rates are lowered and social spending and state borrowing raised, *there will be even worse capital flight*. This is indeed a very serious problem, in terms of both illicit financial flows and licit, legal outflows of profits, dividends and interest (termed the 'balance of payments' within the current account). To pay these flows in hard currency, the Reserve Bank must borrow abroad, resulting in South Africa's total *foreign debt* rising from \$25 billion in 1994 to \$125 billion by 2016 (nearly the same share of GDP as P. W. Botha faced in 1985 when he defaulted), as distinguished from public *domestic debt* which is still manageable and can grow. In addition to illicit financial flows (R330 billion annually from 2004–2013), the licit outflows of profits, dividends and interest in 2015 exceeded R140 billion. (In comparison, the trade deficit was only R34 billion.)

The solution to these pressures is simple: re-imposition of exchange controls. This will be especially important in late 2016 or 2017 when formal 'junk bond' status is likely to be imposed by the credit ratings agencies. Such capital controls worked in the period 1985–1995 when the 'finrand' helped to stop capital flight, at a time when the apartheid state was a victim of successful solidaristic protest in mid-1985 (when P. W. Botha's 'Rubicon speech' meant activists could further delegitimise South Africa). They are also a vital tool for national economic sovereignty in a world beset by extreme financial turbulence. As John Maynard Keynes (1933) once explained, 'In my view the whole management of the domestic economy depends upon being free to have the appropriate interest rate without reference to the rates prevailing in the rest of the world. Capital control is a corollary to this.'

Several other items in the mid-term budget that Nene had advocated were slightly adjusted by Gordhan in 2016, most notably the South African National Defence Force which is taking an R8 billion reduction in coming years. But there could be further cuts, for if South Africa were to become a more peaceful society as a result of higher social spending and lower interest rates (payment of interest at current rates will cost the state R148 billion in 2016–2017), two items could be reduced quickly. Security cluster spending – R182 billion in 2016–2017 – is lower than Nene had offered, in spite of the state allocating itself R3.3 billion extra in 2015 for personnel and armaments against civilians (for example, students), including high-pitch sonic sound cannons (Mabuza and Hosken 2015).

The police epidemic of self-destructive, extreme brutality suggests that weapons should be holstered, not fired. However, the 2016 budget statement by David Mahlobo, minister of state security (2016) was ominous, suggesting a rising degree of paranoia: 'The forces that are opposed to us are hard at work … Some of these protesters are undermining the authority of the state by engaging in acts that seek to provoke the law enforcement agencies hence some people have acted with impunity by killing members of the security agencies.' Mahlobo noted that unspecified NGOs 'work to destabilise the state … They are just security agents that are being used for covert operations'. They have 'very funny names' and fund the student movement, as do others that 'are hard at work in certain parts of our globe using various role players to promote their agenda whilst undermining national security of various countries'.

In addition, as noted, the Treasury's category 'economic infrastructure' includes many ill-considered projects. Aside from the carbon-intensive PICC projects, the biggest current infrastructure bill is for Eskom's coal-fired power plants, backed by a World Bank $3.75 billion loan (its largest ever, but one whose repayment should be deeply discounted thanks to lack of Bank due diligence). Recall that Eskom chair Valli Moosa improperly allowed the ANC's Chancellor House to front for Hitachi on a R60 billion tender that drove the price up by many more tens of billions, as 7 000 welds needed to be redone at Medupi, which fell seven years behind construction schedule (Hunter 2015). And much larger white elephants loom on the horizon: the R300 billion share Pretoria has committed to capitalising a Brics bank for corporate infrastructure (Bond 2016) and the trillion rand estimated for eight nuclear reactors (Faull 2015). Such subsidies to the rich and powerful by corrupt politicians are often openly admitted, for as Zuma himself put it rather unguardedly in October 2015, 'I always say to business people that if you invest in the ANC, you are wise. If you don't invest in the ANC, your business is in danger … This organisation does not make profit, but we create a conducive environment to those who make profit' (quoted in Letsoalo and Hunter 2015).

CONCLUSION

The essence of politics in South Africa is alliance building, and students who mobilised for a zero per cent fees increase in 2016, plus the insourcing of outsourced workers, did a remarkable job in their initial efforts to move across class, to move across space and to move across scale. Much of the obvious political challenge to power in the 2015–2016 protests related to race, decolonisation and the restructuring of university power. A few nominal changes were made, and major demands are still outstanding in relation to curriculum reform, shifting the race and gender make-up of the professoriate, and ending the alienation of black, female and LGBTIAQ+ students (see Chapter 1 of this volume).

However, this chapter has merely addressed the most serious outstanding challenge: achieving free tertiary education by identifying processes associated with the students' adverse class power, the 'state capture' of financial institutions, fiscal options (including the generationally-vital opportunity costs and benefits of defunding fossil-fuel mega-projects in favour of human capital investment), and the politics therein. This review of the political economy of the students' major demand has concluded that to win free education, worker insourcing and genuinely decolonised universities, the students will inexorably demand that #NeoliberalismMustFall and that #FossilFuelsMustFall. And if this transcends #FeesMustFall and #ZumaMustFall, the Fallists will then be joining a major process underway across the world: the 'double movement' to the Polanyian project of resisting the marketisation of society. If Karl Polanyi's (1944) thesis can be updated to account for potential ecological catastrophe (Burawoy 2014), then this student generation will logically link their demands for more university spending to the critique of carbon-intensive infrastructure spending advanced above.

It is true, Naomi Klein (2014) argues, that 'This [climate] changes everything'. Recall, finally, the October 2015 mobilisation of social support across South Africa that contributed to the exceptional pressure mounted against the Zuma government – more than the countervailing pressure of neoliberals in Treasury and the ratings agencies, at least for R2.3 billion's sake. If the argument above is sound, there is every potential for students and their community, youth, labour, feminist and environmental allies to find routes forward to a new society, by building on society's legitimate grievances and demanding the ecological and socioeconomic benefits that would follow an end to both the influence of the neoliberal bloc represented by Gordhan, and the populist patronage of Zuma's last allies. As that battle continues to unfold – as it will for years to come – a progressive alternative stands ready to claim more space, and as #FeesMustFall did on three sunny days in October 2015, to win surprising reforms.

REFERENCES

Africa News Agency (2015) 14 740 service delivery protests in 2014/15. *IOL*, 15 May.

AIDC (Alternative Information & Development Centre) (2015) Lonmin, the Marikana massacre and the Bermuda connection. http://aidc.org.za/lonmin-the-marikana-massacre-and-the-bermuda-connection-seminar-and-press-conference/

Barclays Capital (2012) Global Portfolio Managers' Digest. London.

Bloch, G. (2015) Free education is a worthy goal, but South Africa isn't ready for it yet. *The Conversation*, 22 October. https://theconversation.com/free-education-is-a-worthy-goal-but-south-africa-isnt-ready-for-it-yet-49414

Bloomberg News (2015) $100 billion Brics lender more keen on risk than World Bank. http://www.bloomberg.com/news/articles/2015-07-10/brics-100-billion-lender-seeks-riskier-projects-than-world-bank

Bond, P. (2000) *Cities of Gold, Townships of Coal*. Trenton: Africa World Press.

Bond, P. (2012) *Politics of Climate Justice*. Pietermaritzburg: University of KwaZulu-Natal Press.

Bond, P. (2014) *Elite Transition*. London: Pluto Press.

Bond, P. (2016) Brics banking and the debate over sub-imperialism. *Third World Quarterly*, 37(4), 611–629.

Bozzoli, B. (2015) Wits protests show Nzimande's failure. *PoliticsWeb*, 15 October.

Bracking, S. & Sharife, K. (2014) Rough and polished. Manchester University Leverhulme Centre for the Study of Value. Working Paper 4. http://thestudyofvalue.org/wp-content/uploads/2014/05/WP4-Bracking-Sharife-Rough-and-polished-15May.pdf

Bruce, P. (2016) China checks the SA cards it's played. *Business Day*, 12 February.

Budlender, S., Woolard, I. & Leibbrandt, M. (2015) How current measures underestimate the level of poverty in South Africa. *The Conversation*, 3 September. https://theconversation.com/how-current-measures-underestimate-the-level-of-poverty-in-south-africa-46704

Burawoy, M. (2014) Marxism after Polanyi. In M.Williams and V. Satgar (eds) *Marxisms in the 21st Century*. Johannesburg: Wits University Press.

Carle, J. (2015) Climate change seen as top global threat. *Pew Research Centre*, 14 July. http://www.pewglobal.org/2015/07/14/climate-change-seen-as-top-global-threat/

Creamer, M. (2015) Prevost drops coal bombshell. *Engineering News*, 30 September.

Department of Higher Education and Training (2013) Report of the Ministerial Committee for the Review of the Funding of Universities. Pretoria.

Faull, L. (2015) Exposed: Scary details of SA's secret Russian nuke deal. *Mail & Guardian*, 13 February.

Fine, B. & Rustomjee, Z. (1996) *The Political Economy of South Africa*. London and Johannesburg: Christopher Hirst and Wits University Press.

Flak, A. (2011) South Africa's Transnet eyes 80 mln tonnes on Waterberg line. *Reuters*, 6 October.

Global Financial Integrity (2015) *Illicit Financial Flows from Developing Countries*. Washington DC. http://www.gfintegrity.org/report/illicit-financial-flows-from-developing-countries-2004-2013/

Gordhan, P. (2016) Budget speech. Parliament of the Republic of South Africa, Cape Town, 26 February.

Hosken, G. (2014) World fraud champs. *TimesLIVE*, 19 February.

Hunter, Q. (2015) Hitachi and Chancellor House: How the events unfolded. *Mail & Guardian*, 29 September.

International Monetary Fund (2013) South Africa: 2013 Article IV consultation. 1 October. https://www.imf.org/external/pubs/cat/longres.aspx?sk=40971.0

Keynes, J. M. (1933) National self-sufficiency. *Yale Review*. http://www.panarchy.org/keynes/national.1933.html

Klein, N. (2014) *This Changes Everything*. New York: Knopf.

Letsoalo, M. & Hunter, Q. (2015) Your business is in danger if you don't donate to the ANC – Zuma. *Mail & Guardian*, 9 October.

Mabuza, K. & Hosken, G. (2015) Ghetto blaster. *TimesLIVE*, 22 January.

Mahlobo, D. (2016) Budget vote for Department of State Security Agency. Parliament of the Republic of South Africa, Cape Town, 26 April.

McKinley, D. (2012) *Transition's Child*. Johannesburg: Rosa Luxemburg Foundation.

Nene, N. (2015) Medium-term budget policy statement. Parliament of the Republic of South Africa, Cape Town, 21 October.

Petersen, C. (2015) Free higher learning plans. *Cape Times*, 25 October.

Polanyi, K. (1944) *The Great Transformation*. Boston: Beacon Press.

PriceWaterhouseCoopers (2016) Global economic crime survey 2016: Adjusting the lens on economic crime. http://www.pwc.com/gx/en/services/advisory/consulting/forensics/economic-crime-survey.html

Ramaphosa, C. (2015) Apartheid rulers denied education to black majority. *PoliticsWeb*, 15 October.

Reserve Bank, South Africa (2015) Interest rates and how they work. https://www.resbank.co.za/Lists/News%20and%20Publications/Attachments/5000/Fact%20Sheet%208.pdf

Reuters (2015) South Africa's finance minister says rating agencies watching govt's response to student protests, 21 October.

Shaku, T. (2016) Lessons of fees must fall. *TheJournalist.org*, 20 April.
The Economist (2013) The gated globe. http://www.economist.com/news/special-report/21587384-forward-march-globalisation-has-paused-financial-crisis-giving-way
World Economic Forum (2016) *The Global Competitiveness Report* 2015–2016. http://reports.weforum.org/global-competitiveness-report-2015-2016/

CHAPTER

10

BRINGING CLASS BACK IN: AGAINST OUTSOURCING DURING #FEESMUSTFALL AT WITS

Vishwas Satgar

INTRODUCTION

Most analyses of #FeesMustFall (#FMF) place it in the realm of post-class politics. As is commonly asserted, it was a movement about student identities, inter-generational politics and the return of black consciousness. Yet a class lens reveals a mass politics deeply implicated in class formation. An aspirant middle class wanting meritocratic class mobility is also involved in a complicated relationship with a black working class in precarious, outsourced work. The working class part of the relationship is a fraction of the working class as a whole, constituted from structural changes due to neoliberalisation – particularly the increasing fragmentation and segmentation of the neoliberalised university labour market into core and noncore functions as part of cost reduction. At the same time, though, this working-class fraction is being remade in class terms through defensive struggles, recognition struggles and struggles aimed at reversing structural exclusion.

The dialectic of structure and the agency of outsourced university workers at the University of the Witwatersrand (Wits) will be explored in this chapter in relation to #FMF. A starting point for this exploration is the location of #FMF within a broader cycle of mass politics in the post-apartheid period to highlight the distinctiveness of its politics – this enables an investigation of the central questions in this chapter. Did outsourced workers have agency or were they merely liberated by students? Was Fallism the ideological lodestar of outsourced workers or was there a pre-existing anti-neoliberal politics among outsourced workers? How was solidarity constituted between aspirant middle-class students, workers and academics in the university space? Ultimately, how did working-class interests register in #FMF? These questions lead to an interrogation of the challenges facing #OutsourcingMustEnd/#OutsourcingMustFall.

#FEESMUSTFALL AND THE SECOND CYCLE OF POST-APARTHEID MASS RESISTANCE

During the anti-apartheid struggle, national liberation politics was mass politics, grounded in building class and national popular alliances as a basis of a national liberation bloc. A reading of the strategy and tactics documents of the African National Congress (ANC) confirms the centrality of class agency, particularly that of the working class, while affirming the importance of nonracial unity. The material foundations for this, at least in the 1980s, were mass movements such as trade unions, civic organisations, youth organisations and student organisations. The United Democratic Front (UDF) congealed these forces into a bloc of resistance. However, in this ferment hierarchical forms of organisation were established and, most importantly, vanguardist leadership played a determining role through the ANC and the South African Communist Party (SACP). The idea of an elite vanguard, a centralised underground leadership managing a strategic line of command, defined this politics. The UDF was a mass front for waging a 'people's war' through mass mobilisation. While the UDF had its own democratic grassroots impulses, the Marxist-Leninist imprint and template of this politics was apparent – and not unique to South Africa. The bolshevising of 'national liberation' politics or 'painting nationalism red' was a feature of twentieth-century revolutionary politics because of the influence of the Soviet Union. This is not the politics of #FeesMustFall.

As I have previously pointed out (Satgar 2015), #FeesMustFall emerges as part of a second cycle of resistance (2007 to the present) in post-apartheid South Africa. The first cycle of resistance against neoliberalisation (late 1990s into early 2000s) was marked by the rise of the Treatment Action Campaign, the Landless People's Movement and the Anti-Privatisation Forum. These formations are now either moribund or very weak but, at least in the case of the Treatment Action Campaign, there is an attempt at renewal. At the same time, since 2007 South Africa's civic protest actions against the lack of service delivery have become much more frequent and more violent – the object of analysis of various sociological studies and sometimes vaunted as the 'rebellion of the poor' or 'violent democracy'. These reductive analyses, however, miss the wider range of struggles defining the terrain of counter-hegemonic resistance in contemporary South Africa. Alongside the service delivery protests we have also been witnessing the emergence of new transformative movements that mark out a second cycle of resistance. They include struggles around building solidarity economies; the right to know; equal education; social justice; defence of constitutional freedoms; food sovereignty; rural democracy and rights for women; extractivism; climate; jobs; housing; rights of lesbian, gay, bisexual, transgender and intersexed (LGBTI); struggles against corruption (including a 'vote no' campaign during the 2014 national elections); #ZumaMustFall; moves towards rebuilding a new worker-controlled labour federation; and a growing emphasis on climate justice (350.org, Earthlife, Ground-Up). All these struggles are seeking to engender systemic transformation, advance transformative alternatives and embrace a new constitutive understanding of power. Put more sharply, these are social forces attempting to build and utilise their own capacities to advance transformation from below, informed by the Marikana conjuncture of re-alignment and detachment from the national liberation bloc.[1] As anti-systemic forces, they are not led by any vanguards but are in themselves agents of transformative counter-hegemony.

#FeesMustFall, and its demands for zero fee increases, decommodified education, an end to outsourcing and decolonisation, has to be located in this second cycle of mass resistance. The anti-capitalist impulses in South African society are amplified by all these forces – alongside Marikana, #FMF has brought this to the fore in dramatic ways.

#FMF heralded three new developments in mass politics in post-apartheid South Africa. First, it married social media to mass politics. This enabled telescoped, speedy and cross-campus mobilisation. Students used Twitter, Facebook, WhatsApp groups and even webpages to communicate with each other, but also married situated mass practices to larger political mobilisation. This was new for South Africa and had not existed in 1976. Second, the multitude rising from this political matrix was amorphous but for moments of media representation which presented 'leaders' at the forefront – and yet in practice this was not the case in the university space where various groups jostled for influence and mass mobilisation was catalysed through social media and common resistance activity, providing moments for mass convergence. In many ways, #FMF was leaderless while, at the same time, it had a powerful group and populist logic at work. It was a prototype of a grassroots-driven force with a leaning towards horizontality – but this did not fully mature. At Wits, for example, deliberative processes did not mature into intense democratic group deliberation as they had done in the US Occupy Movement (Hunt-Hendrix and Christie 2015). Instead, final decisions were made through a rather loose assembly format and yes/no procedure around actions (Molefe 2016) and were often driven by particular groups.[2] This weakness and internal tension of leaderlessness existing alongside intense contestation between groups for leadership did not provide much space for debate about strategy and tactics, and ultimately it also fed into divisions within #FMF. Third (and this is a corollary of points one and two), #FMF was about a mimetic politics; it was about copying developments from different campuses, so if students marched and protested at one campus, others followed. Or if students occupied particular spaces at a certain university this was repeated at other campuses embracing the revolt – a copycat practice that also had a life of its own and reinforced the role of social media and 'leaderlessness'. This mass dynamic, however, could have been given greater coherence if #FeesMustFall had moved early on to democratically elect a collective leadership on campuses and nationally. That did not happen, but despite the weakness the mimetic dynamic gave a critical mass to #FeesMustFall and a capacity for mobilisation which culminated at the Union Buildings.

#FEESMUSTFALL BRINGS LIBERATION TO WORKERS?

In the ferment and expression of mass resistance to increasing university fees it is not easy to locate how issues came together. Moreover, #FeesMustFall cannot merely be reduced exclusively to the agency of students. Yet there are three dominant narratives at work in how working-class interests have registered in #FMF. The first narrative suggests that #FMF exposed the weaknesses of unions and eclipsed them. Outsourcing has happened because unions have lost their way in defending workers. By advancing #EndOutsourcing, #FMF achieved what unions had failed to achieve for almost two decades. This narrative is true to the extent that unions have not unionised at least 70 per cent of the South African workforce and have not been able to push outsourcing back – which does not of course mean that unions have not been resisting it. The Congress of South African Trade Unions (Cosatu) has attempted to fight outsourcing through a national campaign against labour brokers that even demanded legislative prohibitions. Struggles led by workers themselves in the Post Office and at universities have been pivotal in confronting outsourcing. However, the failure of organised labour on outsourcing is not just about the internal failings of unions – in fact, unions, particularly Cosatu, have experienced a set of strategic defeats during the post-apartheid transition, losing ground to neoliberal macroeconomic policy and, ultimately, the restructuring of the economy at the expense of workers, the co-option of labour in the context of ANC-led Alliance politics and the limits of neo-corporatist bargaining strategies in the labour market, given the asymmetric power accrued to capital. In short, #FMF did not eclipse unions but, rather, further exposed the strategic defeat of South Africa's organised working class. The extent to which students appreciate this and are willing – together with unions – to take on this challenge and to win back the strategic initiative for the organised working class is still to be seen.

The second narrative suggests that #EndOutsourcing originates with #RhodesMustFall, the student movement that emerged in the public arena in March 2015 with a powerful symbolic act of protest led by Chumani Maxwele. Faeces were thrown on the Rhodes memorial statue and a national conversation was launched about decolonising the University of Cape Town (UCT). In the end, students won the demand to have the Rhodes statue removed. In this narrative it is suggested that the demand for #EndOutsourcing was integral to this struggle and expressed as part of it. Hence the struggle for #RhodesMustFall was the harbinger of the demand to end outsourcing and was how, in October 2015, outsourced workers were given hope of permanent employment. However, this was not the case, as #RhodesMustFall was primarily an epistemological shift from a discourse of transformation to one about 'decolonising the university'. It was about racial exclusion in the university and in society and it spoke symbolically to an important challenge about continued racism. According to Gillian Godsell and Rekgotsofetse Chikane (Chapter 2 in this volume) #RhodesMustFall was about re-igniting a challenge posed by Mahmood Mamdani in 1996 and later picked up in several student-led conversations at UCT since 2011. Chumani Maxwele, in his own recollections, affirms the importance of confronting colonial racism through his symbolic protest actions at the Rhodes statue. As he told the newspaper *City Press* (News24 2015), 'Let's not wrongly personalise the issue and detract from the big picture. This thing is about black people. It is about the history of black people; it is in front of you. It is a political blunder that this issue is even up for debate. In this country, we artificially dance around race and racism and don't address it.'

It would seem that Maxwele's version of #RhodesMustFall is about a return to black consciousness-centred and Africanist politics. Although it had an impact on national discourse, and gave a spur to the rise of Fallist ideology, this was not about class. Instead, it was attempts by the UCT Workers Forum and UCT Workers Support Committee that reached out to #RhodesMustFall (Luckett and Fogel 2015). Without such intersections #RhodesMustFall is a black, middle-class nationalist movement, seeking decolonisation of the system for aspirant black middle-class mobility rather than transformation of class, race and gender as part of reclaiming the public university. In October 2015 it was the developments at the University of the Witwatersrand (Wits), the epicentre of #FeesMustFall, that brought class to the fore in the student revolt, largely due to the efforts of the October 6 movement and solidarities forged between workers, academics and students over a decade and a half which preceded #FeesMustFall.

The third narrative suggests that #FeesMustFall was exclusively about students, led by students and expressed student politics – thus the events triggered on 14 October, including the demand to end outsourcing, were championed exclusively by students. However, empirically this was not the case. #FeesMustFall was about a convergence of social and class forces in the Wits space. Although the protests were sparked by fee increases, and outsourcing was not an immediate issue, it is clear that worker outreach to students quickly affirmed the need for mutual solidarity. Workers supported students in their shutdown of the university; they placed their bodies on the line, provided resources and numbers (Pontarelli and Luckett 2016; Mzobe and Ndebele 2016). Crucial in this regard was also the work done by the October 6 movement, which hosted a massive demonstration on this same date focusing on outsourcing and bringing together student organisations, workers and progressive academics. This unity, however, was shallow, and immediately after the Union Buildings protest, on 23 October 2015, when workers and students wanted to continue protesting to ensure that #EndOutsourcing was firmly on the Wits agenda, a sharp division emerged with the leaders of the student representative council (SRC) (see Chapter 1 in this volume). Unity and solidarity fell apart, revealing also the limited support by some in the student movement to working-class solidarity.

Contrary to these three narratives, it seems that the end to outsourcing found its place in #FeesMustFall through the agency of affected workers; through solidarity relations between workers, academics and students forged before #FMF (over a period of fifteen years at Wits); and through the bonds between workers and students established at the beginning of #FMF. Precarious, outsourced workers were not Fallists, but were betrayed by unions (such as Nehawu, the National Education, Health and Allied Workers' Union) in their long struggle and, also, they were not passive recipients of emancipation but protagonists in #FMF. Why? Where does working class agency in #FMF come from? To answer these questions we have to historicise the remaking of class, race and gender through the neoliberal restructuring of universities, in particular Wits.

THE MAKING OF A NEOLIBERAL LABOUR REGIME AT WITS AND WORKING-CLASS RESISTANCE

To bring class, as a social relation and process, back into social and political economy analysis means appreciating its structural connection to historical processes, and how race and gender have been implicated in class formation. Class, race and gender have been structurally remade by segregation and apartheid, over a century and a half, and through economic, political and ideological struggles. South Africa has a rich theoretical and analytical tradition spanning liberal, neo-Marxist, black consciousness and revolutionary nationalism that have sought to explain the relationship between class and race or, more generally, between capitalism and racism. The polemical relationship between these traditions generally denies not only the strengths of each but also their limited ability to explain South African reality. This is not the place for that discussion. For the sake of this argument, a brief engagement with Harold Wolpe's 'cheap labour thesis' is staked out, to show why class is important but also why we have to go beyond Wolpe in the present to understand why class, race and gender intersections in neoliberalising capitalism and class struggle are important.

In brief, Wolpe, in his seminal works (1972, 1978) brought to the fore the links between super-exploitation of the black working class and the articulation between a capitalist and a pre-capitalist mode of production. For Wolpe's cheap labour thesis, the existence of reserves was essential to the existence of apartheid. He showed how African migrant workers were dominated in the labour market owing to key mechanisms and conditions such as recruitment agencies, pass and influx controls, indebtedness of agricultural producers and the coercive power of chiefs. Essentially, the reserves provided a space for the social reproduction of cheap black labour, which was then fed into a capitalist economy – in other words, South African capitalism needed apartheid to ensure it met its needs for cheap black labour – a structuralist argument derived from Marx's labour theory of value. Wolpe's thesis and argument stimulated a rich outpouring of academic critique and debate (Friedman 2015: 135–175). There are many limitations to Wolpe's thesis but its strength was to show how a crucial dimension of class exploitation worked within a racialised South African capitalism. For our purposes, it prompts us to ask how class exploitation works today in a neoliberalising South Africa, including in its universities.

Three issues come to the fore to enable us to bring class back in but also to go beyond Wolpe. The first is historical specification, which is crucial for this kind of analysis to work, and to understand how exploitation is implicated in particular forms of contemporary accumulation. Wolpe rendered visible the specific racialised mechanisms of exploitation, but this frame of analysis is not relevant to the explanation of contemporary forms of neoliberalised exploitation. The dynamics and conditions of exploitation have changed through globalised restructuring based on privatisation, liberalisation and deregulation. The underlying dynamics of globalised and financialised accumulation have shifted to the extent that direct coercion through a racialised state is not the main mechanism to secure racialised exploitation. Instead, the post-apartheid state sits at the centre of both deracialising and re-racialising processes driven by the ubiquitous market. Universities have taken on board these market-centred dynamics. It is necessary to understand how the historical specificity of racialised exploitation has worked in the university space, in the context of neoliberalisation. This is different from apartheid accumulation or, for that matter, from Frantz Fanon's colonial experience in Algeria.

The second issue is the intersections between class, race and gender. Wolpe did not develop this in his early work and it has to be done beyond abstractions, which means that a class analysis cannot merely be about the structural determination of the working class – it must also take on board the life experiences of the working class. How class, race and gender are expressed in the everyday has to be taken seriously – and this must be brought into Marxist analysis.

The third issue is that the making of the working class cannot be uncoupled from the capital-labour relation. Wolpe did not foreground class struggle (and the contingencies informing it) which must be brought into class analysis in order to understand working class formation at South Africa's universities.

These three issues guide how class is brought back in for an understanding of the place of the working class in #FMF.

FOLLOWING THE UCT NEOLIBERAL STANDARD

The world of the low-skilled or super-exploited workers is mainly the world of African workers, men and women. It is the structural inheritance of a society and labour market designed by apartheid. However, with the end of apartheid and the embrace of the market and logic of econom isation of everything, corporate power has been crucial in maintaining both racialised and de-racialising dynamics in the labour market. The state has provided enabling macroeconomic conditions for this to happen through neoliberal and financialised accumulation policies. Universities have been led on towards neoliberalisation through cuts in public funding, the embrace of public management frameworks benchmarked to standards in the private sector and through their obsession with being 'world class' institutions within a market-centred framework (Pendlebury and Van der Walt 2006). Essentially, South Africa's public universities have been pushed to be more like quasi-businesses, less like public institutions. Students are clients, academics are cost centres and workers are variable costs to be managed through the core and noncore requirements of the university. In the main, workers are expendable, and cost reduction factors in this market-centred managerialism. This was best captured in a Wits academic report critical of outsourcing:

> While internationally the language of outsourcing supports notions of adding value and bringing in expertise, in South African experience research shows that it is generally relatively unskilled work that is outsourced. In a survey conducted by Andrew Levy and Associates blue collar workers comprised more than 90 per cent of employees who were outsourced, while administrative staff accounted for nearly 8 per cent and managers and executives for under 2 per cent. In the South African context, 'core' and 'noncore' has more to do with class and the occupational division of labour – the distinction between administrative/managerial and manual labour – than it does with an honest appraisal of an organisation's functional requirements. In this sense notions of 'core business' may be

understood less as an aspect of good management and more as an ideological justification for cutting blue collar workers and especially for avoiding unions (Adler et al. 2000: 5).

In other words, outsourcing has maintained a racialised labour market pattern but through state fiscal cutbacks and the deracialised managerial power concentrated in the bureaucracy of the university. The origins of outsourcing in South African universities goes back to UCT around 1999 when it started a cost-cutting exercise involving retrenchments and the outsourcing of designated 'support services'. Luckett and Fogel (2015) highlight the callous managerial rationality underpinning this:

> The cost imperative can be seen in the words of Mamphela Ramphele, the vice-chancellor of UCT who pioneered outsourcing at South African universities. 'We had gross distortions in our salary and wage structures,' Ramphele said. 'In a nutshell, we overpaid at bottom level and underpaid at the top. We needed to review and rationalise our staffing structures and numbers to ensure we retained the best and eliminated "dead wood",' she has been quoted as saying.

Wits, together with numerous other universities, followed this UCT neoliberal standard, which derives from the larger neoliberal thrust in government policy, promoting belt tightening, fiscal re-prioritisation, privatisation and public-private partnerships. The ANC government's infamous Growth, Employment and Redistribution (Gear) strategy of 1996 provided the warrant for neoliberalising the universities. Ultimately the challenge of insourcing at universities, together with other #FMF demands, is a direct challenge to this neoliberal framework – a framework that has used the market to further entrench racial inequalities in society and at universities. To explore this further we look at the remaking of class, race and gender through this neoliberal rationality at Wits.

REMAKING CLASS, RACE AND GENDER

Prior to the neoliberalisation, black workers occupied a particular location in the apartheid university workplace, in the division of labour and in the racialised labour regime. This was about a racially segmented labour market in which

African workers were mainly herded into low-skilled, menial and demeaning work (Adler et al. 2000: 33–34). Whites supervised, controlled and had the power to discipline. The racially hierarchised workplace entrenched the humiliation and racial brutality experienced by African workers in the division of labour. For African women it affirmed the triple burden of racialised exploitation at the workplace, racism in society and patriarchal oppression. This structural and lived reality, even in the university labour regime, was ironically also about full-time employment, with low wages and non-wage benefits, such as medical aid, pension funds, access to the university library, maternity benefits, travel allowances and access for education for workers' children. At a macro-level the apartheid state determined, shaped and regulated this labour market regime through its race and gender requirements.

In post-apartheid South Africa, neoliberal leadership at UCT unleashed a nightmare in the lives of the 'dead wood' black service workers. Class, race and gender began operating in ways reminiscent of apartheid – but yet different. Despite the existence of new labour laws and reforms aimed at deracialising and transforming the labour market, university managers chose to perpetuate a racialised and gendered labour regime.[3] A deracialising black managerial layer instituted a shift from a racialised and state-determined labour regime to a market-centred racialised and gendered exploitation regime. Wits adopted it, and introduced outsourcing in 2000. The then vice-chancellor, Colin Bundy, privatised cleaning, catering and electrical and grounds maintenance. About 613 Wits workers were retrenched and only about 250 were to be re-employed by private companies (WSC 2011: 3). This resulted in wages being slashed, and those of cleaners dropped from R2 227 a month to about R1 200. Workers lost most non-wage benefits, precariousness increased and labour rights were also compromised. In short, outsourcing was a quick and efficient way to use the market to depress labour standards for low-skilled and semi-skilled workers.

But what lies behind the numbers and quantitative impacts? How were class, race and gender experienced in the everyday realities of outsourced workers since the infamous introduction of this practice in 2000 at Wits? Andries Bezuidenhout and Khayaat Fakier (2006) capture this brilliantly in exposing the daily cycle of work routines and everyday reproduction imperatives of an outsourced worker, Maria Dlamini. They show that after her twelve-hour-forty-minute work day she continues to work at home, preparing meals and sewing clothes for another two-and-a-half hours, before going to sleep. The boundaries between production and reproduction are completely blurred in the life of an outsourced African women worker. Outsourcing, introduced in the name of efficiency, makes life harder for African women workers with low wage exploitation and precariousness, coupled with patriarchal oppression. 'Economic efficiency' also, in its seeming neutrality, remakes race, class and gender relations – but through corporate power.

Similarly, using photographs, Naadira Munshi, a leading student activist in the Wits Workers' Solidarity Committee, exposed what outsourcing arrangements at Wits entailed: segregated entrances and toilets, hidden and dirty change rooms, and restrictions on the use of public spaces. Deliwe Mzobe, an outsourced worker, also described what she had to live through at Wits. Besides her description of the emphasis on surveillance, invisibility and tight control that workers were subjected to, the palpable feelings of humiliation and brutalisation were vividly expressed when she burst into tears during her narration of this experience to a packed audience at a Sociology of Work Project seminar.[4] In an interview, Deliwe also said:

> I have been a cleaner at Wits since 2008. I was first a temporary worker and then a permanent worker at an outsourced company since 2012. It was very hard. We felt like outsiders because we could not access simple things like the different entrances at Wits. We were only allowed to access Wits through one entrance. We were only allowed to use certain toilets even though we cleaned all of them. We were not allowed to be seen – to sit in the shade, on the lawns and benches. We did not have access to computer and library facilities. We did not have access to Wits buses even if we needed to move from one side of campus to another. Some of it is still like this, but it is better.
>
> Most of all, the money was not good. It was literally nothing. You cannot survive on the wages we receive. I was not able to support my family. I had to choose between lunch and transport money for my daughter. As a result, one resorts to loans from the banks. Sometimes you find people who owe money to almost all the banks. And if you cannot pay, you are blacklisted and have to go to the loan sharks. The loan sharks keep your ID document and your bank card and as soon as money comes in they take a lot of it. Some add 30 percent, 40 per cent, and even 50 per cent. It just becomes a vicious cycle that you are trapped in (Luckett and Mzobe 2016: 95–96).

Besides the imposition of outsourcing as a cost-reduction measure, which further fragmented and divided the working class, it is also the lived experience of outsourced workers through class, race and gender that has provided the material conditions for struggles against outsourcing.

THREE CONJUNCTURAL MOMENTS OF WORKING-CLASS-LED STRUGGLE

Amid this continued onslaught against mainly black workers at Wits, solidarities emerged with academics and students and this played a crucial role in conjunctural moments in which power was shifted against or in favour of workers struggling against outsourcing. History has never moved in a straight line since the imposition of outsourcing and has always been subject to the vicissitudes and contingencies of struggles. Three crucial conjunctural moments stand out at Wits in a fifteen-year struggle against outsourcing.

2000: February to July

With the adoption of the UCT standard on 25 February 2000, the University Council decided to restructure Wits. Retrenchments and outsourcing became a priority. The strategic imposition of this from above solicited resistance from various quarters. First, student and worker resistance unfolded against the retrenchments through critique of the university's plans (Wits Strategic Plan 1999; Wits Restructuring Plan 2001), pickets led by Nehawu, rallies, occupation of the vice-chancellor's office and disruption of the international Urban Futures conference at Wits, involving solidarity from the Anti-Privatisation Forum (see Van der Walt 2000a; 2000b; 2000c; 2000d).

Second, and by May 2000, a powerful academic intervention against outsourcing came to the fore. A report entitled 'The Wits University support service review: A critique', was produced in which the academics positioned to do the following:

> First, we provide a critique of how the restructuring process and outsourcing are conceptualised by UMA [the consultants hired by management]. Second, we assess the quality of data and sources used during the review process, and compare the conclusions drawn by UMA to their own evidence. Third, we show how the review process systematically

ignored evidence, alternative proposals, and valuable insights generated in the review committees. Fourth, we argue that SET's outsourcing proposals will tend to reproduce the legacy of apartheid for both the workforce and the student body (Adler et al. 2000: i).

In this conjuncture managerialist and outsourcing companies prevailed. The management responded with interdicts to neutralise, intimidate and narrow the space for resistance. In the end, the struggle of workers, students and academics did not stop the restructuring. Unions like Nehawu were tamed (it lost about half of its members on the campus after a dismal fight),[5] the university management maintained the strategic initiative and the public university Wits was on its way to becoming a quasi-business.

2011: March to October

The Wits Workers' Solidarity Committee (WSC), formed in 2010 to rebuild worker, student and academic solidarity against outsourcing, was triggered by the 'Armitage affair' about the racist and aggressive behaviour of a senior university official towards workers. A joint student-worker-academic protest put pressure on the management to conduct an investigation. A report was prepared by March 2011. Armitage resigned before his hearing, but admitted guilt in a letter (WSC 2011: 6). According to Thembi Luckett, a leading student activist involved in #FeesMustFall/WSC:

> The WSC managed to bring workers together across companies, with support from students and academics, on specific issues such as racism, unfair dismissals and separate facilities for workers from the rest of the university community. Some key campaigns were won, such as the reinstatement of dismissed Royal Mnandi workers in 2012. Students boycotted the company by cancelling their meals and going on hunger strike. These solidarity actions and victories over the years have built workers' confidence. However, it has been difficult to consistently put on the agenda an end to outsourcing, rather than taking up particular issues to campaign around, especially in the latter years (Luckett 2016).

By October 2011 the WSC (2011: 12) submitted a draft report on the conditions of outsourced workers at the university to the Wits Senate. This report highlighted, *inter alia*, the ban on workers meeting at Wits, segregation practices in relation to working conditions of outsourced workers and the treatment of workers by outsourcing companies – including the intimidation of workers, direct verbal racism and appalling working conditions. In the main, the report recommended that '… Senate should effectively call for the end of all apartheid practices in our university'.

The university was compelled to respond but kept the issue on the Senate agenda for a few years.[6] The issue of ending outsourcing was raised in the Wits Senate in 2012 and 2013 by academics (Senate Member 2016). When Adam Habib became vice-chancellor in June 2013, and when Tawana Kupe became deputy vice-chancellor for finance, an extensive discussion was held in Senate in which Habib made clear that he agreed to insourcing in principle and there was a need to figure out the finances. He was willing to challenge the assumption that outsourcing was cheaper for the institution and called for more research on the options for making insourcing financially viable.

2015: May to October

By May 2015 (see Nkosi 2015), Habib was publicly calling for a campaign involving civil society groups to lobby the state for more resources to end outsourcing. Partly in response, and given that outsourcing was continuing (albeit with regimented and racialised market control, including retrenchments of electricians – see Chapter 4 in this volume), and with the rising decolonising discourse emerging from #RhodesMustFall, the October 6 movement was formed at Wits.[7] It included WSC and workers, academics and students from the University of Johannesburg (UJ). This was an important development for two reasons:

> The October 6 Movement worked to make the demand reach further than Wits and UJ by reaching out to organisations across universities. A national day of action was called for on October 6. Hundreds of students and workers came out at Wits and UJ and solidarity statements and endorsements for the demand and action were received from organisations across the country. Several other organisations also took action at their universities. A Workers Charter (2015) was handed over to Wits and UJ managements, which emerged through a process of years of work. A UCT Workers Forum Charter was developed and updated over the years. At Wits a process had started in 2012. It was restarted in 2015 at Wits and UJ by building on the Wits and UCT Charter through weeks of workers'

meetings and discussions leading up to October 6. For example, debates were held over what the wage demand in the Charter should be – workers decided that it should be R12 500 in solidarity with massacred Marikana workers. It is a charter with a vision of what a university could and should look like (Luckett 2016).

The activism and push from October 6 for a national day of action against outsourcing, and the workers charter it developed, preceded #FeesMustFall and was a crucial precursor for solidarity. Deliwe Mzobe captures clearly the dynamic of solidarity that brought together #FeesMustFall and #EndOutsourcing:

> I think the students realised that it was not only about the tuition fee increase. Students realised that workers were there all the time with them and that there should be a gain for workers, too. They said, 'We can't allow this exploitation of our parents to go on. This outsourcing must end'. It also became a struggle for free education. If you are an outsourced parent, how can you afford to send your children to university, even if there is no fee increase? It is impossible. So it becomes a cycle of poverty (Luckett and Mzobe 2016: 95-96).

While 2000, 2011 and 2015 are punctuated by crucial conjunctural moments that shifted the relations of force for and against outsourcing, three dimensions stand out. The first is that class struggles led by outsourced workers were crucial. The neoliberal labour regime at Wits, while imposed by managerialist forces from above, was shaped and also contested from below. The agency of workers was fundamental in this regard. The second is that alliances between workers, students and academics clearly ebbed and flowed, but constituted power from below at key conjunctural moments, and fed directly into #FeesMustFall – overlaps of student activists, worker solidarity for students and ties to academics all came together from May to October of 2015. The third is that the language of 'apartheid and its continuity' was evoked in historical struggles against outsourcing, emphasising the link between class and race but, more specifically, the continuity of racial oppression experienced by black workers, including women. While for rhetorical purposes this was crucial, and symbolically garnered legitimacy, something more historically specific was at work: the re-racialising of a corporate segmented labour market at Wits (as opposed to a state-segmented one as under apartheid). The neoliberal regime could not find hegemonic roots and its mechanisms of control, discipline and humiliation were a racialised continuity with apartheid – but determined by a specificity of market-centred and economised capitalism. Racism did not die with the end of apartheid but was being remade in the context of neoliberalisation, inside the post-apartheid university labour regime. The exploitation and oppression of the black working class was now implicated in a new mode of accumulation to the benefit of managerialist forces and outsourcing companies.

There was no inevitability or singular determination in how worker-led class struggle, intersecting with race and gender, found its place in #FeesMustFall. The preceding analysis further affirms the role of multiple factors in propelling the place of outsourcing within #FMF: Wits University was a site of a long struggle against outsourcing by workers, worker-student-academic solidarities were key at several moments, #RhodesMustFall found its expression in October 6, in terms of decolonising discourses, but October 6 also took on board the struggle to #EndOutsourcing while, at the same time, Wits management led by Habib was also committed increasingly to resolving outsourcing. Ultimately, student fee increases cut across and electrified political mobilisation in October 2015. In the end, no single political organisation, social group or leader can claim the historical expression and impact of #FeesMustFall. In practice and in its logic it was an expression of multiple determinations and a ripening of several contradictions at once at Wits. Nobody could predict #FeesMustFall nor anticipate its historical ramifications and convergences. As a Wits SRC statement (2015) says: 'When we started our #WitsFeesMustFall protest we had no idea the kind of momentum it would gain or the impact it would make not just nationally, but internationally'.

CHALLENGES FOR OUTSOURCING TO END/FALL

While #FeesMustFall placed insourcing on the state's and university's agenda, it is not a resolved issue. Although there is an institutionalised dialogue with Wits management to find an insourcing solution, the mass factor (of a united, radical nonracial unity) has been displaced with fractures, ideological divisions and personality conflicts within #FeesMustFall. The high point of #FeesMustFall was the display of unity in October 2015 – students, workers and academics stood above political loyalties, ideological divides and racial cleavages as a united force, nonviolently constituting power in the streets and symbolic sites of state power. A discourse affirming the reclamation of the public university resonated across class and national popular forces in the university and society. The legitimacy of the demands made could not be ignored by the state or by university management.

However, without the momentum of united and nonviolent action from below it is not certain that insourcing will be resolved in the interests of workers. Wits, like other universities, has also effectively closed the space for violent protests, which are prevalent among a minority. The tactic of disruption is important, but it also lends itself to uncontrolled violence, which has been lent legitimacy through a simplistic and literal hermeneutic procedure in the reading of Frantz Fanon on violence, for example. The 'revolution of becoming' as verbalised by students in October 2015 needs to reflect on its weaknesses and to rethink, in flexible ways, strategy and tactics to bring back the counter-hegemonic initiative to students, workers and progressive academics. A dogmatic fixation on disruption actually runs counter to the commitment to the unorthodox and non-vanguardist approach of #FeesMustFall. The space for nonviolent action has to be taken as seriously, given the stakes.

The scope of insourcing is proving to be a difficult. It would seem that in its negotiating strategy Wits is making a distinction between different categories of workers: outsourced, vendors and those involved in trading at Wits (Mzobe and Ndebele 2016). This is a challenge to workers as well. The university, either intentionally or unintentionally, will be dividing workers if it sticks to these distinctions and will undermine collective solidarity and agency among workers championing insourcing. However, the Workers' Charter, championed by October 6, could serve as a crucial guide for Wits. It states that everyone whose labour contributes to the university should have:

- A living wage
- A secure job
- Decent, safe and healthy working conditions
- Democratic collective organisation so that they can speak and act together
- A safe place where they can leave children who need care
- Access to the education facilities.

Although the state conceded an end to fee increases for 2016, which was an immediate gain, this does not mean that the state is committed to financing decommodified education, let alone resolving insourcing in favour of workers.

#FeesMustFall needs to make a strong case for fiscal resources and reprioritisation in the national budget in order to secure these gains.[8] This can be done in the context of a contracting economy, given the wasteful expenditure and corruption in the state. With the disarray in #FeesMustFall this case is not being made and universities are going to be left with austerity options and financial deficits if the state does not come to the table with financial support. Reducing wage gaps and cutting the fat in salary structures at the top may yield some resources but will not solve the problem. Thus a united front by universities, #FeesMustFall, parents and broader society, to put pressure on the state, is the only way to win this fight.

Finally, solidarities with the wider organised working class are crucial. Universities like Wits are making some concessions around rolling back outsourcing – which in itself is historic and of crucial symbolic and political significance for class struggles. But this fight has to go beyond universities to all sectors of the economy, and particularly through solidarities with unions. Nehawu, whose commitment to end outsourcing has been dismal, has been kept out of insourcing negotiations at Wits. Apart from unions such as Nehawu, the question still remains: does #FeesMustFall appreciate the extent to which it has revealed the strategic challenges facing the organised working class in society? Students leaving the university, as a new middle class, will be faced with this challenge in the fragmented labour market in which outsourcing is pervasive. Will #FeesMustFall and, more generally, students coming out of this experience, take forward the necessity of rebuilding the power of labour, as was done in the 1970s by mainly white students?[9] To overcome this challenge, students have to also assist unions to rethink their forms and practices. The time is ripe for this to happen, but will students make this choice? History will tell us.

NOTES

1 The Marikana massacre took place on the outskirts of this platinum mining town on 16 August 2012, when police opened fire on striking mineworkers, leaving thirty-four dead and seventy-eight wounded. Marikana was more than an event. It unleashed a realignment of popular and working-class forces against the ANC. It contributed to the 'Vote No!' Campaign in the 2014 national elections, the breakaway of the metalworkers' union (Numsa) from the ANC-led Alliance and the formation of the Economic Freedom Fighters.

2   I remember going to the newly renamed Solomon Mahlangu House on the evening (22 October 2015) before the march to the Union Buildings and speaking to several students in the concourse about what the plans were. No one really seemed to know details of how it was all going to come together at the Union Buildings demonstration.
3   Many of these labour laws were passed between 1995 and 1999 including the new Labour Relations Act, Basic Conditions of Employment Act and the Employment Equity Act.
4   This seminar was held on 15 April 2016, under the title: Students and Workers – Forging a New Alliance. I recorded the inputs made and observed the discussion.
5   It should be noted that Nehawu was an affiliate of Cosatu and supported the Tripartite Alliance with the ANC. Yet the ANC supported the neoliberal restructuring at Wits.
6   This led to the Tokiso Report (2013a) which was an investigation into the issues raised by WSC. Management (2013b) also went on record with a response but was not willing to address issues substantively.
7   I sat in some of the initial meetings of October 6, including the Google list to strongly oppose the use of cooperatives as a solution to outsourcing, given my years of experience in building cooperatives, understanding their failures at the University of Fort Hare and understanding the need for crucial internal and external conditions for success.
8   At the time of finalising this chapter, Wits Council had committed to insourcing (also see Chapter 4). This will require at least R100 million as an upper limit. It has agreed to insource 1 530 workers (cleaners, caterers, security, transport, waste, grounds and landscaping). It has raised the top-up allowance from R4 500 to R6 000 until the end of 2016 and has committed to a minimum wage of R7 500 for 2017. The university has agreed to find income-generating solutions, but it is clear that without state support the university will face difficulties.
9   Mainstream black consciousness in the 1970s did not have a clear commitment and orientation to the working class. It did not contribute to rebuilding unions, particularly black unions.

REFERENCES

Adler, G., Bezuidenhout, A., Buhlungu, S., Kenny, B., Omar, R., Ruiters, G. & Van der Walt, L. (2000) The Wits University support service review: A critique.

Bezuidenhout, A. & Fakier, K. (2006) Maria's burden: Contract cleaning and the crisis of social reproduction in post-apartheid South Africa. *Antipode*, 38(3), 462–485.

Friedman, S. (2015) *Race, Class and Power: Harold Wolpe and the Radical Critique of Apartheid*. Pietermaritzburg: University of KwaZulu-Natal Press.

Hunt-Hendrix, L. & Christie, I. (2015) Occupy and the dialectics of the Left in the United States. In V. Satgar (ed.) *Capitalism's Crises: Class Struggles in South Africa and the World*. Johannesburg: Wits University Press.

Luckett, T. & Fogel, B. (2015) Decolonising labour at SA's universities. *The Con*. http://www.theconmag.co.za/2015/06/24/decolonising-labour-at-south-africas-universities/

Luckett, T. & Mzobe, D. (2016) #OutsourcingMustFall: The role of workers in the 2015 protest wave at South African universities. *Global Labour Journal*, 7(1). https://escarpmentpress.org/globallabour/article/view/2839

Luckett, T. (2016) E-mail interview, 2 May, 07:31.

Molefe, T. O. (2016) Oppression must fall: South Africa's revolution in theory. *World Policy Journal*, 33(1), 30–37.

Mzobe, D. & Ndebele, R. (2016) Interview with #EndOutsourcing/October 6 worker leaders, 19 April.

News24 (2015) Newsmaker – Chumani Maxwele: No regrets for throwing faeces at Rhodes statue. *City Press*. http://www.news24.com/Archives/City-Press/Newsmaker-Chumani-Maxwele-No-regrets-for-throwing-faeces-at-Rhodes-statue-20150429

Nkosi, B. (2015) Wits vice-chancellor says state can help end exploitation. *Mail & Guardian*, 26 May. http://mg.co.za/article/2015-05-26-wits-vice-chancellor-says-state-can-help-end-exploitation

Pendlebury, J. & Van der Walt, L. (2006) Neoliberalism, bureaucracy, and resistance at Wits University. In R. Pithouse (ed.). *Asinamali: University Struggles in Post-Apartheid South Africa*. Trenton: Africa World Press.

Pontarelli, F. & Luckett, T. (2016) #OutsourcingMustFall: Unity in action in South African universities. *The Brooklyn Rail*, 4 March. http://www.brooklynrail.org/2016/03/field-notes/outsourcing-must-fall

Satgar, V. (2015) Between crisis and renewal: Where to for South Africa's Left? *Africa Files, At Issue*. http://www.africafiles.org/article.asp?ID=27893

Senate member (academic) (2016) Interviewed on 26 May.

Tokiso Report (2013a) Final dispute settlement report of discrimination, victimisation and harassment by employees of contractors to the University of the Witwatersrand.

Tokiso (2013b) Management's response to the report on allegations of discrimination against staff employed by contractors.

University Workers' Charter (2015) October.

Van der Walt, L. (2000a) Fighting the privatisation at Wits. *Revolutionary Socialist*. July/August 2000, 13.

Van der Walt, L. (2000b) Neoliberalism comes to Wits University – 600 jobs on the line. *Umsebenzi*, 5 May.

Van der Walt, L. (2000c) Putting profit first. *Sowetan*, 7 September.

Van der Walt, L. (2000d) Wits 2001: Restructuring and retrenchments. *South African Labour Bulletin*, 24(2).

Wits SRC statement (2015) On the #FeesMustFall movement.

WSC (Wits Workers' Solidarity Committee) (2011) Draft Report: Senate discussion on the condition of outsourced workers at Wits University.

Wolpe, H. (1972) Capitalism and cheap labour power in South Africa: From segregation to apartheid. *Economy and Society*, 1(4), 425–456.

Wolpe, H. (1978) A comment on 'The poverty of neo-Marxism'. *Journal of Southern African Studies*, 4(2), 240–256.

CHAPTER

11

BETWEEN A ROCK AND A HARD PLACE: UNIVERSITY MANAGEMENT AND THE #FEESMUSTFALL CAMPAIGN

Patrick FitzGerald and Oliver Seale

INTRODUCTION

> In these challenging times, what is needed is less anecdotal critique of managerialism and more research into how leaders can implement well-considered change.
>
> – *Geoff Sharrock, The Guardian Higher Education Blog,*
> *26 September 2012*

Leadership and management in the contemporary university in South Africa are complex, and take place in a fluid and contested environment. The need and demand for accountable and effective leadership by university executives, in particular vice-chancellors, is becoming increasingly evident. This is manifested and exacerbated by the recent sectoral and institutional disruptions and protests by students, contracted workers and academic staff in the guise of, for example, the #RhodesMustFall, #FeesMustFall and #OpenStellenbosch campaigns. This chapter explores and engages the challenges and complexities of leadership and management at the University of the Witwatersrand (Wits) during the #FeesMustFall campaign. To this end, we identify and reflect on the challenges and issues related to this campaign, its implications for institutional leadership and management, and the lessons learned.

We aim to demonstrate that the conception and practice of accountable, effective leadership in the universities, without the requisite enabling drivers such as adequate funding, have serious consequences for the institutions, given their current context and complex environment. The main contention here is that sectoral and institutional initiatives will fail and not contribute to a sustainable, quality and responsive higher education system without the appropriate level of resources – in particular, funding and requisite governance, leadership and management. We point out that the prevailing crisis with funding and financing of higher education has constrained and compromised university executives, and added another layer of complexity to their required leadership and management capacities.

Significantly, the apparent balancing factor of relatively stable external party political structures, as represented mainly by the African National Congress (ANC) leadership and Youth League structures, have seemingly collapsed. This skein of relationships and networks, which organically connected student politics to the broader considerations and interests of party and government, has all but disintegrated – opening up new possibilities of much more independent and radical perspectives and actions within the campus milieu.

Much has been written on the global impact of change in universities and the requirements for more agile, adept leadership and effective management for institutional survival and success (see Pounder 2001; Duderstadt 2005; Yielder and Codling 2004; Johnson and Cross 2006; Scott et al. 2008). These insights point to a number of common trends, which have provided 'a set of new conventions on the societal value of higher education, and how it should be managed' (Singh 2001: 11). Dominating the existing narratives are pertinent factors such as a decline in public funding; increasing demand for relevance, performativity and financial viability; and increased competition among universities and from private providers. Various distinct national pressures add to these challenges, including (i) a changing, more directed policy and regulatory environment; (ii) transformation imperatives and their impact on institutional legacies; (iii) increased performativity requirements; (iv) managing the pedagogy of underpreparedness; (iv) good governance and effective leadership/management; and (v) intra-institutional competition for staff and students (see Bundy 2006; Johnson and Cross 2006; Badsha and Cloete 2011; Makgoba 2011; Seale 2015;

Habib 2016). The effective leadership and management of the global and local 'wicked problems' has become more pervasive, requiring a different skills set and appropriate, sustainable responses.

FUNDING OF SOUTH AFRICAN UNIVERSITIES

As governments across the African continent experience fiscal constraints owing to the global financial crisis and weak local economies, funding for higher education is becoming more constrained. The current total regional expenditure in this area as a percentage of gross domestic product (GDP) is 0.78 per cent, way below that of Organisation for Economic Cooperation and Development (OECD) member countries, which is more than 1.5 per cent of GDP in at least seventeen countries (Mouton and Wildschutt 2015). The South African government's contribution to higher education funding in the democratic era has been on the increase, R11 billion in 2006 to R26 billion in 2013. However, as experienced elsewhere, it is also declining as a percentage of the government's budget and of GDP (Figure 11.1): from 0.76 per cent in 2000 to 0.69 per cent in 2009 (Hesa 2014; Mouton 2014).

Figure 11.1: State funding for higher education and percentage of GDP 2004–2012 (Hesa 2014).

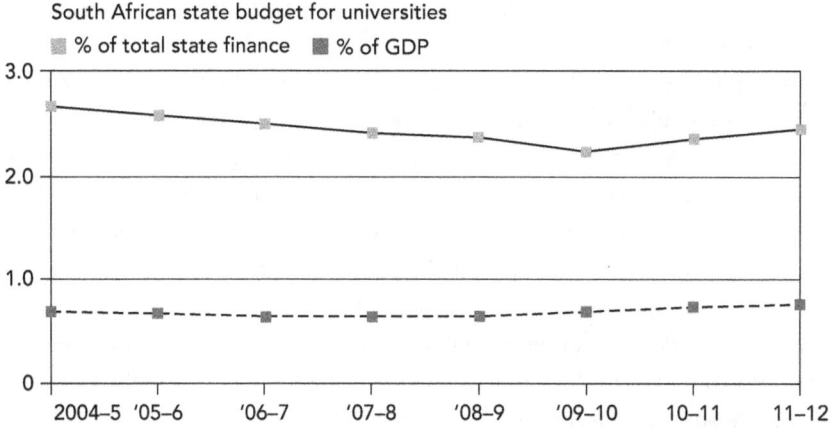

South African universities have a cost-sharing funding model with the main contributors being the government and its primary beneficiaries, the students. As Figure 11.1 illustrates, the declining state funding scenario has negatively affected the other two fiscal sources in universities – tuition fees and third-stream activities. A report prepared by PriceWaterhouseCoopers (PwC) (n. d.) reveals that the state funding component for universities declined from 49 per cent at the turn of this century to 40 per cent at the end of 2012, resulting in an increase in the student tuition fee component from 24 per cent to 31 per cent. While universities have grown their levels of third-stream income to some degree, these increases have by no means compensated for the decline in government support. In fact, universities are facing increasingly worsening financial positions, compounded by crippling student debt which rose from R2.6 billion in 2010 to R3.4 billion in 2012, amounting to an increase of 31 per cent during this period. Student enrolments however only grew by 7 per cent.

> Many of us, vice-chancellors included, have been lamenting the underfunding of higher education for over a decade with little effect. But it was the students with their marches on Parliament and the Union Buildings that shook up the state, changed the systemic parameters and began the process of fundamentally transforming higher education (Habib 2016).

Universities South Africa (USAf) and its predecessor Higher Education South Africa (Hesa) have advised and lobbied government over the past decade or so, on the declining levels of subsidies for public universities. They have contributed to various investigations and the ministerial committee established by government to investigate the funding models and levels in the entire system (Hesa 2011). This committee revealed at the time that universities collectively only received R22 billion in subsidies, whereas they should be getting financial support in the region of R37 billion if they are to be at the world average. For universities like Wits, the institutional impact of this scenario has been quite dramatic in that its subsidy from government has reduced to only 27 per cent of its total revenue, compared to between 50 per cent and 70 per cent at other universities.

These developments, over a period of time, saw universities cutting back on noncore services in order to contain costs and balance their personnel and operational budgets, which in a number of instances were strongly contested by their respective stakeholders, notably unions and elements of the academy. One of the cost saving measures adopted by the sector well over a decade ago was the outsourcing of selected noncore services such as cleaning, security, gardening, transport and catering. The whole-scale re-insourcing of, especially, the most vulnerable contract workers in some of these areas became one of the major demands of protest campaigns, as illustrated in the next section of this chapter.

OUTSOURCING AS A KEY ISSUE

> Outsourcing at Wits University. Apartheid is back!
> – *Deliwe Mzobe, Struggle, September 2015*

As a result of the #RhodesMustFall, #FeesMustFall, and associated hashtag campaigns in 2015 and 2016, the pressures for insourcing (or at least the undoing of previous outsourcing) are extremely strong. It would seem that, in one way or another, university managements are going to have to show willingness in terms of some insourcing movement, be it partly symbolic, partial or thoroughgoing.

The various political and ethical debates around this issue are fully discussed in other chapters in this volume (including in the 'primary voices' section, Part 2). Here, we intend to bring out certain key modalities and ironies constituting ongoing difficulties and dilemmas for the university leadership. The reason for outsourcing at the various universities is normally presented (usually by the opponents and critics of outsourcing) as principally to save money. In most instances this was a significant factor, albeit far from the only one; and even if the direct savings had been negligible or nonexistent it is likely that outsourcing of particular services would nonetheless have gone ahead due to a number of other perceived advantages, such as allowing university management to focus on core academic business, and facilitating much improved services as delivered by specialised and expert providers (see Maree and Le Roux 2014).

Some attribute the widespread outsourcing at universities back to the militant worker actions on many campuses in the late 1980s and early 1990s, when 'liberal' campus managements may have seemed to be soft targets and no real match for well-organised and combative unions. Certainly, the experience of this period could have wielded some influence in disposing university governors and managers towards such outsourcing options, while not in itself constituting the main rationale. Further factors driving outsourcing are outlined below:

Effectiveness and efficiency of services

Some of the functions suitable for outsourcing were being extremely badly managed by some universities, and possibly will always be. After the outsourcing of cleaning at Wits, for instance, many (including some opponents of outsourcing) commented that they could hardly recognise the campus, which had seemed irrevocably scruffy and dirty. In fact, the cleaning technology, material and work techniques that internal Wits cleaners had been using appeared to be entirely obsolete. Similarly, the standard of gardening and sports field maintenance showed immediate improvement in the hands of specialists, who focus on these specific activities as their core business and expertise. Wits actually chose not to outsource their mainstream security function, owing to a history of a well-managed and highly effective security service. However, at other universities the security situation seemingly improved, as it frequently turned out that a fair proportion of the crime on campus had in fact been orchestrated by the previous internal security personnel themselves – which came about because of the amateur security management and oversight exercised by the university leadership. At one university that outsourced security it was contractually agreed that the existing security personnel would be transferred over to the security provider, only to discover that over 40 per cent of such security staff were ineligible for such appointment, because of criminal records.

In the case of the transport function at Wits the effect of outsourcing seemed nothing less than miraculous as old, badly maintained and unreliable vehicles were replaced overnight by well-functioning vehicles which, in terms of the agreement, would never be more than three years old. The constant disciplinary procedures around unauthorised use of the vehicles, dangerous driving and theft of petrol and parts immediately became the problem of the provider – who possessed all the necessary sophisticated systems and technologies to deal with such problems that the university lacked. Moreover, the students were offered a much safer and more reliable transport service.

Releasing university leadership from the management of noncore logistics

University executive teams are predominantly constituted by academics (or academics-become-managers). They are expected to manage difficult and complex issues such as learning and teaching, curriculum development, research, registration, student life and academic human resources (Johnson and

Cross 2006; Seale 2015). As in other industries, such leadership would prefer to focus on areas of core business and core experience, and to manage a host of other services via a high-level contract management capacity. Direct logistical responsibility for this plethora of diverse functions, as well as the responsibility of employing hundreds more personnel was held to constitute a detrimental 'drag' on university managements' capacity to nimbly and strategically apply their minds and make good decisions about the actual 'knowledge business' they believed to be their institutional and social mission and priority.

Skills and staff development

Many staff employed by universities in noncore functions had been left in positions for years without any particular training, development or promotion path. A number of those absorbed or employed in the better service providers immediately experienced opportunities for skills upgrading and promotion, as providers typically operated within an industry context and across a number of sites. In the case of Wits, many cleaning workers absorbed into the industry after 2000 went on to supervisory and junior management positions – actually graduating to higher salaries than they had received as cleaners at Wits, not to mention the advantage of being 'professionalised' – although others, of course, aside from their initial union-negotiated severance payout, found themselves in a much less favourable position in terms of salary and benefits.

University managements now face a variety of dilemmas, such as how to find the financial resources to insource, which services to insource (as there is close political attention to some, but not others) and how to build the requisite capacity to oversee the full logistics of such services rather than just managing contracts and standards. Further, much of the outsourcing procurement had contributed significantly to the BEE (black economic empowerment) procurement scorecard of each university, raising the risk that universities will now receive lower BEE ratings, potentially affecting donor contributions and the ability to win government contracts.

What is brought to the fore by these occurrences, however, is a remarkable parallel to the situation of the universities – and especially the more liberal universities – under apartheid, where pressure from the university community created such universities as small 'welfare states' within the apartheid political economy. That is to say black workers in particular occupations earned considerably more and enjoyed much better job benefits than their counterparts in the same occupation outside these islands of enlightenment. This was true even in terms of activism and rights, and it was no accident that the National Education, Health and Allied Workers' Union (Nehawu) was birthed and nurtured at Wits. This phenomenon was often criticised at the time from the Marxist left who saw it as the salving of liberal consciences, and referred to it as 'plantation management', in the sense that certain plantation owners are less cruel and harsh on their plantation workers than others – without there being any essential change in the societal structural economic and social relationships.

Ironically the tendency is now strongly underway that again the universities will become islands of social welfare in a sea of economic iniquity, as the fierce activism to reverse the outsourcing at tertiary institutions is seemingly not being duplicated or taken further into society in general. So again, as in the apartheid era, we will see a tiny labour aristocracy or elite at the tertiary institutions, without any change whatsoever for those many more workers in the identical occupational class elsewhere. Thus again, the universities will be enlightened plantations and again the consciences of their middle-class (or aspirant middle-class) stakeholders will be salved. The newly insourced workers will no doubt leave their specialised occupational unions and will again join the more politicised and elite general unions active on the campuses, leaving the masses of their erstwhile comrades to carry on without them.

From the perspective of the university fiscus this will simply be experienced as a conscience tax, as higher education institutions will have to pay a not inconsiderable premium in order to purchase services far above the going rate in the rest of the society. Hence universities, as accelerators of a country's ability to compete, innovate and successfully enter the emerging local, regional and global knowledge economies, will find themselves with fewer resources than they might otherwise have had to carry out such a role. One might then pertinently enquire whether these plantations of relative privilege are actually in the overall public good in terms of the knowledge and services the university is expected to provide to society (and the concomitant economic activities and jobs indicatively engendered), as opposed to merely looking after its own inhabitants.

Lastly, for the many writers who have attributed outsourcing to the pervasive trends of 'managerialism' in the universities globally and locally, there appears a further irony. Insourcing will actually bring even more management to the university environment, as human resource and labour relations departments will need to be considerably augmented as, indeed, will finance.

> #OutsourcingMustFall wants outsourced workers to immediately be employed with full benefits and a minimum of R10 000 income per

month and for workers who were recently retrenched to also be offered permanent jobs (Nicolson 2016).

Someone, however, will have to pick up the tab for this. At the University of Cape Town (UCT) for instance, the executive has intimated that the additional costs of insourcing will have to come from the upper end of the current staff payroll (Petersen 2015) which may compromise other positions, especially in the academy. Universities will need to bring back stores to house consumables, tools and equipment, and will require concomitant store-keepers and security. University services departments will have to bring back the various junior and middle management layers, which had been eliminated. And, of course, a plethora of ongoing service management, budgeting and logistical modalities will return to the agendas of management and executive meetings, yet again squeezing out the core business of learning and teaching, research, innovation and the application of knowledge to improve the social and economic prospects of the society beyond the plantation.

Would there have been social space available for a compromise alternative, such as retaining outsourcing while ensuring more favourable remuneration for such workers? This was to some extent implemented at UCT, where for several years wages were 'topped-up' by the university, and likewise at Wits where tender provisions quality assured the human resource and labour relations policies and practices of competing providers. This option, however, would seem inherently unstable and fatally compromised, as it would create a two-tier remuneration within the providing organisation, hampering the ability to rationally deploy human resources between the various organisations they would be servicing, and would also perpetuate an apparent worker aristocracy at the university sites while the bulk of similar workers continued to operate within the socially prevailing labour market conditions.

These developments have major implications for university management.

GOVERNANCE, LEADERSHIP AND MANAGEMENT AND THE UNFOLDING #FEESMUSTFALL EVENTS

> #FeesMustFall completely!!! We reject any per cent including zero
> – *#FeesMustFall student protest poster, 2015*

University management is caught in a strange egg-dance whereby they simultaneously endorse many of the student demands but battle against the impact of often undirected militancy, inappropriate violence and seemingly unreasonable, shifting or utopian demands. Their current dilemma on funding appears to be that in the longer-term perspective, the university managements support key students demands, especially in terms of improving higher education funding across the system, whereas in the shorter term this issue has created a major financial crisis at most universities. Equally disconcerting for university leadership is the unwelcome day-to-day disruption at a number of universities, which seems to have morphed beyond the current protests campaigns, as illustrated by two vice-chancellors, Adam Habib and Sizwe Mabizela commenting in a newspaper article on the fractious and unnecessarily violent character manifested at times during the protest campaign (see *Times Live* 2016).

There are a number of contributing factors that led to what Adam Habib termed the 'perfect storm' in relation to the challenges of tuition fee increases and free education that culminated in the #FeesMustFall campaign. These include:

- Relatively low government funding levels of universities, amounting to about 0.7 per cent of GDP (as pointed out earlier).
- Contribution of tuition fee income that on average amounts to about 30 per cent of total income, compared to 40 per cent for government subsidies, and the remaining 30 per cent accounted for by third-stream income (research, projects, short courses).
- Rising costs of higher education as year-on-year inflation in all university systems worldwide, is typically 1 per cent or even 2 per cent higher than average consumer inflation.
- Inability of the National Student Financial Aid Scheme (NSFAS) to meet the growing demands for student financial aid in the wake of sustained increased access to universities.
- The sector-determined remuneration levels for outsourced workers deployed in universities have been very low compared to those of other university support staff (USAf 2015).

What emerges from an investigation and report produced by USAf is that the protests and disruptions not only focused on student issues such as zero per cent increase in tuition fees and free education, but included labour issues such as the outsourcing of noncore services at universities and its impact on salaries for affected workers (USAf, 2015). Another demand that exacerbated the situation related to insufficient institutional housing for students, which although a perennial issue, resulted in focused protests and sporadic violence at institutions such as UCT (Malgas 2016), and later supported by actions at Wits and other institutions.

University management is therefore challenged to address legitimate demands while moderating others that require either radical policy shifts (free education for all), or more incremental solutions. Achieving operational stability and financial sustainability in the transitional phase to a more appropriate funding model poses wicked problems and dilemmas. Strategic and operational cooperation with the state without loss of autonomy, poses its own difficulties, as witnessed in President Zuma's announcement of a zero per cent fee increase in 2016, which was not within his regulatory ambit to do.

Other imperatives that impact on universities in terms of access and financial sustainability include a target participation rate of 25 per cent, translating to total enrolments of around 1.6 million students in 2030. This is an objective of the National Development Plan and is outlined in the White Paper on Education and Training (DHET 2013) in the light of the steadily increasing matric pass since 1994 and the increasing volume of students who qualify for undergraduate studies.

The state's contribution to student fees in the form of the NSFAS has increased dramatically over the past decade, from R5.1 billion in 2013 to R6.6 billion in 2016, with an additional amount of R6.9 billion provided by government in 2016 to cover the zero per cent tuition fee increase and to assist with NSFAS student debt. However, it still falls well short of the total requirements for qualifying students, especially at the previously disadvantaged institutions. On 15 December 2015, following receipt of a report from the task team investigating the underfunding at universities, and in an attempt to mitigate identified factors that could potentially lead to campus disruptions in early 2016, the Presidency issued a statement announcing:

- R2.3 billion to be made available to universities to address the shortfall resulting from the zero fee increase.
- R2.5 billion (of an identified R4.582 billion NSFAS shortfall) to be provided for the short-term debt relief of 71 753 students who were funded inadequately or were unable to access financial aid over the 2013 to 2015 academic years.
- An acknowledgment of an additional R2.039 billion required in the 2016–2017 financial year to ensure that currently unfunded students receive NSFAS support in the 2016 academic year. The Presidency undertook to find this money from the fiscus, through a re-prioritisation process.

The minister of higher education and training also later announced that a total amount of around R17 billion had been committed by government to support universities in managing the zero per cent fee increase in 2016, addressing NSFAS shortfalls and outstanding student debt. Universities across the board also announced their intentions put in place their own institutional mechanisms to mobilise new funds and thereby provide additional support to financially needy students and their households.

The report presented at the USAf Board in late 2015 on the #FeesMustFall campaign and related institutional concessions and actions taken, revealed that this organisation could have played a far more decisive and prominent role during the protests and disruptions. Following various engagements with a group of vice-chancellors and university executives, USAf developed an operations framework for institutions, which provided guiding principles, and advice on issues such as (i) payment of tuition fees in 2016, (ii) forms of relief in respect of student debt, (iii) registration fees and upfront payments, (iv) insourcing of current outsourced workers, (v) external and internal communication, (vi) protection and security, (vii) empowerment of governance structures and (viii) the role of USAf, especially in regard to much more proactive communication between the vice-chancellors themselves as well as within the sector as a whole (USAf 2015).

A number of commentators have posited that these protest campaigns have a much broader societal motive and agenda, far beyond the realm of higher education. Some forces, they claim, are intent on bringing down the current ANC-led government, as a result of a growing discontent with its leadership and direction (Satgar 2015). Some factions, allegedly inspired by the anti-colonial, revolutionary ideology of Frantz Fanon, have developed disruptive behaviours, not always well synchronised with movement strategy and tactics and demands (News24 2015). Various groupings appeared to be pursuing an agenda primarily aimed at discrediting the previously legitimate institutional decision-making and leadership structures at universities such as governing councils, student representative councils (SRCs) and executive teams in favour of some unspecified direct democracy or populist institutional control.

Whatever the motives of the individuals and groups spearheading these campaigns, there is no doubt that national government and institutional governance structures came under severe attack and were subjected to significant strain. The intensity and coordinated tactical approaches used by the organisers and effective communication platforms of the social media, resulted in the institutional and national leadership being caught off guard, and appearing defensive and reactive. To illustrate the capability of this new form of social media activism, Makgoba (2016) claims that none of the former student protests received this kind of far-reaching support from not only students and academics but also parents, journalists and the broader society. The magnitude and expeditious resolution of the national #FeesMustFall campaign emphasised the power of social media to mobilise peaceful protests in an unprecedented manner. Students at Wits and other universities used a platform that they, their peers and supporters knew would provide maximum impact. Makgoba (2016) points out that '… to give a measure of the broad public support, #FeesMustFall grew to 300 tweets per second, which included tweets from journalists, media houses, protesters and the general public, whereas previous protests had very little national and even less international public recognition.'

Although there were various attempts by government and university leadership to engage the various demands, these were frequently seen or portrayed as retrogressive, short-termist and driven by political convenience. It seemed that at the height of the campaigns the university councils and executive teams spectacularly failed to comprehend the scope and implications of these events, at both institutional and national levels, and fell into a narrow and visionless crisis-management mode (Satgar 2015).

It appears evident that university leadership and management required a different approach and skills set in order to cope with the extent of complexity and crisis with which they were confronted. Vice-chancellors were faced with serious leadership dilemmas in terms of securing and protecting their institutional environments as the bastions of free speech that allow and embrace legitimate forms of protest but, simultaneously, provide adequate safeguards to protect staff, all students and valuable infrastructures. University leaders looked weak and came in for quite vociferous condemnation when they finally resorted to involving the state security apparatus private security services and the courts to deal with a situation that was clearly spiralling way out of control.

The need for coherent and collective leadership by vice-chancellors was acknowledged as one of the key challenges during this time, and resulted in the development of more comprehensive and proactive strategies, focused on providing guidance and support at institutional levels. The vice-chancellors in their individual and joint capacities through USAf acknowledged the extent of the systemic challenges faced, encouraged stakeholders to value universities as national assets, decried the unwarranted violence and destruction of property and called for collective ownership and responsible leadership, in terms of realistic and sustainable solutions (USAf 2015).

CASE STUDY REGARDING STUDENT NEGOTIATIONS

Prior to the #FeesMustFall phenomenon, common conditions applied, which more or less generically patterned the annual tuition fees negotiations. Changing dynamics in terms of institutional modalities – but also in the balance of political power in society, which rapidly altered the previous custom, practice and accepted rules of engagement – are investigated in the case of a particular university with the intention that this case could serve to illuminate analogous changes occurring throughout the system.

Firstly, the SRC in power at Wits was almost always the Progressive Youth Alliance (PYA), a student coalition linked to the ruling party and, concomitantly, to the government of the day. Consequently, the management/student negotiations invariably took place in the virtual political presence of the ruling party and relevant governmental structures. This arrangement, although sometimes uncomfortable, served to provide an implicit limit and safety net for the boundaries that could be meaningfully negotiated and the extent of militant or disruptive actions that could be carried out by the students.

Secondly, as a golden rule all financial documentation, pursuant to the university's budget and budgeting process, was made available by the university administration to the SRC. This was by no means an act of particular transparency, as SRC representatives are full members of the Financial Committee of Council and of Council itself, given that essential recommendations are formulated in the Finance Committee of Council whereas the budget debate at the Council meeting, however pyrotechnic, is the formalisation of a long and arduous process. Further, as SRC representatives are often first-timers in this process, dedicated meetings are convened with them in which appropriate university staff (such as the chief finance officer) systematically take them through the documentation and associated issues. These meetings often facilitate important insights and debate. For example, in the case of this particular university, student leaders were often astounded to 'discover' that the government subsidy is less than one-third of the overall budget. It would be immediately explained that this governmental subsidy is nonetheless a highly significant contribution to the actual core academic tuition process (as opposed to the research, institutes, centres and university companies' budgets). The start of greater understanding is now underway as the complex political economy of a higher education institution gradually emerges. Certainly, during this process, much initial militancy and hostility, based on the notion that the government has provided the universities with the full wherewithal to provide tertiary education for all students, and that student fees are levied for executive salaries, first class air-tickets, luxury catering and assorted unnecessary bells and whistles is dissipated by dint of facts and statistics.

Thirdly, the negotiation process is continued through a number of meetings, some of which last for six or eight hours or longer. On the student side, the negotiators are normally (although not always) new, and they would be hearing the set of arguments for the first time. On the side of management there is a three-person team (including two deputy vice-chancellors) who have done this negotiation many times, and are aware and alert to most student arguments and concerns. During this process leading questions are often put back to the students: for example, where they would cut the budget in order to lower fee increases, reduce academic or support service salaries, cut library resources, eliminate sporting facilities or neglect maintenance. In this process the student leadership often comes to appreciate how little room for manoeuvre there actually is in a university budget, as the largest item by far is the payroll, which is well over 50 per cent, after which municipal rates and taxes, electricity and water, insurance and other items constitute inevitable fixed costs. Further services such as cleaning, gardening and grounds maintenance, transport and so on have to be purchased at a going rate. After adding in library and general administrative costs there is in fact little enough for the university's core mission of academic development, research and public service.

The realisation of the above often causes severe cognitive dissonance within the student negotiators who have a 'mandate' to argue for lower fees (the starting position of the students is invariably a zero per cent increase). An important epistemological moment is habitually reached when one or other student negotiator announces that clearly the government subsidy to higher education institutions is insufficient and the answer may be to lobby the state fiscus accordingly. This invokes a further discussion about the arguments that the institutions, through bodies such as USAf (formerly Hesa), had repeatedly made over long years, and the Treasury's view that higher education is already sufficiently well funded, and should not receive further monies until it becomes more 'efficient' (a reference to the unsatisfactory throughput which characterises the South African higher education system).

What then transpires is dependent on the political chemistry, militancy, or assumed mandate of the particular student leadership group and/or on the general political environment and conjuncture. There are, however, perennial variations on a theme, which can occur either as individual instances or in some combination:

Set-piece speeches and appeals at Council

Depending on the calibre of the student leadership and the amount of preparation they have done, these interventions can be either sensible and persuasive or simply ineffective grandstanding. In the case of well-argued student submissions, council meetings have often sought some concession or compensatory decision that could assist the student leadership to claim a genuine outcome in their favour.

Symbolic or token protest

Some protesting takes place so that the student leadership is being seen to do its job and to stand up to 'management'. This protest may be minimally disruptive of university business, or on occasion there is some more serious disruption of learning activities for a few days.

Appeals to outside forces such as the ruling party or to government

This often set off a most interesting dialogic triangle whereby the parties contacted by the students will themselves contact the university, or individual university managers. These conversations often included a discussion about what form of concession could be given to the students in order that the outside party could assist in calming the situation – usually after allowing some form of militant activity to unfold for symbolic purposes. In the past an underlying concern of such parties, which could have been Luthuli House (headquarters of the ANC) or the Department of Higher Education and Training, was that university negotiators, deliberately or inadvertently may have been facilitating the student leadership to turn their anger and militant efforts towards government, rather than university management.

Indeed, in the case of the 2015 #FeesMustFall 'uprising' this is exactly what occurred, as students went beyond the institutional political economy of their separate universities to challenge the logical underpinnings of national tertiary funding arrangements.

So what changed with regard to the steady state negotiating generic as broadly described above which led to the drastically different pathway and outcome of #FeesMustFall?

Overall climate on university campuses

Detailed discussion of the general state of the university transformation debate is outside the scope of this chapter, but there is no doubt that an incendiary political environment had developed around a range of 'transformation'-related student perceptions and demands.

Negotiation facticities

Fee increases had consistently been above the general inflation rate for over a decade, even if in some years only marginally so. To some extent a ceiling had been reached in terms of the ability of even middle-class households generally to bear such costs, and only an inflation-related increase may have been indicated. Wits in 2015 was proposing a 10.5 per cent increase at a time when inflation was running at 4.8 per cent, which constituted a recipe for confrontation.

Negotiation style

It is not clear that the previous meticulous and mindful process of comprehensively and transparently briefing the student negotiators, along with the dedicated hours of sitting together communing over the university's financial, funding and budgetary dilemmas was followed. By some accounts a more autocratic approach was taken, and busy executives did not see fit to block long days (and nights) out in their diary for iterative and patient conversations with student leadership.

Role of outside parties

Most significantly however, it appeared that by 2015 the 'golden triangle' of political communication (and communion) involving the outside parties had thoroughly broken down in more than one modality. First, personal and/or 'comradely' networks involving university negotiators and key officials in political parties and government may have weakened or atrophied over the years due to natural political entropy and the movement of personnel on one or the other side. Thus the more tactical movement of daily intelligence in regard to fees controversies and potential disruption had been replaced by more formalistic engagement. More importantly however, crucial political authority wielded by the broader party structures outside of the campus environment had significantly waned (see Chapter 1 in this volume). Although nominally in the camp of the ruling party, the SRC leadership felt much less allegiance to a weak and disorganised ANC Youth League, or to an embattled and politically compromised party leadership. Nor had the previous paradigm of cultural reverence and respect for governmental and ministerial authority survived intact in the new and rapidly emerging political era – also fuelled in part by the rise of alternative party political formations vigorously asserting themselves within the student politics.

All the above factors could be seen as part of a 'perfect storm' that arose at Wits in 2015 in response to the attempted fee increases, characterised by a more independent student leadership and the epistemological breakthrough of student leadership overtly locating the real funding problem as essentially beyond the scope or control of university leadership.

However, with the 2015 #FeesMustFall tsunami largely dissipated, and the momentary unity of the student movement in tatters, it seems that the integrated analytical revelation of the demonstrations outside parliament and the Union Buildings has disintegrated. Radical or militant student factions, with varying campus support, are now involved in a series of guerrilla-type campaigns directed at individual institutions (or particular campuses of institutions). However, university management and leadership is again in the firing line in regard to institution-level transformation, financial and academic exclusion, outsourcing, residence space and in some cases language issues – once again, as at the beginning of the #FeesMustFall saga, caught between a rock and a hard place.

CONCLUSIONS

Leadership lessons learned at Wits and across the entire higher education sector point to a need for greater coherence and cohesiveness between the vice-chancellors and their executive teams in managing this structural crisis, more effective approaches to orchestrated disruptions and acts of violence, rapidly responsive communication and security protocols, reinforcing the role of legitimate governance structures, as well as thinking through the implications of institutional agreements and their impact on the entire sector. Moreover, the various components of the university community should also realise that strategic management decisions like no tuition fee increases or insourcing and various transformation measures have serious financial implications, which require sober deliberations and close consideration of complex trade-offs.

The sectoral and institutional disruptions and protests by students and other stakeholders, through the vehicle of the #RhodesMustFall, #FeesMustFall and #OpenStellenbosch campaigns, have illustrated the need for a collective narrative and, perhaps, a national campaign on the future vision and value of universities, led by USAf and involving key stakeholders such as government, business, labour, student leadership, donors, civil society organisations and so on. This national dialogue should focus on the role of universities as major contributors to education, strategic skills-formation, and economic and social development.

Urgent attention should be given to the further 'professionalisation' of governance, along with requisite leadership development efforts being formalised and/or institutionalised for all sub-sectors or stakeholder groups in higher education. USAf should take the lead on this, in cooperation with the Department of Higher Education and Training and the Council for Higher Education, and involving all major role-players, including the universities, which are already researching and/or training in regard to some of these interventions. This is a fundamental need for South Africa's higher education system, since failure to respond appropriately will perpetuate the current governance and management crisis and associated leadership shortcomings. Otherwise, we may well be setting up the vice-chancellors and their management teams for failure, with disastrous, institutional and sectoral implications for South African universities.

REFERENCES

Badsha, N. & Cloete, N. (2011) Higher Education: Contribution to the NPC's National Development Plan, November. Pretoria, National Planning Commission, http://www.chet.org.za/files/HE%20Contribution%20to%20NPCs%20National%20Development%20Plan%20Final.pdf

Bundy, C. (2006) Global Patterns, Local Options? Changes in higher education internationally and some implications for South Africa. In *Kagisano Number 4: Ten years of Higher Education under Democracy*. Pretoria: Council on Higher Education.

DHET (Department of Higher Education and Training) (2013) Report of the Ministerial Committee for the Review of the Funding of Universities, Department of Higher Education and Training, Pretoria, South Africa, October. http://www.dhet.gov.za/SiteAssets/Latest%20News/Report%20of%20the%20Ministerial%20Committee%20for%20the%20Review%20of%20the%20Funding%20of%20Universities.pdf

Duderstadt, J. J. (2005) The future of higher education in the knowledge-driven, global economy of the 21st century. In G. A. Jones, P. L. McCarney & M. Skolnik (eds) *The Changing Role of Higher Education*. Toronto: University of Toronto Press.

Habib, A. (2015) Transcending the past and reimagining the future of the South African university. *Journal of Southern African Studies*, Special Issue: *South Africa in Transition*. Published online, 25 January 2016. http://www.tandfonline.com/doi/abs/10.1080/03057070.2016.1121716

Habib, A. (2016) Goals and means: Some reflections on the 2015 #FeesMustFall protests. *Daily Maverick*, 26 January. http://www.dailymaverick.co.za/opinionista/2016-01-26-goals-and-means-some-reflections-on-the-2015-feesmustfall-protests/#.VsqwgPl95Mw

Hesa (Higher Education South Africa) (2011) Higher education funding in South Africa: Report to the Ministerial Committee, Review of funding to the universities, Hesa, October.

Hesa (2014) Annual Report. http://www.universitiessa.ac.za/sites/www.universitiessa.ac.za/files/HESA%20Annual%20report%202014%20FINAL%20LR.pdf

Johnson, B. & Cross, M. (2006) Academic leadership under siege: Possibilities and limits of executive deanship. *South African Journal of Higher Education*, 187(2), 34–58.

Makgoba, K. (2016) Social media activism #FeesMustFall. *Chica.co.za*. 17 May. http://chica.co.za/career/social-media-activism-feesmustfall/

Makgoba, M. (2011) South Africa: Universities must build a winning nation. *University World News*, 4 December.

Malgas, N. (2016) Protest underway over housing for black students. *Eye Witness News*, http://ewn.co.za/2016/02/15/UCT-students-protest-over-accommodation

Maree, J. & Le Roux, R. (2014) Report on outsourcing at UCT: Findings and recommendations, 14 April. https://www.uct.ac.za/downloads/uct.ac.za/about/governance/Final%20report%20JM%20and%20RLR.pdf

Mouton, J. (2014) South African Higher Education in the 20th Year of Democracy: Context, achievements and key challenges, Hesa presentation to the Portfolio Committee on Higher Education and Training, 22 August.

Mouton, J. & Wildschutt, L. (2015) *Leadership and Management: Case studies in training in higher education in Africa*. Cape Town: African Minds.

Mzobe, D. (2015) Struggle, September. http://workerssocialistparty.co.za/wp-content/uploads/2016/02/Page-4-University-Struggle.pdf

News 24 (2015) EFF playing of the #FeesMustFall card was effective – expert. http://www.news24.com/SouthAfrica/News/EFF-playing-of-the-FeesMustFall-card-was-effective-expert-20151021

Nicolson, G. (2016) Gauteng universities' protests grow. *Daily Maverick*, 14 January, http://www.dailymaverick.co.za/article/2016-01-14-gauteng-university-protests-grow/#.VuKex_l95Mw

Petersen, F. (2015) In B. Stanwix, What are the financial implications of insourcing at UCT, 26 November. http://www.groundup.org.za/article/what-are-financial-implications-insourcing-uct_3551/

Pounder, J. S. (2001) 'New leadership' and university organisational effectiveness: Exploring the relationship. *Leadership and Organisational Development Journal*, 22(6), 281–290.

PriceWaterhouseCoopers (n. d.) Funding of public higher education institutions in South Africa, http://www.pwc.co.za/en/higher-education/Funding-public-higher-education-institutions-SA.html

Satgar. V. (2015) What #ZumaMustFall and #FeesMustFall have in common. *Mail & Guardian*, 18 January. http://mg.co.za/article/2016-01-18-what-zumamustfall-and-feesmustfall-have-in-common

Scott, G., Coates, H. & Anderson, M. (2008) Learning leaders in times of change: Academic leadership capabilities for Australian Higher Education. University of Western Sydney and Australian Council for Educational Research, http://www.acer.edu.au/documents/UWSACER_CarrickLeadershipReport.pdf

Seale, O. (2015) Building leadership and management capacity for deans in South African higher education. Unpublished PhD Thesis, University of the Witwatersrand, Johannesburg.

Sharrock, G. (2012) University management: New finance models need better equipped leaders. https://www.theguardian.com/higher-education-network/blog/2012/sep/26/university-management-professional-development-australia

Singh, M. (2001) Reinserting the 'public good' into higher education transformation. *Kagisano CHE Higher Education Discussion Series*. Issue No.1, 8–11.

Times Live (2016) http://www.timeslive.co.za/sundaytimes/opinion/2016/02/21/Student-protests-when-fear-and-loathing-trump-hope-and-unity

USAf (Universities South Africa) (2015) Report of a special board meeting, 12 December. Intercontinental Hotel, OR Tambo Airport, Johannesburg.

USAf (2016) Statement after the meeting between the Ministry of Higher Education and Training and the vice-chancellors of South Africa's public universities. 20 January.

Yielder, J. & Codling, A. (2004) Management and leadership in the contemporary university. *Journal for Higher Education Policy and Management*, 26(3), 315–328.

CHAPTER
12

FINANCING OF UNIVERSITIES: PROMOTING EQUITY OR REINFORCING INEQUALITY

Pundy Pillay

INTRODUCTION

In the context of the recent student uprisings, perceptions have been created that the state should provide free university education or, at the very least, more funds for universities, and that current levels of state funding for this sector are inadequate. Chapter 2 of the Constitution states that everyone has a right to education (which presumably includes higher education) 'which the state, through reasonable measures, must make progressively available and accessible'. This does not, however, mean that the state has to provide free higher education.

How feasible is it for the South African state to provide free university education? There are at least two important considerations. The first is that in the current economic climate it would not be possible to provide more funding for education in general, and universities in particular, given current and projected low economic growth rates. The growth projections by the National Treasury and private sector experts is of such a conservative nature that the expansionary fiscal policy that has characterised much of the democratic era appears to have come to an end. In other words, the tax base is unlikely to rise significantly to make possible a meaningful increase in education or other social sector spending. The only way in which additional financial resources could be generated by the state at the present time is through increased taxation. However, the chances of this happening are extremely slim given the conservative macroeconomic policy stance of the government especially as regards increasing the tax burden on those at the high end of the income spectrum.

The second consideration, from an equity perspective, and in the context of a stagnating economy, is whether universities should really be getting more public resources in the light of the demand of other more deserving (from an equity point of view) sub-sectors of education such as early childhood development and vocational education and training, as well as other sectoral priorities such as primary healthcare or social grants. As Table 12.1 shows, the technical vocational education and training budget is projected to grow annually by only 4.8 per cent in the Medium-Term Economic Framework (MTEF) period of 2015–2016 to 2018–2019, while university subsidies are projected to increase annually by 9.1 per cent and the National Student Financial Aid Scheme (NSFAS) by 14.1 per cent.

If we are serious about reducing inequality in our society through providing equal opportunities for all *and* ensuring more equal life outcomes, the claims of education sub-sectors such as early childhood development and vocational education and training should surely be prioritised above the demands of universities. Both these sub-sectors are seriously underfunded in absolute terms and as a proportion of the total education budget and of gross domestic product (GDP). This is not to minimise the importance of university education for broader economic and social development. For instance, university education can and does play a critical role in raising the level of economic growth and living standards through education, training, research and innovation.

It is also true that the demand for university education has been increasing at an exceptionally high rate in the post-apartheid era as a consequence of the government's commitment to expanding access and promoting racial and gender equity. As a consequence of this rapid expansion over two decades, the participation rate in higher education expressed as a proportion of the age group eighteen to twenty-four years almost doubled to close to 20 per cent in 2015 (own calculation). With the exceptions of Botswana, Mauritius and Nigeria, no other country in sub-Saharan Africa – where the average gross enrolment ratio is 8 per cent (Unesco 2016) – comes close to the South African figure.

The case for more financial resources for universities, therefore, is beyond question. This is partly why when universities such as the University of the Witwatersrand (Wits) were proposing a 10.5 per cent increase in 2015, when inflation was estimated to be around 5 per cent, it was an obvious recipe for confrontation. It is unlikely that the universities themselves were trying to confront the state. The proposal for a substantially higher-than-inflation fee increase reflects both the higher inflation rate in the university sector and the reluctance on the part of university administrations to address issues of whether they are making the best possible use of the resources they receive from the state and the students. For instance, no university management has dared to propose a salary freeze for 2017 as an alternative cost-saver.

However, the more pertinent question relates to the source(s) of additional financial resources for universities in the light of the constraints on state funding and the political challenges associated with increasing fees. We also need to ask some tough policy questions of the education sector more generally. For instance, are we making the best use of the financial resources allocated to education? For the 2016–2017 financial year, the amount allocated to education is R265.7 billion, or nearly 20 per cent of the budget (National Treasury 2016). It is self-evident that the quality of schooling received by those at the lower ends of the income spectrum condemns those emerging from this system to unemployment and further poverty, or entry into post-school institutions where the vicious cycle of poor quality of education, and poor labour market outcomes, is extended.

In universities, there are serious questions about 'systemic efficiency' reflected institutionally, *inter alia*, in high dropout and repetition rates, and long completion times. In terms of the economy, there is substantial anecdotal evidence (and a little statistical evidence) of graduate 'under-employment' (where students are forced to take jobs that require lower qualifications and/or skills than their education and training suggests, partly because employers see graduates from certain institutions as being of 'poor quality') raising questions about the so-called 'external efficiency' of the university system. An important causal factor here is the current political imperative to focus almost exclusively on quantitative expansion of the system – hence, for example, the policy decision to establish two new universities (mainly to placate the two provinces where there were no universities – as if universities were a provincial competence) when, with limited resources, the more rational decision would have been to expand current university capacity to achieve gains through economies of scale, as illustrated in many countries, both industrialised and developing. Total enrolment in these two universities in their first year of existence was 1 234 (National Treasury 2016) suggesting that there is a long way to go before any 'economies of scale can be achieved' (that is, large enrolments and low unit costs of education).

UNIVERSITY FUNDING

It is argued in some quarters that universities in this country are seriously underfunded and comparisons are often made, for example, with Organisation for Economic Cooperation and Development (OECD) countries where tertiary education is largely free or, at the very least, highly subsidised. For example, a recent newspaper article by the chairperson of NSFAS claims that South Africa's spending on universities is comparatively low. He says that 'in 2011, the state budget for universities (including funding for NSFAS) as a percentage of gross domestic product was 0.75 per cent, just less than in Africa as a whole (0.78 per cent). The budget for the 2015–2016 fiscal year is 0.72 per cent of GDP, lower than it was in 2011. This is also significantly lower than that for OECD countries (1.21 per cent) and the rest of the world (0.84 per cent)' (Nxasana 2016).

These comparisons are not really appropriate. First, most if not all OECD countries do not have the schooling and other pre-university funding challenges that South Africa and other developing countries face, in addition to the intersectoral competition for resources that education faces from health, social development, housing and other sectors. Second, Africa's expenditure on higher education as a percentage of GDP may be higher than South Africa's but this is because sub-Saharan Africa seriously underspends on schooling – the consequence being the poorest outputs and outcomes in schooling internationally. Third, the bulk of higher education funds goes to providing free higher education for the elites in many countries. That is why the gross enrolment ratio in Africa has failed to rise significantly above the 6 to 8 per cent mark during the past few decades.

A more appropriate comparison for South Africa is other 'middle income' countries, which show that current government expenditure on universities in this country is not out of line, especially in the light of the development challenges outlined above. Two interesting case studies on the financing of universities relate to Brazil and South Korea. In both countries, the funding of pre-university education has been prioritised to such a great extent that the university sector is largely privatised. The rationale for this stems from the importance of high-quality schooling for ensuring equal opportunities and outcomes in life for the greater majority of the population. Partly because of increased funding and opportunities for the poor in education, inequality in Brazil, for example, has been falling quite significantly during the past two decades.

None of this is to argue for privatisation of universities in South Africa, although it may well be time to open this debate, especially with regard to not-for-profit private higher education. However, if we are serious about addressing the obscene levels of income, wealth and other inequalities in our society, it is imperative that sectors such as schooling and primary healthcare are prioritised so that individuals can develop the basic 'human capital' for post-school education and for gainful employment in the labour market.

Table 12.1: Post-school education and training expenditure, 2015/16 – 2018/19 (R, m) (Source: National Treasury (2016); 2015–2016 – Revised estimate).

SUB-SECTOR	2015/16	2016/17	2017/18	2018/19	ANNUAL AVERAGE MTEF GROWTH (%)
University subsidies	22 985	24 568	28 069	29 827	9.1
University infrastructure	3 301	3 397	3 538	3 708	4.0
NSFAS	9 247	14 292	13 187	13 722	14.1
TVET	6 843	6 917	7 414	7 866	4.8
Community education and training	1 564	2 070	2 237	2 380	15.0
Skills development levy	18 758	15 894	18 575	20 587	3.2
Total	62 698	67 138	73 020	78 090	7.9

With respect to university funding in South Africa, it is important to distinguish between the subsidies going to universities and the funds provided to NSFAS. In the case of the latter, these amounts have more than doubled in the past five years. In the case of university subsidies, the growth pattern has not been out of line with the increase in the general budget. Moreover, possibly as a consequence of the student protests the subsidies to universities are projected to increase in real terms (9.1 per cent nominal increase – Table 12.1, and the allocations to NSFAS by 14 per cent in the MTEF period 2016–2017 to 2018–2019). Additional spending on higher education for this period is as follows: 2016–2017 – 4.882 billion; 2017–2018: 5.555 billion; 2018-2019: 5.832 billion; total 16.269 billion (National Treasury 2016).

The national budget of 2016 shows the respective average nominal increases for the period 2015–2016 to 2018–2019 as follows: for Basic Education – 7.4 per cent (7.7 per cent 2012–2013 to 2015–2016); Post-school Education and Training – 11.4 per cent (7.9 per cent); and Health – 8.4 per cent (7.6 per cent) (National Treasury 2016).

FINANCING UNIVERSITIES

Table 12.1 shows the allocations (actual and projected) for post-school education for the period 2015–2016. What, then, can be done about addressing the financing challenges of universities? First, we should ask some difficult questions of our universities about how they utilise the resources they currently receive from the state. Institutional inefficiency in the utilisation of resources reflected, *inter alia*, in bloated administrations, as well as high dropout and failure rates and long completion times, results in an enormous wastage of resources in many institutions. Therefore, initiatives to improve this 'internal efficiency' question should be prioritised. The recent proposal by the minister of higher education and training to have universities audited by the office of the auditor-general makes a lot of sense.

Second, with regard to university financing, several options have been put forward in the context of the student protests in the last few months. In this chapter, two options are examined before suggesting a way forward. These options relate to the introduction of a graduate tax and an increase in general taxation.

The graduate tax

With a graduate tax system, university graduates would pay a higher tax rate when they enter and remain in the labour market, the rationale being that they have benefited from the public subsidisation of universities. For example, if a graduate's tax rate is 30 per cent without a graduate tax in place, with the creation of a graduate tax it would rise, say, two to three percentage points higher.

The intention is that the National Treasury would 'dedicate' the revenue from the graduate tax to university education. However, the international experience with such 'dedicated taxes' is not very encouraging. For instance, there is a long history of such funds being raided by government for other purposes as crises emerge on an annual basis. Questions of 'fairness' have also been raised. For instance, more successful graduates will earn more and will therefore pay more. It is also questionable about how much of the benefit that accrues to an individual is actually due to the degree. This view subscribes to the so-called 'screening hypothesis', which suggests that the value of (university) education lies in its ability to identify individuals with greater potential in life rather than providing them with the appropriate skills. Moreover, it is likely that the value of a degree diminishes over time, especially if individuals are in occupations for which they were not educated. Questions have also been raised about whether a graduate tax provides incentives for people to migrate, intensifying the already serious problem of the 'brain drain' in developing countries. Finally, there is the question of whether developing countries have the administrative capability to track all the graduates within a country's borders. This might not be an insurmountable barrier in South Africa given the high level of efficiency of the South African Revenue Service (SARS). However, the graduate tax does provide a strong incentive to deny one's graduate status, especially for the self-employed.

Increasing taxes

The conventional wisdom in South Africa is that it is a country of high taxes and that the burden of taxation is carried by a relatively few individuals. On the first point, the tax-to-GDP ratio is around 29 per cent (National Treasury 2015), which is not high by either industrialised or developing country averages. Second, the personal income tax system in South Africa is not as progressive as it is often made out to be. The marginal tax rate (the highest personal income tax rate paid in the country) stands at 41 per cent for individuals earning just more than R700 000 per annum. What this means is that whether an individual earns R700 000, R7 million, or R70 million, the tax rate that is paid on every extra rand over R700 000 remains at 41 per cent. There is clearly more scope here for increased progressivity in the tax rate for the very rich – but the economic orthodoxy on this will no doubt argue that this provides a disincentive for the rich to remain in the country, work harder, and so on. This orthodoxy needs to be challenged, but it is doubtful whether government has the courage to take the step suggested here, given vested private sector interests, clearly illustrated by its almost apologetic stance for the 1 per cent increase in the marginal rate in the March 2015 budget.

The second pertinent issue is the tax burden that is being carried by a relatively small number of people. This is indeed correct. Eleven per cent of taxpayers are responsible for 61 per cent of all personal income taxes paid. In terms of the highest earners, 2.7 per cent of taxpayers are responsible for 33.7 per cent of all tax (National Treasury 2015).

The question: 'why are so few burdened with taxes in South Africa' is the wrong question. It may be more appropriate to ask why 39 per cent of taxpayers earn less than R150 000, a further 25 per cent less than R250 000, and more than 8.5 million less than R70 000 per annum. These figures illustrate the degree of inequality in South Africa. It is evident that more courageous public finance policies (including higher taxation rates for the very rich) are needed if we are going to bridge the gap between those at the bottom and those at the top of this ladder.

A higher marginal rate of taxation (and hence increased revenues for the state), however, does not necessarily mean more resources for education, or universities in particular, because these funds will go into the general revenue pot to be disbursed through the general budgeting process.

It would be amiss not to say anything about wealth taxes given the current rage around Thomas Piketty (2014, 2015) and his proposals for a wealth tax. Contrary to the view propagated in South Africa, many countries do have wealth taxes and the evidence suggests that the wealthy do not leave the country in significant numbers when such taxes are levied provided they are set at reasonable rates. Nonetheless, the preference here is for increased income taxes (both personal and corporate) rather than a new wealth tax, primarily because of the difficulty of collecting such taxes; assets can be and are swiftly moved, mainly because of the ease of doing so in an increasingly globalised world and especially given the proliferation of international tax havens.

THE NATIONAL STUDENT FINANCIAL AID SCHEME (NSFAS)

In recent years, the state has poured large amounts of resources into NSFAS. In fact, the funding provided to NSFAS has more than doubled in the last five years. The mandate of the scheme is to support poor students. NSFAS and its predecessor, the Tertiary Education Fund for South Africa (TEFSA), awarded R50.5 billion to about 1.5 million students in the form of loans and bursaries between 1991 and 2014 at twenty-five public higher education institutions and fifty technical vocational education and training (TVET) colleges (Nxasana 2016).

However, whether the scheme is funding students in an equitable manner is questionable given the large difference in the numbers of poor students between historically disadvantaged and historically advantaged institutions, or between urban and rural universities (compare Wits with the University of Fort Hare, for example). In other words, is the average poor student at Fort Hare subsidised to the same extent as a poor student at Wits or the University of Cape Town (UCT)?

The state should assess whether NSFAS is producing optimal outcomes with respect both to *efficiency* in the utilisation of the resources provided to it and to *equity* in terms of who benefits. Do poor students actually benefit from this when they are expected to bear the burden of debt for a substantial part of their working career? Is NSFAS really contributing to the attainment of equal opportunities in higher education and more equal outcomes in life for those who graduate? In other words, does providing a loan to a poor student actually contribute to the lowering of inequality?

Moreover, there are serious questions about the viability of NSFAS, particularly in the context of low (or no) growth and appallingly low levels of employment creation in the formal economy. In addition, the evidence of successful loan schemes in the developing world in particular, and across the world is general, is rather scant.

THE GROWTH OF STUDENT DEBT

Related to the provision of student loans, Thandeka Gqubule (2016) has drawn attention to the growth of student debt in South Africa. She argues:

> A disturbing narrative is emerging in higher education in relation to student debt and education financing. The experience of the US has taught the world that student debt is not benign – it has serious detrimental economic and social effects. Students in South Africa owe about R711 million. According to a University of South Africa study that polled 1 220 students from universities around the country, the number of young South Africans with serious over-indebtedness has grown in the past decade. Of

the students polled by Unisa, 77 per cent reported that they depended on their parents and guardians for their income.

Gqubule (2016) goes further to quote from Nobel Prize winning economist Joseph Stiglitz's recent article 'Student debt and the crushing of the American dream', which shows that student debt in the US is more than R1.45 trillion – exceeding credit card debt. The link between student debt and inequality is particularly pertinent for South Africa. Gqubule quotes Stiglitz as saying: 'Like the housing crisis that preceded it, this crisis is intimately connected to America's soaring inequality and how, as Americans on the bottom rungs of the ladder strive to climb up, they are inevitably pulled down – some to a point even lower than where they began.'

Stiglitz points out further: '… in the decades after the Second World War, home ownership and higher education became the symbols of success in the US. But now, debt is delaying household formation, putting a lid on postgraduate studies, and hobbling the housing market. Student debt is dragging down economic growth' (as cited in Gqubule 2016).

Importantly, Stiglitz points to the longer-term economic implications of student debt. As quoted by Gqubule (2016):

> Student debt is not benign and economically insignificant. It affects capital formation – the increase in per capita output, or net additions of capital stock such as equipment, buildings and roads – all of which go to create goods and services and have a direct negative effect on our productivity as a country. People will not start new businesses, invest in capital equipment, manufacture goods and innovate. Student debt can be a drag on GDP. By damping consumption, it hinders economic growth. Therefore we need a solution that will require us to reimagine fiscal priorities, economic management and sustainable financing of higher education.

FUNDING PROPOSALS FOR UNIVERSITIES IN A CONTEXT OF INEQUALITY

Three proposals are advanced here: a) an income-contingent fee scheme; b) conversion of NSFAS into a grant scheme for poor students; and c) introducing measures to enhance efficiency in institutional resource utilisation.

These proposals are made within the following context:
- South Africa is a highly unequal country in terms, *inter alia*, of income and wealth distribution.
- A substantial increase in public resources for university education is unlikely in the short term to medium terms, given low economic growth. However, even if economic conditions did impove, with such high levels of inequality it makes sense for the state to prioritise other sectors above the universities.

Proposal 1: Income-contingent fee scheme – introduce legislation to implement a differentiated fee structure in universities based on socioeconomic status

In other words, the richer your family is, the more you will pay in fees. This could be regarded as 'indirect taxation' and will no doubt be resisted by the more wealthy. However, it would undoubtedly be preferable to raising direct taxes such as personal income taxes (or even, and especially, indirect taxes such as VAT). How could this work in practice? For a start, fees could be linked to the type of school the student comes from and/or the residential area of the student. This type of criterion is preferable to using means (income) testing, which is fraught with problems as NSFAS has amply demonstrated. One possible model is the following, showing declining fees:

(i) Students from private schools (highest fees).
(ii) Students from former Model C schools and former white suburbs.
(iii) Students from former township schools in urban areas.
(iv) Students from peri-urban and rural schools (lowest fees).

There are at least two reasons why this model can be feasible. First, the fees paid by parents for private schools is currently well in excess of what they pay in the most expensive South African universities – even a doubling of fees would not meet what some private schools are currently charging. Second, even if there were a doubling of university fees for this group, it would still be much cheaper than going to a university in the US, for example, or the UK.

It will be argued that there are children from lower socioeconomic groups attending the former Model C schools, in some cases in significant numbers, but exemptions can be created for this group.

The political resistance to this proposal from the elites in society should not be underestimated, but if we are committed to reducing inequality we need to adopt models such as these to show that we are serious about providing equal opportunities for individuals from historically disadvantaged groups to ensure that life's outcomes for them will be much better than they were for their parents. Moreover, this measure of redistribution to fund universities would be less contentious politically than, for example, implementing a wealth tax.

Proposal 2: Convert NSFAS from a loan scheme to providing grants for the poor at the historically disadvantaged institutions, which (as is currently the case) will cater to a larger proportion of economically disadvantaged students as well as for poor students at other universities who are not able to pay fees if they are from groups (ii), (iii) and (iv) above

There are several reasons for rejecting a loan scheme such as NSFAS. First, it serves to entrench inequality. Poor students who invariably will be the first from their families to go to university will have to spend the first five to ten years paying off their loans rather than helping their families to move up the socioeconomic ladder. Second, there is very little evidence that loan schemes such as NSFAS are actually viable in developing countries and there is evidence that NSFAS is struggling to recover payments from students. This is partly because the employment of students from the 'NSFAS category' is not occurring at a sufficiently high level to effect loan repayments owing to low economic growth and, often, the perceived poor quality of graduates from some universities.

Proposal 3: Put in place measures to ensure that universities use state resources in the most efficient way possible

Often, universities hide behind the 'institutional autonomy' banner to prevent external government assessments, but we need to find a way of ensuring that state resources are spent in the most efficient way possible while respecting this jealously guarded autonomy.

CONCLUSIONS

The measures proposed here will undoubtedly be considered 'radical' and impractical in many university environments and in that segment of our society that is being asked to make the greater contribution to this funding model. However, if we want to address the financing challenges in universities currently highlighted by the student protests it will require unconventional thinking that does not pander to vested interests, many of which even deny that inequality is a problem. The alternative is to increase fees in 2017 unless the state significantly increases its university funding yet again.

Education is not the only inequality-reducing factor in society but it is a very important one. At the present time, inequality in schooling reinforces and perpetuates inequality in post-school education and then in the economy and broader society. With the need to prioritise expenditure in a context of limited public resources, the top priority for the state has to be funding improvements in the quality of basic education, primary healthcare and nutrition, the basic building blocks of the nation's so-called 'human capital'.

In the case of universities, the state should move to make better use of the current resources it makes available to universities through ensuring that the poor receive free university education for their undergraduate education (say, four years) while endeavouring to increase such resources as growth levels pick up. In addition, policies should be introduced to induce rich parents to pay a greater share of university costs.

REFERENCES

Gqubule, T. (2016) How student debt leads to slow growth. *Business Day*, 30 March.
National Treasury (2015) Budget Review.
National Treasury (2016) Budget Review.
Nxasana, S. (2016) Planning and financing of universities. *Business Day*, 24 March.
Piketty, T. (2014) *Capital in the Twenty-First Century*. Cambridge, MA: Harvard University Press.
Piketty, T. (2015) *The Economics of Inequality*. Cambridge, MA: Harvard University Press.

PART FIVE

JUSTICE, IDENTITY, FORCE AND RIGHTS – 'WE CAME FOR THE REFUND'

CHAPTER
13

EXCAVATING THE VERNACULAR: 'UGLY FEMINISTS', GENERATIONAL BLUES AND MATRIARCHAL LEADERSHIP[1]

Darlene Miller

INTRODUCTION

In the #FeesMustFall movement, two distinguishing features produce a rupture with the past. The first is that womanhood is a contested space, along with sexual identities. The second is the contestation of forms of leadership, in which representational systems of leadership have been destabilised. These modes of self-organisation and self-expression of students in the #FeesMustFall movement are different to the dominant practices in the recent past of South African social movements. While 'being woman' has been the terrain on which feminists in South Africa and globally have countered gendered political identities, the prevalence of diverse sexualities among women on the university barricades – in protests, speeches, marches, meetings and blogs – is a radical discontinuity with the past.

This gendered difference in the #FeesMustFall social movement is producing a radical feminist political praxis that stands in stark contrast to the 'domesticated feminisms' that characterise older South African political activists today. In various ways – through elite formation, political incorporation, ageing and political fatigue – most of the older feminists who were part of the democratic transition no longer occupy the spaces on the barricades. This may be seen as a natural cycle of social protest. Leon Trotsky is credited with the saying, 'Before forty, a revolutionary. After forty, a rogue!' This chapter contends that the different political positionalities of what I term the 'new African woman' vis-à-vis the 'domesticated feminist' produces a generational rupture and leads to what I call 'generational blues'. By this term I imply that instead of the significant chasm that potentially exists between the 'new African woman' and the older feminist, the older feminist should be the 'organic political elder' of the 'new African woman'.

My chapter focuses on the ways in which lesser-known coloured feminist activists of the 1980s and the 2010s have challenged their social containment as women in order to give fuller self-expression to their political activism. The 2012–2013 Red Tent research project (Miller 2013a, b, c, d) of the Human Sciences Research Council (HSRC) conducted personal interviews with ten middle-class women from 1980s social movements in the Western Cape; a personal interview with a key woman leader from the Proudly Manenberg organisation active in the 2000s; two focus groups with middle-class African women immigrants in Edinburgh; and working-class women (the dominant profile of the male leader, Mario Wanza, has often overshadowed the role of the women's leadership in Proudly Manenberg). Some of the Red Tent research findings are presented here as a way of engaging with our 'vernacular' – the indigenous languages in which we express our political identities. This indigenous language refers to the political lexicons that develop within social movements and national political arenas. We South African feminists have struggled with our identities as 'women', alternately resisting and accepting the socially prescribed roles that would contain and inhibit our self-expression and 'self-activity', a term drawn from the revolutionary text by Vladimir Ilyich Lenin, 'What is to be done'.

The chapter contributes towards a dialogue between older feminists and the 'new African woman', in the hope that some of our struggles with the gendered containment of women in political organisations resonate with the current challenges of heterosexual women and LGBTIAQ+ as they endeavour to forge a new political trajectory for social justice and transformation in South Africa.

THE 'NEW AFRICAN WOMAN' – 'UGLY FEMINIST' OR NECESSARY SCREAM

> In the beginning is the scream. We scream … The starting point of theoretical reflection is opposition, negativity, struggle. It is from rage that thought is born, not from the pose of reason, not from the

reasoned-sitting-back-and-reflecting-on-the-mysteries-of-existence that is the conventional image of 'the thinker' (Holloway 2002).

Black urban women are a force unleashed in the #FeesMustFall movement. Their struggle tactics are radical. Women students at the University of Cape Town (UCT), Rhodes University (Rhodes) and the University of the Witwatersrand (Wits) employed the feminist activist tactic of stripping to show disgust at society. They stood topless at their barricades, most of them young black women. These acts evoked the memory of Laymah Gbowee's Women in Peace movement in Liberia (Gbowee and Mithers 2013). When forcing the warlords and the men to make a truce, they occupied the hotel where the peace meetings were being held and threatened to strip. As the 2012 public furore over Brett Murray's images of the president displayed, revealing intimate parts of the body in the urban context still offends many black South Africans (traditionally, women in rural areas went bare-breasted in public, so taboos around nudity are constructed differently). The 'bare breast' protest by Rhodes and Wits women students thus smashes through prevailing social norms, even activist norms.

Politics begins with the scream. The scream is not pretty. The scream tears at the social fabric of society. 'Ugly feminists' is about the body of the feminist and the necessary ugliness in the feminist and/or radical act. 'Ugly feminists' ascribes hatefulness to the feminist body as it vocalises its radical aggression. The demure African 'girl' has been kicked aside by this advancing movement, and many patriarchs – sweet patriarchs, bullying patriarchs (or both, as is often the case) – are shocked by such temerity. (My personal favourite is the black woman student leader who wears high-fashion suits, has natural hair dyed a blond-orange in a gorgeous fish plait and wears green or blue contact lenses, depending on her mood. I call her the student movement's avatar because of her changeling styles.) Older African women give disapproving looks, and older feminists brought up in the jeans and scruffy union T-shirt traditions of earlier activist movements are bewildered by fashion statements. Activism is as much about image as it is about protest marches for the #FeesMustFall woman and LGBTIAQ+.

The young black women smashing through the barricades of patriarchal society are not alone in Africa. They form part of a rising tide of women activists who are questioning African patriarchal leadership in South Africa and beyond. While evidence of the women demographic in Africa in the twenty-first century is still limited, a number of anecdotal observations about various kinds of struggles can be made. The diversity of the women subjects on the #FeesMustFall barricades defies stereotypes. The women and LGBTIAQ+ demographic in the #FeesMustFall movement is not yet empirically established either. However, in multiple contexts the presence of women and LGBTIAQ+ activists is visually in evidence (at vigils, at marches, in public press statements, in meetings).

The attire of the young, predominantly black activist women (when they have their clothes on) makes loud statements that symbolically scream at society: 'We are here and we have been invisible for too long!' Their choices of clothing are a conscious and assertive part of their activist identity, evident in their public appearances: big African headgear and earrings; Black Panthers-style (the US 1960s African American liberation movement) black pants and T-shirts; bold African prints and, importantly, free black hair. In a society that upholds straight and smooth hair as disciplined citizenship, they have claimed freedom for their hair alongside their rights to activism and activist leadership.

Representational democracy and 'tea-party' negotiations à la those at the 1991 Convention for a Democratic South Africa (Codesa) are decried by the #FeesMustFall students as weak instruments for social change, as the students insist when they say that 'tea-party' change is not part of their agenda. In fact, the students eschew the modified feminisms that have adapted to patriarchy in South African society in which feminists assume conventional roles of mothers, wives, sex(y) objects (one characterisation of the woman who compromises her feminism in this way is that of the 'sexy feminist', who apparently claims her body while she/it simultaneously feeds the 'male gaze' – as was said during the Luhlaza Leadership Initiative Focus Group in September 2015) and various forms of docile labour (Foucault 1995). In this sense, then, they often 'disrespect' African elders by refusing to listen to the cautions of university leaders such as vice-chancellors. Their bodily stance when they do this is often not demure but rebellious, aggressive, angry, resistant. For many in South African society, this kind of *militant irreverence* may be seen as very offensive, even ugly. Feminist activism thus challenges existing gendered hierarchies in society. The womanist activism of the #FeesMustFall students embodies this kind of 'ugly feminism': a radical social challenge that begins with the scream.

The political target identified by the #FeesMustFall students is the system of colonial patriarchy that prevails in all facets of society, including the university. Despite this identification of the patriarchy as the principal enemy, older feminists also find the actions of the students an affront. 'Senseless violence', in referring to the destruction of resources and infrastructure, is one narrative that emanates from new elites – including feminists – both within and beyond the academy. In the act of rage, social movements including the student movements, employ arson as a political tactic. Race narratives in the #FeesMustFall movement offend coloured women for whom nonracialism was a defining principle earned on their barricades in the 1980s (see, for example, Haffajee 2015: 16). Whereas marriage is a dominant social practice among many older feminists, for many in the LGBTIAQ+ community this is seen as 'sleeping with the enemy'. Dominant and codified practices of representational democracy and leadership, such as the Constitution, are accepted by many feminist political subjects in post-apartheid South Africa as the best conduit for transformation. In addition to the above criticisms of the student activists, the emphasis on sexuality and identity has led to the criticism by earlier radicals (many who were active in the 1980s) that the student activists do not focus on fundamental social transformation and social justice.

In various meetings and contexts, the unfolding 'herstory'[2] of the #FeesMustFall woman is an enigma for the generation of both men and women activists who made the transition of 1994. The #FeesMustFall movements are 'lost in translation' for many older feminists, not only patriarchs. Such objections potentially place these older feminists on opposite sides of the barricade from the 'new African woman'. This is not to minimise the importance of the older feminist activist who has continued to occupy the barricades in the new South Africa, such as the Proudly Manenberg women activists who engage in social protests and who participated in the Occupy the Commons protest on the Rondebosch Commons in Cape Town in 2012 (Miller 2013b) – but activist older feminists are an (exceptional) minority. 'Generational blues' becomes the lament of the older activist against the tactics and politics of these younger feminists and revolutionaries. The lament is based on differences in a range of fault lines including nonracialism, class and social transformation, violence in political resistance, participation in socially cohesive practices such as heteronormative marriages, institutions of representational democracy, elite positionalities in the academy and acceptance of dominant and contained versions of womanhood and sexuality. Lest we drown in these faultlines and accept the widening generational chasm, this chapter seeks to share the contestations of older and revolutionary feminists who, unsuccessfully in the main, attempted to challenge patriarchy within social movements in the past.

What has happened to the 'herstories' of the leftist feminists who are not part of the legacy-making cultures of the ruling elites? The research material presented here (the viewpoints of some feminists from the anti-apartheid struggle) emanates from leftist women who screamed and raged in their youth.

Contained in various spaces, including their own revolutionary movements, their voices have seldom been heard in the narratives of post-apartheid South Africa. Lesser-known in the South African intellectual milieu is an émigré in London who has chronicled her experiences as 'faction' (a hybrid of fact and fiction) in novels and articles (Pandit 2002). As one young woman said: 'But I want to know about these coloured women. Tell me. Tell us!' (Thobekile Mbanda, interview, 2012). What I am able to present here are left-wing feminist critiques, from past and present, of the 1980s progressive patriarchal leadership, which go beyond the struggle narratives of male domination and prevalence in liberation movements by illuminating experiences of coloured women activists and revolutionaries. These experiences inform my reaction to the 'new feminists' and their twenty-first-century radicalism. It is here where I express my own generational blues (and the blues of some of my peers) and the discussion is thus deeply interpolated by my own readings of this experience. Some of the revolutionary feminists presented here were members of shadowy, illegal Trotskyist groupings, which had relatively few members (such as the Marxist Workers Tendency and the Workers International League of South Africa) but often had deep roots in mass movements of civics, students and trade unions. Such deep roots found expression in significant political resolutions and policies in South Africa's ANC-dominated organisations.

This chapter thus deals with the reactions of older feminists to issues of patriarchal leadership, motherhood and marriage. The first section discusses the potential chasm between leftist matriarchs and radical young women and LGBTIAQ+ in the #FeesMustFall movement. The second part of the chapter discusses gender and 'being women' as a space of containment and entrapment. The third part of the chapter discusses matriarchal leadership and the 'search for the vernacular' in the way that we present our 'herstories'. The project findings on alternative styles and mechanisms of leadership are discussed in this section.

RESEARCH METHODOLOGY – INDIGENISING RESEARCH PRAXES

The interviews with seven coloured women and one white middle-class woman who were activists and revolutionaries in the 1980s were conducted by young and/or gay interviewees as a conscious, intergenerational research strategy. The interviews were structured to set up a generational conversation in which older feminist activists and revolutionaries told their (as yet predominantly untold) stories to (eager) young listeners. These interviews and life experiences are chronicled in the documentaries of The Red Tent research project.

The documentary 'On Motherhood, Marriage and Activism' (Miller 2013d) begins with the research team washing the feet of the research respondents, women leaders from the organisation Proudly Manenberg. This act is a demonstration of feminist research methodologies in which power hierarchies of researcher and researched are negated. The act of humility and physical lowness symbolises the respect of the researchers for the women they have interviewed. The researchers present an act of thanks by means of an (environmentally friendly) foot massage – sand and water from the beach and the sea were used for the massage. An emotional bond is established between the researcher and the respondent in this act – physical touching and embracing – and highlights the matriarchal nature of the research leadership, in which humility and servant leadership are valued as research team qualities.

This project endeavoured to incorporate indigenous cultural practices into the framing of the research. Juliet Perumal (2007) asserts that feminist research methodologies aspire to 'acknowledge the subjective, emotional and biographical factors that shape the researcher and the researched', and that establish 'non-hierarchical, dialogic, mutually educative encounters' between them. Feminist researchers confront power in society, as well as in the research process, and try to make it visible as well as to limit power from expressing itself in inhibiting ways. So the methods of data collection in feminist research and in this study are used in order to make visible what has tended to be invisible by giving 'voice' to women to illuminate and legitimate their lived experience. Ours is a project of retrieval of what exists but cannot be readily seen.

Elana Buch and Karen Staller (2007: 188) claim that feminist ethnographers find and analyse the 'systematic connections between domains of social life' by 'using the self as much as possible'. Where the researcher is an insider in the community in which she conducts the research, her other roles in the community shape the kinds of responses she could solicit among research participants (Buch and Staller 2007: 202–204), aligning with Mats Alvesson's (2003) warning regarding the constructedness of the research interview. So an important aspect of feminist research methodology entails making visible the biases and interests of the researcher, and the power dynamics inherent in her relationship with research participants and the research question. Ultimately, Buch and Staller (2007: 216) claim, feminist ethnographers select materials that 'reflect their feminist theoretical and ethical positions'.

Three focus groups were conducted in 2012 with different social groups of women:
- Women who were revolutionary activists from South Africa in the 1980s.
- Current African middle-class women immigrants based in Edinburgh, Scotland.
- Current local working-class activists involved in the 'Occupy land' protests in the Western Cape.

The introductory filming for The Red Tent[3] was done under a red Bedouin tent that symbolises *iXhanti*, a safe space for women (*ixhanti* as the term to characterise the research team's understanding of the red tent as a safe space for women was provided by Mr Lebo Mncayi, team member and research assistant). The desert image indicates an oasis for the body of the woman, which is violated in male-dominated society. Her body is a source of social cohesion, providing succour, nurturing men, women, LGBTIAQ+s and children, provisioning and just being present when she is needed. The African woman provides milk, food, fetches water, drives to school, creates colour in her clothing and presence and is an abundant oasis for African citizens. For her own nourishment she must turn to the quiet of the desert in which she restores herself physically, mentally and spiritually. The red tent is therefore a symbolic space of *ixhanti* for women nurturers.

In our research, women were reflecting on their life journeys. A question in this project was how we conceive of the space of the body, important in terms of rights discourses as well. If the body is not temporally finite; if notions of time stretch forward into our planetary futures and back into the past to think of those women who have gone before us – a matriarchal ancestry of sorts – then the safe space is *ixhanti*, where past, present and future intersect, hence the project's isiXhosa name.

There are two explanations of *ixhanti* in Xhosa cultural practices that were explained to the research team. First is the sacred family space in which each home requires an area that is sacred, where important family rituals may be carried out. It is here where people will talk with ancestors to seek guidance and wisdom from the past. Both men and women of the family had access to *ixhanti* and would go to this space for meditation and solitude. Two bull horns, from a beast slaughtered to dedicate the space to the ancestors, were attached to the entrance of the sacred space to mark it out. A more abstract second understanding of *ixhanti* is that of symbolic cornerstone of the home. Many young

Xhosa brides were given the name Noxhanti, as the keeper of family history, secrets and wisdoms, and had the potential to become the family matriarch if they wore these mantras well. When speaking of '*ixhanti lam*', isiXhosa-speaking women are, loosely translated, speaking of a 'secret, sacred place'.

GENERATIONAL BLUES – LEFTIST MATRIARCHS AND TROUBLED RELATIONS

Men and masculine styles of leadership dominate our public culture. The imperative to not be 'emotional'; the preponderance of men in political leadership; the authoritarian styles that often accompany masculinist dispositions – these are the ways in which leadership is generally conducted in the public space. While not essentialising the category of women, our socially constructed binaries lead us to conclude that women (self-identified as such) display gendered behaviours that have particular social qualities. We contend that many women lead differently, by nurture rather than by nature. Socialised into different roles from men – as mothers, wives, aunts and sisters – their collective social wisdom is an important part of the civility through which we adapt and develop as human beings. Patriarchal leadership has been identified by the new young women and LGBTIAQ+ radicals as a brake on radical movements. The contention here is that matriarchal leaders epitomise this alternative kind of African leadership and dispositions, and the 'herstories' of African matriarchs will help to bring these alternative traditions to light, including the nature, practice and potential for the extension of matrilineage in Africa.

Public statements of the #FeesMustFall movement repeatedly decry patriarchy, and anti-patriarchy is linked by the students to the need for decolonisation of the higher education system. Past practices in political organisations are rejected:
- Identifiable leadership is one of the perceived pitfalls of past social movements.
- The overwhelming presence and dominance of male leaders in anti-apartheid organisations and in the post-apartheid government is seen as problematic.
- Suppression of the LGBTIAQ+ movements and individuals is resisted.

Pan-African feminists write about their own troubled relations with their left-wing male leadership, the men in the Africanist movements with whom they shared collective goals, but whose broader politics and leadership styles were often alien in many ways (Davies 2014).

One would expect, therefore, that there would be an organic connection with older black feminists, and to some extent there is. Radical work that focuses on rape and slavery (Dineo-Gqola 2010) has been warmly received by many in the student movement. Postcolonial feminism and its emphasis on narratives of power and their deconstruction occupy a core position in the critique of the young feminists and/or LGBTIAQ+ community. The body is foregrounded as the central unit of political analysis. Where and how the body feels pain is cited as the experience of violence at the colonial campus. Bodily violence and how this stymies the potential for black academic excellence are key ideas in the lexicon of the women and LGBTIAQ+ students in #FeesMustFall, as expressed in meetings, marches and blogs during 2015–2016.

One reason for the chasm between the leftist matriarchs and the young feminist activists is the divergence in their political focuses. Left-wing feminists shared the programmatic vision of their male-dominated organisations and currents. First, the old left wing emphasised (and continues to emphasise) fundamental socioeconomic transformation. Second, the chosen agent of the old patriarchs and the old left-wing feminists was the industrial working class. In their intellectual collaboration on cycles of capital accumulation and hegemonic transitions in the twentieth century, for example, the wife-husband team Beverly Silver and Giovanni Arrighi (Arrighi and Silver 1999) show how the structural location of global forces of labour lead to fresh sites of accumulation and resistance. New countries in which factories grew in number in the twentieth century created sites of militant collectives.

Unlike the divisive particularisms such as xenophobia and provincialism that fragment social movements today, labour in the twentieth century overcame many divisions and was able to turn strikes and protests into revolutionary systemic challenges. Labour was thus the key revolutionary subject of South African Marxism. While divisions were rife and politics was often opaque, there were certainties in questions of revolutionary agency. Battalions of proletarians, supported by youth and intellectuals of various shades, led an onslaught on the capitalist system across the globe in the twentieth century.

The 1980s Marxists criticise the students for being overly focused on identity; and are dismayed at the suspicious approach of many black African #FeesMustFall students towards coloured and Indian students, after two decades of apparent 'nonracialism' in social movements. The focus of the #FeesMustFall movement is criticised as limited in its purview and falling short of the radical programmes that dominated the post-1994 moment (ranging from the Reconstruction and Development Programme (RDP) to calls for expropriation of the means of production). The criticism is levelled by leftists (often academic Marxists now) that the student leaders are inward-looking and narrow in their consciousness while failing to challenge and critique the fundamental aspects of social inequality (CSAS 2015). The contention by leftists is that in order for the students to direct their attention to socioeconomic issues they need to merge their goals with township and working-class constituencies. The student movement has in some cases internalised this leftist criticism and now forms intermittent alliances with workers at the campuses and campaigns around the demands of the workers, particularly for insourcing. However, anti-capitalism is not their key slogan as it is for many on the left.

The movements inspired by labour as the central subject had many successes. Political systems were changed as a consequence. In Africa, workers and peasants/subsistence farmers/petty commodity producers formed revolutionary alliances that began in the early decades of the twentieth century and culminated in independence movements in the 1950s and 1960s. But the twenty-first century, beginning with demoralisation and uncertainty among this labour-inspired revolutionary movement, was routed by capitalism's brutal revival and survival in the late twentieth century (what was termed 'neoliberalism'). Capitalism's crisis became a crisis of the left, a conjunctural collapse of alternative political economic systems and a physical ageing of the twentieth-century left. The 'new ones are not yet born', you could have said of the late twentieth century, but *not of the twenty-first century*. Sites of radical openness have blossomed each year as this century has evolved its own *lineages of freedom*, beginning with the radical Occupy movement in Western Europe and North America and currently spreading into a global anti-racist student movement such as the #FeesMustFall movement.

Political certainty had a gendered character among the revolutionary Marxists. Men were both subjects and leaders of revolutionary transformation. The privileged political subject for these revolutionary Marxists was the male proletarian, the factory or blue-collar worker. Marxist men dominated their social movements. South African Marxists found an accommodation with feminists in revolutionary organisations and labour movements. Women's leadership was a matter of quotas and quantity rather than a question of political style and integrity. While many women revolutionaries were disgruntled with male leadership, this dissent was suppressed in the main, and male leadership prevailed, as is evident in post-apartheid society. Older left-wing feminists who now occupy matriarchal spaces as wives, mothers and respected academic elders were thus unable to transform the hierarchy of gender in their own political praxis.

WOMEN'S SPACE AND WOMAN'S 'PLACE' – 'BEING WOMAN' AS A SPACE OF CONTAINMENT

Women today are smashing through the containment of patriarchal spaces that make African women quiet, demure and invisible. In a range of radical organisational spaces, women prevail and dominate. In the struggle over land grabs in Africa in the early 2000s and after, women villagers have been vocal in resisting foreign investors and their own governments (Miller 2014). Coloured working-class women in the Western Cape were pivotal in the Occupy protests in 2012 (Miller 2012). In WOMIN (Women in Mining) and the Rural Women's Assembly, women battle mining companies and combine to fight for better wages for farmworkers. In many different contexts in Africa and globally, these women's movements are challenging the expanded accumulation of capital and may be seen as sites of radical openness. But the transition from patriarchal leadership to womanist/feminist/LGBTIAQ+ leadership faces many difficulties, as do all fundamental transitional challenges.

In southern Africa today, patrilineage and patriarchal styles of leadership place both hidden and visible restrictions on the accumulation of power for women in the public space. African democracy equates leadership with male, patriarchal and formal democratic leadership. Alternative and everyday practices of democracy are often invisible in these mainstream practices. Women's leadership and women's participation in political processes can be stymied by these dominant masculine modes of governance. Power thus rests on gendered binaries in which men are the favoured political leaders. Categories of women and men and their respective positions in public and private spaces create gendered hierarchies in the practice of representational governance.

Gendered spaces contribute towards social cohesion: we are all safely in our place. Docile bodies and male-dominated governance are ensured. Society functions in key social institutions in which the family, the church and marriage contain the independent, self-expression of women and LGBTIAQ+s. These institutions play a supportive function for *citizens under siege* (my own term for the precarious and 'bare lives' (Agamben 1998) of citizens under declining and crisis-ridden twentieth-century capitalism) in declining global and national economies. But these institutions are also profoundly conservative in that they uphold the gendered containment of women.

The first part of this chapter contended that women and LGBTIAQ+ are at the forefront of twenty-first-century political activism in South Africa (and Africa). These observations use biological identifications of women based primarily on the physical attribute of breasts – that is, you know if someone is a man or a woman *mainly* by whether they have physical protrusions on their chests. There are of course other attributes that help identify gender. This kind of gender assignation is termed 'biological essentialism' inasfar as we look at a body's physical form and assign a gender based on this physical essence.

But gender and sexuality are much more than the physical form. How, then, do we defend the use of these binaries – women and men – in society and in our discussions of gender and social movements? Even the term 'male-dominated' is then subject to scrutiny, as sexuality is a continuum – so who is dominant if sexuality is a fluid continuum? In this chapter, we support the categories of woman, LGBTIAQ+ and man as forms of self-identification. The subject's own understanding of their sexuality and gender becomes an important way of discussing gendered roles. The spaces we occupy assign our power in society. Feminist women are often marginalised in society because of patriarchal social dominance (or male-dominance). Women and LGBTIAQ+s who do not question mainstream ideologies and social structures rise to positions of power and prominence.

Gender binaries have created stereotypical notions of men and women. Sexualities are very divergent, as the acronym LGBTIAQ+ indicates. However, we ignore such differences in sexuality and use only the binary categories. One of the reasons we ignore sexual diversity is that it conflicts with prevailing social hierarchies and values. These categories – 'men', 'women', 'mom', 'dad' – create forms of social entrapment through social expectations of appropriate behaviour for men and women. So, if many of us understand the conceptual limitation of the category 'woman' and the potential limits that this category places on the self-actualisation of women, why do we still use the term 'women'? What alternative categories are we suggesting that dispense with the binaries of this gendered social condition – and is research in the name of 'women' still defensible?

One of the major gendered divisions produced by the stereotyping of the sexes is that women and men are assigned to different social spaces (Spain 1992). Reena Patel (2010: 8) contends that 'the distinction between the public and private spheres gained popularity in the 1970s as a means to explain a woman's place, or lack thereof, in society' but there was so much that was uniquely individual or overlapping that these distinctions made no sense. However, the notion of separate spheres remains an important illusion, she argues. Indeed, as demonstrated by the popularity of books that perpetuate sexist beliefs about masculinity and femininity, such as *Men are from Mars, Women are from Venus*, the illusion of separate spheres certainly remains real and relevant in the lives of men and women, despite the fact that there is difference and overlap at the individual level (Patel 2010).

These perceptions of women's place have a consequence for her status in society, downgrading it. When the public space is the place of accumulated power and influence, the realm of the home becomes less significant. Other studies, however, point to the prevalence of women's unpaid household labour in the care of society (Ally 2009) and that, in fact, in terms of labour hours women are spending more time at home. Among professional and working-class women there is much evidence to show that the bulk of childcare and home management or cleaning falls to the working woman, even when domestic help is acquired. The way that the service sector functions today increases the household management and administration, requiring a range of tasks and skills in the home.

If the burden of home care and organisation falls to wives, mothers, aunts, grannies and the various social roles ascribed to women by these categories, then the social reproduction of daily life still takes place within these broad binaries. Irrespective of your sexual preference, therefore, your social role is mainly biologically determined. Gay, bi-, transsexual, etc., you will still be expected to do the dishes or cook and will be transgressing if you don't. The fluidity and inter-relationality of gender traits therefore mostly breeze over society's head, and to be a woman in our society has particular meanings and connotations, so to develop radical notions of womanhood we need to begin from the premise of the real, lived experience of binary realities. When you walk into a public toilet, men and women are apart, for good reason in the here and now, given how deeply entrenched are gendered hierarchies in our society.

These assigned spaces correspond to particular gendered traits. Table 13.1 demonstrates these socially ascribed gender differences.

Table 13.1: Gender socialisation in the public and private spheres (Source: Andersen 1983; Runyan and Peterson 2014).

PUBLIC SPHERE	PRIVATE SPHERE
Masculine	Feminine
Production of goods and services	Reproduction – childbearing
Paid labour	Unpaid labour
Leaders	Followers
Visible	Invisible

Occupying the masculine space of paid labour in the 'public sphere' does not, however, automatically increase the status of women in society. Instead, society can retain a residual resentment towards those outside of their ascribed gendered spaces and deny women the space of leadership. A social expectation has been violated, and the double role of 'birthing person' and senior colleague can prove too conflicting for those around women, placing them in a space of transgression. Work, then, can mean that women find themselves torn between these traditional roles and their workplace commitments, and the reproductive role in the household and paid labour in the workforce thus compete for a woman's body. Patel (2010: 10) also argues that while cultural practices may produce different conceptions of the public and private, higher status attaches to masculine traits despite these differences. These traits are then spatialised in terms of what constitutes a feminine space and what constitutes a masculine space. Socially constructed differences are then naturalised and made to appear as an essential part of women's sex, and thus become entrenched social myths: 'myths in this case are essentialised ideas of difference – such as women's "natural" capacity for nurturing – that takes on the status of biological destiny, thus erasing the history of their complex social construction' (Patel 2010).

But more than that, people around them can be a constant disciplining force reminding them that they are still carrying the 'woman's burden'. Society resists the integration of women into the public space in large and small ways – in the reticence of administrative assistants to women professionals, in the dismissiveness of male colleagues, and in the public ridicule of women in leadership positions (for example, the recent 'big panties' display by teachers against the minister of basic education (Masombuka 2013)). An overall low status level for women can then express itself in gestures of humiliation and indignity for those women in power, while other women are afforded respect as 'mothers', *'umama'* or *'moeders'*.

MATRIARCHAL LEADERSHIP AND 'MAMA-WE': SEARCHING FOR THE VERNACULAR

In the politics of the new student movements, 'Mama-we' has become an iconic figure for whom poems are written and songs are sung. During the student occupation of 'New Azania House' at UCT in 2015, for example, poems to 'Mama-we' were posted on the doors. Songs incorporating 'Mama-we' are sung frequently at protests and mass rallies. Disaffection with male and masculinist leadership has seen women and 'womanism' re-emerge as a political reference point in the #FeesMustFall movement. These terms refer to biological woman rather than sexualities, which are widely divergent (suggesting the need for the acronym 'LGBTIAQH+', linking heterosexual women to this range of sexualities and disrupting the sexuality binaries). However, many women leaders, globally and among our own unique brand of 'femocrats' in Africa, are anti-democratic and neoliberal (Mama 2001). If patriarchal leadership has been found wanting, what, if any, are the lessons of the matriarchs? Which of the past experiences of feminist activists are relevant for the struggles of young feminists today?

On leadership

In the introduction to the Red Tent documentary, women activists discuss their conceptions of leadership. This leads us to the need to conceive of leadership differently and in less individualistic terms. 'Crowning' leadership places the individual above the mass and emphasises the need for social distance between leader and follower. The leader is something 'über-special', invested with qualities that normal citizens do not have. If leadership could be held differently – as a shroud rather than a crown – the character of political cultures might change. But leadership that is a shroud is exercised fluidly and may shift from individual to individual. A more collective construction of leadership becomes possible, therefore, with various qualities called upon at different times in different spaces (Miller 2012; Knowles in *Red Tent* Introduction and Part 1; Miller 2013c).

In the organisation Wasa (Women's Academic Solidarity Association) formed by women academics in 2005 at Rhodes University, the emphasis was on rotational leadership (Miller 2012). Chairpersons held their position for six months and then vacated before egotistical distortions could become entrenched. Subcommittees were issue-based and led by those who were most affected by or most passionate about the problem in question. The organisation was constructed nonracially and was 'womanist' in orientation. Men were sometimes allowed to participate, but the membership, leadership and activities were led and dominated by women (Miller 2012).

Rather than abdicating leadership and creating a vacuum, which could lead to confusion and disorganisation, this fluid and rotational approach to leadership had immense organisational potential. Instead of leadership as a reified social category, it becomes something more fluid and can be imbued with different qualities within different contexts. Leadership may rotate among individuals within different spatiotemporalities (space-time contexts).

MOTHERHOOD AND ABORTION

Many feminists have ambivalent relationships to potential motherhood. For feminists, men are the physical bearers of patriarchy and childhood is predominantly created through sexual intercourse. Conceiving children in this way can therefore be seen as an act of compromise with patriarchy. The different ways in which activist women have resolved (or not resolved) these tensions of marriage and motherhood may be of interest to younger women, including the radical feminists at the helm of the new barricades.

Individual interviews were conducted with women activists of the 1980s on the parts of their life history that are relevant to the documentary titles. The women discuss their ambivalent relationship with motherhood and pregnancy. The video airs the taboo subject of abortion. Many women revolutionaries saw motherhood as a constraint on revolutionary activism. Attitudes to marriage are also discussed, with many of the partners emerging as 'good patriarchs' who accepted their partners' activist roles and gendered choices such as abortion. The orientation against childbearing was concretised into a political statute of the illegal revolutionary organisation to which some of the interviewees belonged

(Pandit 2002)[4] – some women had abortions even though they didn't want to terminate their pregnancies. In this sense, they were forced, and some nurse a lifelong grievance against that organisation.

Abortion is an ugly face of feminism. In order to claim her bodily freedom, the woman chooses to deny the actualisation of another human being. This is a violent suppression of someone else's coming into being; an 'untimely ripping-from-the-womb,' as Shakespeare or the Bible would term it. This is not a peaceful act as it is physically invasive for the woman, cuts short the life of the embryo, and the operation is often performed in brutally unhealthy, racially violent or unsympathetic environments such as the money-making surgeries of crooked white male doctors, or the dirty rooms of hardened township women. In order to claim back control of her body, the feminist woman negates the existence of another. In order to be, she has first to destroy, a controversial ethical act.

While Pandit's account presents herself as victim of the revolutionary organisation and its patriarchal leadership – while her 'good patriarch' husband watches helplessly in the face of her violation – she fails to indicate why she followed loyally, making her account vulnerable to accusations of revolutionary 'brainwashing'. For many women in these organisations, abortion was an act of self-actualisation and revolutionary agency, in which they elected not to conform to social containment through motherhood. A particular kind of revolutionary strength and volunteerism was present in these choices. In the United Kingdom, legal abortions allowed the citation of 'political activism' as a reason in the forms filled in prior to the state-paid-for legal abortions that were available free to citizens and non-citizens. Women thus made conscious political decisions to desist from motherhood as an expression of their political agency and personal strength in denying this socially accepted norm of childbirth. Pandit's account thus potentially feeds an anti-revolutionist ideological machinery in providing only one side of the decisions made in the act of abortion.

The Red Tent research project utilised radical feminist methodology to excavate notions of motherhood among older feminists and activists. #FeesMustFall students have also critiqued the colonial pedagogies that underpin knowledge systems in institutions of higher education. The Red Tent, *ixhanti* research project sought to retrieve these 'herstories' through ethnographies of present and past women leaders. Through a series of focus groups (in Cape Town, Eastern Cape, Edinburgh), this research showed the different styles of 'doing leadership' that suggest the potential resourcefulness of African matriarchal leadership traditions against corrosive and egotistical African patriarchy – both patrimonial and left-wing variants. The focus groups aimed to bring to light the qualities of alternative leadership by identifying African matriarchs in different contexts who exercise leadership at a local level or beyond.

The playful energies of the women at the end of the video on Motherhood, Marriage and Activism (Part 3) speak of a bodily freedom and happiness; a bodily state distant from angry or aggressive feminisms. Perhaps the decades of searching have produced feminists who have found peace within and dispelled the restlessness of gendered containment. How helpful is this, though, when society still places women in social containment? It would seem that the aggression of the young feminist is required to smash down walls that hold the majority of women in confinement. Theirs, then, is the way of the future. But the symbolism in the colour and diversity at the end of the video suggests, along with the singer, that 'a whole new world' is one that will not play out in black and white but will be a burst of colours and sexualities. Unlike the sterile binary genders of the earlier anti-apartheid movements, the gender of #FeesMustFall changed, with a heterogeneous sexuality unfolding that sees personhood ranging from heteros to lesbians to intersex to feminist men. The angry counterpoint of 'ugly feminism' may be a necessary conduit to the beauty of the becoming of the 'new African LGBTIAQH+', alternatively, the 'new African being', free of the constraints of a defined and socially contained sexuality, race and humanist identity.

CONCLUSION

This chapter is a conversation presented by an older radical feminist who has set aside the rage and the scream, hoping that the young ones who are being born draw on our stories presented in the findings of the research project, The Red Tent, and the documentaries and focus groups conducted in this project. The research methodology relies on multiple research sources, including fieldwork, activist research, documentary film footage, traditional literature reviews and my own grounded experience in left-wing revolutionary movements. This contribution seeks to revise the 'struggle narratives' in South Africa by addressing a lacuna in feminist history/'herstory', revealing a small slice of the experiences of revolutionary and coloured feminists.

This chapter presented some of the experiences of the older feminists in order to set up an imagined conversation between young and old. Issues and challenges that may have some purchase for young feminists today are highlighted in the discussion, as well as points of divergence and rupture. As much as older revolutionary feminists would like to share their experiences with the younger generation of women and LGBTIAQ+ activists, these 'lessons of the matriarchs' may be considered superfluous. As one of the Luhlaza Leadership Initiative women/LGBTIAQ+ participants put it in a writing workshop conducted in Stellenbosch in September 2015, 'I don't feel like sucking on anyone's old teat!' While the older left patriarchs are socially incorporated into academic and power structures, and the 'domesticated feminist' stands in the grey space between, the #FeesMustFall students are making 'herstory'.

While we, the older feminists, have mostly been unable to resist the domestication of our feminism in the *longue durée* of life, or even the succumbing to Trotsky's rogue status, this article gives examples of our resistance as self-styled revolutionaries and activists in the 1980s to our spatial and social containment as women. That we were so-called 'coloured' is perhaps just historical accident. What is not an accident is the subsequent erasure of our voices – which happened because we were women coloureds and 'far-left', dissidents from the majoritarian ANC movement in the 1990s when the birthing of the new South Africa took place. We were cast aside – or elected to step aside – as a piece of ruptured umbilical cord, severed rather than buried in the soil and embedded in the legacy, history and 'herstory' of South Africa's transition. Like the 'new African woman' in the #FeesMustFall movement who screams her pain, this article also challenges the postcolonial and post-apartheid erasures of left-wing, coloured women revolutionaries and activists – in the hope that our 'herstories' will help their new stories unfold.

NOTES

1. I would like to acknowledge the research funding support of the Rosa Luxemburg Foundation and the National Research Foundation. I also acknowledge Professor Sandra Rein for her part in the Red Tent project, and Red Tent research team members Lebo Mncayi, Pamela Harris and Corinne Knowles for their leadership and assistance. Thanks also to the Rhodes Allan Gray Centre for Leadership Ethics. I also acknowledge Professor Patrick Bond and my old alma mater, Wits University, for making this chapter possible.
2. This is a term used by other feminists as well. It reminds us of the masculine focus in historical accounts.
3. The name of the project is drawn from Anita Diamond's novel, a counter-factual writing of Old Testament and matrilineage. Women were sent to a separate tent in

the Old Testament days when they were in menses as they were considered unclean. Diamond's novel shows the women reclaiming this space as a site of matrilineal power.

4   The illegal revolutionary organisation was WILSA (Workers International League of South Africa). The actual archival documents will need to be excavated, if they still exist, in order to prove this claim with written documentation but the feminist methodology in my research relies on the oral testimonies of women members as one scientific representation of the truth.

REFERENCES

Agamben, G. (1998) *Homo Sacer: Sovereign Power and Bare Life*. Redwood City: Stanford University Press.

Ally, S. (2009) *From Servants to Workers*. Ithaca, NY: Cornell University Press.

Alvesson, M. (2003) Beyond neopositivists, romantics and localists: A reflexive approach to interviews in organisational research. *Academic Management Review*, January, 28(1), 13–33.

Andersen, M. L. (1983) *Thinking about Women: Sociological perspectives on sex and gender*. Boston: Allyn & Bacon.

Arrighi, G. & Silver, B. (1999) *Chaos and Governance in the Modern World System: Contradictions of modernity*. Minneapolis: University of Minnesota Press.

Buch, E. & Staller. K. (2007) The feminist practice of ethnography. In *Feminist Research Practice: A Primer*, pp. 187–221: New York: Sage Publications.

CSAS (2015) Colloquium, University of Cape Town September.

Davies, C. B. (2014) Pan-Africanism, transnational black feminism and the limits of culturalist analyses in African gender discourses, *Feminist Africa*, 19, 78–93.

Dineo-Gqola, P. (2010) *What is Slavery to Me?* Johannesburg: Wits University Press.

Foucault, M. (1995) *Discipline and Punish: The Birth of a Prison*. New York: Vintage Press.

Gbowee, L. & Mithers, C. (2013) *Mighty be our Powers: How Sisterhood, Prayer, and Sex Changed a Nation at War*. New York: Beast Books.

Haffajee, F. (2015) *What if There Were No Whites in South Africa?* Johannesburg: Picador Africa.

Holloway, J. (2002) *Change the World Without Taking Power: The Meaning of Revolution Today*. London: Pluto.

Mama, A. (2001) Challenging subjects: Gender and Power in African contexts. Plenary address. *African Sociological Review*, 5(2): 63–73.

Masombuka, S. (2013) Angie has fit over panties. *Times Live*, 30 April. http://www.timeslive.co.za/thetimes/2013/04/30/angie-has-fit-over-panties

Mbanda, T. (2012) Interview.

Miller, D. (2012) WASA's founder and first chairperson. In *The Company of Women. Ten Years of WASA and the Way Forward for Women Academics*. Women's Academic Solidarity Association, Grahamstown: Rhodes University.

Miller, D. (2013a) *The Red Tent: Rough diamonds, Who's got your back?* https://www.youtube.com/watch?v=yE-tC9jOljw

Miller, D. (2013b) *On Women's Leadership (Parts 1–3)*. https://www.youtube.com/watch?v=ro4qJ00zoq0

Miller, D. (2013c) *Red Tent 1: Research Project Introduction (Part 1)*. https://www.youtube.com/watch?v=_G__UmyU6sM

Miller, D. (2013d) *Red Tent 4: On Motherhood, Marriage and Activism (Parts 1-3)* https://www.youtube.com/watch?v=yE-tC9jOljw

Miller, D. (2014) *Speak, Lioness, Speak: Pan-African tribunal on land grabs in Africa*. Documentary. University of Western Cape, Bellville: PLAAS.

Miller, D. & Harris, P. (2012) The Red Tent: Regional dispositions and women's leadership in post-apartheid Southern Africa. In *Waiting To Be Heard*. IFE Equity Report for Rio + 20 Earth Summit.

Pandit, S. (2002) Women and oppression in South Africa. *Journal of Gender Studies*, 11(1), 67–78.

Patel. R. (2010) *Working the Night Shift: Women in India's Call Center Industry*. Redwood City: Stanford University Press.

Perumal, J. (2007) *Identity, Diversity and Teaching for Social Justice*. European University Studies, Series 11: Education. Bern: Peter Lang.

Rent Tent Research Project (2012) Introduction (Part 1) YouTube. https://www.youtube.com/watch?v=_G__UmyU6sM

Runyan, A. S. & Peterson, V. S. (2014) *Global Gender Issues in the New Millennium*. Boulder: Westview.

Spain, D. (1992) *Gendered Spaces*. Boulder: University of Colorado Press.

CHAPTER

14

THE SOUTH AFRICAN STUDENT/WORKER PROTESTS IN THE LIGHT OF JUST WAR THEORY

Thaddeus Metz

INTRODUCTION

In this chapter I evaluate the South African university student and worker protests of 2015–2016 in the light of moral principles that are largely uncontested in contemporary philosophies of just war, violence and threats. I speak of 'protests', 'uprisings' and the like in the plural, to deny any suggestion that there was a single, coordinated movement. I do not seek to provide an all-things-considered judgement of the protests across the nation, or even at a given institution – that is, I do not conclude anything of the form that a given struggle was, on balance, just or unjust. Instead, I work in a more piecemeal fashion, appraising representative instances of protests and drawing conclusions about which of them are plausibly deemed to have been morally sound, and which have not been.

I do argue that some ways in which students and workers expressed their resentment and sought to rebut perceived injustice were not merely less than ideal, but wrong, should have been undertaken in other ways and, frankly, merit contrition. That point is compatible with recognising that many of the goals they aimed to achieve have been legitimate and that much good has probably resulted from disruptive protests.[1] Ethically speaking, the ends do not always justify the means. Such is implied by moral principles about why, when and how to use force that are among the least controversial in both the African and Western political philosophical traditions. It is not merely those with 'middle-class sensibilities' (Sacks 2016) or 'liberal old farts' who believe, or should believe, that some of the means that university students and workers took to fight against injustice were themselves unjust and should be avoided in the future.

Others have addressed the issue of ends and means as they pertain to the protests, and have concluded that often the coercion of innocents and the destruction of property was unjustified (February 2015; Jansen 2015; Bilchitz 2016; Habib 2016; Pamla 2016; cf. Mbembe 2016). My analysis aims to be more philosophically thorough, including responding to attempts to defend coercion, destruction and violence as a reaction to injustice, to be more comprehensive when it comes to the types of protest that were and could have been undertaken, and to be grounded on moral principles salient in much of the sub-Saharan anti-colonial and anti-apartheid tradition.

In the rest of this chapter I spell out and apply five principles that I submit should normally regulate the use of force against adults, where force includes issuing threats to others, vandalising others' property, aiming to prevent others from exercising rights such as to move, to vote and to obtain an education, and subordinating or harming others in severe ways ('violence' in a usefully narrow sense). (Perhaps verbal abuse and vilification belong here too.) The five principles are neither pacifist (categorically forbidding force) nor collectivist (treating individuals merely as a means to a greater good). Together they add up to the claim that force is *most clearly permissible if it is the least amount necessary and likely to rebut a greater injustice and is directed against those particularly responsible for the injustice.*

This approach is grounded on a variety of sources, including compelling African moral thought about how to resist white oppression (Kaunda 1980; Mandela 1994) as well as Western just war theory (to be distinguished from the West's practice of war, of course; for an overview, see Orend 2005) and the influential Siracusa Principles on how to limit rights in the International Covenant on Civil and Political Rights (International Commission of Jurists 1985). I also draw on some of my previous philosophical work in which I have articulated the principles and applied them to debates such as whether routine HIV testing is permissible (2005), whether the death penalty is just (2010) and which violence directed against apartheid was justified (2016). Although I sometimes allude to these sources below, I avoid intricate textual analysis and expect readers to find the position to be intuitively plausible, or at least attractive upon some brief motivation that I provide.

I apply the five principles to a wide array of protests that were undertaken in 2015–2016, ranging from the boycotting of classes, to the barricading of entrances and exits, to the hostage taking of council members, to the expression of slogans such as 'kill all whites', to the production of a film and the erection of a symbolic shack, to the marches on major sites of political power, to the throwing of petrol bombs at buildings and buses, to the burning of books, tyres, artworks, buildings and cars, to the spread of human faeces on a statue and in lecture halls, to the blocking of traffic on roads outside university campuses and the throwing of bricks at motorists, and to the threats to shut down polls during municipal elections. I answer the questions of which of these means were just, which were not, and why one should think so.

Along the way, I address suggestions from 'revolutionaries' in South Africa who have sought to defend the use of violence by the university students and workers. In particular, I provide reason to doubt the commonly expressed view that systematic injustice (or 'structural violence') on the part of universities and brutality by private security forces justified an equally violent reaction. With one of the most insightful theorists of the May 1968 student and worker upheaval in France, I think that reflection on the history of radical social change in places such as the Soviet Union and Mao's China reveals that one 'can no longer combat alienation with alienated forms of struggle' (Debord 1967: 122). By this token, it would be counter-revolutionary to seek to change oppressive fee requirements and academic culture according to views such as this: 'Violence will bring an end to the world as we know it and cleanse all the evil, give rise to a completely new world where the only race that matters is the human race' (University of the Witwatersrand #FeesMustFall quoted in Nicolson 2016a).

JUST CAUSE

When thinking about whether a disruptive protest or other use of force is permissible, the natural thing to ask first is whether its purpose is appropriate, or, in the just war theory lingo, whether its cause is just. If one is going to actively prevent students from entering campus, or staff from leaving a meeting, one had better have a good reason, an end that would be of the right sort to justify such a means.

When it comes to current thinking about which purpose justifies war, many these days maintain that only the aim of rebutting aggression, understood roughly as the use of armed force to violate a state's territory or citizens' human rights, can do so in principle (for example, United Nations 1945; Walzer 1977). Not all aggression justifies a military response, but only aggression can justify it, so the post-Second World War view goes. Rebutting aggression is obviously too narrow a category to account for when force less severe than warfare is justifiable. Here, many would suggest that non-military force, such as disruptive protest, can be justified insofar as it is in some way directed against domination, oppression, exploitation or injustice more generally. Preventing or compensating for such negative conditions might not be the only just cause for non-military force, but it is the least controversial one.

Recall that protesters were largely seeking the following: to make education more affordable (perhaps free); to make decent student accommodation more affordable; to pay cleaning, security and other staff a living wage; to have the curriculum imparted with more African sources and perspectives; to have lecturers be more demographically representative of the South African population; to have universities use languages that would be more inclusive; to remove symbols of colonialism and apartheid; to create mechanisms by which management would engage with students and workers directly; and generally to reduce the amount of 'black pain' that is a foreseeable consequence of financial hardship and alienation from institutional culture.

I have no interest in questioning these ends here, most of which I have sought to defend philosophically elsewhere (for example, Metz 2009; 2012; 2015). The above ends not only justify protest, but also provide a *prima facie* justification for using force of certain kinds (at least if non-disruptive protests had been shown to be ineffectual, as I argue below).

Other ends have occasionally been voiced, such as removing all police and private security presence from campus (Isaacs and Petersen 2015; #FeesMustFall quoted in Pretorius 2016). A related goal has sometimes been for management to refrain from disciplining protesters and for police not to prosecute them, with the University of the Witwatersrand (Wits) student representative council (SRC) once having proclaimed, 'we demand that any student, worker or academic involved in any form of protest must not face any disciplinary charges whatsoever' (2015; see also #FMF Parents Solidarity Committee 2015). These ends are obviously more controversial, with much depending on what counts as a legitimate form of protest. If some forms of protest were morally unjustified, as I argue in this chapter, then certain kinds of defensive and punitive force against them were in principle justified, and the sort of blanket demand quoted above is unreasonable. (It does not follow, of course, that in practice the police and private security forces have always themselves responded to wrongful protests in appropriate ways. Where they have not, then a certain kind of defensive force – different from retaliation – by students and workers was permissible.)

There is no doubt that some activists had broader ends, too, concerning the advancement of certain political parties or labour movements. As long as there were ends, such as improving access to education and changing institutional culture, that *did* justify disruption on university campuses, then, if additional ends were pursued within the permissible parameters of pursuing *those* ends, doing so was not unjust. This point leaves open the questions of whether the more questionable, political ends were indeed pursued within such parameters, and also whether universities were in a position to cope on their own in the face of exogenous influences.

LIKELY SUCCESS

A second standard criterion for a just war is that, supposing it is undertaken for a just cause, it must be likely to succeed in advancing it. Although a disruptive protest does not of course threaten anywhere near as much mayhem as war or even a handful of military strikes, it still seems right that it must be likely to achieve the end of rebutting injustice. It is not enough merely to have good intentions; if force is to be justified by a certain end, it must have some reasonable prospect of realising it. Otherwise, costs are imposed for no good reason. At the very least, a certain means must not be counterproductive with respect to the end sought.

It can be difficult, in practice, to tell which means are likely to be effective and which are not. But the principle remains sound, and should guide practice as much as possible. Someone who tried to abide by the principle and failed would have acted much less wrongfully than someone who simply ignored the principle. Which forms of protest were likely to advance the ends accepted as just in the previous section, which were likely to be ineffectual, and which downright counterproductive? Although it would take some substantial social science to answer these questions conclusively, risks of counterproductivity are easier to judge than those of mere ineffectiveness.

Basically, any form of protest that inhibited students from obtaining an education should be seriously questioned as having hindered the ability to obtain the just end of increasing access to education. Brief stayaways from lectures and even temporary shutdowns of a campus would not be serious impediments to achieving the goal of providing more education. However, protestors routinely undertook other means that they knew would substantially retard others' ability to obtain an education, and so were probably unjust. For example, at times indefinite shutdowns of a campus were sought out (Morrissey and Monama 2015), or at least were a foreseeable result of widespread disruption and destruction (Sesant 2016). At other times, protesters not merely prevented students from attending lectures or writing exams by erecting barricades at university entrances, but also threatened them for seeking to do so (Fisher and Mortlock 2015; GroundUp 2015). On still other occasions, protesters blocked those new to varsity from registering and so from becoming students at all (Habib 2016; Nicolson 2016b; Pamla 2016). And, finally, lecture venues, entire buildings and student buses have been strewn with human excrement, set on fire or otherwise destroyed, to the point of reaching R300 million in damages as of April 2016 (see Chernick, Exstrum and Molosankwe 2016, who translate this amount into the numbers of degrees that could have been funded).

Furthermore, these kinds of tactics risked bringing certain effects in their wake detrimental to the cause of more and better education in South Africa. For one, talented academics would have strong reason either not to come or to leave (Jansen 2016). For another, it was predictable that university managers would spend what it took to protect staff and students from intimidation, petrol bombs and the like, where substantial funds have now been spent on security (Sesant 2016) that could have been spent in more productive ways, and might well have been, given other kinds of pressure. Finally, for a third, it was foreseeable that upon using the above kinds of means, other students, staff and much of the broader society would withdraw their support for the cause, where unity is a particularly effective means for achieving radical change.

In reply, one might point out that access to education was not the only goal, so that even if the above tactics frustrated this aim, perhaps they were likely to have advanced other aims. In addition, some have suggested that the present generation of students needs to make serious sacrifices for the sake of future generations (Hassan, quoted in Nicolson 2016b).

The serious problem with these two replies is they fail to consider the possibility of forms of protest that would not only have advanced all aims simultaneously, but also would have done so for both present and future generations. The implicit premise of the replies is that trade-offs had to be made among aims

297

as well as beneficiaries, but that is far from obviously the case. In addition to temporary stayaways and shutdowns, there was a range of other tactics that could have been undertaken in lieu of interfering with the ability of students to obtain their degrees. Consider mass marches to sites of political power, mass sit-ins and teach-ins on campus, petitions, civil disobedience – and negotiation. In particular, changing institutional culture would require speaking to students, staff and managers about how it tends to make black people feel, as did the *Luister* film (this documentary features interviews with more than thirty students at the University of Stellenbosch about their experiences of racism and exclusion, and has been viewed about 400 000 times on YouTube).

Of course these kinds of means were used. My points are that they were far from the only means used, and that had they alone been employed in systematic and creative ways they probably would have been more effective at advancing a variety of just aims (broadening educational access, changing institutional culture, insourcing workers) and for all affected by injustice (present and future generations) than the riots, petrol bombs and indefinite lockdowns, which ended up frustrating the aim of educating (black) students.

Others have replied that the protests have been 'for' the students, and that pointing out that many have been prevented from registering, attending lectures or writing exams (for example, Habib 2016) consists of:

> masking of the true nature of the objectives of #FeesMustFall. It is precisely these potentially vulnerable students, and their families, that #FeesMustFall is composed of … A 'grandfather from Limpopo' should ***not*** have to save and use all of his money, as well as the money from his family, for his one grandson to register. The meaning of the #FeesMustFall campaign is precisely to advance the rights of this student to be able to register for free (Vally and Godsell 2016; cf. Godsell et al. Chapter 5 in this volume).

One problem with this reply is paternalism. It implies that it is justifiable for protesters to coerce and otherwise violate the rights of other, innocent parties for their own good; specifically, it suggests that prospective students may forcibly be prevented from registering so that they could benefit from no fees. A second problem is that it suggests that the odds were high of the protests eventually enabling *this* grandson to register for free, but that is extraordinarily doubtful.

The 'objectives' and 'meaning' of the protests do point to a just cause – of improving access to education – but that is not sufficient to justify a means that impedes many innocent parties from obtaining an education. Instead, the means should avoid undermining education in serious ways. Or so Cosatu (Pamla 2016) as well as Abahlali baseMjondolo and the South African National Civic Organisation (both quoted in Nicolson 2016a) are naturally read as maintaining – not merely vice-chancellors, government officials and the occasional moral philosopher.

PROPORTIONALITY

A third core principle for evaluating the use of force is the idea that the means must not be disproportionate to the end sought. Even if a certain end would in principle justify the use of force, and even if the latter were likely to succeed in advancing the end, the cost of using the means must not be greater than the benefits expected from the end. Roughly speaking, the positives must be worth the negatives employed to achieve it. The cure must not be worse than the disease.

There are two ways in which the proportionality criterion might not be satisfied. First, the just cause might not be good enough to outweigh the bad of the forceful means. On this score, I am sympathetic to those who have pointed out that many have inappropriately become more upset about the burning of artworks and vehicles than they have about the oppressed lives of hundreds of thousands of black students and workers (see, for example, Kamanzi 2016). My claim is not that such burning was justified, but rather, in the present context, that it was not obviously disproportionate to the injustice done; it was not unjustified clearly for *that* reason.

That said, while oppression outweighs property damage much of the time, death usually outweighs oppression. There were unfortunately some forms of protest that seriously risked killing people, and those I find disproportionately severe, relative to the degree of injustice done. There was palpable hate speech during some protests, with one protester wearing a T-shirt with 'kill all whites' emblazoned on it (Lewis 2016), and with some of the very first social media broadcasts from #RhodesMustFall sporting the slogan, 'one bullet, one settler' (Ismael 2015; see also Price 2015). Bricks and other projectiles were thrown at passing vehicles, and it is sheer luck that no one was seriously injured (Wicks 2016). That is particularly true of those incidents in which buses filled with students were petrol bombed (Gernetsky and Mashego 2016; Masuabi 2016), and in which petrol bombs were thrown at and left inside university buildings (Aboobaker 2015; Van der Merwe 2015).

There is a second respect in which some of the protests were, or at least risked being, disproportionately more severe than the injustice they were fighting. Sometimes there are situations in which, even though the just cause would be good enough to outweigh the bad of the forceful means considered in itself, there would be large unintended but foreseeable bad side-effects of pursuing it or of doing so in this way. What this means for the student/worker protests is that when evaluating them, one must look not merely at the degree of injustice they were struggling against and the degree to which their means were forceful, but also at unintended but nonetheless likely harms of fighting that injustice and using a particular means do. One has to look at the larger effects on society, and especially on the worst-off socioeconomic classes in it.

Here, one should consider the effect of widespread violent protests on investor confidence and the exchange rate (TMG Digital 2016), where there is good reason to believe that a severely weakened rand would mean higher food prices and hence more hardship for the poor. In addition, it is worth reflecting on the suggestion that the students by and large were not among the most needy or deserving of aid from the state, and that their victory has meant losses for others. Relatively few (though surely some) of the students have been among the 12 million South Africans living in extreme poverty, unable to meet their nutritional needs (Nicolson 2015). Perhaps the funding needed to cover the zero per cent increase to university fees in 2016 should have rather been directed systematically towards the latter.

No doubt, the wealthier members of society and the state should fund both higher education and the poor more than they currently do. But, then, they are unlikely to do so, and it was perhaps foreseeable that the benefits undergraduate students have wrought would come at the expense of other downtrodden social groups, such as primary school students (Paterson 2016) and postgraduate students (Nzimande, quoted in Presence 2016) (as well as at risk to others such as the unemployed, on which see Cokayne 2015).

LAST RESORT

Even if an end would in principle justify a certain forceful means (just cause), even if this means were likely to achieve this end (likely success), and even if the good of the end outweighed the bad of the means itself and what it would foreseeably bring about (proportionality), the means would be unjustified if there were another available means likely to achieve roughly the same good but with no or less bad.

That is, defensive force must be *necessary* to rebut injustice in order to be justified, and, furthermore, it must be the *least amount* needed to do the job.

Such a principle guided Nelson Mandela and Umkhonto we Sizwe (MK), the armed wing of the African National Congress (ANC), in their fight against the apartheid regime. Mandela repeatedly said that he and the ANC had turned to destructive means only because other means had failed to work. Mandela had used peaceful forms of struggle against apartheid for about fifteen years, and the ANC and black resistance movements generally had used them for several decades. However, they had been ineffective – the historical record is clear on that. Most famously, consider Mandela's statement at the Rivonia trial: 'It was only when all else had failed, when all channels of peaceful protest had been barred to us, that the decision was made to embark on violent forms of political struggle' (1964) (for many additional citations and discussion, see Metz 2016).

MK sought to use the least force necessary to accomplish the aim of achieving freedom and equality for all those in South Africa. In *Long Walk to Freedom* Mandela states:

> Our intention was to begin with what was least violent to individuals but most damaging to the state ... It made sense to begin with the form of violence that inflicted the least harm against individuals: sabotage ... strict instructions were given to members of MK that we would countenance no loss of life. But if sabotage did not produce the results we wanted, we were prepared to move onto the next stage (1994: 325, 336; see also 441).

What goes for fighting apartheid and colonialism surely goes for fighting injustice in the post-apartheid, post-independence era. Those engaging in protests against injustice in university settings are obligated to use the least disruptive or forceful means necessary.

Admittedly, it can be difficult to know in practice which degree of severity is the smallest degree essential to advance a just cause. It is therefore usually apt to 'ratchet things up', to start with no force at all, and next the smallest amount of force, and then to increase the amount incrementally over time, as Mandela suggests. It is not always possible to do, as sometimes there is not enough time, but it should be the default position and disregarded only in emergencies.

There have been some recent defenders of violent protest who have implicitly rejected the idea that it must be a last resort in order to be justified. The mere fact of structural violence or heavy-handedness by security forces on campus has been seen as sufficient to warrant a comparable reaction. For instance, one group has said:

> When students get excluded, that serves as violence unto them. Hence our response is and will forever remain legitimate ... we reserve the right to respond with just as equal forms of violence as the system subjects us to (University of the Witwatersrand #FeesMustFall, quoted in Nicolson 2016a).

Similar advocates of violence have spoken of 'fighting fire with fire' (Tiro 2015) and of 'violence as self-defence' against a university management labelled 'the coloniser' (Manzini 2016).

However, while it is true that the logic of defensive force (force used to rebut violence or other injustice) can permit force comparable in degree to the injustice it is counteracting (that is, proportionality), it further requires using the *least force necessary*. The mere fact that another agent has acted unjustly does not permit one to react to him in a comparable way, if doing so is not needed to get him to stop and to make restitution. For example, if a thief enters my house, and I have two ways to get him to leave, by merely threatening him with a *sjambok* or by injuring him with one, I am morally obligated to use the former means, even if the latter would be an 'equal form of violence'. Otherwise, I am not acting in self-defence, but rather punitively (usurping the role of a judge in a constitutional democracy) and likely out of retaliatory vengeance.

It has also been suggested that negotiation would have been ineffective, and that only violence would be successful:

> Violence is always relevant given the nature of structures we are dealing with. When one looks into history, negotiating was tried and tested and it clearly does not work ... History has taught us that the oppressor is not going to willingly give us our freedom and will eventually call us into a negotiation table and you will be outfoxed and still remain subservient to his rule (University of the Witwatersrand #FeesMustFall, quoted in Nicolson 2016a).

Here, I would just say that it would be prudent for a negotiator to take a proposal back to his or her constituency, which should decide whether to ratify it. That way, the wisdom of collective reflection and discussion would prevail, making it less likely that a small group would be hoodwinked by slickly-talking bureaucrats (in addition, doing so would honour the value of collective self-governance). The best way to know that negotiation will not work is first to try it. After all, Rhodes did fall, and did not need fire to do so.

DISCRIMINATION

Fifth, and finally, there is the issue of against whom force may be directed. Just war theorists speak of 'discrimination' in this context, which does not mean something like racism or sexism but, rather, drawing distinctions between who is morally liable to be threatened or harmed and who is not. It is standard in the context of war to maintain that only aggressors should be targeted – roughly, those who are responsible for the violation of a state's territory or of citizens' human rights, most clearly high-ranking politicians who have militarily embarked on an unjust cause and combatants who have volunteered to fight for it (for example, McMahan 2004). It is the violation of this principle that leads people to judge the nuclear attacks on Hiroshima and Nagasaki to have been gravely unjust.

Transplanted to a non-military context, the principle is that force should be directed only against those responsible for injustice. Note that 'perfection' is not expected or even morally required. Sometimes innocent parties, those not responsible for the injustice, will get caught up in the course of a fight, especially a political struggle. However, the basic point is that, normally, innocents *at least* should not be *intentionally* threatened, subjugated or harmed, even if doing so would be expected to promote a just cause.

It is not always certain, in a given context, who counts as responsible. For instance, are those who voted for an unjust leader responsible for his injustice? As a rule, though, force ought to be directed against those who are *particularly or obviously responsible*, that is, against the easy cases and not the hard ones. On this score, university senates, senior management teams and councils are fair game, at least when it comes to matters of institutional culture. When it comes to funding, more on the hook are the Department of Higher Education and Training, the Ministry of Finance and the ANC more generally as having been in control of the state for more than twenty years.

Several of the kinds of counterproductive tactics discussed above, preventing innocent students from obtaining an education, targeted the wrong parties. In addition, threatening the white population as a whole with 'kill all whites' and 'one bullet, one settler' was objectionably indiscriminate. Still more, smearing human faeces in lecture halls, where poorly paid workers were surely going to be the ones to clean it up, was wrong for misplacing burdens (Calderwood 2016). And then there was, beyond the recurrent stopping of traffic, the throwing of bricks at passing motorists (Wicks 2016), the attacks on them with sticks (February 2015), and the threat to act on the slogan, 'no free education, no elections!' (Germaner 2016), all of which targeted random citizens with no connection to higher education. The purposefully indiscriminate nature of the imposition of burdens has been clear, with the Wits SRC president having said, 'We are here to frustrate the city' (quoted in Zwane 2015).

In sum, reflection on the proper conduct of war, justified anti-apartheid rebellion and moral common sense indicates that force is *least controversially* permissible when it is *the smallest amount essential and expected to counteract a larger injustice, and targets those directly responsible for it*. I have not quite argued that this approach captures the only occasions in which force is justified. However, the burden of proof is plausibly on those who maintain that force is permissible in cases beyond those allowed by the five principles. I have argued that these principles entail that several forms of protest that students and workers took over the past year were wrong and should not be used again.[2]

There was a broad range of options available to students between being silent, accepting their fate, or even merely negotiating – and burning down buildings to prevent new students from registering (unlikely to succeed at increasing educational access), throwing petrol bombs at buses full of students and threatening death to all white people (disproportionate severity), smearing human excrement across lecture floors (hardly a last resort), and attacking passing motorists with bricks and threatening to disrupt democratic polls (indiscriminate). As I have acknowledged, these are not the only means that students and workers took over the past year, but, then, they were far from sporadic, too. I have mentioned some alternatives to these kinds of means. Which additional ones might thoughtful, strategic activists come up with and ideally use in the future to advance their just cause?[3]

NOTES

1   For a list of recent changes at the University of Cape Town, see Price (2016). See also Habib (2015) for the point that students 'have had more success in the last week than many of our collective efforts since the dawn of our democracy'.

2   There remains the issue of how various actors might prevent wrongful forms of protest or 'violence', but that is for the social scientist and not the moral philosopher to address (cf. Kamanzi 2016).
3   Thanks to Dee Cohen for compiling much of the empirical data that I have cited, to Susan Booysen and Adam Habib for giving me things to think about with regard to the ethics, and to several copy editors for sharing judgement.

REFERENCES

Aboobaker, S. (2015) UJ under 'mini state-of-emergency'. *IOL*, 15 November. http://www.iol.co.za/news/crime-courts/uj-under-mini-state-of-emergency-1945385

Bilchitz, D. (2016) Recent student protests are entirely counterproductive. *South African Jewish Report*, 9 March. http://www.sajr.co.za/news-and-articles/2016/03/09/recent-student-protests-are-entirely-counterproductive

Calderwood, I. (2016) Wave of violent student demonstrations has erupted across South Africa. *Sankofa Sofa*, 25 February. http://www.sankofasofa.com/docs/feed/item/wave-violent

Chernick, I., Exstrum, O. & Molosankwe, B. (2016) #FeesMustFall damages bill: R300 302 848.58. *IOL*, 13 April. http://www.iol.co.za/news/south-africa/feesmustfall-damages-bill-r300-302-84858-2008936

Cokayne, R. (2015) Raiding Setas not welcome – industry. *IOL* 19 October. http://www.iol.co.za/business/news/raiding-setas-not-welcome---industry-1937390

Debord, G. (1967) *The Society of the Spectacle* (trans. D. Nicholson-Smith). New York: Zone Books.

February, J. (2015) Why is the state not a target of student protests? *eNCA*, 20 October. https://www.enca.com/opinion/why-state-not-target-student-protests

Fisher, S. & Mortlock, M. (2015) Student protests continue at UCT and CPUT. *Eyewitness News*, 27 October. http://ewn.co.za/2015/10/27/Student-protests-ongoing-at-CPUT-and-UCT

FMF Parents Solidarity Committee (2015) Our children aren't violent hooligans – #FeesMustFall parents. *PoliticsWeb*, 16 November. http://www.politicsweb.co.za/politics/our-children-arent-violent-hooligans--feesmustfall

Germaner, S. (2016) #FeesMustFall protesters threaten polls. *IOL*, 14 January. http://www.iol.co.za/news/south-africa/gauteng/feesmustfall-protesters-threaten-polls-1970686

Gernetsky, K. & Mashego, P. (2016) Vice-chancellors say most students want to get academic 2016 under way. *Business Day Live*, 18 January. http://www.bdlive.co.za/national/education/2016/01/18/vice-chancellors-say-most-students-want-to-get-academic-2016-under-way

GroundUp (2015) Universities closed and exams postponed. *GroundUp*, 26 October. http://www.groundup.org.za/article/universities-closed-and-exams-postponed_3440/

Habib, A. (2015) Wits University supports students' demand for more funding for higher education. *VC's Post*, 22 October. http://blogs.wits.ac.za/vc/2015/10/22/wits-university-supports-students-demand-for-more-funding-for-higher-education/

Habib, A. (2016) Goals and means: Some reflections on the 2015 #FeesMustFall protests. *Daily Maverick*, 26 January. http://www.dailymaverick.co.za/opinionista/2016-01-26-goals-and-means-some-reflections-on-the-2015-feesmustfall-protests/

International Commission of Jurists (1985) Siracusa principles on the limitation and derogation provisions in the International Covenant on Civil and Political Rights.

http://icj.wpengine.netdna-cdn.com/wp-content/uploads/1984/07/Siracusa-principles-ICCPR-legal-submission-1985-eng.pdf

Isaacs, L. & Petersen, C. (2015) Vow to shut down varsities. *Cape Times*, 21 October. http://www.iol.co.za/capetimes/vow-to-shut-down-varsities-1933208

Ismael, Z. (2015) 'One bullet, one settler', says RMF. *iAfrica.com*, 14 April. http://mobi.iafrica.com/uncategorized/2015/04/14/one-settler-one-bullet-says-rmf/

Jansen, J. (2015) South Africa: When student activism turns to gangsterism. https://martinplaut.wordpress.com/2015/10/25/south-africa-when-student-activism-turns-to-gangsterism/

Jansen, J. (2016) Why I fear for the future of our universities. *Rand Daily Mail*, 3 March. http://www.rdm.co.za/politics/2016/03/03/why-i-fear-for-the-future-of-our-universities

Kamanzi, B. (2016) Demythologising campus violence. *Daily Maverick*, 6 March. http://www.dailymaverick.co.za/opinionista/2016-03-06-demythologising-campus-violence-towards-a-united-front-for-free-education/

Kaunda, K. (1980) *Kaunda on Violence*. London: Collins.

Lewis, C. (2016) UCT investigates as T-shirt with racist slogan seen on campus. *Eyewitness News*, 11 February. http://ewn.co.za/2016/02/11/UCT-investigating-latest-incident-of-racism

Mandela, N. (1964) Statement by Nelson Mandela from the dock at the opening of the defence case in the Rivonia Trial. http://www.mandela.gov.za/mandela_speeches/before/640420_trial.htm

Mandela, N. (1994) *Long Walk to Freedom*. London: Abacus.

Manzini, Z. (2016) Violence is a necessary process of decolonisation. *Mail & Guardian*, 2 March. http://thoughtleader.co.za/mandelarhodesscholars/2016/03/02/violence-is-a-necessary-process-of-decolonisation/

Masuabi, Q. (2016) Fourteen arrested for 'unlawful activities' at Wits. *Eyewitness News*, 19 February. http://ewn.co.za/2016/02/19/14-arrested-for-unlawful-activities-at-Wits

Mbembe, A. (2016) Theodor Adorno vs Herbert Marcuse on student protests, violence and democracy. *Daily Maverick*, 19 January. http://www.dailymaverick.co.za/article/2016-01-19-theodor-adorno-vs-herbert-marcuse-on-student-protests-violence-and-democracy/#.Vw8tZmNWdcY

McMahan, J. (2004) The ethics of killing in war. *Ethics*, 114, 693–733.

Metz, T. (2005) The ethics of routine HIV testing. *South African Journal on Human Rights*, 21, 370–405.

Metz, T. (2009) African moral theory and public governance. In M. F. Murove (ed.) *African Ethics*. Pietermaritzburg: University of KwaZulu-Natal Press, pp. 335–356.

Metz, T. (2010) Human dignity, capital punishment, and an African moral theory. *Journal of Human Rights*, 9, 81–99.

Metz, T. (2012) Developing African political philosophy. *Philosophia Africana*, 14, 61–83.

Metz, T. (2015) Africanising institutional culture. In P. Tabensky & S. Matthews (eds). *Being at Home: Race, Institutional Culture and Transformation at South African Higher Education Institutions*. Pietermaritzburg: University of KwaZulu-Natal Press.

Metz, T. (2016) A life of struggle as *ubuntu*. In S. Ndlovu-Gatsheni & B. Ngcaweni (eds). *Nelson Rolihlahla Mandela: Decolonial Ethics of Liberation and Servant Leadership*. Trenton: Africa World Press.

Morrissey, K. & Monama, T. (2015) #WitsFeesMustFall protest to continue. *IOL*, 15 October. http://www.iol.co.za/news/crime-courts/witsfeesmustfall-protest-to-continue-1930243

Nicolson, G. (2015) South Africa: Where 12 million live in extreme poverty. *Daily Maverick*, 3 February. http://www.dailymaverick.co.za/article/2015-02-03-south-africa-where-12-million-live-in-extreme-poverty/#.VqcP2MdWdcY

Nicolson, G. (2016a) Violent protests: Community organisers weigh in. *Daily Maverick*, 22 February. http://www.dailymaverick.co.za/article/2016-02-22-violent-protests-community-organisers-weigh-in/#.Vs08QMdWdca

Nicolson, G. (2016b) Fees must fall: Reloaded. *Daily Maverick*, 12 January. http://www.dailymaverick.co.za/article/2016-01-12-fees-must-fall-reloaded/#.Vw9CXmNWdcY

Orend, B. (2005) War. In E. Zalta (ed.) *Stanford Encyclopaedia of Philosophy*. http://plato.stanford.edu/archives/fall2005/entries/war

Pamla, S. (2016) Students must allow new students to register – Cosatu. *PoliticsWeb*, 18 January. http://www.politicsweb.co.za/politics/students-must-allow-new-students-to-register--cosa

Paterson, K. (2016) Limpopo education department: More money, same problems. *GroundUp*, 21 April. http://www.groundup.org.za/article/limpopo-education-department-more-money-same-problems/

Presence, C. (2016) Nzimande: SA can't afford fee free universities. *IOL*, 21 April. http://www.iol.co.za/news/politics/nzimande-sa-cant-afford-fee-free-universities-2012885

Pretorius, W. (2016) #FeesMustFall leaders present list of demands. *News24*, 13 January. http://www.news24.com/SouthAfrica/News/feesmustfall-leaders-present-list-of-demands-20160113

Price, M. (2015) UCT boss: I am dismayed at settler chants. *Rand Daily Mail*, 10 April. http://www.rdm.co.za/politics/2015/04/10/uct-boss-i-am-dismayed-at-settler-chants

Price, M. (2016) How UCT is stepping up transformation. *PoliticsWeb*, 11 March. http://www.politicsweb.co.za/documents/how-uct-is-stepping-transformation--max-price

Sacks, J. (2016) South Africa: Keep calm and let the students disrupt injustice. *The Daily Vox*, 25 January. http://allafrica.com/stories/201601252244.html

Sesant, S. (2016) Universities spend millions beefing up security. *Eyewitness News*, 7 March. http://ewn.co.za/2016/03/07/Universities-spend-millions-in-beefing-up-security

Tiro, M. (2015) Blackness & violence. *Vuka Darkie*, 26 November. http://www.vukadarkie.com/blackness-violence-a-view-from-the-ground/

TMG Digital (2016) Two months of student protests resulted in R92m in damage claims: Sasria. *TimesLIVE*, 9 March. http://www.timeslive.co.za/local/2016/03/09/Two-months-of-student-protests-resulted-in-R92m-in-damage-claims-Sasria

United Nations (1945) Charter of the United Nations and the statute of the International Court of Justice. https://treaties.un.org/doc/Publication/CTC/uncharter.pdf

Vally, N. & Godsell, S. (2016) A response to Wits VC's open letter on university protests. *The Daily Vox*, 27 January. http://www.thedailyvox.co.za/a-response-to-wits-vcs-open-letter-on-university-protests/

Van der Merwe, M. (2015) #FeesMustFall Thursday: Promises vs petrol bombs. *Daily Maverick*, 30 October. http://www.msn.com/en-za/news/featured/supernumberfeesmustfall-thursday-promises-vs-petrol-bombs/ar-BBmAGVh

Walzer, M. (1977) *Just and Unjust Wars*. New York: Basic Books.

Wicks, J. (2016) Tuks students hailed for bravery after #FeesMustFall march turned ugly. *News24*, 15 March. http://www.news24.com/SouthAfrica/News/tuks-students-hailed-for-bravery-after-feesmustfall-march-turned-ugly-20160315

Wits SRC (2015) Wits SRC on Habib's plan and the R40K. *IOL*, 29 October. http://www.iol.co.za/news/wits-src-on-habibs-plan-and-the-r40k-1937718

Zwane, T. (2015) Student protest: 'Even if they point their guns at us, we are going'. *Mail & Guardian*, 23 October. http://mg.co.za/article/2015-10-22-student-protest-even-if-they-point-their-guns-at-us-we-are-going

CONCLUSION: *ALUTA CONTINUA!*

Susan Booysen

'The owl of Minerva spreads its wings only with the falling of the dusk,' wrote Hegel in *The Philosophy of Rights* (1821). Like Hegel's owl of Minerva we might only gain our full understandings much later in our processes of probing, in our case, South Africa's #FeesMustFall revolt of 2015–2016. The chapters in this book are offered with a view to optimising our understandings at an early point in time, roughly a year since the first explicit manifestations of #FMF in October 2015, and just over a year from the point of renewed worker struggles at the University of the Witwatersrand (Wits) in May 2015. We have no illusions; we do not want to pre-empt Hegel's owl – we do not fully understand as yet, but we hope that both individual contributions in *FeesMustFall: Student Revolt, Decolonisation and Governance in South Africa*, and the book as a collective constitute one substantive step towards the full understanding.

Many questions remain about South Africa's 2015–2016 higher education war on fees, funding and outsourcing. It will only be with hindsight that we shall know whether #FeesMustFall is a case of '*Aluta continua, victoria ascerta*', or simply '*Aluta continua*'. Only history will bring the confirmed answers to the questions of 'who won and who lost', 'what was won and what lost' and 'what were the exact configurations of causes and triggers?' The answers, for now, depend on the lenses worn and the directed angle, and this volume offers a collection that opens the doors to stocktaking and further questioning.

From whichever angle it is approached, however, it is evident that governance in South Africa and its higher education institutions has been irrevocably altered.

#FeesMustFall, along with #OutsourcingMustFall, changed aspects of government and sociopolitical culture in South Africa. Like other student uprisings, especially in sub-Saharan Africa, the rising did not expel the government (nor, probably, was ever intended to) but served notice of a powerful post-liberation generation that does not live a reality of liberation and rights. Students in sub-Saharan Africa had begun to act as the social conscience and voice of the broader society, responding to and shaping responses to externally driven and internally driven political and economic events in particular historical periods. In South Africa, the 2015–2016 students saw the deficits, and demanded that the narratives of the generation of promise-makers be fulfilled. The footprints of #FMF are tentative and, in some instances, reversible. They were realised across the domains of policies on access to higher education, funding and national budgeting, conditions of workers, institutional cultures (ranging from coloniality to misogyny), the sociopolitical compact of 1994, and government approaches to dealing with dissent. Collectively, and with some changes manifested across all campuses, others not, there are twelve such changes at least.

As student activists, worker solidarity for students, and ties to academics all came together at the conjunctural moment from May to October of 2015, the #FeesMustFall movement won important higher education funding concessions and policy elaborations from the ANC government. There was a zero per cent fee increase for 2016, possibly beyond, implemented across the higher education sector for all public institutions. Registration fees were moderated and debt negotiated or covered by new sources from the National Student Financial Aid Scheme (NSFAS) and, in some cases, the private sector. The students themselves stepped in and fundraised to help cover the costs of the missing middle. The students of 2015 took on the ANC-led state, and won important gains – at first – and then faced the challenges to sustain momentum, broaden the struggle, and ensure that public sympathy was not lost. These challenges come, as David Everatt argues in Chapter 6, at the time when the movement has been fragmenting into various Fallist factions, calling alternately for patriarchy to fall and white supremacy to fall, with others focusing on their particular institution (whether colonial heritage or language is at stake).

A far greater awareness and wide range of action arose to help bring better access to students of unambiguously poor and missing-middle-poor backgrounds. The state reordered education funding priorities – in effect, raided (or 'used surpluses' available in) other educational budget items – to channel extra funding into the neglected higher education sector. New investigations were launched, the findings of which will help determine the next round of fees-insourcing struggles. Multiple future funding models were being explored. There were also deadends. The 2016 university funding formula was not sustainable, but there was no going back to the *status quo ante*. University managements were converted away from budgeting processes that looked at fee increases as the answer to rising costs. Never again will fee increases be considered or introduced in blasé managerialist styles and without consideration of human suffering (and potential student action). In the process, universities entered a new phase of cooperation with the state, recognising their institutions' dependency afresh, but nevertheless campaigning to affirm their intellectual independence.

University cultures changed, or started a long-term process of change. Alienation and decolonisation entered the intellectual vocabulary and found roots in the society-wide recognition that the shortcomings of the 1994 political and economic settlement have come home to roost. Demands for far-reaching change in higher education institutional culture and curricula came to rule the institutions. Numbers calculated by South African race category were no longer being used as evidence of 'transformation achieved'. Decolonisation and Africanisation went hand in hand.

A new generation confirmed a new ideological consciousness, even if it often employed rhetoric and implied inconsistency. The intersectionality of continuous oppression was the foreground in a crusade against injustices of continuous exclusion through funding, alienation, structural violence and discrimination. This generation of youth came together in the course of the #FeesMustFall (and antecedent and subsequent hashtag struggle formations), spurred on by a deepened campus-based worker consciousness. They settled in and gave notice – albeit in multiple iterations that spanned much of the political spectrum – that they would no longer, or at least not much longer, or no longer patiently, or silently, live the compromises entered into by their liberation-credential predecessors. One of the solidifying cores of the generational change (even as it fought to retain centrality in #FMF) was a new and assertive African feminism, and LGBTIAQ+s stepping into spaces created in the new struggle movement. General institutional-level change was still to become concretised but without doubt this societal foundation started to move, as was evidenced in the unyielding anti-rape and sexual abuse protests of 2016.

Change spanned the student–worker spectrum. A change came in multiple university managements changing their governance paradigms to settle on phased insourcing of categories of university workers (cleaning and maintenance, gardening, electrical) who had been subject since 2000 to neoliberalised outsourcing regimes. The process would still be slow, and universities were figuring out how to budget without compromising the academic project, but there could be no going back on commitment. The worker–student solidarity had been advancing the gains on all of the student-fees, institutional-decolonisation and worker-insourcing fronts.

These sets of changes – recorded across the chapters in this volume – combined to challenge several of the foundations of the post-apartheid, democratic-era political and economic dispensation. Rainbowism was discarded as an insulting fallacy. New forms of solidarity came via hashtagism with its Fallist elixir. A good cause in the new spirit of the times – the solidarity issues of zero fee increases, decolonised education or free education for the poor – could raise disruptive solidarity protests at any campus around the country and select international ones. The social and economic compact of the post-1994 dispensation was dismissed, even if inconsistently and on occasion in rhetoric more than in action. The actions asserted that the trajectory ahead was unlikely to unfold as it did in the past. Redistributive economic justice, pursued with the vigour of newly-confirmed power, seemed to drive the campaign.

It is at this point that the effects and changes wrought by #FeesMustFall stall and spew out questions. Several chapters in this book analyse the strain that the ANC and government experienced, put under severe pressure by the anti-fees campaign that became a revolt (instead of remaining a *campaign*, as the ANC had imagined it would) and showed insurrectionary potential for a short while. The ANC felt threatened, stepped in and counter-mobilised – as government and as political party. As party it facilitated concessions and as government it was quick to formalise offers, to bring in additional funding, to reorganise NSFAS and work with universities to contain the additional 2016 outbreaks. The ANC called on its loyalists and divided much of the student movement in its late-2015 configuration. Beyond the point where the #FMF-Wits was partially subverted back into the ANC fold, the #FMF movement lost much of its radical thrust and, as core strains moved back into conforming with the ANC, it also stopped pushing the parameters of ANC governance (as had happened at the height of #FMF). When the remainder of the party-politicised segment of the #FMF movement veered towards the Economic Freedom Fighters (EFF), the Pan Africanist Student Movement of Azania (Pasma) and Black First Land First (BLF), it became easier for university managements and their private security contingents to pull the movement back into the safe mode of protest against fees, colonial-apartheid legacies of society and universities, and feminist and LGBTIAQ+ activism. In the end, as Vishwas Satgar observes (Chapter 10), 'no single political organisation, social group or leader can claim the historical expression and impact of #FeesMustFall. In practice and in its logic it was an expression of multiple determinations and a ripening of several contradictions at once'.

It was ideal territory for the governing party, testifying to a 'full circle': the radical rhetoric and insistence on far-reaching change to rid South Africa of the structural legacies of colonialism and apartheid came to dominate the 2016 political agenda. This was well aligned to the style of propagation and campaigning that the ANC has been assuming in recent times. Frustrated ideals and unfulfilled policy promises have been blamed increasingly by the ANC and its government under President Jacob Zuma on the deep-seated and wicked persistence of colonial and apartheid (inclusive of racist and white capital) disorders. The student movement, in large part, was now breathing this exact rebellion. In its 2016 phase, the big, latent question for the student movement became whether it would be captured, contained and be a *de facto* part of the ANC's project for political hegemony, or whether it would in time and in numbers again assume an insurrectionary if not 'revolutionary' character.

The #FMF revolt opened up contradictory spaces. As Lynn Hewlett, Nomagugu Mukadah, Koffi Kouakou and Horácio Zandamela conclude in Chapter 7, the possibility arises of alliances with other sectors of society for resistance to try and bring about different economic and/or political orders, besides the possibilities for co-option by political parties and elites distributing patronage. The spectrum of arguments in this book highlights further the contradictions of #FMF, including the question of violence and the justification of violent means of protest (which can also be indiscriminate), and the ideological contradictions when class and race come to intersect. There was no inevitable and singular determination in how #FeesMustFall intersected with worker-led class struggle, and further intersected with race, gender, black consciousness and the young generation's aspiration for improved education and middle-class life opportunities. As Satgar observes with regard to Wits, there was a ripening of several contradictions, all at once.

Students' lived reality as well as observation of fellow students' academic aspirations being thwarted through combinations of repressive and reactionary financial and cultural conditions contributed to the conditions for #FMF. At the same time there was a rising cohort of student intellectuals ready to interpret the budding struggles in terms of philosophies of change. The leaders, those who suffer directly and those who sympathise, had grown up in South Africa's epoch of 'guaranteed' human rights and a dominant, former liberation party insisting that these are being delivered (gradually) and cautioning simultaneously that outside and hostile forces of racism and colonialism were sabotaging the emergence of the economically-liberated post-apartheid society. Much of this sentiment reverberated in #FMF. The students had also grown up in a country rich in protest culture and had learned that protest, peaceful or not, brings government attention. The rise of significant new political parties furthermore helped to legitimise opposition and dissent – in fact, the ANC at the time of the student revolt had much less authority over the youth and student generation than it had had a decade or so earlier. Finally, and as Manuel Castells (2012) also remarks about social media and the youth generally, improved networking communication among student protest movements fortifies solidarity with and among student movements on university campuses globally.

The next phase in student mobilisation will be a delicate balancing act. The analyses of Sizwe Mpofu-Walsh and of Gillian Godsell and Rekgotsofetse Chikane show both the substance of and the lines of tension in the student movement. 2015–2016 has changed the rules of operation beyond the growth of student power. University managements have been sensitised, are budgeting (somewhat and selectively) more transparently and are cooperating with student leaders (some student leaders are co-opted, albeit largely on terms favourable to #FMF objectives); extensive security on campuses has been legitimised; the student movement is fragmented; re-insourcing of university workers is unfolding, curriculum reform is taking hold and advanced racial change in the academy has commenced ... to cite but a few changes associated with #FMF. By 2016, students were taking stock, returning to their immediate and base issue: poor students are still paying fees, still accumulating debt, still feel alienated, and are still going hungry and lacking accommodation conducive to studying. University managements and government were considering finance options, pleading for acceptance of fee increases.

And the wheel was turning towards a next round of revolt, then still underdetermined in form but unfolding on a terrain of struggle that had evolved from the moment of October 2015. Students and workers had tasted the power of direct action. They now knew the sway of solidarity and the weakness of divisions – yet in the next revolt, beginning on 19 September 2016 following Minister of Higher Education and Training Blade Nzimande's announcement about fees for 2017, they would be facing university managements and a government that had learned lessons in the containment of revolt, by both force and persuasion. In a next round of revolt the stakes would be higher and attitudes would have hardened.

REFERENCES

Castells, M. (2012) *Networks of Outrage and Hope: Social Movements in the Internet Age*. Malden: Polity Press.
Hegel, G. W. F. (1821) (transl. 1896 by S. W. Dyde) *The Philosophy of Rights*. London: George Bell & Sons.

APPENDIX

1

ANNOTATED TIMELINE OF THE #FEESMUSTFALL REVOLT 2015–2016

Susan Booysen, with Kuda Bandama

Acknowledgement: I thank Shaeera Kalla, former Wits SRC president and key figure in the student protest movement, for her detailed comment, suggestions on, and corrections of, an earlier draft of this timeline. Her first-hand knowledge of and insights into the Wits leg of the revolt, especially, have been invaluable. The responsibility for interpretation of content in the table nevertheless rests with me, Susan Booysen.

Sources: Direct observation; a wide range of media coverage; and corroboration against, for example, South African History Online 2016; University of the Witwatersrand student protests 2015 timeline, http://www.sahistory.org.za/article/university-witwatersrand-student-protests-2015-timeline.

KEY TO ACRONYMS OF UNIVERSITY NAMES USED IN THE TIMELINE				
CPUT	Cape Peninsula University of Technology	TUT	Tshwane University of Technology
DUT	Durban University of Technology	UCT	University of Cape Town
NMMU	Nelson Mandela Metropolitan University	UFH	University of Fort Hare
NWU	North West University	UFS	University of the Free State
RU	Rhodes University	UJ	University of Johannesburg

APPENDIX 1

UKZN	University of KwaZulu-Natal	UWC	University of the Western Cape
Unisa	University of South Africa	VUT	Vaal University of Technology
UP	University of Pretoria	Wits	University of the Witwatersrand
US	University of Stellenbosch	WSU	Walter Sisulu University

Additional acronyms in the timeline	
ANC	African National Congress
ANCYL	African National Congress Youth League
CIA	Central Intelligence Agency (USA)
Daso	Democratic Alliance Students Organisation
DHET	Department of Higher Education and Training
EFF	Economic Freedom Fighters
FMF	FeesMustFall/#FMF
Habib	Professor Adam Habib, vice-chancellor of Wits University
HE/HET	Higher Education/Higher Education and Training
NSFAS	National Student Financial Aid Scheme
Nzimande	Dr Blade Nzimande, minister of higher education and training
PAC	Pan Africanist Congress
PYA	Progressive Youth Alliance (ANCYL + Young Communist League + Sasco)
RMF	RhodesMustFall/#RMF
Sasco	South African Student Congress (ANC-aligned)
Saso	South African Students' Organisation
Seta	Skills Education Training Authority
SRC	Student Representative Council
USAf	Universities South Africa
VC	Vice-chancellor
Zuma	President Jacob Zuma

DATE	SELECT #FEESMUSTFALL EVENTS AND EXPLANATIONS
	Antecedents
	Multiple historical events have impacted on the core issues in the #FeesMustFall revolt of October 2015 to 2016. The focus of this timeline, however, is on the #FeesMustFall protest. We acknowledge (without replicating a wealth of activist and scholarly reports) the roots of financial exclusion and cultural alienation in colonial and apartheid times, and the resistance that was manifested in youth ranks over many decades. As a mere and a respectful nod in the direction of the roots, we note the formation of the South African Students' Organisation (Saso, articulating the politics of black consciousness) and the Soweto student revolt, emanating from the need to emancipate the black student from separatist oppression. Between 1994 and 2004 many events shaped the student movement, and many fees protests took place. At Wits, the fight against outsourcing started in the early 2000s; the police were on campus in 2007 and 2009 to quell fee protests; several student leaders were arrested in the course of fees protests at various times. Most recently, the timeline specifically also acknowledges the '1month1million' campaign and the #RhodesMustFall and other campus-based protests against racism and financial exclusion. Equally, government's engagement with the idea of free higher education has vacillated. As one illustration, the minister of higher education appointed a working group to investigate the feasibility of 'fee-free' university education, but the pro-free-education-for-the poor report of December 2012 gathered dust.
2014–2015 generally	In the context that Sasco has over many years protested nationally for free education, and had made historic contributions to progressive education generally, non-ANC-aligned student organisations started asserting themselves. To illustrate, while the ANC-led PYA remains dominant, the EFF Student Command wins **University of Limpopo Turfloop** campus, defeating the PYA. Subsequently it wins two core portfolios in the **NWU** (Mahikeng) SRC elections, but ties 6-6 with Sasco. Daso wins the **Fort Hare** SRC elections by 52.5%, taking the campus leadership from Sasco leadership (Sasco regains the majority in April 2016). The EFF wins the **VUT** SRC elections against Sasco. At **Wits** the EFF contests (on a manifesto that is about decolonisation rather than free education) and loses to Sasco.
February 2015	The Wits SRC's '1month1million' campaign brings to national attention the higher education funding crisis. This was an important moment: broader society accepted that this is a problem in the higher education sector. Whereas '1month1million' focused on the decommodification of higher education, #RMF centred attention on decolonisation and its links into alienation and cultural exclusion.

APPENDIX 1

March 2015	#RMF starts at **UCT**, spreads to **RU** through the Black Student Movement championing for transformation through #RhodesSoWhite. On 9 March, Chumani Maxwele protests at the UCT site of the Cecil John Rhodes statue and begins a week of events that leads to the occupation of Bremner Building, UCT administrative headquarters. **Wits** students join the campaign through #TransformWits. Open Stellenbosch begins at the **US** with the objective of erasing the remnants of apartheid, calling for a 'truly African University'. The Black Student Stokvel at **NMMU** joins the cause rallying for the re-creation and attainment of a socially responsible NMMU. Transform Pukke at **NWU** (Potchefstroom), and Tuks UP-rising at the University of Pretoria follow.
April 2015	At the **US** the Open Stellenbosch Movement challenges the hegemony of white Afrikaans culture (and 'normalised' institutional racism), the exclusion of black students and staff, and the slow pace of transformation. Students speak about their experiences of racist abuse and their struggles with learning under the language policy that favours Afrikaans speakers. They tell the university and its management: 'After years of empty promises and hollow commitments, we no longer trust what you say. Speak to us with your actions because your words will fall on deaf ears, as ours have for over a decade.' Subsequently in August the documentary Luister (Listen) follows and takes the issue into the national domain. It trends on social media.
27–29 May 2015	Workers and students occupy the **Wits** vice-chancellor's office in protest against the lack of response by university management in the dismissal of the outsourced MJL electrical workers. Wits settles by paying the workers outstanding wages, but refuses to insource them.
22 August 2015	**Wits** management suspends students from the EFF Student Command and one from the PYA for disrupting an SRC election debate, including Vuyani Pambo, who became one of the faces of the #FMF movement. Pambo argues that Wits had been brutal to the black students, workers and lecturers. Wits SRC leaders over many years had been targeted with disciplinary procedures, arrests and suspensions (for fees action, protest with workers, solidarity with the Palestinian cause, etc.); such action therefore is not exceptional. The difference is that by 2015 there is a change in political and socioeconomic consciousness and student revolt potential is accumulating.
26 August 2015	The build-up of a new zeitgeist in student ranks continues. At **TUT** several students are injured in a clash between EFF and Sasco supporters (Pretoria West campus). The clash arises after a pre-SRC election address by Julius Malema.

14 September 2015	Protest erupts at Westville campus, **UKZN,** and spreads to other UKZN campuses. At Westville police and security guards engage in running battles with students who set fire to buildings (administration and security structures) and destroy vehicles. SRC president Lukhanyo Mishingana is charged with public violence, and several SRC members are arrested. The protests concern NSFAS funding and lack of accommodation. Pietermaritzburg campus SRC President Richard Mhongo qualifies the protest actions as a reflection of the students' dissatisfaction with UKZN's position on further increasing tuition fees and burdening poor students.
14–16 September 2015	Rioting at **UKZN** leads to campus closure for two days. UKZN spokesman, Lesiba Seshoka, states that all academic programmes would be suspended, effective Wednesday 16 September.
	October 2015 – the height of the revolt
2 October 2015	On the agenda of the **Wits** council meeting are fee increases. SRC president Shaeera Kalla is accompanied by Nompendulo Mkhatshwa (incoming president, with observer status at this stage). The meeting disagrees on the proposed fee increase and those opposing it are defeated in a vote.
6 October 2015	October 6 (a movement of students, workers and progressive academics) gathers an estimated 2 000 people across party political affiliations to march against outsourcing at **Wits, UJ** and **UCT**. The Workers' Charter is presented to Wits and UJ managements. Zuma announces a presidential task team to explore 'solutions to short-term student funding challenges'. The October 6 movement helps solidify the relationship between students and workers.
8 October 2015	A Wits SRC statement declares that the university has taken 'a deliberate and anti-progressive decision to once more entrench the financial exclusion of poor students'.
13 October 2015	**Wits** students stage a sit-in at the Wits St David's Place campus, protesting Wits plans to do away with much of this campus' student accommodation to replace it with mostly lecturing venues. Wits VC arrives to negotiate with students.
14 October 2015	**Wits** students start a systematic shutdown of the university, executing a decision by the PYA-led Wits SRC. Students protest and block Wits entrances after the announcement that fees would be raised by 10.5% for 2016. The events constitute the formal start of the #FeesMustFall movement, and Day One of entrance blockades at the main Wits campuses. In the same week **UCT** announces a fee increase of 10.3%. Protest is taken to Twitter as #WitsFeesMustFall. As Wits SRC president at this time it was ultimately Shaeera Kalla's decision to launch the protest. Along with Kalla, Mcebo Dlamini (former Wits SRC president), Wits SRC president-elect Mkhatshwa, and Pambo emerge as leading figures in the no-leadership-structures student movement at Wits.

APPENDIX 1

15 October 2015, for several days	Day Two of the systematic shutdown of **Wits** entrances and facilities, particularly East and West Campus, Braamfontein and Education Campus, Parktown. The South Gauteng High Court grants Wits an interim interdict for police to interfere on campus, if requested, to assist with regulating student protests.
16 October 2015	VC Habib leaves the HE summit in Durban to go and address the protesting Wits students. Habib and Wits Executive Team members are held hostage in Senate House (later Solomon Mahlangu House) by students. A meeting of the executive committee (Exco) of council takes place at then Senate House. It is the first time an Exco meeting takes place in front of students.
17 October 2015 (Saturday)	Social media speculate about an **RU** shut-down. At **Wits**, Dr Randall Carolissen, chairperson of the Wits Council, and Kalla meet and an agreement is signed that results in the fee increase for 2016 being suspended. It is also agreed that disciplinary action would not be taken against participating students or staff members.
19 October 2015 (Monday)	The Wits shutdown continues. Negotiations were to have started, but Council boycotted the meeting. #FeesMustFall protest spreads to all campuses around the country. **UCT** management secures a court interdict against protesters. RMF students occupy the UCT administration building and riot police are called in to evict students forcibly. **RU** students barricade themselves into the university, shutting off access. **UP** students plan to lock down three of the UP campuses on 21 October.
20 October 2015 (Tuesday)	Minister of HE, Nzimande, meets with university VCs at the Western Cape Parliament. He announces a 6% cap on the increase of 2016 fees. **Wits** students reject the compromise proposal, demanding that there should be no increase. **UCT** students march to Rondebosch police station to demand the release of fellow students. **CPUT** students protest and shut down their campus. **FH** students commence protesting and go into lockdown, refusing to sit for exams. **US** students hand a memorandum of grievances to university management.
21 October 2015 (Wednesday)	About 5 000 students mostly from **UCT** and **CPUT** march to Parliament, gaining access to the parliamentary grounds, and attempt a sit-in on the steps. They are forcibly removed through stun grenades, riot shields and batons. Several are arrested, and charged *inter alia* with treason and contravening the National Key Points Act. Nzimande tries to address the crowd but is booed. At **NMMU,** students block the entrances to the Summerstrand campuses. Police use rubber bullets and teargas to push students back onto campus. At **Sol Plaatje University** in Kimberley chaos erupts after students register their objection to an 8% tuition fee increase. Students throw stones at the police. Stun grenades are fired. Students at the Mbombela campus of **TUT** join the #FMF campaign, emphasising the issues of accommodation and NSFAS only benefiting a small number of students.

22 October 2015 (Thursday)	**Wits** and **UJ** students march en masse on the ANC's Luthuli House downtown Johannesburg headquarters, forcing ANC secretary general Gwede Mantashe to listen to them and receive their memo. They demand a no-fee-increase for 2016, free quality education and no outsourcing of staff at universities. **NMMU** students disrupt classes, block entrances and shut down access. Lack of trust causes negotiations with management to fall flat. At **FH**, students light bonfires at the entrances. In **Cape Town** students gather at the magistrates' court for the appearance of 29 arrested students.
23 October 2015 (Friday)	**UCT** students cooperate with *Cape Times* to produce an all-student-contribution issue. Robed academics join a charge across **UCT** campus. **NMMU** classes are cancelled. In Pretoria invited student leaders and university VCs meet with Zuma (**Wits** SRC leaders choose not to be part of the meeting). Outside the Union Buildings large numbers of students assemble, joined by many 'non-students' and probably some agents provocateurs. Zuma announces just before 15:00 from within the Union Buildings complex that there will be no fee increases for 2016. Immediately after the president's announcement, Wits SRC president Kalla responds through a Facebook posting: 'The government has addressed 0%. Let it be known that we are not satisfied with it. We are still waiting to be addressed on ending outsourcing at universities and on free education.' (0% was supposed to be a symbolic commitment towards free education.) The crowd is angered by the fact that Zuma does not descend to the grounds to address them. Rioting, including the burning of police vehicles and mobile toilets, break out in downtown Pretoria. The police disperse the crowd with rubber bullets and teargas. This minority crowd re-groups several times, and the police retaliate with teargas and flash-bangs. Approximately 6 000 **Durban** students march through the city, stopping at City Hall, and proceed to ANC regional headquarters in Stalwart Similane Street. In **Stellenbosch,** after a march management comes out in support of the 0% demand. Students demand the release of the *No Varsity Fee* report. They also demand explanations for police brutality. In **London** hundreds of South Africans gather at the SA High Commission in support of #FeesMustFall.
24 October 2015 (Saturday)	Wits management expresses its disappointment in the students' decision to continue protesting despite the announcement of the 0% fee increase.
25 October 2015 (Sunday)	ANC national structures intervene in the **Wits** struggle in particular. A meeting is held and it is reported that the ANC instructs its PYA campus partners to take the gains and suspend/end protest. This is a great divisive moment in the movement. Wits SRC members deny that any decisions were taken in their meeting with the ANC. It is largely non-SRC members nevertheless who continue the next week's struggle towards the insourcing of workers. Subsequently, multiple SRCs' authority to speak on behalf of students would be questioned.

APPENDIX 1

26–29 October 2015 (Monday)	Student formations across the country take stock and a number of higher education campuses postpone examinations; some close for the summer vacation. Protests against outsourcing continue on several campuses, including **Wits**. Wits management proposes a 9-point plan to address ongoing student concerns (26 October). Wits #FeesMustFall lists 18 demands.
30–31 October 2015	Wits University reaches an agreement with students and workers over the contending issues surrounding the protest.
Rest of 2015 – Victories for insourcing, factions emerge	
1 November (Sunday) 2015	#OutsourcingMustFall formations at **Wits** meet under conditions of legal orders prohibiting campus gatherings, while the Wits Council deliberates. Wits commits in principle to insourcing and the creation of a task team to work out the modalities by 6 November so as to ensure 'sustainability' of the university. It also agrees to write off the debts of financially needy 2015 final-year students who owe less than R15 000; students will no longer pay a R1 500 fee for each supplementary exam they write; the children of outsourced workers who gain entry to Wits on academic grounds can study there for free. It is proposed that examinations be postponed for a week, subject to Senate approval.
5–9 November 2015	The #OccupyUJ movement takes off and Wits #FeesMustFall support the movement by co-protesting and assisting with food and refreshments (5 November). UJ occupation ends after 163 students and workers are arrested and held at Brixton police station, 7 of whom are **Wits** students (6 November). The first of the arrested students and workers are released, and #Brixton163 and #Brixton141 start trending on Twitter. **UJ** holds a night vigil to show solidarity with the struggle to end outsourcing (8 November). The state withdraws charges against the remaining 141 students and workers (9 November).
15–26 November 2015	The USAf board meet to reflect on student protest and plan strategic responses.
November 2015 generally	Classes resume and catch-up falls into place across South Africa. Multiple examinations are disrupted, rescheduled or postponed. Students are offered the option of deferred exams. At most sites exams unfold under heightened security, services are often rendered controversially by private security firms.
3 December	SRC presidents and secretaries meet Nzimande at invitation of the parliamentary portfolio committee on HE. Some student leaders are angered and walk out, saying they are tired of talking without progress. They are also still awaiting the results of Zuma's task team investigating the feasibility of free education (set up upon the first round of protest).

12 December 2015	A special board meeting of USAf takes place. It releases a report on members' support for quality and increased access to HE, along with financial support for poor students. It also denigrates violence and condemns the destruction of university property (12 December). The **Wits** SRC (15 December) announces that all students with R15 000 (or less) outstanding fees will be allowed to graduate. It also releases a call to students who have been academically excluded to appeal to the SRC for assistance (22 December).
	2016 – The struggle continues and diversifies
3–4 January 2016	Students of the **Wits** #FeesMustFall movement begin occupying Solomon Mahlangu House and taking up residence there (3 January). **Wits** SRC meets with the management (4 January 2016) and reaches agreements on deferred and supplementary exams, academic exclusion, finance, the SRC Humanitarian Fund, the First Payment Plan, accommodation, residence vacancies, and timing of residences opening.
11 January 2016	The struggle moves into a phase of securing free post-secondary education for poor students. Registration fees and financial exclusion remain an issue as the registration process is disrupted at **Wits** and **UJ**, prompting management to bring in increased private security on the basis of threats made to them by students. **UP, TUT, Tshwane South College, Tshwane North College, Unisa** and **Sefako Makgatho Health Sciences** are closed by worker-student action against outsourcing.
14 January 2016	Zuma announces a commission of enquiry into free higher education in South Africa, to be chaired by a retired supreme court of appeal judge, Jonathan Heher. They have eight months to complete the task. SRC leaders again meet Nzimande – some do a walkout, stating that there will be protest if they enter into compromises. Nzimande announces that R17 billion has been set to back the 0% fee increase for 2016, and universities pledging mechanisms to support this effort.
15 January 2016	**Wits** management gets a court interdict to prevent further disruption of registration and brings in additional private campus security. The court order outlaws (in the words used in the order): unlawfully occupying 'Senate House' or any other offices, buildings, facilities or lecture halls; disrupting normal activities including registration, classes, lectures, tutorials; obstructing or preventing any person from entering or leaving the university or any Wits buildings and facilities; causing damage to property; participating in, calling for, inciting or encouraging unlawful behaviour; harassing, intimidating, threatening or assaulting any person on campus; and being in possession of any dangerous weapons including knives, sticks or the like. The order also enables management to bring police onto campus.
18 January	The OutsourcingMustFall committee representing tertiary institutions and municipal workers on contract threatens mass action if workers' demands are not met.

APPENDIX 1

	Workers at **UP, TUT** and **Unisa** promise to intensify their actions. The Workers and Socialist Party (WASP) says these demands must be met or mass action will follow.
19 January 2016	Students threaten to boycott the 2016 local elections. The ANCYL says such a boycott will be met with the 'wrath and might' of the state's law enforcement agencies. Sasco says that 'CIA-trained dark forces' want to use #FMF for regime change. Sasco blames disruptions on EFF students. Allegations of a third force under #OutsourcingMustFall disrupting and hijacking student protest for political ends gains momentum.
31 January 2016	**Wits** SRC launches a R10 million-target fundraising campaign to help cover education costs of the missing middle.
15 February 2016	**UCT** students erect a shack on campus, to protest the lack of student accommodation. UCT management states that 75% of residence accommodation is allocated to black students and ascribes the shortage to the higher number of returning students, given better affordability due to the successes of #FeesMustFall. At **NWU** following violent clashes between campus security and students affiliated to the EFF Student Command, lectures at the Mahikeng campus are suspended. At **WSU** students burn vehicles and loot for food.
16–17 February 2016	**UP** is closed after a worker protest. EFF and AfriForum Youth students clash over Afrikaans as language of instruction. **UCT** students firebomb VC Price's office and a Jammie shuttle bus after being angered by an instruction to move the shack. Anger and violence escalate and students burn art works – seen as colonialist relics – from UCT residences Jameson, Smuts and Fuller. Eight students and some 'non-students' are arrested. UCT obtains an interdict against 16 students and suspends three. #FMF students vow to continue their protest until the university commits to 'a clear decolonisation project' including better psychological counselling services, clear timelines and frameworks for curriculum change, reform of the academic staff profile, and representation of black students in arts and culture. The accommodation situation is dire, also at **Wits** where one of the results of the 0% increase is an influx of students coming into Johannesburg without prior planning and requiring accommodation. Gift of the Givers steps in to help some students who have been going hungry. A Wits inter-campus bus is burned outside a residence in Parktown (17 February). A small group of students briefly occupy Solomon Mahlangu House but are evicted. **UWC** students protest about inclusion, debt relief and fees. Management refuses to shut down the campus, and protesting students are served with eviction notices. At UWC many students are also living in libraries, computer labs and other student facilities.

	NWU protest includes the use of petrol bombs at Mahikeng campus, over an SRC leader's suspension. **NMMU** students threaten protest. Their #FMF plenary uses the hashtag #DecoloniseOrPerish. **WSU** shuts down; accommodation protests happen at its East London campus. **RU** protest comes in the form of a march under #Nisixhoshelani ('Why are you turning us away?'), accusing management of breaking promises.
18 February 2016	**NSFAS** states that if students meet the criteria, NSFAS will pay for private accommodation. Chief Executive Msulwa Daca says NSFAS is awaiting completion of registration across SA and will then review how many students with historic debt NSFAS can pay for. Meanwhile DHET asks institutions to register NSFAS-qualifying students who have historic debt. NSFAS cements its relationship with Seta, organisations that contribute R365 million towards bursaries awarded through NSFAS. At **UP** the SRC launches a fund-raising campaign to raise R10 million for education fees for poor students from the missing middle. **UCT** students demand that management addresses effectively the issues of police brutality against students, sexual assault, patriarchy and accommodation.
19 February 2016	**UP's** Hatfield and Groenkloof campuses close while demonstrators clash and burn tyres. Police use rubber bullets to disperse students at the Hatfield campus. 14 students are arrested and held at the Brooklyn police station.
23 February 2016	**UKZN's** Howard College, Westville, Edgewood and Pietermaritzburg, and **DUT** campuses have protest action when outsourced workers down tools.
24 February 2016	Several buildings at **NWU**, including a science centre and administration building, are destroyed through arson. Classes are suspended. The former SRC president of its Mahikeng campus is suspended for three years for misconduct. Violence started when the university administration replaced the elected SRC with an appointed one.
March 2016	The North West High Court rules that an interim order against former **NWU** SRC president Benz Mabengwane and 11 other students be made permanent (3 March). The Open and Access Movement at NWU's Mahikeng Campus threatens to take the management of the institution to court. **Unisa** contract workers continue protesting, saying that management had not responded to their demands as they had expected (4 March). **TUT** outsourced workers demand permanent jobs, and far better wages. They block entrances, preventing students from entering campus. Strike action continues at TUT Pretoria West and Soshanguve campuses (8 March). TUT is closed and students required to vacate residences (9 March).

April 2016	About 30 students protest at the **Wits** main campus fees office. An empty lecture hall at the Umthombo Building at **Wits** University is set ablaze by people believed to be politically commissioned and classes are disrupted (4 April). Wits SRC condemns the current protest, arguing that political opportunism has taken hold at the institution. Students from other universities, as well as EFF and PAC members join in. Students protesting against rape culture and sexual assault at **RU** successfully pressure the administration into accepting some of their demands. Students from the #RUReferenceList movement drive the protest (22 April) against rape culture and sexual violence on women. They identify perpetrators and demand broader definitions of sexual violence in university policies. **Wits** students also take part in an anti-rape and rape culture protest outside the campus' Great Hall (25 April).
May 2016	At **UJ** arson fire destroys the Sanlam Auditorium and a computer centre. **UFS** VC Jonathan Jansen resigns.
June 2016	**Wits** Council endorses insourcing with effect from January 2017, a R7 500 minimum wage for workers, and wage top-ups in the interim. **University of Stellenbosch** formalises the adoption of a new language policy. Reports emerge that university VCs had struck an accord not to announce fee increases (inflation-linked) for 2017 prior to the local government elections of August 2016.
Ongoing	

APPENDIX 2

STUDENT PROTEST GLOSSARY OF TERMS[1]

Source: Busisiwe Nxumalo (student protester). 23 October 2015. #ShutItDown...; verbatim conceptualisations from http://www.iol.co.za/news/south-africa/western-cape/shutitdown-1934399 [accessed 24 October 2015].

Black: All racially-oppressed people of colour. This political identity goes against the divisive racial categories that were formed during apartheid, such as Indian, coloured and African. 'Black', as a political identity, unites all people of colour who have been socially, politically and economically oppressed.

Black feminism is a consciousness highlighting black women's experiences in society, which often go unnoticed because black women face alienation based on race, gender and other social factors. This leads to an experience only black women can speak and write about, and from which knowledge can be created.

Black pain is the dehumanisation of black people, a daily struggle that comes from the violence that exists in systems that privilege whiteness or is institutionally racist.

Decolonisation is the removal of all unjust systems such as patriarchy, racism and capitalism in society and the restructuring of society to reflect African systems.

Gender conforming people operate a system that privileges men and oppresses everyone that does not conform to the gender roles that society expects.

LGBTIAQ+ stands for lesbian, gay, bisexual, transgender/transsexual, intersex, asexual, queer and other sexual orientations and gender identities.

Patriarchy is an unjust political-social system that insists that males are inherently dominant and superior. Everyone else is deemed weak – especially females.

Violence is an experience of structural oppression. This experience can translate into physical violence, emotional and psychological violence through violent words, institutional processes, actions and behaviour that are directed at black people in order to dehumanise them. A reaction to this violence is not violence itself, but a defence against dehumanisation.

Whiteness is a system that privileges white people at the expense of black people. It is present in all institutions in South African society and it is assumed to be the standard of how things should be, but it is inherently racist.

White privilege is a set of advantages or access to certain benefits that have been exclusively developed for white people. White people have white privilege because a system of whiteness is present in South Africa and across the globe, which means that society is structured around white people and their culture.

NOTE

1   The current listing highlights the unaltered student movement's use of the terms, as articulated in the student-authored edition of *Cape Times*, 23 October 2015. Scholarly and analytical conceptualisations used by individual authors in this volume may differ from the exact conceptualisations in this Appendix. Several of the chapters in this book, particularly in the 'Primary Voices' section, add to and elaborate on Appendix 2.

APPENDIX 3

KEY FEATURES OF STUDENT PROTEST ACROSS HISTORICAL PERIODS IN SUB-SAHARAN AFRICA

Compiled by Lynn Hewlett, Nomagugu Mukadah, Koffi Kouakou and Horácio Zandamela

Summary of key features of student protest in different historical periods in Africa

Chronology (time)	Key features across the three entities (Anglophone, Lusophone and Francophone)	Driving forces	
		External	Internal
Colonial era 1900–1960s	Politics • Student movements developed outside of the countries of residence while the elite were studying in colonies. Exposure to international political movements and ideologies – African diaspora in higher education influenced by these debates in the metropole. • Internally, little evidence of overt/ significant student protest – emerging scattered historical accounts of protests pointing to nascent student population joining forces with emerging nationalist movements to fight for independence. Earlier establishment of higher education institutions in North Africa especially in Algeria, Morocco and Egypt created a stimulus for student protest – gave voice and legitimacy to student movements that came later elsewhere in Africa.	Colonisation First World War and Second World War.	Struggle for independence.

APPENDIX 3

Chronology (time)	Key features across the three entities (Anglophone, Lusophone and Francophone)	Driving forces	
		External	Internal
	Policies • Broad colonial educational policies in relation to higher education. • Purpose was to train up an elite layer of bureaucrats to serve the colonial system – children of the colonial bureaucrats. • French and Portuguese education policies focused on assimilation and control. • Top-down approach to educational systems. • Class, gender, territorial/spatial and racially-based education systems, elitist, small and selected. **Governance** • Some elements of autonomy of institutions vs. political centralisation. • Differentiated governance system – assimilationist approach, to produce bureaucrats Anglophone and Francophone. • External capacity/resources to operate the institutions of higher education.		
Nationalist/ post-independence era 1960s–1980s	**Politics** • One party rule and implications for student political subservience/co-option to party, expectation of reward from government – jobs, elite status. • Influence of socialist/Marxist ideologies – equitable access. • Student movements/organisations as informal expansion of the party; student organisations perceived as the early stage of the youth and student political engagement; notion of political progression.	Socialist countries dominated by Soviet Union – socialist ideological orientation. African governments expand education systems along Soviet lines.	Massification of higher education (overcrowding, scarce resources, infrastructure decline, poor quality of education, critical staff shortages). Deteriorating sociopolitical and economic conditions.

Chronology (time)	Key features across the three entities (Anglophone, Lusophone and Francophone)	Driving forces	
		External	Internal
	• From co-option to contestation to protests. • Protesting students in later stages were no longer exclusively of the elite and had more allegiance with rural and worker struggles. Policies • Africanisation – higher education systems as vehicles to create African identity and knowledge acquisition. • Free education, zero fees (zero tuition, bursaries for all, free or subsidised meals, accommodation and transport) – gradually becoming curtailed by IMF structural adjustment, internal corruption and inefficiencies. • States influential in constructing the role of higher education (production and distribution of resources, financing higher education, employing graduates). • Higher education sector largely responsive to state demands. • Reduced priority to higher education, cost-recovery principles. • Developmentalist reform followed by market-based reform. Structural Adjustment Programmes (SAPs) • In line with SAPs, governments advised to cut public funding of higher education and focus on primary and secondary education. • Higher education marginalised and perceived as an elitist preoccupation; deprived of both international and domestic support.	Structural adjustment programmes. Socialist ideology of equitable access to education; funding from socialist countries. Priority re-orientation in funding support – to primary education.	Widespread corruption and administrative and technical inefficiencies. Economic crisis led governments to rely more on international financial institutions. Experiences of and allegiance to liberation movements. Underfunding, access inequality, corruption, capacity challenges; inequitable social structure.

APPENDIX 3

Chronology (time)	Key features across the three entities (Anglophone, Lusophone and Francophone)	Driving forces	
		External	Internal
	Governance • Centralised governance system of education became relaxed with the economic dictates of international institutions to privatise education and liberalise higher education on fee-based access for sustainability – mix of centralised and liberal policies. • Higher education faced challenges of inadequate funding and finance. • Students challenge power configurations of governments imposing high-level state control of universities. • The liberalisation of politics in some universities enables students to engage more actively in how institutions were governed.	Less external funding support to higher education.	Local politics
Multiparty democracy era 1990s to present	Politics • Multiparty politics (alignment of student bodies to different parties); pluralistic political environment. • The growing wave of multiparty systems, with term limits, throughout Africa created open and transparent nations that struggled to accommodate old centralised systems of politics and newer approaches to broader-based inclusive participation in societies. Idea of the democratic language starts to permeate political practices and forces reluctant changes. Capitalism and economic growth become the new ideas that shape politics. Globalisation, liberalisation, and privatisation enter the political arena in Africa. • From socialism/Marxism to contestation of rampant exclusive elitist capitalism to student protests.	Globalisation – universities linked to wider global communities. Regime change Liberalisation Globalisation	Inequality, access challenges, social change, party politics. Emergence of different student movements that are culturally, socially and politically driven.

333

Chronology (time)	Key features across the three entities (Anglophone, Lusophone and Francophone)	Driving forces	
		External	Internal
	Policies • Education systems move from one-tier, mono system to diversified dual system that incorporates both private and public institutions. Bid to expand educational access. With expanding access came issue of equity in terms of gender, finances, locations etc. • Privatisation • Fee-paying education gradually becomes *de facto* policies – the motto is that there is not enough money for everybody and someone has to pay for it. • Elitism of higher education – exclusiveness and its consequences. The gap between those who have and do not have increases. Resource-rich with quality education and poor universities with poor quality education. Discontent grows at poor universities and student protests increase. Governance • Differentiation in student movement/organisations. • Centralised governance system of education became relaxed to privatisation of education and liberalising higher education on basis of fee-based access for sustainability.		

APPENDIX
4

Memorandum of Understanding between the University of the Witwatersrand Management, Outsourced workers and Students

The University of the Witwatersrand like all universities in the country has been witness to historic student led protests which have drawn on the energies of exploited black outsourced workers. Together with the exploited outsourced black workers students in this university dared to imagine a different society, a society in which free quality education will be provided to all, and a society where the unethical labour regime of outsourcing would not only be outlawed but abhorred by all for its dehumanising effects on black workers. Following weeks of political protestation and agitation by students and outsourced black workers, intense but productive negotiations aimed at returning normalcy to the university were entered into. Convinced of the legitimacy of the grievances university management, outsourced workers and students worked earnestly and have arrived at a point of mutual agreement on the following issues:

1. Insourcing/Outsourcing

Recognising that the practice of outsourcing is an exploitative and dehumanising practice an agreement was reached after a University Council deliberation and decision that in principle the University should insource. Cognisant of the above and the imperative to maintain a financially viable institution it is hereby agreed that;

1.1 In pursuance of the principle of insourcing the university will not be renewing any contract that lapses except in instances where it secures the concurrence of the insourcing task team.
1.2 An insourcing task team will be constituted to work out the modalities (details) of the whole process including an analysis of cost structures.
1.3 Whatever decision the insourcing task team arrives at, it must ensure that it does not undermine the intent of the overarching principle which is to end the dehumanising practice of outsourcing.
1.4 The task team must report back on progress made to at a general meeting exactly a month after it is officially constituted.

1.5 The insourcing task team will be constituted as follows:

1. Chairperson of the Task Team	To be chosen by Task Team
2. Council Representative	Randall Carolissen
3. Council Representative	Theunie Lategan
4. Management Representative	Linda Jarvis
5. Management Representative	Imraan Valodia
6. Worker Representative	Elizabeth Deliwe Mzobe
7. Worker Representative	Matthews Lebelo
8. Worker Representative	Johannes Dlamini
9. Worker Representative	Vusi Masondo
10. Union Representative (NASAWU)	Sam Ndou
11. Student Representative	Vuyani Pambo
12. Student Representative	Ntokozo Moloi
13. Student Representative Council	Nompendulo Mkhatshwa
14. Student Representative Council	Thabo Boom
15. Academic Representative	Shireen Ally
16. Academic Representative	Noor Nieftagodien
17. Independent Expert	To be chosen by Task Team

1.6 At its first sitting the task team will deliberate and agree on an external person to chair its proceedings and an independent expert.

1.7 At its first sitting the task team will have to work out a quorum to ensure that it is not paralysed by lack of attendance of some members at anyone meeting.

1.8 The following key items it is expected are going to be prioritised in the work of the task team; lock-in clause (meaning companies that provide outsourced services may not move workers to other sites outside of Wits in manner that deprives these workers an opportunity to be insourced), MJL workers, ownership of the Matrix, and dispute about Campus Control night shift allowance.

2. Dependants of Outsourced Workers

Dependants of outsourced workers who are admitted to the university will be able to study tuition free until they complete their studies. The onus will be on the University to find the resources with which to support these students.

3. Supplementary Exam Fee

The supplementary exam fee of R 1500 will no longer be levied.

4. With-held Qualifications

It has been agreed in principle that students with unpaid fee accounts who have completed a qualification will be issued their transcripts and be permitted to graduate, subject to entering into an agreement and payment plan with the University. The University will work out how this provision will be implemented in a way that ensures that it does not place its finances at risk.

APPENDIX 4

5. Deferred Exams

Those who for reasons pertaining to protests feel inadequately prepared for exams will be permitted to sit for these in January 2016 in accordance with rules for deferred exams which allow for deferral on these grounds.

6. University General Assembly

It was proposed that a University Assembly composed of all stakeholders be constituted as the overarching institutional authority. It did however emerge that the structure that was envisaged may be at variance with past practice in the University. Hence this matter could not be conclusively dealt with within the parameters of the negotiations. It was therefore resolved that continued engagement on the matter is pursued and finality be reached at least by June 2016.

7. Disciplinary Action

No disciplinary action will be pursued against any student for taking part in the protest. Furthermore no outsourced worker or university employee will be victimised in any way for taking part in or supporting the protest.

8. Underwriter

It was agreed that an underwriter to the agreement be nominated. The person will play the role of arbiter of the agreement. More precisely in the eventuality of a disagreement or dispute the person nominated will be the mediator. Advocate Mojanku Gumbi has since been nominated for the role and position of underwriter to this agreement.

Signed on the 13th day of November 2015, at the University of the Witwatersrand, Johannesburg.

_____
University Management

_____
Outsourced Workers

_____
Student Representative

CONTRIBUTORS

PATRICK BOND

Patrick Bond is a professor of political economy at the Wits School of Governance. His recent books include *Elite Transition* (3rd edition, 2014); *South Africa: Present as History* (with John Saul, 2014); *Politics of Climate Justice* (2012); and *Durban's Climate Gamble* (edited, 2011). He is also honorary professor at the Centre for Civil Society at the University of KwaZulu-Natal. Prior to 2016, he directed the University of KwaZulu-Natal Centre for Civil Society. His radicalisation during the 1980s came thanks to United States student movement solidarity with black South Africans.

SUSAN BOOYSEN

Susan Booysen is a professor at the Wits School of Governance. She is the author of *Dominance and Decline: The ANC in the Time of Zuma* (2015); *The African National Congress and the Regeneration of Political Power* (2011); the e-book *The ANC's March on Mangaung* (2012) and is the editor of *Local Elections in South Africa: Parties, People, Politics* (2012) and *Compendium of Elections in Southern Africa, 1989–2009: 20 years of Multiparty Democracy* (2009, with Denis Kadima). Her specific focus is on politics, power and public policy; her 1989 PhD was on change in student political consciousness. Susan's political life in the 1980s and early 1990s was in the United Democratic Front (UDF) and the Union of Democratic University Staff Associations (Udusa). Mobilisation and protest came in daily doses.

REKGOTSOFETSE CHIKANE

Rekgotsofetse (Kgotsi) Chikane is the national president of InkuluFreeHeid, a nonpartisan youth organisation that works to enhance social cohesion, deepen democracy and create innovative solutions to socioeconomic problems. He completed his Bachelor's and Honours degrees in Social Science at the University of Cape Town and is currently pursuing a Master's in Management at the Wits School of Governance. He is a former Mandela Rhodes Scholar and board member of the South Africa Washington International Program. Kgotsi has been recognised by *Mahala* magazine as one of ten young South Africans leading the way to making change in our country.

DAVID EVERATT

David Everatt is a professor and the head of school at the Wits School of Governance and was formerly in the Gauteng City Regional Observatory (GCRO). He has authored a book on white liberalism, has edited a number of books, edited two special editions of *Politikon*, and was formerly employed by the Community Agency for Social Enquiry (Case). He has participated in several large-scale youth surveys.

PATRICK FITZGERALD

Patrick FitzGerald has served in various capacities in political and community organisations, academia, government and university management, and is a past SRC vice-president, national director-general and deputy vice-chancellor for finance and operations at Wits. He has published a number of books, book chapters and journal articles on topics relating to public administration, development, strategy, leadership and university management. Also a published poet and playwright, he is currently an adjunct professor at the Wits School of Governance and also serves as chair of the Group Performance Audit Committee for the City of Johannesburg.

GILLIAN GODSELL

Gillian Godsell studied at the universities of the Witwatersrand, Stellenbosch, Leiden and Pretoria. She has a PhD from Boston University. She has worked at the Council for Scientific and Industrial Research (CSIR), the Centre for Developing Business at Wits, the Faculty of Education at the University of Johannesburg and currently works at the Wits School of Governance. Since being elected as the first woman to chair the youth wing of the Progressive Party in 1972, she has served on NGO and professional boards, including chairing school governing bodies at Auckland Park Preparatory School and Parktown High School for Girls. She hosts a weekly programme on the community radio station Radio Today.

WILLIAM GUMEDE

William Gumede is an associate professor in the Wits School of Governance as well as a senior associate and program director at the Africa Asia Centre in the School of Oriental and African Studies (SOAS) at the University of London. He is the chairman of Action Aid and the founder and chairman of the Democracy Works Foundation (www.democracyworks.org.za). He is the author of a number of books including *Restless Nation: Making Sense of Troubled Times* (2012).

LYNN HEWLETT

Lynn Hewlett is a senior lecturer at the Wits School of Governance and currently convenor of the PhD programme. Prior to joining the Wits School of Governance she worked in further and higher education in South Africa and the UK. Her current research interests encompass higher education policy and practices, curriculum, capacity building and development, literacy and language studies and educational development and evaluation of learning and capacity-building programmes. Previous work has included research and development in relation to curriculum, education and training, academic literacies, developing workplace learning initiatives, and student learning.

KOFFI KOUAKOU

Koffi Kouakou, an African analyst and scenario strategist, is a former senior lecturer at the Wits School of Governance, where he taught strategic government communications and scenario planning. He is the former director of the Unilever Mandela Rhodes Academy for Communications and Marketing (UMRA) at the University of the Witwatersrand. He is an associate member of the African Futures Institute and the South African Millennium Programme, a foresight collaborative network of African futurists. He was the coordinator of the Program on Environment Information Systems in Sub-Saharan Africa, with the World Bank, from 1992 to 1998. He is a co-author of *AfricaDotEdu: IT Opportunities and Higher Education in Africa*.

REFILOE LEPERE

Refiloe Lepere is a postgraduate research coordinator teaching critical reflexive praxis in Drama for Life at the University of Witwatersrand. She is also a dramaturge at the South African State Theatre. She received her MA from New York

University. Currently, her PhD looks at performance as a research method in documenting the oral histories of domestic workers in South Africa. In her work as a journalist, director and playwright, she weaves history, statistics and personal narrative to address issues of social (in)justice, intersectional identities and black people. Refiloe travels across the country performing, presenting, and facilitating workshops on writing political theatre, race and diversity.

SWANKIE MAFOKO

Swankie Mafoko is an Honours student at Drama for Life at Wits, studying applied theatre. She is an actress and dancer with over six years of ballet experience, and has performed in a number of plays. Her work aims to educate and empower different communities. She recently performed in a one-woman play entitled 'Nine to Fivers Anthem' at the prestigious So Solo Theatre Festival. Swankie co-hosts DFL Life.Beats, a radio show, on Voice of Wits (VOWFM) and is also a news reporter on the station. She is passionate about her art form and using it to influence the world.

THADDEUS METZ

Thaddeus Metz is distinguished professor (2015–2019) and research professor at the University of Johannesburg. He writes on a variety of moral, political and legal topics, including interpreting African moral thought analytically and applying it to contemporary issues; engaging in comparative philosophy among non-Western traditions; addressing normative issues in higher education; enquiring into what makes a life meaningful; and developing theoretical accounts of mental health. Among his more than 150 professional publications are three books, *Meaning in Life* (2013), *A Relational Moral Theory: Africa's Contribution to Global Ethics* (forthcoming 2017), and *Jurisprudence in an African Context* (forthcoming 2017).

DARLENE MILLER

Darlene Miller is a senior lecturer at the Wits School of Governance. She completed a Doctorate in sociology at Johns Hopkins University in Baltimore, USA. Her focus was on regional political economy and the expansion of South African firms in post-apartheid southern Africa, with a specific focus on labour in Zambia and Mozambique. In her early career she was the national education coordinator of Saccawu, a Cosatu retail affiliate. She was also the director of the Institute for African Alternatives (IFAA), a research and training nonprofit organisation. Her recent work includes film documentaries on women's leadership and project management of land grabs in southern Africa.

SIZWE MPOFU-WALSH

Sizwe Mpofu-Walsh holds an MPhil in international relations from the University of Oxford, and an Honours degree in politics, philosophy and economics from the University of Cape Town. A Weidenfeld scholar, he was one of the *Mail & Guardian's* 'top 200 young South Africans' in 2013. In 2010, he served as president of the UCT student representative council. He is currently pursuing a DPhil in international relations at the University of Oxford, and writing a book of essays on South African politics.

NOMAGUGU MUKADAH

Nomagugu (Gugu) Masuku-Mukadah is a researcher at the Centre for Learning on Evaluation and Results in Anglophone Africa based at the University of the Witwatersrand. She is presently focused on establishing an evidence base on emerging social movements in Africa to enrich emerging African theories and practices on monitoring and evaluation. She holds a Master's degree and postgraduate diploma in monitoring and evaluation methods and a Bachelor of Science degree. A former Nuffic Fellow, Gugu is adept in project and programme management and has extensive experience in development and humanitarian work, having worked for international agencies such as World Vision and several grassroots nongovernmental organisations.

AYABONGA NASE

Ayabonga Nase is a candidate attorney at the Centre for Applied Legal Studies based at the University of the Witwatersrand. He holds an LLB degree from the University of Fort Hare and a certificate in advanced administrative law from the Mandela Institute at Wits. He is a Fellow of the Bertha Justice Initiative, a movement that supports organisations that practise public interest law.

OMHLE NTSHINGILA

Omhle Ntshingila hails from the small town of Dundee in northern KwaZulu-Natal, where she also matriculated. She moved to Johannesburg to pursue a degree in political studies and anthropology at the University of Witwatersrand and is currently in her final year of study. She hopes to further her studies and obtain Honours and Master's degrees in development studies. In her early years at Wits she frequently fought to improve conditions for students on campus. She was elected to the Wits student representative council in 2014–2015 and became deputy president and student governance officer. Together with her SRC colleagues, she was a planner of the #WitsFeesMustFall protest.

PUNDY PILLAY

Pundy Pillay is a professor of economics and public finance, and research director at the Wits School of Governance. His previous positions include senior economist at RTI International; head of the Policy Unit in the Office of the President; director of the Financial and Fiscal Commission and senior lecturer in economics at the University of Cape Town. He has worked in Bangladesh, Egypt, Kenya, Iran, Lesotho, Namibia, Nigeria, Pakistan, Rwanda, Uganda and Zambia. His research interests are public finance, the economics of education, inequality and poverty, and public policy.

VISHWAS SATGAR

Vishwas Satgar is an associate professor of international relations at the University of the Witwatersrand. He is the editor of the Democratic Marxism series of books. He recently edited *Capitalism's Crises: Class Struggles in South Africa and the World* and co-edited *Cosatu in Crisis: The Fragmentation of an African Trade Union Federation*. He has been an activist for over three decades.

OLIVER SEALE

Oliver Seale has a keen interest in university governance, leadership and management, organisational development, performance management and leadership development. He holds a Master's degree in Higher Education Studies from the University of the Free State and a PhD in Leadership Development from Wits. His former positions include acting CEO of Universities South Africa (USAf) and director in the vice-chancellor's office at Wits where he provided strategic advice, project management and administrative support. He was also deputy director-general for training delivery at the Public Administration Leadership and Management Academy (Palama) and director of the Higher Education Leadership and Management Programme (Helm) at Higher Education South Africa (Hesa).

HORÁCIO ZANDAMELA

Horácio Lucas Zandamela, born in Mozambique, obtained his Master's and Doctoral degrees from the Wits Graduate School of Public and Development Management, now the Wits School of Governance. In the process of the research work that he undertook, he was familiarised with a range of development issues including local economic development, local government, unions and civil society participation, gender, development training, electoral monitoring, urban water provisioning, micro-credit and small business development, rural development, natural disaster management, and curriculum development.

INDEX

#ANCMustFall 3
#FeesHaveFallen 3
#FeesMustFall (#FMF) 1–2, 8, 18–19, 33, 37
   against outsourcing at Wits 214–233
   ambiguities 84–85
   anarchists and arsonists capturing 46
   at Wits 5, 214–233
   case of *Aluta continua, victoria ascerta* 309–315
   cleansing 32
   demands and claims 31
   documenting 102, 108, 114–116, 118, 120
   education policy 31
   educational institutions 31
   Euro-America 74–75, 77, 79, 83–85
   foundational ranking 31
   in London 74–75
   in sub-Saharan Africa 160
   just war 294–295, 298, 302
   matriarchal leadership 270, 272–275, 278–280, 285, 287–289
   October 2015, 22–23
   outsourcing 30, 32, 61–67, 87–90, 95, 98, 106, 108, 192, 217–220, 222–232
   police and security brutality 14, 32, 109, 197, 209, 294, 326
   protest of shame 116–118
   revolt 2015–2016 (appendix) 316
   revolt, issue progression 31–32
   roots of revolution 59–60
   select events and explanations 318–327
   social movement in SA 192–193, 196, 204, 206, 210–211
   through eyes of outsourced workers 98
   university management and 235–253
   youth sacrifice, generations of 133–136, 142, 145–146
#FeesWillFall 3
#Hope 118–119
#KingGeorgeMustFall 2
#NationalShutDown 3
#OpenStellenbosch 2, 235, 253
#OutsourcingMustEnd 215
#OutsourcingMustFall 26, 215, 242, 310, 323, 325
   through eyes of workers 87–99
#PatriarchyMustFall 3, 120
#RainbowIsDead 118
#RhodesMustFall (#RMF) 2, 33, 37, 56–59, 74–77, 79–81, 83, 120, 134, 171, 218–219, 228, 230, 235, 239, 299, 318
#RhodesSoWhite 2, 319
#TheStatueMustFall 2, 76
#Transformation 119–120
#TransformWits 2, 319
#ZumaMustFall 195, 210, 216

A

abortion/s 287
   excavating the vernacular 286–288
   in UK 287
   motherhood and 286–288
academics (faculty)
   precariousness of 61–63
   roots of revolution 61–63
accountability 17, 29, 64, 185–186
   direct 29
   forced 37
   lack of 44
   political 29

activist-scholars 4
Africa
   autonomy and university governance, learning about 162–164
   multiparty tensions and student activism, learning about 161–162
   policies, funding and access, learning about 159–161
   rising against liberators 125–185
   South Africa in 125–185
   student protests, learning about 159–164
African National Congress (ANC) 8, 23, 126, 129, 146, 178, 197, 215, 236, 301, 317, 339
   pushing out of comfort zone 35–36
   retaining control with safe-zone protest 36–38
African National Congress Youth League (ANCYL) 26, 36–37, 46, 126, 317, 325
   #ANCMustFall 3
African welfare society 151
Algeria 7, 172, 175, 177–178, 180, 183–185, 221, 330
Altbach, Philip 152
Aluta continua, victoria ascerta
   #FeesMustFall a case of 309–315
ambiguities
   #FeesMustFall 84–85
ANC, *see* African National Congress
ANC governance
   foundational and ideological impact of revolt, subversion of comfort zone of 30
ANCYL, *see* African National Congress Youth League
ANC Youth League, *see* African National Congress Youth League
Anglo American Corporation 200
Anglophone Africa 158
Angola 152, 157
Arrighi, Giovanni 279
autonomy
   learning from African countries 162–164
Azanian People's Organisation (Azapo) 13, 15

B

Baader Meinhof Gang, *see* Red Army Faction
Ben Ali, Zine al Abidine 170, 176–177, 179, 183
Bertelsen, Eve 64–66
Bezuidenhout, Andries 56, 66, 224
Biko, Steve 7, 13, 34, 135, 143
Black Consciousness Movement (BCM) 10, 13, 143
black consciousness, revolt positioning 3–4, 7–8, 12–13,15, 26, 28–31, 33–34, 59, 82, 128, 134, 214, 219, 220, 233, 313, 318
Black Economic Empowerment (BEE) 241
black feminism 328
Black First Land First (BLF) 15, 26, 30, 47, 313
black pain 14, 25, 76, 295, 328
black power, revolt positioning 13–15
BLF, *see* Black First Land First
Bloch, Graeme 194
Boal, Augusto 111
Botswana 257
Bouattia, Malia 55
Bouazizi, Mohamed 169, 171, 177
Bouteflika, Abdelaziz 172
Bouzid, Sidi 169
Brazil 203, 207–208, 259
British Labour Party 11
Buch, Elana 276
Bundy, Colin 63–65, 87, 224, 236
Burawoy, Michael 153, 210

Burke, Penny 68–69
Burundi 157

C
Cameroon 154, 158
Cape Peninsula University of Technology (CPUT) 15, 321
Cape Verde 152, 157
case studies, student negotiations 248–252
Central Intelligence Agency (USA) (CIA) 37, 325
change impact categories, revolt 27–32
Chenoufi, Moncef 151
Chikane, Rekgotsofetse 6, 9, 45, 54, 77, 218, 314, 340
China 55, 200, 203, 294
CIA, *see* Central Intelligence Agency (USA)
Class 3, 90–91, 116–117, 134–135, 140, 313
  redefined 191–268
  remaking 223–226
classification, of uprising, revolt or revolution 2–4
Codesa 273
Coleman, James 152
Commonwealth countries 158
communication, *see* documents of protest
  listen to us 191–268
Congress of South African Students (Cosas) 26, 37
Convention for a Democratic South Africa, *see* Codesa
Côte d'Ivoire 158, 164
counter mobilisation 30
CPUT, *see* Cape Peninsula University of Technology
cultural cleansing 32

D
DA, *see* Democratic Alliance 15, 26, 47, 192, 198–199
Daso, *see* Democratic Alliance Student Organisation
debt
  growth of student 264–265
  precariousness of 62–63
decolonisation 25, 28, 34–35, 38, 47, 54, 58–59, 84, 102, 111, 115, 146, 205, 210, 216, 219, 278, 325, 328
  roots of revolution 58–60
Democratic Alliance Student Organisation 26, 318
Department of Higher Education and Training (DHET) 245, 326, 250, 253, 330
  2012 report 41
  2013 report 198
  white paper for post-school education and training (2013) 40
Dergham, Raghida 170, 182, 185
Destourian Socialist Party (PSD) 176
DHET, *see* Department of Higher Education and Training
direct accountability, governance changes related to 29
direct action
  governance change through 45–47
  governance change related to 29
discrimination, just war 303–304
documents
  of protest 102–114
  themes from 114–120
Du Preez, Max 117
Duncan, Jane 116
Durban University of Technology (DUT) 326
DUT, *see* Durban University of Technology
PSD, *see* Destourian Socialist Party

E
Economic Freedom Fighters (EFF) 15, 26, 93, 98, 133, 206, 232, 312, 318–319, 325, 327
economic inequalities
  contributed to uprisings in North Africa 174–176
EFF, *see* Economic Freedom Fighters
Egypt 149–150, 171–172, 174–176, 178–182, 185, 330

Elbelghiti, Rachid 178, 182
Employment
  precariousness of 61–63
  roots of revolution 61–63
equity, promotion of 256–268
Ethiopia 149
Euro-America, 'MustFall' moves to 74–85
European Union (EU) 157, 181, 207

F
Fallism 2–3, 58–60, 215
  definition of 4
  philosophy of 56, 58–60
  post-#RhodesMustFall 23
  theory of 82–84
Fanon, Frantz 7, 33, 34, 46, 58, 99, 111, 135, 221, 231, 246
FDI, *see* Foreign Direct Investment
#FeesHaveFallen 3
#FeesMustFall (#FMF) 1–2, 8, 18–19, 33, 37
  against outsourcing during at Wits 214–233
  ambiguities 84–85
  anarchists and arsonists capturing 46
  at Wits 5, 214–233
  case of *Aluta continua, victoria ascerta* 309–315
  cleansing 32
  demands and claims 31
  documenting 102, 108, 114–116, 118, 120
  education policy 31
  educational institutions 31
  Euro-America 74, 75, 77, 79, 83–85
  foundational ranking 31
  in London 74–75
  in sub-Saharan Africa 160
  issue progression 31–32
  just war 294–295, 298, 302
  matriarchal leadership 270, 272–275, 278–280, 285, 287–289
  October 2015, 22–23
  outsourcing 32
  police and security brutality 32
  protest of shame 116–118
  revolt 2015–2016 (appendix) 316
  revolt, issue progression 31
  roots of revolution 59–60
  select events and explanations 318–327
  social movement in SA 192–193, 196, 204, 206, 210–211
  through eyes of outsourced workers 98
  university management and 235–253
  youth sacrifice, generations of 133–136, 142, 145–146
#FeesWillFall 3
feminism/s 3, 9, 12–13, 30, 270, 273
  aggressive 288
  angry 288
  assertive 7, 311
  assertive African 311
  black 328
  domesticated 270, 289
  ideologies of 3
  modified 273
  post-colonial 279
  radical 4, 59, 82
  radical black 59
  revolt positioning 12–13
  ugly 273, 287–288
feminists 11–12, 146, 270–290
  African student-activist 9
FET *see* Further Education and Training
financing, *see also* funding
  of universities 256–268
  promoting equity 256–268
  reinforcing inequality 256–268

345

Fine, Ben 202
fiscal investments
　in youth, arguments against 199–203
　in youth, arguments for 196–199
FitzGerald, Patrick 8, 47, 65–66
Flacks, Dick 11
FMF, *see* #FeesMustFall/#FMF
FMF, *see* FeesMustFall/#FMF
force
　refunding 269–315
Foreign Direct Investment (FDI) 181
formal agreements, documents of protest 106–108
fossilised neoliberalism, must fall for free education 192–268
foundational and ideological impact of revolt
　demands and alternatives 29
　ideological subversion 30
　on governance 27–28
　subversion of comfort zone of ANC governance 30
　symptoms 29
France 150–151, 172, 184, 207, 294
Francophone Africa 155, 157–158
Frasinelli, Pier Paolo 116
free education 6, 38, 41–42, 44, 79, 97, 111, 153, 229, 244–245, 304, 318, 322–323, 332
　for the poor 31, 38, 41, 312, 318
　fossilised neoliberalism must fall 192–211
　meaning of, 79
Fukuyama, Francis 149
funding
　free education, uniting with other constituencies 203–210
　higher education and percentage of GDP (2004–2012) 237
　proposals in context of inequality 265–267
　SA universities 237–239
funding, *see also* financing
Further Education and Training (FET) 40

G

Gabon 157
Gauteng City-Region Observatory (GCRO) 136
GDP, *see* Gross Domestic Product
gender
　conforming people 329
　matriarchal leadership 270–290
　remaking 223–226
　socialisation in public and private spheres 284
General Union of Tunisian Workers (UGTT) 171
generational blues 270–290
Ghana 152, 154–155, 157, 164
glossary of terms (appendix) 328
Gold Coast Students Union 151
Gordhan, Pravin 194–196, 201, 203, 207, 209
governance, *see also* university governance
　and #FeesMustFall events 243–248
　change impact categories 27–32
　change through mass direct action 45–47
　changing in South Africa 22–48
　evidence of change impact categories 27–32
　foundational reconsideration of 33–38
　impact of revolt 27–32
　revolt impact on 24–27
　through lens of student activism 17–19
government
　dissatisfaction with three spheres of 143
Gqubule, Thandeka 264–265
graduate tax 261–262
Gross Domestic Product (GDP) 136, 237, 257, 259
Gross Enrolment Ratio (GER) 257, 259
Guinea-Bissau 152, 157

H

Habib, Adam 19, 43–44, 68, 74, 93, 115, 117, 176, 228, 230, 237–238, 244, 293, 297, 304–305, 321
Haffajee, Ferial 60, 62, 108, 274
Hani, Chris 131
HBIs, *see* historically black institutions
headspace, 2015 student movement 141–145
Hesa, *see* Higher Education South Africa
higher education
　actual and projected allocations for 260–261
　burden of fees 77–79
Higher Education South Africa (Hesa) (later Universities South Africa (USAf)) 237–238, 249
higher education systems
　1900s–1960s 149–153
　1960s–1980s 153–156
　neoliberal and democratic period (2000-present) 156–159
　pre-independence phase and colonial era (1900s–1960s) 149–153
historical periods
　key features of student protest across in sub-Saharan Africa (appendix) 330
historically black institutions (HBIs) 60
historically white institutions (HWIs) 60
#Hope 118–119
HSRC, *see* Human Sciences Research Council
Human Sciences Research Council (HSRC) 132–133, 271
HWIs, *see* historically white institutions
Hypervisibility 112

I

Identity 29, 60, 153, 178, 273–274, 279, 288, 328, 332
　refunding 269–315
ideological impact of revolt
　on governance 27–28
IDP, *see* Integrated Development Plan
ILO, *see* International Labour Organisation
IMF, *see* International Monetary fund
Indonesia 208
inequality 27, 33, 55, 63, 68–69, 76, 97, 118, 156, 170–171, 174, 179–180, 256–257, 259, 263–268, 280, 332–333
　funding proposals in context of 265–267
　reinforcement of 256–268
institutional change
　tentative emerging 43–45
institutional impact
　revolt on governance 28
Integrated Development Plan (IDP) 142
International Labour Organisation (ILO) 181
International Monetary fund (IMF) 158, 199
investing, *see* fiscal investments and funding

J

Jansen, Jonathan 45, 327
JEP, *see* Joint Enrichment Project
Johnston, Hank 114, 117
Joint Enrichment Project (JEP) 129
Jonas, Mcebisi 196
just war
　last resort 300–303
　likely success 296–299
　proportionality of 299–300
　SA student/worker protests in light of 292–304
justice, refunding 269–315

K

Kenya 152–154, 157
Keynes, John Maynard 209
#KingGeorgeMustFall 2
Kundu, Tadit 61

L

leadership
  and #FeesMustFall events 243–248
  matriarchal 270–290
Legal Resources Centre (LRC) 104
Lephatsa, Lerato 35–36, 45
LGBTI, Lesbian, Gay, Bisexual, Transgender, and Intersexed 216
LGBTIAQ+, Lesbian, Gay, Bisexual, Transgender, Intersexed, Asexual and Queer 25, 30, 146, 210, 271–275, 277–279, 281–282, 285, 288–289, 311, 313, 329
liberators
  rising against 125–185
Liberia 272
life circumstances
  2015 student movement 138–141
Lipset, Seymour 152
LRC, *see* Legal Resources Centre
Lusophone Africa 7, 157

M

Mabizela, Sizwe 244
Madagascar 158
Mahlobo, David 36, 209
Makerere College 151
Malaza, Nqobile 55, 109
Malik, Khalid 17
Mamdani, Mahmood 56–57, 59, 148–149, 163, 218
management
  and #FeesMustFall events 243–248
managerialism 5, 56, 63–66, 119–120, 242
  ideologies 55
  market-centred 222
Mandela, Nelson 130, 293, 301
mass direct action
  governance change through 45–47
mass politics
  #FeesMustFall and anti-apartheid struggle 215–217
massive open online courses (MOOCs) 161
matriarchal leadership 270–290
Mauritius 257
Maxwele, Chumani 57, 76–77, 218, 219
Mbembe, Achille 2, 27, 34–35, 43
Medium-Term Economic Framework (MTEF) 257
Memorandum of Understanding
  between Wits management, outsourced workers, and students (appendix) 335
methodology
  2015 student movement 136–138
MJL electrical maintenance service company 87, 89, 91–94, 319
Mncayi, Lebo 277, 289
Molepo, Mmamalema 109
Monageng, Virginia
  in conversation with 87–99
  story of 95–97
MOOCs, *see* massive open online courses
Morocco 150, 175, 177, 179–183, 185, 330
motherhood
  excavating the vernacular 275, 286–288
MoU, *see* Memorandum of Understanding
Mouffe, Chantal 18
Mozambique 152–153, 155, 157
MTEF, *see* Medium-Term Economic Framework
Mubarak, Hosni 171–172, 176, 178, 182
multiparty tensions
  learning from African countries 161–162
Munshi, Naadira 225
Mzobe, Deliwe 66–68, 106, 219, 225, 229, 239

N

Naidoo, Leigh-Ann 34, 38, 45
Naidoo, Prishani 206
Naidoo, Shan 66
Namibia 152
National Development Plan (NDP) 41, 201, 203, 245
National Education, Health and Allied Workers Union (Nehawu) 220, 242
National General Council (NGC), of ANC 40, 42
#NationalShutDown 3
National Student Financial Aid Scheme (NSFAS) 40–41, 60, 78, 117, 198, 244, 257, 263–264, 310
National Union of Metalworkers of South Africa (Numsa) 37, 92, 206
NDB, *see* New Development Bank
Ndebele, Richard
  in conversation with 87–99
  story of 90–95
NDP, *see* National Development Plan
negotiations
  case study regarding student 248–252
Nehawu, *see* National Education, Health and Allied Workers Union
Nelson Mandela Metropolitan University (NMMU) 59
Neoliberalism 25, 28, 30, 55, 97, 117, 148, 156, 159–60, 214–215, 218, 223, 229–230, 280, 285, 312
  labour regime, at Wits 220–222
  must fall for free education 192–211
New Development Bank (NDB) 203
New Left, revolt positioning 11–12
New Public Management 64–68
  at Wits 64–68
NGC, *see* National General Council, of ANC
NGOs, *see* non-governmental organisations
Nhlapo, Tokelo 88
Nigerian Progress Union 151
Nkrumah, Kwame 34, 152
NMMU, *see* Nelson Mandela Metropolitan University
non-governmental organisations (NGOs) 134, 209
non-partisan nature, of revolt 24–27
Nonxuba, Athabile 4
North Africa
  conditions that contributed to uprisings 173–179
  impact of 2007–2008 global financial and Eurozone crises 180–181
  sparks of 171–173
  unfinished revolutions 169–185
  uprisings 169–185
  uprisings, unfinished democracy 181–185
North West University (NWU) 31–32, 45, 85, 318–319, 325–326
NSFAS, *see* National Student Financial Aid Scheme
Ntshingila, Omhle
  Richard Ndebele's story 90–95
  Virginia Monageng's story 95–97
Numsa, *see* National Union of Metalworkers of South Africa
NWU, *see* North West University
Nzimande, Blade 6, 29, 35, 37, 42–44, 192, 194, 197, 300, 315, 321, 323–324

O

occupy/occupation
  as documentation of protest 112–113
  revolt positioning 11–12
OECD, *see* Organisation for Economic Cooperation and Development
open letters, of protest 105–106
#OpenStellenbosch 2, 235, 253
Organisation for Economic Cooperation and Development (OECD) 139–140, 198, 237, 259

outsourced workers 31, 68
   #FeesMustFall brings liberation to 215–217
   memorandum of understanding between Wits management, workers and students (appendix) 335
   skills and staff development 241–243
outsource companies
   at Wits University 89
outsourcing 32
   against during #FeesMustFall at Wits 214–233
   as key issue in funding universities 239–243
   at Wits 63–68
   challenges to end/fall 230–233
   conjunctural moments of working class-led struggle 226–230
   following UCT neoliberal standard 222–226
   non-core logistics management 240–241
   roots of revolution 63–68
   through eyes of workers 87–99
   workers 31, 68
#OutsourcingMustEnd 215
#OutsourcingMustFall 26, 215, 242, 310, 323, 325
   through eyes of workers 87–99
Old Left, revolt positioning 11–12

P

PAC, *see* Pan Africanist Congress
Pakistan 208
Pambo, Vuyani 47, 319–320
Pan Africanist Congress (PAC) 15, 26, 134, 327
Pan Africanist Student Movement of Azania (Pasma) 15, 26, 313
Pan-Afrikanism
   revolt positioning 12–13
participation/mobilisation change 30
party politics
   particularities, revolt positioning 15–17
   revolt impact on governance 24–27
Pasma, *see* Pan Africanist Student Movement of Azania
Patel, Ebrahim 201
Patel, Reena 283–284
Patel, Shirona 104
Pather, Christina 58
patriarchy 329
   patriarchal leadership 272, 275, 281, 285, 287
#PatriarchyMustFall 3, 120
performance art
   as documentation 110–112
Perumal, Juliet 276
Peters, B Guy 18
PICC, *see* Presidential Infrastructure Coordinating Commission
Pierre, Jon 18
Piketty, Thomas 263
Polanyi, Karl 210
police/security brutality 32
policy/ies
   and institutional impact of revolt on governance 28, 30
   base, higher education 39–41
   change, #FMF impact 38–43
   concessions, unpacking 42–43
   extension, higher education 39–41
   funding and access, learning from other African countries 159–164
   impact of revolt on governance 28
   implementation, higher education 39–41
   initiatives, unrealised towards free and accessible higher education 41–42
political inequalities
   contributed to uprisings in North Africa 176–179
Portugal 60, 157

post-school education,
   actual and projected allocations for 260–261
power
   redefined 21–48, 191–268
   what happened to governance 21–48
precarious
   employment 61–63
   roots of revolution 61–63
Presidential Infrastructure Coordinating Commission (PICC) 200
Pretoria-Witwatersrand-Vereeniging (PWV) 127
PriceWaterhouseCoopers (PwC) 77–79, 199, 238
private sector 63–64, 98, 222, 256, 263, 310
   bargaining councils 98
   counter mobilisation 30
Progressive Youth Alliance (PYA) 24, 26, 93, 193, 248
proportionality
   of just war 299–300
protest/s
   direct action and direct accountability, governance changes related to 29
   documents of 102–114
   governance changes related to 29
   protesters' documents 108–110
   value of action affirmed 46–47
PSD, *see* Destourian Socialist Party
PWV, *see* Pretoria-Witwatersrand-Vereeniging
PYA, *see* Progressive Youth Alliance

R

race 6–8, 18, 25–26, 55, 59, 85, 109–110, 133, 173, 193, 198, 210, 219–221, 229–230, 274, 288, 294, 311, 313, 328
   American critical race theory 7, 135
   critical race theory 108
   inequality 55
   prejudice 60
   relations on campus 57
   remaking 223–226
   UK activists 80
   war 128
RAF, *see* Red Army Faction
#RainbowIsDead 118
rainbowism 30, 118, 312
Rakei, Simon 4, 43
Ramaphosa, Cyril 195, 198, 200–201
Ramos, Maria 202
Ramphele, Mamphela 223
RDP, *see* Reconstruction and Development Programme
Reconstruction and Development Programme (RDP) 40, 129–131, 139–140, 279
Red Army Faction (RAF) 132
Red Tent research project 271, 276–277, 287–289
redistributive economic justice 312
regional inequalities
   contribution to uprisings in North Africa 179
relatives
   precariousness of 61–63
   roots of revolution 61–63
revolt, *see also* student action
   annotated timeline of #FeesMustFall 2015–2016 (appendix) 316
   foundational impact on governance 27–28
   ideological impact on governance 27–28
   impact on governance 24–27
   non-partisan nature of 24–27
   policy and institutional impact on governance 28
   rising against liberators 125–185
   classification of 2–4
   positioning of 10–17
revolution/s
   classification of 2–4
   documenting 101–120
   primary voices roots of 53–120

roots within SA society 60–61
roots of 54–69
student roots of 54–58
unfinished 169–185
unfinished in North Africa 169–185
#RhodesMustFall (#RMF) 2, 33, 37, 56–59, 74–77, 79–81, 83, 120, 134, 171, 218–219, 228, 230, 235, 239, 299, 318
#RhodesSoWhite 2, 319
Rhodes University (RU) 12, 59, 272, 286
Rhodes, Cecil John 23, 58
  Oxford monument 75, 80
  Rhodes Building of Oriel College 80–81
  Rhodes House, All Souls College 81
  Rhodes memorial statue 57, 58, 75–77, 80, 218, 319
RhodesMustFall in Oxford (RMFO) 80–82
RhodesMustFall/#RMF (RMF)
RMF, *see* RhodesMustFall/#RMF
RMFO, *see* RhodesMustFall in Oxford
Rollock, Nicola 55
Ross, Marc Howard 177–178
Royal Mnandi 87, 89, 227
RU, *see* Rhodes University
Russia 10, 203, 207, 208
Rustomjee, Zav 202
Rwanda 157–158

S
SACBC, *see* Southern African Catholic Bishops' Conference
SACC, *see* South African Council of Churches
SACP, *see* South African Communist Party
safe-zone protest
  ANC retaining control 36–38
Sankara, Thomas 22, 34
SAPA, *see* South African Press Association
SAPs, *see* Structural Adjustment Programmes
SARS, *see* South African Revenue Service
Sasco, *see* South African Student Congress (ANC-aligned)
Saso, *see* South African Students' Organisation
scholar-activists 4
Senegal 154, 158
SERI, *see* Socio-Economic Rights Institute of South Africa
Seta, *see* Skills Education Training Authority
shame
  protest of 116–118
Silver, Beverly 279
Skills Education Training Authority (Seta) 326
social inequalities, *see also* inequality
  contributed to uprisings in North Africa 179
social media 14, 29, 45, 75–76, 80, 105, 118–120, 159, 169–170, 216–217, 246–247, 299, 314, 319, 321
  as documentation of protest 108–109
society
  roots of revolution within SA 60–61
Socio-Economic Rights Institute of South Africa (SERI) 105
songs
  as documentation of protest 113–114
South African College 151
South African Communist Party (SACP) 36, 44, 206, 215
South African Council of Churches (SACC) 129
South African High Commission (SAHC) 74
South African National Civic Organisation (Sanco) 205, 299
South African Revenue Service (SARS) 262
South African Student Congress (Sasco) 26, 36–37, 46, 318–319, 325
South African Students' Organisation (Saso) 318
South Korea 259
South Sudan 257
Southern African Catholic Bishops' Conference

(SACBC) 129
Sprague, Ralph 102
SRC, *see* student representative council
Staller, Karen 276
state agencies 193
  counter mobilisation 30
Steinberg, Jonny 33
Stiglitz, Joseph 265
structural adjustment programmes (SAPs) 155, 332
struggle (2015–2016)
  revolt positioning 15–17
student action, *see also* student revolt/protest
student activism
  governance through lens of 17–19
  learning from African countries 161–162
student debt
  growth of 264–265
student movement (2015) 132–145
student negotiations
  case study regarding 248–252
student protest/s
  in light of Just War Theory 292–304
  in sub-Saharan Africa 148–164
student representative council (SRC) 28, 89, 134, 193, 246, UCT 57, Wits 219, 295
student revolt, *see also* student action/protest
  (2015–16) impact on governance 29
sub-Saharan Africa
  higher education systems,1960s–1980s 153–156
  higher education systems, 1900s–1960s 149–153
  higher education systems, neoliberal and democratic period (2000-present) 156–159
  higher education systems, pre-independence phase and colonial era (1900s–1960s) 149–153
  key features of student protest across historical periods in (appendix) 330
  student protests in 148–164
subversion 30, 84
Supercare 66–67, 87, 89, 95
Symonds, Richard 80

T
TAC, *see* Treatment Action Campaign
Tambo, Oliver 137
tax increases
  funding universities 262–263
TEFSA, *see* Tertiary Education Fund for South Africa
terminology
  student protest, glossary of (appendix) 328
Tertiary Education Fund for South Africa (TEFSA) 264
#TheStatueMustFall 2, 76
Timbuktu 149
timelines
  of #FeesMustFall revolt 2015–2016 (appendix) 316
#Transformation 119–120
#TransformWits 2, 319
Treatment Action Campaign (TAC) 43, 192, 215–216
Trotsky, Leon 270, 289
Trotskyist groupings 275
Tshwane University of Technology (TUT) 23, 46, 98, 194, 319, 321, 324–326
Tunisia 108, 169–171, 175–179, 181, 183–184
Turkey 208
Turok, Ben 46
TUT, *see* Tshwane University of Technology

U
UCT, *see* University of Cape Town
UDF, *see* United Democratic Front
UFH, *see* University of Fort Hare
UFS, *see* University of the Free State
Uganda 151, 154, 157
UGTT, *see* General Union of Tunisian Workers
UJ, *see* University of Johannesburg

349

Ukweza 89, 96
UKZN, see University of KwaZulu-Natal
Unesco, see United Nations Educational, Scientific and Cultural Organisation
Union Buildings 217
  #FeesMustFall (#FMF) revolt 23, 27, 37, 46, 75, 84
  Zuma's offices on 23 October 2015, 38, 43–44, 193, 219, 233, 322
Union of African Descent 151
Unisa, see University of South Africa
United Democratic Front (UDF) 128, 134, 215
United Kingdom 55, 150
  abortions - political activism 287
United Nations Educational, Scientific and Cultural Organisation (Unesco) 156
Universities South Africa (USAf) 19, 238, 244, 246–249, 253
university financing 256–268
university funding 259–261
university governance, see also governance
  learning from African countries 162–164
university management
  and #FeesMustFall campaign 235–253
  roots of revolution 63–68
University of Cape Town (UCT) 2, 3, 194, 196, 218, 243, 264, 272
  #RhodesMustFall 75–77
  Neoliberal standard 222–226
University of Fort Hare (UFH) 23, 233, 264
University of Johannesburg (UJ) 2, 98, 101, 104, 228
University of KwaZulu-Natal (UKZN) 194, 197
University of Lourenco Marques 151
University of Luanda 151
University of Nairobi 58–59
University of North West 47
University of Pretoria (UP) 41, 98, 319
University of South Africa (Unisa) 264–265, 324–326
University of Stellenbosch (US) 298, 327
University of the Free State (UFS) 98, 327
University of the Western Cape (UWC) 32, 44, 325
University of the Witwatersrand (Wits) 2, 23, 55, 78, 87, 95, 101, 135, 197, 214, 219, 235, 257, 272, 294, 295, 302, 309
  against outsourcing during #FeesMustFall 214–233
  memorandum of understanding between Wits management, outsourced workers, and students (appendix) 335–338
  Workers Solidarity Committee (WSC) 88, 93, 225, 227–228, 233
UP, see University of Pretoria
uprising/s
  classification of 2–4
  North African 169–185
US, see University of Stellenbosch
USAf, see Universities South Africa
UWC, see University of the Western Cape

V

Vaal University of Technology (VUT) 318
Veriava, Ahmed 206
violence 6, 9–10, 329
  revolt positioning 13–15
  structural 10, 16, 294, 302, 311
  theme from protest documentation 115–116
VUT, see Vaal University of Technology

W

Wagle, Swarnim 17
Walter Sisulu University (WSU) 325–326
Wanza, Mario 271
Wasa, see Women's Academic Solidarity Association
West African Students Union 151
WhatsApp Groups
  as documentation 110
white privilege 97, 329
whiteness 328–329
  revolt positioning 13–15
WILSA, see Workers International League of South Africa
Wits School of Governance (WSG) vii, viii, ix, 2
Wits, see University of the Witwatersrand
Wolpe, Harold
women
  matriarchal leadership 270–290
Women in Mining (WOMIN) 281
Women's Academic Solidarity Association (Wasa) 286
WOMIN, see Women in Mining
worker documents
  of protest 106
worker protests
  in light of Just War Theory 292–305
workers
  #FeesMustFall brings liberation to 215–217
  #OutsourcingMustFall through eyes of 87–99
  precariousness of 61–63
  roots of revolution 61–63
  struggles through student lens 97–99
Workers International League of South Africa (WILSA) 290
Workers Solidarity Committee (WSC)
  Wits 88, 93, 225, 227–228, 233
working class resistance
  at Wits 220–222
working class-led struggle
  conjunctural moments of 226–230
WSC, see Workers Solidarity Committee
WSG, see Wits School of Governance
WSU, see Walter Sisulu University

Y

YCL, see Young Communist League
Young Communist League (YCL) 26
youth cohorts
  2015 student movement 138
  dissatisfaction with government 143
  racial attitudes by 144
  status of 137
youth struggles 127–132
  at onset of democracy 129–132

Z

Zambia 159
Zille, Helen 26
Zimbabwe 152, 157, 162, 164
Zuma, Jacob 27, 29, 36, 39, 42, 44, 48, 84, 193, 195–198, 201, 203, 210, 211, 244, 313, 320, 322–324
#ZumaMustFall 195, 210, 216

www.ingramcontent.com/pod-product-compliance
Lightning Source LLC
Chambersburg PA
CBHW020240030426
42336CB00010B/561